P9-DML-223

Into the Breach

DOROTHY AND CARL J. SCHNEIDER

Into the Breach

AMERICAN WOMEN OVERSEAS IN WORLD WAR I

VIKING

NEW CUMBERLAND
PUBLIC LIBRARY

79995204

VIKING
Published by the Penguin Group
Viking Penguin, a division of Penguin Books USA Inc.,
375 Hudson Street, New York, New York 10014, U.S.A.
Penguin Books Ltd, 27 Wrights Lane, London W8 5TZ, England
Penguin Books Australia Ltd, Ringwood, Victoria, Australia
Penguin Books Canada Ltd, 2801 John Street,
Markham, Ontario, Canada L3R 1B4
Penguin Books (N.Z.) Ltd, 182–190 Wairau Road,
Auckland 10, New Zealand

Penguin Books Ltd, Registered Offices:
Harmondsworth, Middlesex, England

First published in 1991 by Viking Penguin,
a division of Penguin Books USA Inc.

1 3 5 7 9 10 8 6 4 2

Copyright © Dorothy Schneider and Carl J. Schneider, 1991
All rights reserved

Pages 349–351 constitute an extension of this copyright page.

LIBRARY OF CONGRESS CATALOGING IN PUBLICATION DATA
Schneider, Dorothy.
Into the breach : American women overseas in World War I / Dorothy
and Carl J. Schneider.
p. cm.
Includes bibliographical references and index.
ISBN 0-670-83936-1
1. World War, 1914–1918—Women—United States. I. Schneider,
Carl J. II. Title.
D639.W7S36 1991
940.3′15042′0973—dc20   90-50751

Printed in the United States of America
Set in Plantin
Designed by Francesca Belanger

Without limiting the rights under copyright reserved above, no part of
this publication may be reproduced, stored in or introduced into a retrieval
system, or transmitted, in any form or by any means (electronic,
mechanical, photocopying, recording or otherwise), without the
prior written permission of both the copyright owner and the above
publisher of this book.

For Marian

PREFACE

THIS BOOK RECORDS the participation of American women abroad in World War I—and their efforts to end it. Most of these 25,000 women have vanished from memory. Identifying them and discovering their records exercised our ingenuity and kept us wandering through space and time.

Fortunately, that letter- and diary-writing generation laid a wide paper trail. But the publishing practices of the time strain the detective skills of the researcher. Books appeared anonymously or pseudonymously, without clues to the qualifications of the writer. Many a proud father turned over bundles of his daughter's letters from overseas to a printer unedited, pausing only to blank out all the proper names, leaving the reader to wonder when and why his daughter had gone overseas. Sometimes the letters (dated only by month and day) stop in the middle of her experiences, without explanation. Often the reader cannot tell whether she was British or American until page 145—if ever.

Letter and diary writers in the custom of the time, to protect other women from unladylike publicity, often identified them only by an initial. Edith Gratie Stedman wrote of working with a Dr. C., an American who had driven an ambulance in Salonika and "an all round corker." A corker indeed, but who was she, what kind of doctorate did she hold, and what was she doing in Paris?

Or one catches a tantalizing glimpse of adventure in a sketch, the details of which the writer has forgotten or never knew, as in her son's reminiscence of Helena Crummett Lee, in the Schlesinger Library at Radcliffe College: "At the outbreak of World War I she and her daughters helped found a hospital in France, worked with the French women in the fields, and brought about the capture of a German spy in an unused tower of their château."

Circumstances like these complicate the problem of judging credibility and ultimately drive researchers to rely on an educated sense of probability. Take, for instance, the enthralling story told by Chief Nurse Stevens in "Under the Red Cross Banner," in Elaine Sterne's *Over the Seas for Uncle Sam* (New York: Britton Publishing Co., 1918). In these stories collected from patients in government hospitals, Stevens claimed service under the flags of France, England, and the United States. She alleged that she had seen on the battlefield the bodies of Frenchwomen dragged to their trenches by the Germans—a ubiquitous atrocity story. A British friend, she said, helped her to a job as matron of a British hospital ship of four thousand beds loaded with casualties from the Dardanelles, in which post she was to be gazetted a major in the British army. She threw in also a tale of shipwreck, in which her ship was torpedoed and she stayed in the water three hours. Well, maybe. But the "eyewitness account" of the familiar atrocity story, the improbability of the British appointing an American to such an important post, and the editor's inability to vouch for her kept us from using Stevens's evidence.

Or consider the anonymous *War Nurse, The True Story of a Woman Who Lived, Loved and Suffered on the Western Front* (New York: Cosmopolitan Book Corp., 1930). The author's candid remarks, particularly because they incorporated some information we already knew to be reliable, tempted us to hope that in this book, published twelve years after war's end, we might find illumination on subjects that the inhibitions of women writing a decade earlier had obscured. "I think there was less living together among Americans on war service than there was among the English and the French. This was partly due to the fact that it was the unconventional type of woman who originally went in for war work in France, the woman who had already stepped outside the hard and fast rules laid down by society. The pre-war nurse was suspect as *peut-être pas femme honnête* [perhaps not a respectable woman]. The correct young girl, who was the first to find her way into American war work, was the last to find her way into French war work." (pp. 151, 162) But alas, the patness of the melodramatic plot and the rather sensational style drove us to conclude that we were dealing with fiction: fiction that certainly contained much fact, but offered us no way to distinguish.

But judging on the basis of style also presents its difficulties, so much have fashions changed. The researcher must take care not to be derailed by the sentimentality of a Grace Livingston Hill, who after all had access to the best sources of the Salvation Army women.

We made several arbitrary decisions on parameters. Most importantly, we chose to write only about Americans. But we salute here the brave British women whose initiative and daring inspired the sympathy and emulation of our subjects. It's heartening that scholars like Diana Condell, Jean Liddiard, Gail Braybon, and Penny Summerfield have begun to tell the British women's stories.

We confined ourselves almost entirely to the duration of the fighting, from August 1914 to November 1918, resisting the impulse to follow the postwar work of women in reconstruction. We included American women married to Europeans: their work was distinguished from that of Frenchwomen, for instance, not only by the necessities the war imposed on many French women but also by the American tradition of volunteerism and by the Americans' Stateside connections, which enabled them to produce all sorts of help on request.

We have relied heavily on primary sources, though when well-researched secondary sources are available—notably in organizational histories—we have not hesitated to use them. We have documented all direct quotations, and most incidents that cite a particular woman. Our undocumented statements, including our generalizations, are just as firmly based on evidence, not on speculation. Because this book focuses on the experience of individual women, we have not mentioned many of the organizations employing American women overseas who did outstanding work. In spite of the widespread publicity given Edith Cavell and Mata Hari, we found no trace of American women agents overseas, but the American intelligence system, then in its infancy, confined itself largely to domestic concerns. We hope that we have neglected no profession or occupation in which American women overseas engaged (though we stumbled across female news photographers at the penultimate moment), but we sadly acknowledge that we have omitted mention of thousands of individual

women with stories just as significant, adventurous, and engaging as
those we include.

As we write, the terminology for Americans known during
World War I as "Negroes" or "colored people" is in flux. Afro-
Americans? African-Americans? Blacks? After much hesitation and
some consultation, we have decided to stay with the well-established
usage of "blacks," except, of course, when another term is used in
a quotation.

Librarians have been our lifeline. We particularly thank Ann
Penniman and her staff of the Essex, Connecticut, public library,
who have fielded questions ranging from the spelling of Lifebuoy
soap to an allegation of a peace conference in Vienna in 1917, and
who have exploited the marvelous resources of the interlibrary loan
system, enabling us to do much of our work at home. We also deeply
appreciate the help of Eva Moseley and the other knowledgeable
women who assisted our work at the invaluable Schlesinger Library,
even in their temporary quarters with the thermometer up and the
air conditioning down; of Elizabeth Norris, Librarian/Archivist at
the YWCA National Headquarters; of David Koch, Archivist of
Special Collections at Southern Illinois University; of Gloria Gavert,
Archivist at Miss Porter's School; of Margaret Jerrido and Jill Smith,
Archivists at the Medical College of Pennsylvania; of Maynard Brick-
ford and his staff in the Archives of the American Library Association
at the University of Illinois; of David Keogh and Pamela Cheney at
the Military History Institute; of Barbara Paulson of the Health
Science Library at Columbia University; of Elaine Trehub, the Archivist at Mount Holyoke College; of Jean Berry of the Wellesley
College Archives; and of Millie Ettlinger, the Archivist for the American Telephone and Telegraph Company. Our debt extends also to
the staffs of the Houghton Library, the New York Public Library,
the Bentley Library at the University of Michigan, the Friends'
Historical Library at Swarthmore, the Nebraska State Historical Library, the Indiana State Historical Library, the Smith College Library, the Vassar College Library, the Library of Congress, and the
library of Yale University—especially to the people there who scur-
ried after an extension cord so that we could establish our computer
at the refectory lectern in their Gothic reading room.

We think with special gratitude of the irreplaceable guidance given us by Helene M. Sillia, longtime historian of the Women's Overseas Service League. Our agent, Elizabeth Knappman, has always been our staff, never our rod. Amy Mintzer read our work with sympathetic insight, helped us identify gaps, and challenged us into thought. Michael Millman efficiently fostered the book through the press.

We appreciatively acknowledge a travel grant from the National Endowment for the Humanities which enabled us to spend an invaluable week at the Schlesinger Library.

Finally, we bow to that third person created by and dominant in a collaboration.

CONTENTS

Into the Breach

CHAPTER 1

The Entrepreneurial War

UPWARDS OF 25,000 American women, ranging in age from twenty-one to their sixties, served overseas in World War I, the "Great War" of 1914–18. Beginning in August 1914, long before the United States joined the conflict in 1917, American women took it upon themselves to assuage the suffering inflicted by the war. At first singly or with a few companions, then in larger groups under the aegis of organizations like the YMCA or the American Red Cross, and only years later at the behest of the United States government, they streamed across 3,000 miles of submarine-infested ocean. As one of them, the sixty-year-old Margaret Deland, wrote: ". . . of all the amazing things that have come bubbling and seething to the surface of life during these last three and a half years, there has been nothing more amazing to me than this exodus of American girls! Has such a thing ever happened in the world before: A passionate desire on the part of the women of one people to go to the help of the men of another people? Would any other nation, I wonder, if we were at war, send its girls across the ocean to serve us?"[1]

At that moment in history those notoriously independent and self-reliant Americans, the "New Women" who had been developing in the late nineteenth and early twentieth centuries, discovered in the public sphere of action (which they had already entered) a desperate need for the quality with which tradition uniquely endowed women: the ability to nurture and to heal. Well educated, often professionally experienced, self-motivated, they set out to find their own niches, devise their own methods for service. For them the "Great War" was an entrepreneurial war. And by its nature World War I called for entrepreneurship.

It was a curious war, one that took people aback in its onset and in its prolongation. Many, especially Americans, had believed that the Western world, triumphant in its industrialization and the growth of its social conscience, had progressed beyond war. Even after the war began, both the Allies and the Central Powers denied that it could last more than months, or that it would last more than weeks.

An odd war in other ways, too, continually contradicting itself. The greed, stupidity, and carelessness among both the Allies and the Central Powers that caused it were mirrored in its conduct; yet at the outset the soldiers who fought it were inspired by enthusiasm and a passionate idealism, marching off to war with flowers in their rifles, decorating their transports with garlands. Never in history have so many credulous or fatalistic young soldiers been sent to their deaths by such obstinate, callous, and unimaginative old men, unable to devise any battle plan other than a war of attrition. Three times as many British soldiers died in World War I as in World War II; 60,000 of them died in just one day on the Somme. When after enduring years of the unspeakable horrors of trench warfare French troops finally mutinied in April 1917, their generals unflinchingly ordered them shot. Yet even in 1917 many Americans believed that they were joining a crusade to save Western civilization, end wars, and make the world safe for democracy.

In every respect, a catastrophic war. Catastrophic in terms of the 37,000,000 casualties among its soldiers. Catastrophic for the millions of civilians it killed, wounded, orphaned, widowed, and displaced. Catastrophic economically and politically. Catastrophic for the Western civilization it was supposed to save, but whose value system it undermined. It not only destroyed families, but weakened the family structure. It drove a wedge between generations that ultimately split them. We Americans must count ourselves fortunate that our involvement was no greater. Our country was not a battlefield. More than 10,000,000 Europeans died in battle, but "only" 115,000 Americans. The United States declared war in April 1917 and eventually mobilized 4,355,000 men, but it took almost a year to equip, train, and transport the 2,000,000 men sent to Europe. Full American participation in the war thus was limited to about six months. But we too inherited the social, political, and economic whirlwinds it roused.

It was indeed a world war. It involved millions of people, and many countries: Russia, Turkey, the Balkans, Japan, as well as the nations of western Europe and their widespread empires, and eventually, of course, the United States. Russia, Serbia, and Italy as well as France and Belgium endured its ravages. Yet for long periods the war was fought in fixed trenches, leaving much of Europe open to the wanderings of civilians. Soldiers in France made and won bets that the trench lines would not change by more than a mile in two years, but meanwhile thousands of American women, among others, moved about the Continent with startling freedom. The Europe of 1914–18 more nearly resembled the Civil War America in which Oliver Wendell Holmes set out from New England to seek his wounded son in the South than the *Festung Europa* of World War II. (Indeed, as Marie Van Vorst reported, Robert LeRoux went on just such an errand in World War I, only to find his son lying in a hospital with 700 other wounded men, unattended save for three nurses.[2]) Sometimes European authorities, made wary by spy scares, insisted on strip-searching innocent relief workers traveling on their missions. At other times they allowed civilians like the cartwheeling singer Elsie Janis to treat the war as a spectator sport, vying with each other in efforts to get closest to No Man's Land, and, best of all, to pull the lanyard on a cannon.

A bumbled war. As logistically inept as strategically stupid, the ill-assorted men responsible for its organization and management aggravated the chaos that always accompanies battle. The generals stumbled over their own political maneuvers, failing to coordinate their plans. When John J. Pershing went to France commanding the American forces, with his soldiers still desperately in need of training, he had to devote much of his time to repelling the attempts of his British and French counterparts to absorb American men into their own ranks. Despite the lessons of the Crimea and the Civil War, military preparations for the care of the wounded had been abysmally inadequate. The hospital supply system was a thing of rags and patches, loosely stitched together by individual enterprise.

War's onset in 1914 at once tugged at the emotions of Americans,

Americans related to Europe by blood, marriage, education, friendship, common languages, and shared modes of thought. And, of course, both the Allies and the Central Powers sought American support and help. Americans gave it, more and more generously as they heard of the suffering the war spawned, in reports carefully constructed in the propaganda offices of Berlin, Paris, and London. At first America, determined to stay out of the war, offered relief to both sides, sending out a Red Cross "Mercy Ship" staffed with American nurses to care for the sick and wounded of the Central Powers as well as those of the Allies. But gradually American sentiment swung overwhelmingly to the Allies.

American women as well as American men went to the rescue. The problems the belligerent nations had not prepared for and could not handle attracted volunteers, and allowed them wide scope to devise their own ways of helping. The need for their services found the "New Women" well prepared.

> By 1890 a "New Woman" had "reached her stride. Decidedly middle-class, if not upper-class, she was usually a town or city dweller, the wife or daughter of a business or professional man, and better educated than the average. Perhaps she was even a college graduate. . . . She was more likely to be single than was any other group of women at any time, before or since, in American history; even more so if she had been to college. If unmarried, she might be employed outside the home. . . ."[3]

In the latter part of the nineteenth and the early twentieth centuries, American women had been changing their ideas and their life-styles, moving more and more into the public domain. Quite a lot of them had begun to work outside their homes. The Civil War necessitated this move for a good many: with casualties greater than in any other American war, it forced the women whom it had rendered widows, spinsters, and wives with disabled husbands to try to support themselves and their families. By 1910 8,000,000 American women were paid to work in the marketplace—more, in proportion to the population, than in 1920.[4] The ranks of educated women were swelling, and women had invaded the professions. In medicine, in fact, women becoming doctors had already aroused the fears of males to the point of backlash, so that the number of women physicians was actually on the decline from an earlier high point.

As their families diminished in size, American women had more time to work for the well-being of their towns and cities. Over the course of time American women as volunteers expanded their sphere out of their homes into their communities, assuming there the same kinds of moral and domestic responsibilities they had long borne at home. Quite right that they should, argued many a man glad to abdicate the throne of virtue: it should be up to women to maintain morality, since by nature they are purer and face fewer temptations than the stronger sex. Women associated themselves in clubs dedicated to self, community, and even national improvement. By 1914 women's volunteer work was a familiar fact of American life, regarded as work peculiarly appropriate to their gender. (Of course, it kept them out of competition for paid jobs as well.)

By that time, too, American women were close to winning the vote—indeed, had won it in several states. The suffrage movement, whether or not they supported it, had raised their consciousness and their confidence. Industrialization and urbanization were freeing them from small-town scrutiny and inhibitions. The development of "domestic science," washing and sewing machines, and prepared foods helped women run households more efficiently, but also enabled them to rely more on themselves and less on servants. The bicycle and automobile gave them mobility. Their clothes became looser, their skirts shorter, to allow for their increased activity.

What with all this, and many another cultural change, American women were perceived at home and throughout Europe as almost uniquely determined, competent, and independent. Perhaps this myth arose in part from the pioneer experience, when women were forced to assume equal responsibility for the security and sustenance of the homesteads, and men were forced to acknowledge the necessity of their work. Doubtless the atmosphere of rugged individualism and the mobility of American society strengthened the concept.

Such a perception of women allowed for the possibility of relationships between women and men untinged by sexuality—

friendships rather than flirtations; working partnerships rather than romances. Louisa May Alcott, that feminist in sheep's clothing, by the end of the 1860s was portraying, and praising, girls and boys, women and men working and playing together. A bit later Henry James embodied the legend somewhat differently in his young American women flouting the conventions of a corrupt European society. Journalist Dorothy Dix in 1915 described the American girl attractive to the modern young man as a "husky young woman who can play golf all day and dance all night, and drive a motor car, and give first aid to the injured. . . ."[5] By the outbreak of the "Great War" there had evolved in the collective mind an image of "the independent American girl," who could engage in work and play unthinkable to her European sister, associate freely with men, and remain a "nice girl." She was, said legend, doubly protected by her own virtue and the chivalry of American males—wherever they went, whatever they did, recognition of their moral superiority would earn America's daughters gallant treatment.

> ⚑⚑⚑ *In the wars of the seventeenth, eighteenth, and the early part of the nineteenth century, while the hospitals had a moderate share of fair ministrants, chiefly of the religious orders, the only female service on the battle-field or in the camp, often the scene of fatal epidemics, was that of the* cantinières, vivandières, filles du régiment, *and other camp followers, who, at some risk of reputation, accompanied the armies in their march, and brought to the wounded and often dying soldier, on the field of battle, the draught of water . . . or the cordial.*[6]

Shifts in American women's ways of participating in wars paralleled (and sometimes propelled) the changes in their roles in the society at large. American women have, of course, worked in all American wars, often on or near the battlefields. Although George Washington inveighed against the women (and children) who followed their menfolk into the camps of the Continental Army and had to be fed and moved with the army, he knew that the army needed them as cooks, nurses, laundresses. Indeed the army hired other civilian women as well for such tasks. American women accompanied their husbands onto American fighting ships, and on occasion fought by their sides or in their places.

In the Civil War women served on both sides as soldiers, spies, scouts, couriers, cooks, laundresses, prostitutes, and, in one case, a chaplain. Some wives fought openly alongside their husbands; about 400 other women passed as male soldiers.[7] After service as a nurse, Dr. Mary Walker was commissioned a lieutenant in the Army Medical Corps. The efforts of Clara Barton, Elizabeth Blackwell, Dorothea Dix, and hundreds of nameless women mitigated the suffering of the sick and wounded; ultimately, despite opposition from doctors, the Northern and Southern armies employed 3,200 nurses, white and black, free and slave.[8]

Linus Pierpont Brockett and Mary C. Vaughan's *Woman's Work in the Civil War* is indeed, as its subtitle declares, *A Record of Heroism, Patriotism and Patience*. Its chapter headings suggest the breadth of women's activities: "Superintendent of Nurses (Dorothea Dix), Ladies Who Ministered to the Sick and Wounded in Camp, Field, and General Hospitals, Ladies Who Organized Aid Societies, Received and Forwarded Supplies to the Hospitals, Devoting Their Whole Time to the Work, Ladies Distinguished for Services Among the Freedmen and Refugees, Ladies Distinguished for Services in Soldiers' Homes, Volunteer Refreshment Saloons, on Government Hospital Transports Etc., and Ladies Distinguished for Other Services in the National Cause."

Among the last of these was Annie Etheridge, who served with the Second, Third, and Fifth Michigan regiments as daughter of the regiment. Her nursing brought a general's promise that she should be made a regimental sergeant—that is, receive the pay and rations of a sergeant. Wounded men were shot in her arms. She seldom used the pistols she carried, but repeatedly she rallied the men; at Chancellorsville, for instance, she rode along the line of shallow trenches, urging, "Boys, do your duty and whip the rebels." Her division general trusted her so implicitly that he gave prisoners into her keeping. "During the battle of Spottsylvania, Annie met a number of soldiers retreating. She expostulated with them, and at last shamed them into doing their duty, by offering to lead them back into the fight, which she did under a heavy fire from the enemy."[9]

Although individually they vanished into the mists of women's accomplishments, the deeds of "Gentle Annie" and her ilk in the Civil War *may* have enhanced perceptions of women's capabilities. Clara Barton thought so. "At the war's end," she claimed in 1888, "woman was at least fifty years in advance of the normal position which continued peace would have assigned her." At any rate, although the reputation of nurses remained questionable, the Civil War saw the advent of middle-class women into war work that extended far beyond the drudgeries most frequently assigned women in earlier wars. Moreover, as the record compiled by Brockett and Vaughan indicates, women's contributions had begun to attract recognition and honor.

In the Spanish-American War, an epidemic of typhoid fever forced the army to hire civilian women as nurses, efforts to recruit men to care for the sick having failed. About 1,500 women served Stateside, overseas, and on the hospital ship *Relief*.[10] Finally, after more than a hundred years of such experiences, the army and navy in the early twentieth century established an auxiliary nurse corps.

So when the United States entered the "Great War," for the first time in its wartime history women were already officially affiliated with its army and navy. Now too for the first time the navy and the marine corps gave women military rank—enlisted rank, of course. The navy recruited into its active reserve some 13,000 women, known popularly as Yeomanettes but formally as USNR(F) or Yeomen(F), to do clerical work, Stateside. And the marine corps similarly enrolled 305 Women Marines—USMCR(F).

But long before 1917 the war had engaged the sympathies and enlisted the labor of millions of American civilian women. From 1914 on they formed literally hundreds of organizations like the Woman's Committee of the Commission for Belgian Relief, the Vacation War Relief Committee, the Surgical Dressings Committee, the National Patriotic Relief Society, and the National League for Woman's Service. They even started national service training camps, which offered leisured middle- and upper-class young women courses in dietetics, camp cookery, map reading, motor car driving and repairing, bicycling, signaling, and agriculture.[11] As Ida Clyde Gallagher Clarke somewhat wearily noted, "Even the animals have not been forgotten in the war relief work of American women. Mrs. Elphinstone Maitland is at the head of what is known as the Blue Cross Fund, designed to help suffering horses in wartime."[12]

Almost immediately the women who ran all these committees and commissions at home and the American women in Europe who organized such groups as the American Ambulance in Paris and the American Women's War Relief Committee in London recognized the necessity for Stateside women to go to Europe, to act as liaisons, to survey needs, and to conduct the work itself.

American women were ready. More surprisingly, so were their families and the society generally. Parents of course did sometimes object, expressing their entirely reasonable concern for the interruption of a promising career, their understandable fears for the physical safety of their daughters, and in one case a familial complaint that the young woman was setting out with an unbecoming hat! But whatever qualms they felt about their daughters' sexual safety and reputations were apparently soothed by the myth of the competent and pure American girl and her protection wherever she went by the chivalrous American male. The myth was assiduously touted in such publications as the journalist Mabel Potter Daggett's *Women Wanted: The Story Written in Blood Red Letters on the Horizon of the Great War.* "As he puts me in my taxicab and lifts his hat . . . ," she exulted, "he only knows that I am his countrywoman. And he is an American man. The Lord seems to send them when you need them most."[13]

And, daughters reassured their parents, some of the older American women in Europe took it upon themselves to hold high the standard: upon her arrival in Paris Marian Baldwin, extraordinarily young for her canteening job at twenty-two, was told "what is proper and . . . given . . . a list of restaurants where one can lunch safely with a man!"[14] Meanwhile the military newspaper *Stars and Stripes* was counseling its servicemen readers "to hold all women as sacred."[15]

Realism suggests also that parents may have had less authority in 1914–18 than nostalgic memories of the past attribute to them. Margaret Deland, on her way to France as a canteen worker and a correspondent for the *Woman's Home Companion*, remarked on "the parental bewilderment which is one of the hallmarks of the twentieth century. . . . I am inclined to think that this special expression of [the high adventure of altruism], which has started a little army of girls over to France, could not have happened anywhere but in the United States, where fathers and mothers have so very little to say as to the behavior of their daughters. . . . they cannot hold their girls back from the gray sea, where heaven only knows what may meet them!"[16]

What's more, the crisis of the times justified unconventional behavior. American society generally was exhibiting considerable idealism about the purity of the Allied cause. An ancient concept of war persisted—war as a necessary and redemptive exercise of strength, virility, and chivalry, for the country and for its individual citizens.

True enough, many Americans in 1914 and 1915 energetically opposed the war. Some isolationists, in Barnard Dean Virginia Gildersleeve's words, wrapped their oceans around them and left it to Europeans to settle Europe's quarrels. Others argued that the war was bad for business. And many—especially women—struggled with all their might to restore the peace out of pacifist conviction; some of them indeed argued that women had a special moral fitness and responsibility to end the war which men's passions had induced.

But German militarism, broken faith, and contemptuous usurpation of the rights of other nations combined with the effectiveness of French and English propaganda to overwhelm American opponents of the war. By 1917 mainstream American public opinion so ardently idealized the cause and the men who fought for it that Americans crucified anyone, even a Jane Addams, who spoke so much as the plain truth about the war and its conditions. The Allied cause having been transmogrified into a crusade, it was right and proper for American women to serve in it.

As usual, society found itself able to adjust to changes in women's roles when they suited society's ends—particularly when, as in the "Great War," they could be read as ways to help and nurture men and children.

Not that women escaped the censure and opposition of some men in their enterprises. Women librarians had to cope with the pompous explanations of some of their male colleagues that only the male was suited to the physical demands of libraries on military sites. Women physicians faced the determination of the military establishment to exclude them from service. But by and large, society approved, and the women's families were proud.

What with all the genuine advances women had made and the developing recognition of the need for their services, by 1914 it was possible for thousands of American women to go overseas to relieve the sufferings of the civilian victims of war, to support and nurture troops, and to report the war. Belief in the purity of the cause and the indefatigable chastity of American women combined to put the imprimatur of society on their undertakings.

They were the right women at the right time: they moved into an environment that would afford them scope for independence, for initiative, for entrepreneurship. The lack of coordination among welfare and relief agencies in the early years of the war and their reliance on volunteers meant that women could move freely among them, and within them could establish their own objectives, adopt their own agenda, devise their own means. The profound inadequacies of foreign medical services called out for women to take charge, to solve problems, to find supplies where they could, to launch their own projects to feed, clothe, and comfort their patients. World War I enveloped far more people and more territory than the wars that preceded it, but without the controls, coordination, and centralization of World War II. The resultant chaos, aggravated by disagreements among allies and uneven applications of policy, left women surprisingly free to meet in their own way, through their own enterprise, some of the desperate needs they discovered.

So American women stepped off into the blue of World War I. Armed and defended by their birthright, eager to serve, of no mind to be excluded from the action, the work, and the danger, American women set sail for England, or better still, for the Continent.

But their experiences overseas differed markedly from those of their American foremothers in earlier wars.

First, they went in numbers—some 25,000 of them.[17] The numbers are impressive in themselves, even more so in that all the women volunteered, and most so in that recruiting efforts were strictly limited, and sporadically counterbalanced by adjurations to women to stay at home. The Red Cross did actively recruit nurses, especially in the later days of the war, but the military wholeheartedly repudiated the efforts of women doctors to sign up. When a call for telephone operators went out, ten times as many qualified women as could be used responded. Welfare organizations usually restricted their recruiting to quiet networking. Overwhelmingly, women went to the "Great War" spontaneously.

Second, for the first time some were service members. More than 10,000 nurses served in Europe in the Army and Navy Nurse Corps. A handful of the navy's 13,000 Yeomen (Female) also worked in hospitals in France. And the Army Signal Corps deployed in Europe more than 200 women telephone operators, later—much later—acknowledged to be veterans.

Third, most of the women went on their own, not because of a relationship with a male combatant. In fact, most organizations rejected women with male relations overseas. A few women, to be sure, accompanied their prominent husbands and then became caught up in war work—like Grace Thompson Seton, who organized and directed a motor unit in France financed by the New York City Women's Club; like Ruth Bryan Owen Rohde, who served for fifteen months as secretary-treasurer of the American Woman's War Relief Fund in London, then in 1915 went with her two-year-old son to Cairo, where she worked for three years as an operating room nurse in a military hospital. But far more women traveled independently.

Fourth, they performed more jobs, and more different kinds of jobs, than women had in previous wars. Although by far the largest group were nurses, American women also worked in Europe as physicians, dentists, dietitians, pathologists/bacteriologists, occupational and physical therapists, administrators, secretaries, "chauffeuses," telephone operators, entertainers, canteen workers, interpreters and translators, searchers (for soldiers reported missing), statisticians, decoders, librarians, supervisors of rest homes for women munitions makers, directors of recreation, accountants, publicity directors, social workers, distributors of supplies, journalists, peace activists, small factory and warehouse operators, refugee workers, interior decorators, laboratory technicians, and architects.[18] Some women concentrated on one job; others shifted occupations mid-war. Magda Layton, for instance, signed up originally as nurse's aide and interpreter, and wound up as resident social worker for a Parisian affordable-housing project for workingmen's families.[19] A few were unique in their occupations, like the prominent suffragist Vira B. Whitehouse, who as director for Switzerland of the United States Committee on Public Information not only did an outstanding job of work but also won an epic battle for women against her own State Department.

Fifth, they traveled afar, not merely to Yorktown or Gettysburg. They crossed the seas to range over Europe, not only in England, France, Belgium, Germany, and Italy, but into improbably remote situations in the Balkans, Russia, and the Near East. Belle Breck in 1916 took a job with the State Department as a dollar-a-year woman when America as a neutral was caring for the Central Powers prisoners of war in Siberia. With America's entry into the war, she was transferred to Moscow and then to Petrograd, where she lived through the Bolshevik Revolution.[20] Nurses and doctors practiced under the most primitive conditions in war-swept Serbia, succoring civilians and the soldiers of three or four armies as the fortunes of war shifted. Other American women went to those parts of the world where the Allies and the Central Powers were battling to increase their empires, like Dr. Caroline Carle Lawrence, who in February 1918 enlisted with the American Red Cross Expedition to Palestine, to take charge of the Children's Hospital in Jerusalem.

Sixth, American women went to help other warring nations *even before the United States was officially involved*. In 1914 Red Cross nurses went to relieve suffering impartially, neutrally, in the Central Powers as well as among the Allies. But as time passed American women increasingly directed their efforts toward helping the peoples of the Allied nations.

🎺🎺🎺 *When the drums beat, most women go to war with their men—and upper and middle-class women who do war work get from war man's excitement minus the danger.*
—Mary Heaton Vorse[21]

Who were they, these adventurous and enterprising women who crossed the Atlantic over German submarines and worked through air raids and shellings? It's hard to sort them out. No point in dividing them into military and civilian, for the lines between fade under examination: Red Cross nurses labored alongside army nurses, doing the same work under the same conditions. No point in separating them by uniforms, since everyone who could garbed herself in the most attractive uniform available, authorized or self-designed. Alice B. Toklas fashioned her coat after a British officer's many-pocketed jacket, and topped it off with a pith helmet, while Gertrude Stein chose a Russian model, emphasizing her imposing figure with a great-coat and a Cossack hat.

Overwhelmingly they were upper- or middle-class women. Some were the daughters of the wealthy, who abandoned luxury and ease for anonymous drudgery. The daughters of George Washington Hill (the tobacco tycoon) and Henry Frick (the steel magnate) assisted Molly Dewson in her Red Cross work: she described them as "good steady serious minded young women, who are willing to learn and who are willing to be on the road all day, and writing letters and arranging things until about twelve every night."[22] By no means were all the American women war workers rich: some had to scrimp, save, and risk their life savings to get overseas. Others were subsidized by their alumnae associations or organizations like the General Federation of Women's Clubs. But entries like this occur frequently in the letters home: "11/26/16. One of our greatest needs is a small motor-car—we take great heavy packages and heavy furniture all over town, and then in the visiting work we have to go everywhere, and we get really more tired than I ever thought it possible to get and we waste so much time walking. . . . here [cars] are too expensive to buy and mostly too poor in quality." "12/16. We were all electrified at Father's cable about the Ford. Did any girl ever have such a good father!"[23]

Some of the women were professionals, usually in medicine or journalism or social work. Almost all of them were white, for all but four or five black women were denied the opportunity to serve. Many of them were educated above the norm. In other words, they were the privileged, either by birth and upbringing, or by professional training. Helene Sillia, longtime historian of the Women's Overseas Service League, speaks of the overseas women of World War I as "a breed apart—women of means; they had to be." They could afford, or they had equipped themselves, to engage in what they considered the most absorbing and significant experience of their generation.

Many of them were single and unencumbered. But even women with family responsibilities managed to get away—sometimes at the cost of extraordinary hardships for themselves and their families. Horror at the terrible suffering in Europe and patriotism surged to overcome their usual caution and override their domestic concerns. Some left children at home. "In view of the fact that nearly all the women [physicians] had dependents, aged parents, invalid relatives, brothers or sisters, nieces, nephews, or their own children to educate," wrote Dr. Rosalie Slaughter Morton, "their patriotism was the more evident in the assurance that almost every one could be ready to sail within two weeks!"[24]

They were not young girls. In contrast with the many American nurses and Red Cross workers who went to Vietnam in their early twenties, those American women in World War I who scrubbed floors, fried doughnuts, took dictation, operated switchboards, and drove ambulances in the Europe of World War I were typically in their middle to late twenties, their early thirties. Their supervisors, some of the nurses, the doctors, the founders of private hospitals or relief agencies, the journalists, and the money raisers were often older, sometimes much older—like Florence Kendal, whose son, bidding her good-bye, remarked ruefully to bystanders: "I'm too old to fight, but I'm sending my mother."[25] The novelist and war correspondent Mary Roberts Rinehart told a story about her son Stanley and his general. "Stanley was furious at being kept in a training camp. 'If the General pleases, I would like to be sent to the front.' 'The front? What's the idea, lieutenant?' 'I would like to see my mother, sir!' "[26] As Dr. Esther Pohl Lovejoy commented when she sailed for France, "The official old age limit [of the Red Cross] for men was 55, and the large number of mature commissioners aboard suggested that this ruling had been made by men who could qualify under it. But 40 was the feminine limit and all the women on the

Chicago were doing their best to conform to this requirement."[27]

Many of the women knew each other, particularly those who came from the East Coast, and those who shared a profession. "I do verily believe I see here and in camp the old friends in greater numbers, specially the scattered college boy acquaintances and the girl friends that I knew at school and at home, than I would have met in the same length of time had I never come to France," wrote a YMCA canteen woman. "The fact is that a large part, I guess the majority of our acquaintances of my age are 'Somewhere in France' or about to come over."[28] If the women didn't know one another individually, they at least recognized their own kind.

But why did these American women choose to go? For as many different reasons as their brothers. Beyond a doubt, the example of European women inspired many an American: the fortitude of Frenchwomen and the courageous and unconventional work of British women filled the pages of American women's magazines. The achievements of the Scottish Women's Hospitals and the adventures of such women as the British Flora Sandes, who became a captain in the Royal Serbian Army and was photographed in uniform, swagger stick in hand, thrilled the imagination. Yet until 1917, at least, the situation of American women differed drastically. The United States was not at war. What's more, American women could go to war only by a journey of at least some 3,000 miles—and a perilous journey at that. Going required initiative, courage, and a determination approaching obstinacy, tinged with recklessness.

Convoluted logic motivated women like the social worker Chloe Owings: "Finally I realized that although I was opposed to war, I could not understand the world situations in which I would forever afterward live if I did not help in meeting them."[29]

But most of the women discussed their reasons in patriotic terms. Ruth Holden, with an M.A. from Radcliffe and a fellowship at Newnham College, Cambridge, in 1916 explained to her parents her reasons for volunteering for war work in Russia: "Now, every Englishman & girl, worth his or her salt, have chucked everything to help in this war, and if I were to sit tight at Newnham, continuing my research on fossil botany, of all things, getting the benefit of their sacrifices, don't you think it would look like the height of selfishness? And the more spectacular the thing I do, the more people will hear of it, and they won't think that every American is looking for profit from this war."[30] Juliet Goodrich, a socialite and world traveler, wrote: "It may have been my instinct for adventure which, as soon as war was declared, made it seem possible that I should go. I like to think, however, that it was patriotism. I had always been strongly pro-ally, believing that Germany represented the negation of those principles of freedom and democracy, faith in which has always been one of the abiding lights of life, for me. I had done a good deal of war work, particularly for France, now with my own country fighting for Liberty, I felt that I had a right, a duty indeed, to take a more direct part in the struggle."[31]

Love of country similarly motivated American women resident in France when the war broke out in 1914. American expatriates inspired by a dual allegiance to France in its hour of need and to the United States in its vaunted mission of salvation for democracy improvised their own forms of service. Gertrude Stein and Alice B. Toklas, for example, knew the Chicago millionaire Mary Borden Turner, who operated a hospital near the front. And their friend Jo Davidson's wife, Yvonne, was running a hospital for wounded officers near Perpignon. Stein and Toklas persuaded Stateside Americans to buy a Ford van which they specially equipped; Stein learned to drive; and they established depots from which they distributed supplies to hospitals. (Their facility at combining such trips with gastronomical tours only illustrates their entrepreneurial ingenuity.)

Sheer longing for adventure of course mingled with patriotism and Franco- and Anglophilia. As Elizabeth Shepley Sergeant observed, ". . . whether war be good or bad, whether it means purgation or damnation for civilization, it is still the adventure of these years."[32] Determined not to miss war's experiences and its opportunities, American women went where the action was. Head nurse Julia C. Stimson exulted, ". . . to be in the front ranks in this most dramatic event that ever was staged, and to be in the first group of women ever called out for duty with the United States Army, and in the first part of the army ever sent off on an expeditionary affair of this sort, is all too much good fortune for any one person. . . ."[33]

Beyond question, war rescued some women from lives of invalidism and a sense of uselessness, though few of these, the record suggests, went overseas. A handful of women unable, in the Alice James fashion, to function, found a temporary salvation in war service. Elizabeth Shepley Sergeant's friend Peggy "has never been so well and happy as while nursing."[34] And Lucy Stockton's physician in a letter to her father advocated her going to France: "Both 'Mlle Miss' & Miss Harper were nervously unstable when they went to France. Both improved in health under the strain of work." Stockton too improved in health and succeeded in her overseas work—the last success she was to know. After that she tried over and over, but apparently never again succeeded in living and working independently.[35]

For some the war experience provided a respite from boredom. "The most tragic discovery of all to any woman," wrote Mary Roberts Rinehart, "is that she is no longer needed, and many women were no longer needed. Brutal as it sounds, the great war came as a boon to those women, to millions of them; and its ending as a tragedy. Once more they were not needed."[36] And Marie Van Vorst recognized that for some women war provided a welcome escape from domesticity: "Here is Countess ———, for instance, *happy for the first time in her life*, nursing wounded in a military hospital, whilst in order to keep her husband peaceful and satisfied, she has imported a beautiful cousin from the United States."[37] (A hitherto-unrecognized form of war work.)

A few American women, despite the dangers they experienced overseas and the horrors around them, found the war a giddily inebriating round of adulation and romantic adventure. Seldom did they speak as bluntly as a character in Gertrude Atherton's *The White Morning*: "Gott, how German wives would rejoice in a war! Think of the freedom of being a Red Cross nurse, and all the men at the front."[38] But Mary Louise Rochester Roderick, giving up an incipient career in opera to tour the trenches as a singer, found that "Being the only girl is really fun, and it all seems quite natural," and "Whatever anyone may say, war is fun if you are right up where things are happening. Only fun for the onlookers, however, not the soldiers."[39]

The "chauffeuses" of the American Women's Hospitals, Dr. Esther Lovejoy said, were "manifestly ladies of the new school,

. . . not sitting in balconies, gazing at the sympathetic stars and longing for the hero to return. No, indeed, they were following him in a motor car. Bright-eyed, red-cheeked and beautiful, albeit a bit ruffled and mud-bedaubed, one of these ladies emerged from under her car . . . on a memorable occasion. . . . lying on her back in the mud under the car, looking for 'trouble,' she spied it in the sky, and out she came just in time to catch a glove that fell from a passing plane. A sky pilot's glove! Poor Romeo and Juliet! They lived too soon."[40]

Above all, though, American women went overseas in the "Great War" to serve. Independent "New Women" though they might be, they clung to the belief that the highest calling of women is to serve. They wanted to serve suffering humanity. They idealized the "cause," and wanted to serve it. Although the jingoistic rhetoric of the early twentieth century may ring hollow in our ears, it often accurately expressed a widespread, if naive, contemporary belief in the absolute justice of the Allied cause, the correspondingly absolute evil of the Hun/Boche/Kaiser Bill, and the efficacy of making the world safe for democracy by war.

In such a war, no service could suffice. "I was in the hospital from eight in the morning until seven, or often, eight in the evening, working steadily," wrote Juliet Goodrich, "and yet I was never able to feel that I had done even a small part of what should have been done for the comfort of the men."[41] And, triumphing over the harsh prejudice directed at them, the black women Addie Hunton and Kathryn Johnson wrote: ". . . we had the greatest opportunity for service that we have ever known; service that was constructive, and prolific with wonderful and satisfying result. For the privilege of serving in this capacity we shall ever be grateful."[42] (All sisters under the skin of Gertrude Atherton's protagonist in *The White Morning*, a German countess, who at war's outbreak "forgot her personal experience of the German male, forgot herself. Her beloved Fatherland was attacked, and the German male in his heroic resistance, his triumphal progress, was become a god. *Dienen! Dienen!* [To serve! To serve!]")[43]

Whether motivated by idealism, patriotism, longing for adventure and romance, escapism, or a desire to function in the public domain, the American women who served overseas in World War I were a determined lot. Some came from the ends of the earth, like the Red Cross nurse Elizabeth J. Miller, who in a hospital 1,600 miles in the interior of China received orders to join a unit leaving Shanghai for Russia. In China she traveled four days in a rowboat, three in a launch, and three in a steamer to Shanghai; then four days in an ocean-going vessel to Vladivostok, and finally thirty days by train to Tiumen, Siberia.[44]

Once American women had made up their minds to go overseas, what were their options? Where could they look? First, to British and French relief and medical organizations, and, in a handful of cases, the British and French military. Second, to private charities established by individuals, usually wealthy or famous or both, like Edith Wharton. Third, to a multiplicity of new organizations created independently to meet a felt need, like the American Relief Clearing House. Fourth, to large, preexisting service organizations, some with semiofficial governmental status, others only loosely coordinated with the military: the American Red Cross, the Salvation Army, the YMCA and YWCA. Fifth, to relatively small new groups sponsored by existing institutions: the Quakers; individual American hospitals; some women's colleges; the Junior League. Sixth, to the American military, where they enrolled in the Nurse Corps, or, with little chance of service overseas, in the Naval or Marine Reserve; others worked for the military as secretaries, stenographers, clerks, or Signal Corps telephone operators. Seventh, to publications which would print their reports of war and war work overseas.

Because they were self-selected adventurous women, because officialdom excluded them from many kinds of institutional participation, or simply because they confronted the general haste, disorganization, and lack of preparation, many American women enterprisingly found their own work, improvised their own tools, modified or created their own jobs overseas. Usually they sailed in groups, but some women set out alone, planning to find jobs when they arrived. Usually they worked in organizations, but often they switched at will from one to another. They improvised, argued, persuaded, and scrounged for supplies. They created new organizations where none had existed. So fluid and freewheeling was the situation as to alarm the State Department; by February 1918 it was trying to transmit the message "No Free Lances Wanted in France."[45]

Even those women who worked in long-established institutions frequently had to improvise, to strike out on their own. Their often-minimal training could not prepare them for the situations they would actually encounter: Barnard College trained women as YMCA overseas canteen workers in a course "covering just *one week*. In this time women were given instruction in French, hygiene, setting-up exercises, simple games, stories and storytelling, canteen cookery, recent history, manners and customs of our British, French, and Italian allies, conditions in the 'huts' and among our soldiers overseas, and *how not to be a nuisance*."[46] One untrained woman after another spoke of having to learn basic nursing skills with little supervision, working on desperately wounded men.

Occasionally the women's daring and enterprise cost them dearly. Some of the women who hurled themselves into the breach suffered rejection, and there was no system and no safety net to save them—only their own exertions. "There is a whole group of people over here I really feel sorry for," wrote Elizabeth Ashe in September of 1917, "they came a year or two ago as volunteers paying all their own expenses, now money has given out and they are stranded. The majority don't know enough French to be useful in our work [at the Children's Bureau of the Red Cross], the army doesn't want them, the canteen people won't support them, as they can get shoals of non-paid people and here they are, some very clever, capable girls."[47]

> ✄✄✄ *It isn't exactly an alluring prospect to be exiled in the back woods of Russia for a couple of months with only 2 English speaking people, to run an infectious hospital, but it will be rather fun.*
>
> —Ruth Holden[48]

Nevertheless, most of the American women who went overseas were glad they went. In their accounts the word "fun" turned up repeatedly. In part a word endemic in the language of the young American woman, in part a reassurance to anxious families at home, it assumed a variety of meanings. Much of the fun lay in participating in public life, working in the center of affairs.

Some women found their fun in romantic exploits, some in hardship and danger. Here is Ruth Holden in Russia: "We had a grand time getting here, first 12 hrs from Kazan by boat down the Volga to Simbirsk, 7 hrs on the train to Noarlat (3 A.M.) & then 3 hrs driving. The roads are awful,—deep ruts & rivers to ford, & it was raining. We rode in 3 'tarantes,'—a sort of a springless vehicle, where you half sit half lie down on a pile of straw, & jolt & joggle till every bone aches. We were inches deep in mud by the time we arrived, but it was lots of fun."[49]

And Mary Lee, later a novelist and a journalist, ended her description of the shelling of Paris at twelve-minute intervals by the German cannon Big Bertha: "You mustn't be sorry for us over here you know. If we take the chances of the war, at least we get all the fun of it too, & the moments of Hell sprinkled in are short and peppy ones."[50]

When they wrote less exuberantly, American women often spoke not of fun but of privilege. From somewhere in France Chief Nurse Julia Stimson wrote: "No one should be sorry for any of us who are here in connection with the army. . . . oh, dear people, no greater thing can ever come into any one's life than this chance of ours. . . ."[51] Lida A. Little of the Vassar group considered it "the greatest privilege of my life that I should have been here last night to give out to these men even the smallest gift."[52] And Elizabeth Shepley Sergeant, hospitalized for two years by a grenade wound, wrote, "we who did share in it, in greater or lesser degree, are not martyrs and heroines but privileged people."[53] Shades of Henry V! Apparently it's not only men who are to "think themselves accursed they were not here, / To fight with us. . . ."

Intermingled with the fun and the sense of the privilege of service was a discovery or an affirmation of the value of work. Some of these women had never before worked in any adult sense; some had never touched physical work. Yet they responded to the needs they perceived with enthusiasm and amazing perseverance.

Now and then flibbertigibbets and incompetents showed up. Chief Nurse Carrie May Hall expostulated: "I'd like to come home and give somebody a few points on selection. . . . I would insist on a more complete physical examination . . . and . . . on the candidates being able to demonstrate that they knew the value of a day's work and that they were willing to buckle down to doing that day's work *every* day. These people who manage to get over here to get *thrills get my goat.* Of course I know that the majority of the women over here are perfectly game, plodding away somewhere, unseen, doing their work and doing it well. . . ."[54] Alice Lord O'Brian, canteen director, reported: ". . . I have shipped two off for good. They were tabby cats and upset everybody. . . . When people first come over, they are very sentimental and full of good but impractical advice and ideas. . . . One young lady . . . told me with such feeling that she had longed for months to work for the soldiers, nothing was too lowly, scrubbing floors or washing dishes, all she asked was a chance. She finally admitted, however, that she never got up for breakfast and wondered if that could be a drawback. I . . . told her we could overcome that by having her right on night duty so she would already be up for breakfast."[55]

But far more commonly reports emphasized the hard, consistent, and responsible work of the women, in danger, discouragement, and seas of mud. Being useful, being appreciated enabled women to find significance and reward in all kinds of work, as Elizabeth Potter passionately declared: "Canteening dull? Do you think it dull to hear all day long that the sound of your voice is balm and honey? . . . [The soldiers] are never fresh, only rarely flirtatious, but so friendly, so glad to see one. . . ."[56] Mrs. P. D. Lamson, distributing comfort bags to soldiers departing for the front, doubted her usefulness until one officer said, "almost with tears in his eyes, '*Ah, Mesdemoiselles, vous avez fait du bien* [You have done well].' "[57] Such assurance of its usefulness made work satisfying, whatever its environment and its intrinsic appeal. As Carrie May Hall wrote: "For the first two months I felt as if I were more or less wasted. . . . But now I know that our strongest, most forceful women are needed over here."[58]

The more challenging the work, the more these women had to learn, the more enthusiastic their reactions. The brilliant Ruth Holden, who loved learning hospital work but with mastery found it boring, flourished as, in her words, "a man of all work," setting up hospitals for refugees in Russia, learning Russian and Polish, traveling about Russia, negotiating with Russian customs officers, and chivying Russian workmen to complete their tasks.

The American women in Europe during the "Great War," clearly patriotic, hardworking, and eager to serve, at the same time repeatedly exhibited—however unconsciously—the elation of power, of having assumed control over their own lives, of taking charge. They were escaping the traditional women's patterns and places, enlarging their spheres, exploring new ways to be, re-creating themselves—acting in the public, rather than the domestic, domain.

They offered their gifts of their professional skills, their time, their energies, their health, and their lives—for more than 300 of them died overseas. Their creativity, imagination, and entrepreneurship in identifying and meeting needs led them to exceed the limits of the past and adventure on unknown frontiers of achievement. They certainly earned, though they never received, the flag for women war workers at home and abroad for which the Daughters of the American Revolution vainly petitioned Congress. For the women demonstrated a remarkable courage, as with the Smith College Relief Unit workers, whose valor rescued French peasants caught in the German invasion of the Somme, and the YWCA worker in the Russian revolution, who, describing the danger and devastation, coolly commented: "Altogether it was some revolution, but I wouldn't have missed it for a farm."[59]

CHAPTER 2

Common Experiences

THE AMERICAN WOMEN who served in Europe during the "Great War," despite wide variations in their occupations and geographical situations, shared many hazards and hardships.

Our ship was fired upon by a German sub after our convoy left but our ship was well armed and fired back and escaped unharmed.
—Irene Wilkinson O'Connor[1]

Getting there was difficult. Even the Atlantic crossing, plain sailing in comparison to the journey to Russia via the Pacific and the Trans-Siberian Railway, was forbidding. The chances of a ship's being attacked by a submarine in the Atlantic sometimes rose alarmingly: in the first quarter of 1917 one ship in four that left the British Isles did not return. But at any time the possibilities were daunting. Members of the Wellesley unit standing at their lifeboat stations watched destroyers sink two submarines before their eyes.

Most American women, however, treated the dangers nonchalantly—even though some of them carried rubber suits designed to support a survivor upright in the water and protect her against the cold. "These last two nights we have been in utter blackness outside, where we sleep, or try to in our chairs, while the 'vigilantes' pace up and down to marshall us into the boats if necessary," wrote Molly Dewson of her crossing in November 1917. "However, there is not 1% of tension on the boat. In fact we have not a sensation—except of all men—the bishop who 'has a premonition' that we are going down. Imagine his trying to start a panic—the bishop! But it is sort of picturesque with the life boats swung out, the gunners at their posts and the white banded vigilantes and our general with his revolver at his hip. But you can't make yourself believe there is as much danger as in driving out to Berlin [Massachusetts] on a wet night."[2] Marian Baldwin was acutely aware of the passengers' absurdity as they bumped "into each other's life preservers on the crowded upper deck. . . . Every one is checked off and each man is told what woman he is to save. (Great excitement at this point as no one of the men wants to save the lady detailed to him, but some one in another boat!)"[3]

Quite possibly the catastrophic flu epidemics which broke out on ships transporting troops and workers in 1918 posed an even greater threat than German submarines. Grace M. Bacon, representing Mount Holyoke, lived through a nightmare of a voyage in October 1918. Her ship, carrying 130 women and the flu, but no doctor, lost its convoy in a storm. Her colleague Ruth MacGregor was among those who died and were buried at sea.[4]

On many ships meetings and lectures distracted the passengers from contemplation of danger. Mrs. J. Borden Harriman reported that on one crossing in 1918 the busy British suffragist Mrs. Pankhurst was making speeches; Aileen Tone, "lovely in her uniform," was singing twelfth-century ballads; and Harriman herself was giving French lessons and practicing choral singing with the soldiers.[5] Edith Gratie Stedman, lying seasick in her bunk, listened skeptically to "a group of youths under our window doing their best to learn French in ten days. They are still conjugating 'avoir' and the prospect of ultimate success looks to me doubtful."[6] (As Anna Steese Richardson, staff writer of the *Woman's Home Companion*, commented: "Telling Americans they can pick up French is like telling foreigners they'll pick up gold on the streets when they get to our country."[7])

Once in Europe, war workers met with varying degrees of discomfort. The pinched diet of wartime: ". . . you are hungry all the time here," wrote a YM worker from Paris in January of 1918. "Last night I went with some of the Y.M.C.A. office crowd—a good collection—to a place for dinner, and when we finished we began all over again." Travel in unreliable cars: "I drove the Ford Y.M.C.A. wagonette filled up in the back with secretaries, nice ones—all egging me on. In some strange way the darn thing got on fire on the way over, but we all turned to and put it out with snow."[8] Or train travel: sitting up three nights in a week on trains packed "like a Harvard-Yale game, but not so polite a crowd. 'The devil take the hindermost Ho!' "[9] Sleeping "on the floor of the train corridor but one sardine in a box of foreign soldiery, which however by daylight and examination of the head in my lap proved to be Italian speaking, 100 per cent Americans from New York City. . . ."[10] Dirt: "I was billeted in a peasant's cottage which looked clean but alas, there were bed bugs, which kept me awake until 4:00 when I killed the last (?) of them."[11]

The gluey mud: "In spite of the fact that we were provided with rubber boots and in addition took with us one or two extra pairs of rubbers," wrote Army nurse Iva Lehman, "we were soon in need of more rubber footwear. Fifty days of continuous rain made the mud almost bottomless, and it was impossible to step out of our quarters without being protected. A few walks were made with broken stones and cinders, but the broken stones were hard on shoes. Many of us wore rubbers issued from the quartermaster's, but they were so large and heavy that we could scarcely carry them."[12]

Worst of all, cold: Bessie Baker in France heard tales of patients freezing in their beds; when winter came, she began to believe them. Often she would find a nurse who could not stay on her feet until she had soaked them in ice water to ease their aching. Some talked "of starting a Chilblain Club, but such rivalry for the presidency arose between one of the surgeons and the assistant chief nurse that it had to be abandoned."[13] In Siberia, Elizabeth J. Miller of the American Red Cross remembered, "The temperature reached as low as 65 below zero and stayed for weeks at 20 to 30 below. . . . The blizzards were so severe and blinding that we tied ropes from the hospital to the Nurses Home and held on to these for safety. I recall one time being in a train that was side-tracked in a blizzard, and we had only a small wood stove to use. Our hands were so cold we could not fasten the buttons on our sweaters, and a bucket of water would freeze solid in a few moments' time. We practically lived on oatmeal until the blizzard was over."[14]

Even in Paris life was straitened, and, with the air raids and the

German long-range gun Big Bertha, perilous. Just living in a country at war was difficult—particularly for those who, like Mary Smith Churchill, wife of an American military attaché, had to maintain a household and struggle with shortages; they soon learned that "things that seemed necessities really are not." The lack of conveniences like gas and electricity was reduced to insignificance by an air raid. "I have just put my first experience in a Zeppelin raid behind me," Churchill wrote in January 1917, "and right here let me tell you it is, without exception, the most helpless and horrible sensation you can imagine. . . . about seven, came the horrible fire-engines through the streets, preceded by bugles, which only means one thing—put out your lights, the Zeppelins are coming! . . . At the same time the telephone central turns a buzzer on all the wires and in an instant *'tout le monde'* knows the 'Zepps' are arriving. . . . Moll [her little girl] said, 'I wish there never was such a thing as war; I wish we weren't so far from home.' "[15]

▞▞▞ *Some of the Americans here, particularly the women, are quite hysterical when they talk about Wilson's policy, and war in the United States between Americans and Germans; they say they are ashamed of being Americans.*
—Mary King Waddington[16]

Before 1917 Americans abroad suffered the strictures of Europeans who resented American neutrality. "Wherever I went I heard mention of 'Traitorous America,' " Margaret Sanger noted, observing that anyone who wanted to remain safely in England must agree with England.[17] "I don't think I should have had the face to come over here before our entry into the war," Marian Baldwin confessed. "Americans who have been here since the beginning say that the situation grew very strained. . . ."[18]

Some Americans tried to compensate by devoting themselves to war work. Feelings of guilt at least partially motivated women like Mrs. Robert Bliss, whose husband served at the American embassy in Paris: enormously generous to war causes with her time and money, she thought that "any American who comes out of this crisis with his income what it was before the war is an 'honte,' a disgrace.

What have we done to show we took part in what others are enduring—I mean to say, what have we done that has cost us anything
at all?"[19]

Others tried to escape censure by denouncing their own country.
". . . nothing is a more unlovely spectacle," wrote Elisabeth Marbury,
"than to find one's compatriots in a foreign land so disloyal to their
own country as to throw the balance of their influence against it.
The traitors to the United States were not only to be found in the
enemy's camps, but in the most luxurious drawing rooms of the
American colony in Paris. . . . our home government was too often
made the target of American criticism, and its short-comings were
noisily described and derided by our compatriots who were the loud-
est in proclaiming their allegiance to the Allies."[20] In England the
American poet Louise Imogen Guiney raged at being "an Alien neutral. Would I were at the front. . . . If England doesn't pull through,
no more will liberty and civilisation." Even the armistice did not
quench this fifty-seven-year-old's bellicosity: ". . . why did the
wretched soft-soapers interrupt Foch by granting that Armistice,
when another three weeks of him would have cut the claws of all the
Devils forever! *À bas les civiles!*"[21]

> ▶▶▶ *It was the "Three thousand mile disease" again [the*
> *difference in outlook between England and America].*
> —Mrs. J. Borden Harriman[22]

English and French people who castigated the United States for
not entering the war also contributed to the atmosphere of suspicion
that traveling Americans encountered. From Scotland Ruth Holden
wrote on October 1, 1914, ". . . behold me now in Fort William—
held up & forbidden to go to any more islands, because I'm an
American citizen. For 2 days I cussed, telegraphed the Home Secretary, & the Aliens Inspector, but all to no purpose. In Bruiescan,
all the children shouted 'German spy' at me, & to further the illusion,
I jabbered German at them. Then someone informed the Home Sec.
that the steamship co. was carrying German spies disguised as Am.
citizens, & I'm the goat. It really is quite a sensible provision, for if

the Germans wanted a base, those unfrequented & sometimes un-
inhabited islands, would be just the thing."[23]

Jessica Lozier Payne in 1916 described for *The Brooklyn Eagle*
her travels in the British Isles and France. In Liverpool, where she
had to register at the police station before she could get a hotel room,
a police official told her, "Madame, our orders are to regard every
American as a German spy until proof is given us to the contrary."
A Scots official was even more difficult, insisting that she provide an
identifying mark for her "Identity Book," rejecting a mole as too
small. She was ready to give up: "Well, I am very sorry, but I cannot
mutilate myself just to give you a mark of identity to write in your
book." But finally they found a small scar of recent date on her wrist,
carefully measured and described it, and "I devoutly hoped it would
stay by me and not fade away before I left the land of the cautious
and canny Scot."[24]

The irrationalities of spy fears exempted no one—not even the
wildly popular Elsie Janis, on tour to entertain the troops, when the
French stopped her and sent her back to Paris under suspicion. In
1916 Gertrude Atherton was detained more than once because she
was blond—just the way the French pictured Germans. Mrs. J.
Borden Harriman on a trip through England in December 1917 forgot
to register with the police. When they found that she had been visiting
ammunition factories and that her police pass was improperly made
out, their suspicions waxed, despite her American passport and her
blanket pass from the British Minister of Munitions. "Over in the
corner in a very high seat like a pulpit sat an extraordinary elderly
man in uniform—one of the handsomest men I had ever seen. . . .
He took my passport, looked down at me and looked back at my
passport, and said, 'And what is Robert Lansing to me?' 'Nothing,'
I said, 'except that he happens to be the American Secretary of State.'
. . . The man in the pulpit said, 'How do we know that you didn't
pick these passes up somewhere?' I told him to turn over the paper
signed by the unknown Robert Lansing; maybe I would look like
the photograph on the front page."[25]

All sorts of bureaucratic regulations hampered movement—
though so unevenly enforced that the lawless Americans often successfully circumvented them. After early 1916, all foreigners in

France had to register as aliens and get permission to travel—even doctors, nurses, and ambulance drivers in American units.[26] Women who had to travel extensively in the line of duty, like Chief Nurse Elizabeth Ashe of the American Red Cross, repeatedly came under suspicion as spies; their credentials were questioned; sometimes they were detained, sometimes strip-searched. Ruth Farnam, on a trip to take relief to Serbia, equipped with every possible paper of authorization, at the Italian frontier faced an official who was "peculiarly insulting while his manner was that of one who was dealing with a particularly vicious criminal. . . . I gathered [he] had decided the minute he saw me that I was a spy, and his manner made me believe that my ultimate (Latin) destination would be the rock-hewn, undersea dungeons of some noisome Italian jail."[27]

🕊🕊🕊 . . . *not only does that dreary and dangerous region [the war zone] exert a sinister fascination but . . . it seems to expel fear from your composition. It is as if for the first time you were in the normal condition of life, which during the centuries of the ancestors to whom you owe your brain-cells, was war, not peace.*

                                        —Gertrude Atherton[28]

Despite the hazards, "frontline fever" infected almost everyone. Whether for a brief visit or a tour of duty, American women competed to get as far forward in the war zone as they could. "I was so afraid they would locate me in some place in the western part of France, far away from the front," wrote the twenty-two-year-old telephone operator Adele Louise Happock. "I much preferred to be as near the lines as possible. . . . it is the most interesting place of all, because it is near the Front."[29] Instead of their important administrative work for the YMCA, Edith Gratie Stedman and Mrs. Theodore Roosevelt, Jr., would have preferred, said Stedman, "to run a doughnut and coffee route out from Toul, she making the doughnuts and I peddling them around to the boys back of the 3rd line in a little Ford. . . . I do hope to get closer to the Front after another month."[30] And Agnes Gilson, Wellesley '10, envied Wellesley Professor Margaret Jackson, who had been assigned "nearer the front, the only woman within thirty miles, or something like that. It pays to be old and harmless."[31]

The disease of frontline fever was easy enough to diagnose in others. Particularly obnoxious were the "never ending collection of worthies from the States on tours of inspection," whom the war workers dared not offend but could only fulminate against. One day, observed Edith Stedman, "our treat consisted of four fat pompous civilians from Pittsburgh and its environs representing some mysterious Order of the Moose. Fatuous fools—one looked at me up and down and asked me if I enjoyed my work."[32] The expatriate American writer Natalie Barney, an inventive opponent of the war, reduced the fever to a surrealist absurdity by turning expeditions to the front into a kind of sport, which her friend Jean Cocteau satirized in one of his plays.[33] Edith Wharton, who frequented the front for journalistic and charitable purposes, could imagine nothing "ghastlier & more idiotic than 'doing' hospitals en touriste, like museums!"[34]

Dr. Esther Lovejoy commented that "everybody in service hated the war tourist"—but she might equally accurately have added that everyone wanted to be one. As she confessed, she herself would have been if she could: "The contemplation of my impeccable itinerary [away from the front lines] is a joy in retrospection. This evidence of rectitude gives me a great advantage and whenever I hear a war tourist talking about Verdun or Rheims (especially a woman) . . . I can ask myself with the consciousness of a blameless schedule what he was doing there. 'But conscience doth make cowards of us all,' and that psychological inconvenience compels me at this moment to acknowledge that the credit for my record in this respect is due to the regulations, and an utter inability on my part to circumvent them."[35]

All American women overseas in World War I shared experiences like these, labored under such stresses and strains. But they did different kinds of work, associated themselves with different organizations, assumed different responsibilities, and spread out across Europe.

CHAPTER 3

To the Rescue

The American Community Abroad

THE "GREAT WAR" wreaked its cruelties not only on the men who fought it but equally terribly on the civilian populations whose homelands it invaded. Inevitably starvation and epidemic festered around it. Children, women, and old men fled before it. And the Germans, taking and killing hostages, importing able-bodied laborers from France and Belgium, deporting from the territories they conquered the people they found useless, displaced millions more. The refugees immediately overwhelmed European relief agencies.

In a trickle, then in a spate, Americans surged to the rescue. Tourists, students, and expatriates discovered an enormous need and a thousand ways to help. Soon volunteers arrived from the States to multiply their efforts.

True enough, some tourists joined a panicky flight for home, usually uncomfortable because of the crowds, the lack of preparation, and the spy hunts conducted by both the Allies and the Central Powers. Others went on as planned, slightly discommoded by troop movements and suspicions, now and then landing in considerable difficulty—like Ruth Pierce, who on a visit to Russia got herself charged with espionage for describing in a letter home the harsh Russian treatment of imprisoned Jews on their way to Siberia. For a while it looked as if she would join them.[1] Other American women continued to travel on business: in April, 1916, Ruby Goodnow and Nancy McClelland, representing Wanamaker's Department Store, were buying antiques in England and porcelain in France, and persuading the Italian government to grant army leave to Murano glass-makers. And Bella da Costa Greene in the same year journeyed to England for treasures for J. P. Morgan's art collection.

But frequently travelers were drawn into war work. The suffragist Harriot Stanton Blatch, on a trip to England to settle her late husband's affairs, was persuaded that the war would improve women's status and urged American women to help—though events, she felt later, proved her wrong.

The hundreds of American women students, particularly of music and art, in England, France, Germany, and Italy seemed at first inclined to stay where they were. After all, almost no one predicted a long war, and the United States was not a participant. So a good many of them just went about their business—business that sometimes seemed incongruous in a world at war; in Paris "a young girl, a Californian (University of Berkeley and Oxford)," wrote the journalist Inez Irwin, "is learning the Latin shorthand which is used in manuscripts of the middle ages, learning it in preparation for her study of mediaeval cities."[2]

Others turned to war work. Sylvia Beach, later to found the Paris bookstore and publishing house Shakespeare and Company, in 1917 lived with her sister in the Palais Royal while she studied contemporary French literature. "During the nightly air raids, Cyprian and I had the choice of catching the flu in the cellar or enjoying the view from the balcony. We usually chose the latter. More frightening was 'Big Bertha,' the Germans' pet gun, which raked the streets during the day." As a change from her life in the Parisian literary world: "One whole summer I worked as a volunteer farm hand. . . . After harvesting the wheat, I picked grapes in the vineyards of Touraine. Then my sister Holly managed to get me a job in the American Red Cross. We went to Belgrade, where for nine months I distributed pajamas and bath towels among the valiant Serbs."[3]

Ruth Holden, a young paleobotanist at Cambridge University, ready to abandon her studies to work in an ammunition factory but rejected there as an alien, trained as a Red Cross nurse and volunteered in British hospitals through 1915 while still living in college and enjoying a fringe benefit of war: "One result of the war is that profs who last year wouldn't admit girls to their lectures, are this yr only too glad to have them. Some of the courses are attended almost exclusively by girls."[4] In January 1916 she went to Russia with a British hospital unit.

Because they could see the needs at first hand, and because their sympathies as a rule lay strongly with their host countries, the women in the American communities abroad were usually at the forefront of efforts to succor war victims. In the capitals of the warring nations from the beginning of the war, their wives and daughters promptly joined resident American businessmen and diplomats in relief work of all kinds. In Germany they ran a soup kitchen in Berlin, a hospital in Munich, a bazaar for the German Red Cross in Dresden. In Paris they started numberless relief enterprises, including the American Relief Clearing House and the famous hospital called the American Ambulance at Neuilly. In Brussels Ambassador and Mrs. Whitlock led relief efforts, conducting "themselves with wonderful discretion & wisdom . . ." which gained the affection of the Belgians and the respect of the Germans.[5] In Italy Americans formed a branch of the American Relief Clearing House, met regularly to make hospital supplies, and found work for the wives and widows of Italian soldiers. In London Mrs. Whitelaw Reid not only headed the chapter of the American Red Cross, but also imaginatively devised ways to ease the lives of American nurses—sending them down-filled sleeping bags, fighting to get them colored uniforms to free them from hours at the washtub at the hopeless task of restoring blood- and mud-stained uniforms to whiteness.

The American missionaries resident in the Balkans were a special case in the expatriate community. Understandably, the American Board of Commissioners for Foreign Missions did not take war work as their province. But missionaries to Bulgaria and Serbia had long been relieving the victims of disease and hunger as part of their work in the service of Christianity, and as long as they remained in middle Europe during the war they continued as best they could to succor its victims, sometimes in cooperation with the official and unofficial war-relief agencies.

In her report from Monastir Station, for instance, the missionary Delpha Davis wrote that while the station had had to operate under two different governments, Bulgarian and Serbian, "Mrs. Clarke" had engaged in industrial relief among poor Turkish women and distributed food to the needy, and "Sister Hilda Hawley has spent the whole of the past year . . . in the military hospital where she has rendered noble service." Meanwhile, though, "Miss Matthews was instrumental in distributing numbers of Bibles and tracts in various hospitals. . . ."[6]

The missionaries, that is, while responding to the emergencies that war forced on the populations they sought to minister to, continued to envision their mission as they had before the war. Unlike the women who flocked to Europe from the United States and the expatriates who devoted themselves to war work, they did not understand their lives and priorities differently because of the war.

Besides the travelers, the students, the diplomats' and businessmen's wives, and the missionaries, the American community abroad included women who worked there: like Mary Cassatt; like the sculptor Malvina Hoffman, assistant to Rodin; like the journalist/ writer Mildred Aldrich, who found French plays for American producers and French singers for American operas. Of no mind to desert in wartime the countries they had loved in peace, many of them did what they could to help. The artist Anna Lea Merritt joined her friends and neighbors in making hospital supplies for the wounded and joked about being harassed by circulars issued from British society matrons "proposing that I, aged then seventy-two years, should register for agricultural work; the government would . . . provide a first outfit, including tunic, gaiters and breeches. I constantly regret not having accepted this generous offer, as it is just what I need for my garden work."[7] The classicist Lily Ross Taylor, who in 1917 became the first woman fellow of the American Academy in Rome, joined the American Red Cross to serve in Italy and the Balkans. The interior decorator Elsie de Wolfe and the theatrical agent Elisabeth Marbury converted the historic gem of a house they shared with Anne Morgan at Versailles into a hospital and devoted themselves to war work. The actress Maxine Elliott depleted her private fortune to outfit and operate a barge in the canals of Belgium to carry food and clothes to the poor.

Of course some women in the international set reacted differently. "I would gladly have been a nurse," wrote Isadora Duncan, who reveled in dancing in the Place de la Concorde during an air

raid, "but I realised the futility of adding what would have been a superfluous force when the applicants for nursing were waiting in rows." Instead she enjoyed a "blissful time . . . gladdened by my archangel [her current lover], surrounded by the sea [in the south of France], living only in music. . . . Now and then we issued from our retreat to give a benefit for the unfortunate or a concert for the wounded, but mostly we were alone. . . ."[8] As for the heiress Mabel Dodge, then emotionally involved with John Reed, the war "didn't interest or excite me, or even reach me. . . . I made one feeble attempt to connect in some way with the Red Cross Society. But either I was too half-hearted or they were too organized."[9]

The poet Natalie Barney as a matter of principle advocated that people should go to "love the way they go to war." In her "Amazon's salon" in Paris she and her friends denounced the mindless slaughter of the war. Saying "I rejoice in being completely useless," she refused all forms of war service. In the spring of 1917, at the time of the mutiny of the French army, Barney convened a woman's congress for peace, at the end of which she proclaimed: "We must create a civilian cross [a decoration] for those who have neither sought nor too eagerly fled the danger, for all those who have borne the war with a somber amazement, silently. In waiting for humanity to become human again, keeping a civil and personal equilibrium in the confusion and monotony is to act as a good citizen, which, equal to an iron cross or a wooden one, is a distinction in itself."[10]

But most of the expatriate American women distinguished themselves by their war work. Mary Dexter's mother collected money from the States to form a "War Club for Soldiers' and Sailors' Wives . . . in a slummy part of Southwark. . . . Mrs. Parker gets the house from the County Council for the rent of a shilling a week! They give a house warming while it is still unfurnished, and invite people in, the result being that everybody gets interested and sends furniture."[11]

Grace Monks, in 1916, a time when propagandists were touting the life of munitions workers as healthful, recognized the dangers of industrial disease and chemical poisoning, and enterprisingly opened a hostel in England for prevention and care: "We take cases suffering from Tri Nitro Toluol [T.N.T.] poisoning, mercury poisoning, and fatigue, also a few convalescent cases, women suffering from burns, septic fingers, or women who are recovering from operations. . . . we aim to take in women who have been working on poisonous substances before they break down, to build them up by a diet recommended by the doctors, to save them from what might have been a serious illness, and to send them back to work and the service of their country." For the thirty women in her care at any one time, Monks tried to create a democratic, stimulating haven: "I often think as I sit at the head of the table pouring out thirty cups of tea, what a free and equal lot we are. We discuss all sorts of industrial questions. . . . above all we like to speculate on what is going to happen to industry after the war."[12]

American expatriate women of wealth and influence accomplished miracles in organization and fund-raising—including the many highly influential women who had married European men. Wealthy American women romanticizing European culture and noble rank had married titled—though sometimes impoverished— Europeans in such numbers that Bessie Marbury jested about "the denationalization of our women. This contagion spread so rapidly that there are now many American grandmothers and even great-grandmothers whose names appear in the peerage."[13] Names like Mme. la Marquise d'Andigne (Madeleine Goddard of Providence), Mme. la Marquise de Talleyrand-Perigord (Elizabeth Curtis of New York), the Comtesse de Roussy de Sales, and the Princesse Poniatowska (Elizabeth Sperry of California) headed the list of officers in organizations like Le Bienêtre du Blessé (The Welfare of the Wounded).

Mary King Waddington may here represent many other expatriate Americans who all during the war dedicated themselves to war work. The daughter of a president of Columbia College, she had long before married a Frenchman who served as ambassador to England for ten years; a grandmother when the war broke out, with a son in the French army, she plunged into multiple relief activities. In her mid-seventies, she charged about Paris and the countryside around her estate: "Her plackett was always open in the back, her hat on any way, and she had not bought a new hat since the beginning of the War."[14] Early in August 1914, with her American friend "Mrs. Mygatt, who has lived a great deal in Paris," and is very anxious to give some help to the poor women of France, she established an *ouvroir* (workroom), in an effort to employ a few of the thousands of Parisian women thrown out of work by the war. (The French, convinced that the war would be short, shut down banks, businesses, even some ammunition factories for the anticipated duration.) Waddington and Mygatt planned to employ "not only soldiers' wives, but quantities of young women and girls left with no work and no money. . . . It is always the same story with that class in Paris. They spend all they earn on their backs. Three or four of them club together and have a good room, and they live *au jour le jour* [from day to day], putting nothing aside. . . . In our rooms we could easily employ sixty, perhaps more, women, give them fr. 1.50 a day, and one good meal. They could work all day, making clothes for the sick, the wounded, and the refugees. . . ."[15]

Money was a problem; generous as the American community were, they had first to think about the American Ambulance and the needs of Americans stranded by the war. So, with the help of a woman correspondent of *The New York Times*, Waddington, already known for her book *Château and Country Life in France*, composed an appeal to Americans Stateside, both for her workroom and for the Mme. Waddington Relief Fund for the refugees who were beginning to flood into Paris. Americans responded.

Mme. Waddington led a complicated life. In the fall of 1914 she had to make a decision about the family estate at the village of Mareuil, whence her daughter-in-law and grandsons were soon forced to flee, to get her invalid sister out of Paris, which itself was threatened by the Germans, and to arrange for the operation of the workroom in her absence. By mid-October 1914 she was back in Paris, sickened by what the Germans had done to her estate: they had lived there eight days, sacked the houses, left them unspeakably filthy, and stolen, among much else, the whole *batterie de cuisine*. In mid-December Mme. Waddington took down relief supplies for the village and sent a truckload ahead; she had tried to shop for people individually.

By late January 1915, "Our stuffs [materials for the workroom] are giving out, and our poor women increasing in number. Some of them look too awful, half starved and half clothed. I didn't like to ask one poor thing who came with two children, both practically babies, four weeks and one year old, if she had any clothes on under her dress—I don't think she had. She knew nothing of her husband; had had no news since the beginning of December. . . . We must start a Women and Children's Department—and have ordered from London a thousand yards of flannel and a thousand of cotton."[16]

After most of her estate was requisitioned in May 1915, Mme. W. had endless problems with the French military authorities. But she continued to accept responsibility for the village people, maintaining a nursery school for their children, getting assistance from young women at the American embassy to help clothe them, opening a workroom for village women. By June 1916 the country and the city workrooms had sent 20,000 packages to soldiers. The village work was compounded by an influx of refugees from the invaded districts. The Waddington estate was on their line of escape, so "they simply camped in the park and in the garage. Of course they had to be clothed, fed, and generally assisted."[17]

That wasn't all. Mme. Waddington, that energetic septuagenarian, also sponsored and helped manage a clinic at St.-Rémy and converted the upper floor in her stables into a hospital ward of twenty-four beds which she operated under the supervision of an attending military doctor and with the aid of one trained nurse.

And Mme. Waddington served in other organizations as well, most importantly as president of the Comité International de Pansements Chirurgicaux des États-Unis (International Committee for Surgical Dressings of the United States). "It is entirely an American work. All the pansements [dressings], blankets, old linen, etc., are sent direct from America . . ." though sometimes goods sent from America made the trip back again, because the ports were shorthanded.[18]

Like Mme. Waddington, Edith Wharton at the outbreak of World War I already bore many responsibilities. At fifty-two she was a widely read and critically admired novelist, and a settled expatriate with a house near Paris and another on the Riviera, and a wide circle of distinguished friends. She quietly committed herself, her resources, and those of her friends to private, entrepreneurial solutions to the problems created by the war. Though, as she commented to

Bernard Berenson, she found that "it takes a great deal more time to do good than to have fun," she managed to accomplish without fuss or fanfare an enormous amount of relief work demanding organizational finesse even while she continued to impress her friends as a woman of leisure.[19]

She too responded to the plight of displaced workingwomen by starting a workroom which eventually employed a hundred seamstresses. She too aided refugees, by borrowing houses from her wealthy friends to establish the American Hostels for Refugees, renting the refugees rooms at modest fees, feeding them, providing them with a free clinic and dispensary, opening for them a clothing depot and fitting up a workroom where sixty women made clothes for it. Concurrently Wharton and a friend set up a distribution point where refugees could buy groceries at a 40 percent discount, arranged for coal delivery to them, created a day nursery, held classes in singing, sewing, and English, and started an employment agency for them. By the end of 1915, a year after she founded the American Hostels, "9,300 refugees had been assisted . . . 3,000 of them on a permanent basis; 235,000 meals had been served, and 48,000 garments handed out; 7,700 persons had received medical care; jobs had been found for 3,400. The whole undertaking had cost $82,000 in the first year, and monthly expenses ran to $6,000. . . . she had collected more than $100,000 in the preceding twelve months."[20]

In April of 1915 Wharton, responding to the request of the Belgian government, on forty-eight hours' notice undertook the care of sixty refugee children, later adding another six hundred, starting classes in lace making for the girls and industrial training for the boys, teaching the Flemish children French. Five times in 1915 she toured and wrote about the front lines from Dunkirk to Belfort. She arranged benefit concerts in France and in the United States, rummage sales, art exhibitions.

Emotion fueled this frenetic but efficient and productive activity. She chose hard work as an escape from "the sadness of all things." But equally she was driven by her disgust with the posture of neutrality assumed by the American president and by the pope: "two such Pantaloons as Wilson and Benedict the Last (I hope). . . ."[21] She considered her work and that of other Americans in Europe

essential to compensate for the failure of the United States to enter
the war.

In the spring of 1916 Wharton initiated a new effort, a cure
program for people who had contracted tuberculosis during the war,
later turned over as a going institution to the International Red Cross,
while she went on to establish two American Convalescent Homes
and two more homes for children. Meanwhile she and her friends
continued to support financially and to oversee all her other enterprises. Only in the summer of 1917, with the United States now in
the war, did she feel free to vacation in Morocco and to turn her
attention primarily to her writing, as the Red Cross took over some
of her programs and others seemed almost to run themselves.

Many other American women living abroad who were neither
wealthy nor particularly influential also thought up ways to help the
war's victims. Of course not all succeeded. Valentine Thompson, a
journalist living in France, was inspired to start at Passy a school
designed to teach hotel keeping to young French women of good
family whose marriage prospects were ruined by the war. It eventually failed for lack of funds.

But an American doctor, wife of an Italian physician who had
upon the outbreak of war abandoned his practice in Chicago to serve
on the Italian front, was living in a town in Sicily. When refugees
swarmed in, the mayor asked her to run a "hospital," comprised
entirely of a building and twenty beds. "She at once . . . moved over
her private equipment . . . and finding a couple of promising looking
refugees she dressed them in sheets and called them nurses. . . ."
She also opened an outpatient clinic. After the Red Cross took over,
the doctor remained to direct the hospital, and to start up and run
a refuge for a hundred small children, an industrial school for women,
a carpenter shop, and a music school. Another American woman in
Italy, wife of a Red Cross district delegate, organized a playground
for the boys running wild on the streets.[22]

Janet Scudder, the sculptor, who had lived in France since 1909,
in 1914 at the age of fifty-four engaged successively in several different
kinds of war work, pausing only to earn enough money to continue.
When the United States entered the war, Scudder undertook to
lecture for the troops and to manage concerts for the singer Camille

Lane. They spent an arduous six months at it. "We were delighted to have the chance to do our bit . . . but often the indifference and even heartlessness of the Y.M.C.A. secretaries in charge of the camp huts were more than we could bear in silence." The YM men disgruntled Scudder particularly one evening after Mrs. Lane, at a doctor's request, had spent a long afternoon singing to soldiers to help them through the painful process of having their wounds dressed. Back at the hotel the women could get nothing to eat, so Scudder went foraging. At the Y quarters the table was laden, but the YM men refused to share their food without a written order from an absent authority. Scudder acted: "I grabbed a napkin from the sideboard and reached over the heads of those feeding secretaries, dumped the contents of a sugar bowl in it, picked up several pieces of bread and finally appropriated a plate of butter. . . . what I thought of an American organization and American men who could permit themselves to reach such a state of bad manners. . . ."[23]

When Lane's voice gave out, the two women spent a few weeks in canteen work, then took a job decorating YM huts: "We went from camp to camp, mixed colors, climbed ladders, hung curtains and accomplished a lot of work," work that they enjoyed more after they managed a transfer to the Red Cross, where ". . . there was not nearly so much red tape and never any stupid interference with our work. . . ."[24]

Mme. Berard, formerly Miss Dana of Boston, with three sons in the French army, after nursing at the front for three months devised a scheme that brightened the lives of many soldiers. For those who—often because of war losses—had no families to write them and send them small comforts, she embarked upon the career of *marraine*, or godmother, herself corresponding with several hundred men. As the work grew beyond her own powers, she called upon her friends to help out. The practice of adopting a *filleul*, a godson, spread widely both in Europe and in the States.

(In time, rascals exploited the relationship. In November 1916, Mary Dexter warned a would-be *marraine:* ". . . really there are no lonely soldiers now. There are clubs, and everything is systematized. And people who had a 'lonely soldier' have found they were one of several writing to him! . . . I didn't go to the Fairy Godmothers'

League—isn't the name enough to put one off—this is no time for sentiment! . . . Dr. C——, of the R.A.M.C., told me that when he was out at the front a man in his regiment advertised as a lonely soldier, as a joke, and Dr. C—— said that hundreds of answers came from girls. The man was a rotter, and when Dr. C—— overheard him joking about it, he made him sit down and answer every letter!"[25])

Despite the vast display of generosity, initiative, and administrative ability, not all American women abroad leave such an impression. Katherine Blake, for instance, wife of an American Army doctor, felt that people at home underestimated the hazards she faced, decided that her services were not really needed in the established welfare organizations, and criticized severely the relief and rescue services, as well as the ARC and YMCA women workers, whom she thought of as kept women or wives in disguise.[26] Edith L. O'Shaughnessy, wife of an American diplomat, emerges from the pages of her travelog as a woman chiefly interested in seeing how many times she could get to the front. She is highly critical of her betters, calling the Quakers engaged in reconstruction work "ugly traveling salesmen," and alleging that the Annamites, French colonials who had been brought to France to work on the roads, were "of little use when the cannon sounds."[27] She and her companions, meanwhile, on their trips to the front, now and then walked through a hospital distributing cigarettes and talking to the wounded, but spent much of their time drinking coffee and eating candy fresh out from New York. Best of all, they visited a battlefield, where O'Shaughnessy experienced *frissons* over the feel of *warm* shrapnel and the elastic sensation of scarcely buried bodies under her feet.

What a contrast with Mary Smith Churchill, another American Army officer's wife! She comes engagingly off the pages of her book to typify the personal care and concern that American women abroad showed the victims of war. During her stay in Paris, from August 1916 to January 1918 (her husband was originally assigned as an observer), she filled her life with her household, her young daughter, and a variety of imaginative services to soldiers and civilians. Most of her energies went to her increasingly responsible job for the American Fund for French Wounded, a clearinghouse for hospital supplies sent from America to be distributed to French hospitals.

But Churchill also ventured into all sorts of private undertakings on her own. She wrote to friends at home offering to act as liaison: "If they would like to have their work more personal by sending it to me, and through me hearing about the hospital and the use their things are put to, and about the various cases, I shall be only too glad." She went to departing troop trains to distribute cigarettes, turning all her money into cigarettes and wishing she had more to give. She encouraged her daughter Mollie to adopt a soldier "godson"; when on his leave he came to visit the family, they talked with him by the hour, took him to the cinema, sewed on his stripes, and felt sorry when he had to go back.[28]

One evening Churchill and her friends threw a party at the canteen in the Gare du Nord, whence troop trains departed: "We provided sandwiches, coffee, red and white wine, cigarettes and candy . . . and had a piano sent there. . . . They were like children in their joy and appreciation. . . . They all sat at this one table, and we were kept busy pouring wine and coffee for them and listening to their chatter. . . . Many asked if they could sing solos, having been on the stage, or in the opera before the war, so each was given a chance to do his parlor trick." The party broke up at midnight. ". . . you only wished you had the strength and the money to do it every night."[29]

One Saturday morning she ventured into the poorest part of Paris to distribute the fifty surprise Christmas bags assigned to her of the 50,000 the American Fund for French Wounded had prepared. These "comfort" or "Blighty" bags, often containing soap, razors, writing paper, or smoking materials, gave the men a place to keep whatever small possessions they had managed to salvage.[30] Churchill looked for and found a really poor hospital, supported principally by the poor people in its section of Paris; some had even sent their beds for the comfort of the wounded and sick soldiers, while they themselves took to sleeping on the floor. ". . . the men . . . were so excited that I felt quite sure a visitor was a rare thing. . . . I can't tell you what joy was in their faces as they opened the bags and examined each little thing. As always I had my big box of cigarettes and made my second round with those. This was a long process for they all wanted to show me what they had in their bags, and always to read the address [of the donor] they found within. And the ones who didn't find any address almost wept. A line written with an address is the most personal letter to them, as most of them haven't had a letter since the war began, and they almost blew up with excitement."[31]

With money from home Churchill organized a concert for the blind: "I had hoped to have a hundred . . . but one hospital didn't want to allow theirs to come, as the authorities do not like to have many seen at a time on account of the effect on the people at large. . . . Of the forty-seven there were all kinds and descriptions—African cavalry with their red fez, chasseurs, men in red and men in blue; many were without one arm, but all had both legs. One Moroccan about seven feet tall, with his head all bandaged up, and with hardly a square inch on his face, which wasn't a big dent, made by fragments of shell, was beaming with happiness. . . . Mrs. L——, who brought one from Val de Grace, went to see him the next morning and he said, 'Please tell madame for me that I feel thirty years younger. For the first time since I lost my eyes I felt that life was worth living. I didn't know I ever could enjoy anything again; I am a new man!'"[32]

✄✄✄ . . . *though I am a member of the Royal Serbian Army I am also a true American.*
—Ruth S. Farnam[33]

Some American women abroad adventured along more danger-ous paths. Ruth S. Farnam before World War I had twice visited Serbia, where on her second visit she had worked in the primitive hospital founded by Mme. Grouitch, an American woman married to a Serbian diplomat. In early 1915, in England, Farnam responded to a call for volunteers at a meeting of the Serbian Relief Fund but was rejected because of her lack of training, "my knowledge of the people, their customs and the practical experience I had gained among them, being apparently of little value." But if Farnam couldn't have bread, she would eat cake. Princess Alexia Kara-Georgevitch, the American wife of Prince Alexis of Serbia, invited her to go to Serbia with them, the money and supplies they had collected for Serbian relief, their English maid, their French chef, chauffeur and chambermaid, a pair of bulldogs, an Italian dog, a Pekingese, and thirty-eight trunks.

In Serbia they found typhus raging, with thousands dead. Even the life-style of the prince and princess was cramped: their French chef had scant materials on which to exercise his arts. "So there might be no danger of my springing to the table and greedily devouring all the . . . 'dinner' for four," Farnam remembered, "I would retire to my own room before the meal was served and, locking the door, swallow three or four spoonfuls of rich, cloying honey and then take my place at the table with a politely dulled appetite. I never want to taste honey again!"

Farnam took charge of the storeroom of a hospital in Vrgntze staffed by Greeks, Frenchwomen, Americans, English, and Russians, and supplied by shipments from English and American sympathizers. By segregating the patients and destroying vermin, they managed to reduce the mortality of typhus from 80 percent of those attacked to 20 percent. Then Farnam was sent back to England to solicit funds, because supplies from Britain were faltering.

While she was gone, a strong Austrian offensive forced the prince and princess to flee, in a dramatic escape that the American-born princess described in her book, *For the Better Hour*. On November 2, 1915, the prince and princess left in their car, their five foreign servants following in an ambulance. As the roads worsened, they destroyed the cars and took to springless carts, then to horseback, then to foot. One hundred fifty thousand refugees, droves of sheep, oxcarts loaded with ammunition and supplies, and packhorses carrying the gold of the Serbian government impeded their progress. They climbed mountains and forded streams, sometimes trying to persuade the horses onto "ferries" made of two hollowed logs lashed together. They stayed at an Eastern Orthodox monastery (pausing to celebrate the feast day of the metropolitan's [bishop's] patron saint), at filthy inns, in a loft over a stable, in an Albanian hut, where "I feel sure that the presence of our fourteen fearless [Serbian] soldiers, with guns and knives, was all that saved us to tell the tale."

When they met a procession of Serbian army wagons carrying bags
of flour, "it gave me a thrill of joy to see on the sacks, in big black
letters, 'New York,' 'St. Louis,' etc., and to know that my country
was providing this valiant army with its staple food." Finally an
Italian destroyer conveyed them secretly, by night, to Brindisi.[34]

Meanwhile, Farnam crossed to the States, where she lectured
to raise money to help Serbian refugees in Corsica and to establish
the American Unit of the Scottish Women's Hospital, other units of
which were already working in Serbia. Called back to England on
personal business, Farnam volunteered to extend her trip, and, east-
ward ho! off she went to Paris, Geneva, Berne, Naples, Athens—
whence she traveled to Serbia to survey conditions there for the
Serbian Relief Committee of America. "When I started back [to
America] to face my Committee, if there was anything that I did not
know about refugees or hospitals for Serbians or general relief in
refugee camps, that thing was not worth discussing! My work was
done."

But not before she had finagled a trip to the front. With Colonel
Dr. Sondermayer, head of the Military Medical Service of the Serbian
Army, whose German speaking often placed them at hazard on the
trip, she traveled to Ostrov. Farnam, wearing a Red Cross brassard,
and Sondermayer would " 'dash' along at a good speed, hit a rock
or a big hole, slow down a minute to make sure that our engine was
still in its place, then 'dash' on until we struck another obstacle!
After a couple of hours' ride, we halted before a gap in the low hills.
. . . Imagine a group of white tents, with neat walks bordered by
stones running before and between them, and . . . great trees spread-
ing their branches over an altar before another, much larger tent:
among them busy women in gray, or white, or khaki. . . . This was
the American Unit of the Scottish Women's Hospitals [financed by
Americans, but staffed largely by women of other nationalities]."
The Prince-Regent Alexander, visiting the hospital, suggested that
Farnam might like to go to the front.

Welcomed by the Commander-in-Chief of the Serbian Army,
Farnam and her escort advanced toward the front. "Where two
stones, rudely set in the earth, marked a boundary, Major Todorovitch saluted. 'Madame,' he said, 'I have the honor to inform you

that you are the first woman of any nationality to enter reconquered Serbian territory.' "

From a hillside they watched a battle, then crossed a protected part of No Man's Land on foot. The commander of the Serbians said, " 'Will you go further into Serbia than we have yet been, Madame? . . . Give me your hands,' he said, 'and lean out.' So, bending out over the valley from the brow of the precipice, I went, by the length of my own body, further into Beautiful Serbia than the soldiers had gone." Farnam thrilled to the view from the observation post, whence she could see a "welter of maimed and bloody forms" and "a group of men, perhaps eight of them, mashed to a gory pulp. . . . Still dazed and gasping, I heard Colonel Milovanovitch ask, 'Would you like to give the signal for our guns to recommence firing?' and, shaking with emotion, I nodded assent. So, in the name of American Womanhood, I gave the signal which sent shells roaring over the valley to fall in the Bulgarian trenches. . . . I was shaking from head to foot with excitement and the lust of battle. Major Todorovitch spoke—'Calm yourself, Madame; they have not just got our range up here yet. When it grows *too* dangerous we will take you away.' 'Do you think I am afraid?' I cried. 'I never *lived* before.' "

When the commander-in-chief told her that she should have been a soldier, " 'Make me one,' I promptly responded. The Colonel of the First Cavalry Regiment instantly put in his word. 'I want her to be made a member of my regiment,' said he. And so, with the shells screaming over our heads at the most exciting moment of my life on that famous battlefield of Brod, in October, 1916, I was made a member of the first Cavalry Regiment of the Royal Serbian Army. I was no longer a woman helper. I was now a soldier, and, as I write this—the only American woman soldier in this great war."[35]

Ad Hoc Organizations

While Americans in London, Paris, and points east were launching their war-relief efforts, Americans back home were setting up their own networks and committees, many of which soon developed into full-fledged organizations. Some functioned as fund-raisers for overseas organizations; others operated on their own. They shipped abroad not only money and tons of clothing, hospital supplies, trucks, and ambulances, but also personnel to evaluate needs and more personnel to meet them. In the jumble many of these agencies duplicated the work others were doing—though the vast needs swallowed up whatever aid they furnished. Eventually American women served, according to the Women's Overseas Service League, in "some 52 American and 45 foreign agencies and war organizations."[36]

Their range covered the whole spectrum of interests among the American population. The American Huguenot Committee, running mate of the Franco-Belgian Evangelization Committee, sent Grace Marling and Catherine Wetmore to France; since they could not go directly to the Belgian towns occupied by the Germans, they were "loaned" temporarily to La Société Secours d'Urgence (The Society for Emergency Relief). The Christian Scientists sent women to engage in relief work with their coreligionists in France. Mrs. Charlotte Kellogg went to Belgium in 1916 with Herbert Hoover on the Commission for Belgian Relief, undertaking particularly to write a book in tribute to the women of Belgium.[37] In 1914 the International Women's Relief Committee, needing a citizen of a neutral country, appointed the American Henrietta B. Ely as its agent to bring out from Belgium English children at school in Belgian convents when the war began, who had not since been heard of; in the seven weeks she spent there she also rescued some British nuns, and emerged with seventy-four in her "excited, frightened, homesick, and happy . . . troop."[38]

Le Comité Franco-Américain pour la Protection des Enfants de la Frontière, with Mrs. Cooper Hewitt as its honorary president, rescued refugee and repatriated children, identified them (if they could), fed them, clothed them, housed them in colonies, and trained them, while its American counterpart, Children of the Frontier, collected and shipped money and mounds of clothing. In the crises arising from the influx of thousands of refugees, the Comité supplied not only material aid but tender loving care. Its American women workers met the trains and comforted the children—down to the "dirtiest little specimens" with runny noses and lice. The Franco/

American Committee for Devastated France did similar work among other refugees, adults as well as children.

The American Relief Clearing House (ARCH), Le Bienêtre du Blessé, and the American Fund for French Wounded, among other American agencies, performed an invaluable service in furnishing and distributing hospital supplies at a time when the French hospitals would otherwise have had few, if any—partly because the French transport system broke down completely. ARCH alone afforded "5,000 relief organizations, societies, schools, churches and individuals at the head of small circles in various parts of the United States, Canada, Hawaiian Islands, Cuba and Bermuda . . . its free facilities for transferring material to France."[39] ARCH also operated the American Ambulance Service.

In 1915 at the request of the French health service, a group of prominent French, French-American, and American women established Le Bienêtre du Blessé, Société Franco-Américaine pour nos Combattants (The French-American Society for the Welfare of Wounded French Soldiers). Its mission was to provide special diets for convalescent French soldiers unable to stomach army food, either by transporting delicacies from some central point to the hospitals, or by running special kitchens in the larger hospitals. Gertrude Atherton learned of a second reason for these kitchens: "Military discipline closes every hospital kitchen in the war zone . . . promptly at 6 P.M. and does not open it again until 7 the next morning. If a blessé is brought in after 6 there is not so much as a teaspoonful of milk to give him, and if, as sometimes happens, he is passed on to another hospital early in the morning, he leaves without having had sustenance of any sort."[40] From December 1917 onward the New York City Women's Club provided and supported a motor unit for the organization and recruited "socially agreeable" women with a knowledge of the Ford mechanism to drive for it.

All of these were, it's important to remember, volunteer efforts. Their ad hoc, seat-of-the-pants, off-the-cuff operations not only had to respond to successive unanticipated crises, but also depended on coopting the necessary services. Thus when Le Bienêtre du Blessé needed a Stateside fund-raiser, the American-born Mme. d'Andigne conscripted Gertrude Atherton, who had gone to France as a reporter. Atherton had firmly resolved not to be drawn into any organization, because "Possibly no one ever lived who hates sitting at a committee table as I do. However, escape was impossible then or later; and, by degrees, I became infected with . . . enthusiasm. After my visits to military hospitals in the war zone I promised . . . willingly enough that I would do what I could to put the thing through in [the United States]."[41]

The success of the American Fund for French Wounded (AFFW), as well as similar organizations, suggests a high degree of tact and efficiency in its administration—especially since it numbered among its many volunteers the likes of Gertrude Stein and Alice B. Toklas, with their distinctive, not to say eccentric, style. "Gertrude Stein," wrote Alice B. Toklas, "commenced driving Aunt Pauline [their car] for the American Fund for French Wounded, she was a responsible if not an experienced driver. She knew how to do everything but go in reverse. She said she would be like the French Army, never have to do such a thing. . . . Aunt Pauline—Model T, bless her—made no more than thirty miles an hour, so we were always late at inns, hotels and restaurants for meals." Eventually Stein and Toklas opened an AFFW depot at Perpignan, using a hotel banquet hall as a distribution center, warehouse, and office, where hospital representatives came to collect what they needed.[42] They went on to work at Nîmes, where Stein evacuated the wounded who came in on the ambulance trains. Stein and Toklas continued their work until well after the war, when they found that "we had largely overdrawn at our banks to supply the needs of soldiers and their families and now the day of reckoning had come. We would live like gypsies, go everywhere in left-over finery, with a *pot-au-feu* for the many friends we should be seeing."[43]

But if the necessity for handling all kinds of volunteers demanded flexibility from the administration of these organizations, changing needs also required that quality in the volunteers themselves. For instance—from the time of its founding in the spring of 1915, the American Fund for French Wounded expanded its functions, responding to the needs of refugees as well as of soldiers. The tasks assigned workers multiplied and diversified. "We go often to see refugee families," Amy Owen Bradley wrote, "and Miss Wells, of the Red Cross . . . has promised shoes and beds for them. We are doing the clothing part and are cooperating with the Red Cross practically, as well as theoretically, here. . . . The Red Cross has now made us part of their Casualty Bureau, to look up U.S. soldiers who have somehow got lost, and are 'missing.' "[44]

Bradley found herself in her "leather coat with shoulder straps, marked A.F.F.W., and a blue felt hat with A.F.F.W. on the hatband" now delivering hospital supplies, now at the request of the French government removing from comfort bags the religious tracts deposited in them by the American ladies who packed them, and again driving for the American "Dr. Alice Brown, of Winetka, Ill., on her rounds of dispensary work. She visits six towns, each twice a week, to look after the women and children, who have had no medical care since the war. . . . I wish I could keep on with this work as it is the kind I like best."[45] Wherever she went in her "Lizzie" Bradley met with a delighted welcome. After the American troops arrived "I rescued five United States cooks, who were lost from their regiment on its way to the front, and restored them to their convoy. The next day, coming over the same road, I saw a car stopped and surrounded by soldiers—'more cooks,' I thought. So in my rattling and muddy Ford, with the wash bouncing around like a huge white balloon behind, I slowed up, at the same time calling out, 'Are you broken down; can I help?' Imagine my horror when a general came forward and saluted me. He said, 'No we aren't broken down, but we are in trouble. The trouble with us is, we haven't had the pleasure of speaking to an American lady for a long time, so I am delighted that you have stopped and given me that pleasure and opportunity.' Wasn't that nice of him?"[46]

Organizations proliferated, and this spontaneous outpouring of American concern, dedication, money, materials, and assistance expanded from the summer of 1914 to the spring of 1917. With the entry of the United States into the war, the situation of the ad hoc organizations changed abruptly—thanks to the American Red Cross (ARC).

The American Red Cross

In the history of relief work in World War I, as in its medical record, the American Red Cross looms over all other organizations. Its enormous financial resources and its quasi-official status empowered it to go unto all the world, to be all things to all peoples, and to subordinate and extend the efforts of others under its aegis. It served both soldiers and civilians in every imaginable way. It undertook vast educational enterprises, particularly in public health, concerning itself especially with children and the tubercular. It not only cared for soldiers during their hospitalization, but also manufactured artificial limbs for them and reeducated the blind and the crippled. It succored refugees from the time they were displaced until they were reestablished in their homes. In France alone its table of organization rivaled or exceeded in complexity and diversity those of the military:

1. Department of Requirements: Bureaus of Supplies, Transportation, Manufactures, Personnel, Permits and Passes, Construction
2. Medical and Surgical Departments: Hospital Administration, TB and Public Health, Children's Bureau, Reconstruction and Reeducation, Nurses
3. Medical Research Intelligence: Research, Medical Information, Library, Publications
4. Army and Navy Service: Canteens, Home Hospital Service, Outpost Service, Field Service
5. French Hospitals: Requirements and Supply, Visiting
6. General Relief: Refugees, Soldiers and Families, War Orphans, Agriculture
7. Public Information: News and Public Information, Reports and Pamphlets, Photographs and Moving Pictures
8. Administration[47]

At the beginning of the war, though, from the summer of 1914 until the spring of 1917 when the United States declared war, the American Red Cross chose to confine its war-related activities to rather limited medical missions and to massive financial support of the works of other organizations.

But as time passed and its people recognized the likelihood of the United States' entering the war, the American Red Cross geared up to expand its own projects and to take over the supervision and in some cases the assets of other groups involved in relief work. In June 1917, the Red Cross was charged by the French and American governments with the major responsibility for distributing funds and supplies for civilian war relief. The private relief agencies were "invited" to affiliate with the Red Cross as closely as possible.[48] Since the Red Cross controlled so much of the available shipping space and so much money, few of them could afford to refuse.

Many in other organizations bitterly resented losing control of institutions they had founded and funded. Edith Wharton called the Red Cross "that blatant scourge."[49] Women with more than two years of experience watched in horror as new supervisors blundered. Sometimes the transition went smoothly, with the Red Cross tactfully and profitably utilizing the skills that workers had developed. At other times a straight power play drove the old-timers into disillusionment. In the enormous expansion of the Red Cross—from twenty people in Europe at the start to 6,000 women and men by January 1919—some of the new workers brought with them professionalism, expertise, and a generous appreciation of the work accomplished by other organizations. Other ARC workers bungled, damaging what had been built up with years of effort and patience.

Peer organizations also protested and despaired at the petty machinations of some officers of the ARC, determined to implement the policy of centralization, and rejoicing in the exercise of the authority conferred upon them by their affiliation with the most powerful organization for the welfare of both soldiers and civilians. The YWCA reports from workers in the field to their National Board, for instance, teem with polite accounts of their work's being obstructed by the Red Cross. A local Red Cross official resented the idea of having a YW administrator. The YW experienced difficulties in getting huts and equipment, because of the ARC's control over all activities on hospital grounds.

Beyond a doubt, the political maneuverings that ensued sometimes disrupted efficiency and victimized the very people the welfare organizations were seeking to help.

But despite their resentments and apprehensions most groups simply had no choice. If they wanted supplies, if they wanted shipping space for personnel and materials, they had to "cooperate." So the Society of Friends discovered; so the Smith College group; so the American Ambulance at Neuilly; so independent operators. At best they could negotiate to retain some control, some autonomy, and some identity. Private enterprise gave way to systematization, with all the benefits and all the faults of one huge overarching organization.

The system worked splendidly, for instance, in the enormous effort to save orphaned and abandoned children. In Marseilles, where the death rate among them had reached 49 percent, the Red Cross secured the cooperation of fifty French institutions in a comprehensive program of child-welfare work which continued even after the war.

The generous-minded among the ARC workers, especially those with power, could and did turn its resources to the benefit of other organizations and the individuals who otherwise might slip through the patchwork of safety nets. Elizabeth Ashe, chief nurse of the Children's Bureau of the ARC, helped out the American Fund for French Wounded by stopping off to inspect military hospitals when she went on Red Cross trips. "I can often help," she remarked "[by lending nurses] where most of the R.C., although doing splendid work in their own pursuits, do not realize how much is going on outside. I chum with all kinds of people, exchanging ideas and workers with them."[50]

But if in some degree civilian and military victims of the war benefited by the elimination of duplicate efforts and the systematization that it effected, if the organizations under the Red Cross aegis benefited financially, the American Red Cross also owed a monumental and sometimes unacknowledged debt to the American workers first on the ground. Chloe Owings, for example.

Owings, at thirty-three already a well-thought-of director of a social agency in Poughkeepsie, sold her household goods, took her savings and a gift from a board member, and in October 1916 went to Paris to work for the American Relief Clearing House. She volunteered to scrub floors, but fortunately her recommendations had preceded her, and the ARCH director hired her as his secretary. Living frugally with a French family, and struggling to learn French, Owings soon put the ARCH office in order. Then she turned down tempting offers for Stateside jobs, including one from the Rockefeller Foundation, in order to organize offices and other systems for a Red Cross hospital and for the American Society for Relief of French War Orphans. She also undertook to receive all requests for help coming to ARCH and prepare the dockets for the ARCH committee's decision. After the United States entered the war, she helped lay the ground for the arrival of the Red Cross, the Salvation Army, the YMCA and YWCA, and the Quakers. For the Red Cross she translated and organized fifty file cases of material about French war-relief agencies, identifying their boards, summarizing what each did. Eventually she went to work for the Red Cross, providing invaluable continuity as well as her superb organizational skills.

The story of American Red Cross World War I activities in Italy presents a paradigm for what happened on a much larger scale and in more diversified and better organized ways in France and other countries. As elsewhere, a freewheeling period of individual effort and ad hoc agencies was followed by a time when work was centralized under the ARC. When in mid-October 1914 the American community rallied to undertake rescue efforts, they formed an Italian branch of the American Relief Clearing House. The Red Cross financially assisted ARCH, and designated this organization its representative in Italy. After the disastrous defeat of the Italian Army at Caparetto in October 1917, the American ambassador sought help in Washington; the War Council of the Red Cross gave him $250,000, sent a small Emergency Commission from France, and backed American consuls in various Italian cities in starting up canteens for refugees and wounded soldiers and organizing the American community to help. The contributions of other groups in America, sending ambulances and relief supplies, paralleled this work.[51]

The Permanent Commission of the Red Cross did not arrive until December 1917. "Obviously the first thing necessary was to recruit a force to carry [the job] through, and that at once. The

Commission set out to enlist the services of available Americans who
were on the ground, artists, connoisseurs and dilettanti, and men
and women of leisure who had made Italy their home, Americans
married to Italians, travellers caught and held by the war—here a
professor of Logic from a Western University, there a chorus girl
who had sung in a popular light opera, here a well known impressario,
there a singer who as Carmen or Aïda had delighted audiences at the
Metropolitan, etc., etc., and large drafts were made on the students
and teaching force of the American Academy at Rome."[52] The numbers of American workers in Italy for the Red Cross went from 31
to 949.

Picking up ongoing efforts or branching out, the Red Cross then
ran rest houses, schools, workshops, sewing rooms for unemployed
lace makers. They undertook the construction of a town near Pisa
for refugees. With American nurses they opened one hospital and
took over an existing one. With Italian women they had trained they
started a Children's Health Bureau. They fought the influenza epidemic in the fall of 1918. When they discovered in the Pontine
marshes a small town with no medical facilities, "Within forty-eight
hours . . . the American Red Cross had a hospital of forty beds,
thoroughly equipped, established in a building that had formerly
been a convent, with three American nurses and an American doctor
in charge."[53] In Capri the Red Cross helped an American woman
who had long lived there to find work for soldiers' wives and care
for their children.

In all these activities, American women participated. In the
Home Service, they guided bewildered, non-English-speaking Italian
mothers of soldiers in the American army through the bureaucratic
wilderness, locating their sons and straightening out allotment problems. In Taormina: ". . . one young fellow walks up and says in
English to one of the Red Cross women in charge [of distributing
milk and clothing], 'Is this Miss ———?' He turns out to be an old
protégé of hers from the east side of New York." In Pádova, a letter
from an army chaplain related, "One of our men had died at your
hospital. . . . On the day of the funeral it rained, it literally poured
rain. . . . There were three American Red Cross nurses marching
in the procession carrying flowers to place on that soldier's grave. I

said to them, 'You should not do this; the weather is too severe.' 'But, chaplain, we are taking the place of the mother, sister and sweetheart.' "[54]

The American Red Cross was duplicating work like this, and initiating other services, not only in Europe, but in the far corners of the earth. Everywhere this organization provided ways for American women to exercise their talents—like Anna L. Johnson, self-described as "educated in French, Spanish, Arabic languages," who in January 1918 enlisted in the ARC Commission to Palestine and the Near East, serving at Headquarters, Jerusalem. The Commission to Palestine sailed from New York in March 1918 by way of South Africa, East Africa, India, where they transshipped for Port Said, Egypt, arriving in mid-June. There, serving directly under General Allenby, the commission did civilian relief.[55]

In many ways, it mattered little to the experiences of individual women in which organization they chose to serve. Obviously women like Edith Wharton, who for years made almost all the decisions for her many charities, faced dramatically different roles once the Red Cross had moved in. And members of small, cohesive groups with distinctive philosophies, like the Friends, or previously established ties, like the Smith College Relief Unit, experienced their work and related to their coworkers differently than those affiliated with large, heterogeneous operations. But most women were just as likely to serve happily and effectively in the Red Cross as in ARCH: they did the same kind of work, faced the same frustrations, and won the same rewards. Indeed as we have seen many, many workers changed from one organization to another in the course of their overseas life.

 The anguish of war for me was between its declaration and the time I got to work. . . .
                                                —Molly Dewson[56]

Molly Dewson might have contributed equally in another organization, though she happened to sign up with the Red Cross. She and her "partner," Polly Porter—with whom she lived, ran a farm, and worked for women's suffrage—sailed in the early fall of 1917, wearing their Abercrombie and Fitch "Red Cross uniform: tailored suit jackets, long skirts, plain blouses with neckties, and large square hats. This severely masculine outfit was modelled on the style favored by professional women of the day."[57] First assigned as a delegate for the Red Cross, in January 1918, by war's end Dewson held the position of director of general relief for about a third of France.

The eminently capable Dewson and Porter worked long hours, "trying to get the families who have been living under German rule on American bread without any work, back into a wholesome way of living. . . . we were running an employment bureau, sending out work on army clothing to the women in little places, starting kitchen gardens, potato patches, rabbit hutches . . . helping out the sick, halt and blind; hunting lost trunks, not to mention relatives, and most important, softening the mayors up to find them better lodgings, selling them furniture at ⅔ value on installment plan, etc. etc."

With the German spring offensive of 1918 Dewson and Porter switched to coping with refugees fleeing before the advance. "We thought we were busy before the offensive," Dewson wrote her family, "but now with all the people from the Oise and Somme flooding down here we just gape. We could not work any longer hours so we have shifted our job to trying to buy camp beds and bedding, stoves, chairs and tables, and 'batteries de cuisines.' #1 If we could find the things, #2 if the merchants could produce them after they had sold them to us, #3 if the railroads were not too overloaded to carry them it would really be a much easier job than our old one. . . . This is the way it works. A week ago Tuesday I had a meeting with the Drome Départemental Comité des Réfugiés. They had just had word that 1000 refugees were expected; I offered them my stock of 1000 sheets and 1000 blankets and several hundred beds if they would use lots of empty houses I know about rather than cantonments. Quite a lively meeting!"

Traveling in impossibly crowded trains, or through a rainstorm in a Ford Camionette minus a windshield, in which "My hat became a sponge and my raincoat a marsh and Miss Spaulding's a sluice way," Dewson went from camp-bed factory to bureau of placement to vestiaire, injecting energy, efficiency, and enthusiasm into French businessmen and officials and American volunteers. "And then a telegram saying that I was to have charge of the Red Cross aid to the 1000 réfugiés coming into the Jura, also the 1000 in the Doubs and a French ajoint. Also a telegram from my assistants in the Drôme saying one was sick and both had gone to Paris to consult a doctor. The third was on sick leave. Also got a telegram from the bed man saying he could not deliver the beds, letter following. Alone and four departments taking as much time to reach as it takes to go from N.Y. to Boston to Buffalo to Cleveland! I felt like a fly behind a cow's ear; I could stick but I was not very useful."[58]

But Dewson and Porter's hardest job, in their view, was dealing with French bureaucrats and those of the American Red Cross, the International Red Cross, and the AEF. It was a toss-up, Dewson thought, between the representatives of the French government, and those of the United States Army, "these funny old business men, all tricked out in uniform, running around ordering and counter-ordering, and saluting and Majoring and Captaining. . . . I never thought men were any smarter than women, and I now think their organizing ability is enough to make a dressmaker smile." To add to her exasperation, she had to fend off their advances: "Really a decent American man is better at home."[59] Porter seconded her, calling military requirements "rigmarole," commenting, "It may be annoying to have Paris bombarded and Amiens about to fall, but all this is entirely obliterated for us by our local mole hills;" finally, driven beyond her limits, Porter went "running away" to Lyons to find out for herself what was happening, since they wouldn't answer her letters. But Dewson charmed the local citizenry and coped with her administrative problems by making "a joke book for relief workers that always broke the ice in a French Committee meeting. Oh those good old faithful jokes in my terrible French!"[60]

All the while Dewson and Porter, who had envisioned themselves handing out doughnuts and chocolate at the front, yearned for the wartime adventures of the canteen workers. Dewson complained that she had been "hoisted up into the red tape ranks, so that my days of usefulness are numbered. . . . This running here and there, eating with a bunch of old brokers every night, does not amuse me."[61]

All the more credit to these women that, like hundreds of other administrators—and secretaries and clerks—they stuck to their jobs behind the lines and, against lethargy and inertia, made the wheels turn. As Dewson put it, ". . . on we roll, and the underlings turn off great gobs of work wherever they are out in the field right next to the real thing ready to be done; everywhere in refugee work, canteen, or hospital, no matter how tied up with red tape and lack of supplies, they find a way. Of course some are pretty slick little advertisers and sob stuff writers, but there are hundreds who just bone right to, and no one knows and no one cares what they do. They work for the joy of working, and let the heads take care of the bureaucracy. They forget about commendation because they never get noticed at all. As one woman said, 'I hope, when the war is over, they will remember to send for me.' "[62]

The American Friends

In the "Great War" as in other wars, the American Society of Friends, bound by loyalty and conviction to their traditional Quaker principle of pacifism, centered their work on help for the suffering. Consistently they designed their activities to promote healing and peace rather than in any sense to support the war. They wanted to help war victims back to independence as soon as possible, so whenever they could they chose reconstruction rather than relief.

Up until 1917, rather than undertake "war work" on their own, they cooperated with British Quakers on their projects in western Europe and in Russia, benefiting from the British experience, and multiplying their own effectiveness. With the United States' entry into the war, the American Quakers significantly increased their participation, in money and personnel.

At the same time they had to cope with new problems of conscience presented by America's declaration of war. Their young men were being drafted, an act that violated two basic convictions of the Friends—against war, and against taking an oath. With their deep respect for the individual conscience, the Society of Friends wanted their young men allowed whatever other form of service each thought right, but many suffered physical and mental abuse before the society succeeded in persuading the government to accept the legitimacy of

conscientious objection. Reconstruction work abroad eventually provided a satisfying alternative for many a Quaker youth.

The Friends faced another problem of conscience in France in
not being allowed to bring the consolations of their religion to the
war victims they aided. Nations at war, for obvious reasons, did not
welcome expositions of pacifism.

Nevertheless, the American Friends Service Committee
(AFSC), formed in 1917, sent to France all in all some six hundred
persons, of whom fifty-odd were women. "It seems an unfair proportion," wrote Rufus Jones, "but . . . the work in the main was
agriculture and reconstruction, and secondly . . . the young men
who were of draft age were eager to find service abroad. . . . We
always sent, however, all the women workers for whom we received
calls from Paris and for whom they had openings for service. It
was a definite policy that no woman should go into that maelstrom
unless there was positive evidence that her skillful hands were
needed. . . ."[63] The workers received their support from the AFSC,
but no other compensation.

The women Friends participated in medical, agricultural, transport, building, and relief programs. They gathered up and looked
after children and old people. They paid refugee women for
plain sewing, and taught them to embroider and "to make mattresses, pillows, and that curious contrivance which the French call
duvet. . . ." At Charmont, Frances Ferris reported, they did more
than "furnish a shelter for a handful of stranded old refugee women.
The doctor holds a weekly clinic here and considerable amateur
medical work is done in the village. A shop has been opened where
stuffs, bedding and furniture are sold at reduced prices to refugees.
Recently an *ouvroir* has been opened at Bettancourt, near by, where
cut-out clothing is distributed for sewing, the same to be sold afterward in the shop later in the Spring. . . ." Edith Moon oversaw the
work of helping the refugees to reestablish more than ninety schools,
furnishing school supplies and libraries.[64] A handful of Quaker
women in the Somme area distinguished themselves during the German offensive of March 1918, feeding wounded soldiers and helping
fleeing civilians.

And, of course, the women helped take care of the male workers.

"Lillie F. Rhoads (Mrs. Charles J. Rhoads) and her cousin, Anita Bliss, of New York, came nearly every day to the Hostel [for reconstruction workers], usually in time to serve afternoon tea to the men who could be there. They looked after their mending and in a multitude of ways they brought a beautiful atmosphere of home and fellowship to the Hostel."[65]

The cultural differences between the British and American Friends working together occasioned some problems. So too did the individualism and rugged consciences traditional among the Friends. "Miss A. G. Jacob is feeling that her object in coming out is not yet obtained and that Bettancourt does not give her an opportunity. . . . we are releasing her to come to Paris, where she proposes to offer her services to the *A.R.C.* This is not our general policy by any means, but in this special case may we hope, work out. She has also mentioned that she might feel it right to return to her school in America."[66]

Mary Elkinton Duguid's letters, filled with details of her life and work, glance sidewise at such difficulties. Duguid, a graduate of Wellesley who had studied at the Harvard School of Design, and her British husband, William, had tried since the fall of 1915 to get to France. Finally, in June 1917, they sailed with the first American contingent of Friends. In time William became the head of the mission at Ornans.

Mary managed a household of forty: she went on expeditions to buy food, took care of visitors, and tended the sick—mostly American men over thirty who got colds or upset stomachs, she said. The children she cared for were so spoiled "that it takes a strong hand to lead them to see that when the Great Aunt Mary says go to bed (coucher an lit) it means to stay on [the] bed and not talk to a dozen boys out of the window. . . ." That strong hand was exercised also with the women refugees, whom she gave "a glass of milk for every meal and as we give them no wine they are glad to have it. . . . We have very lively times, sometimes it is someone that has forgotten to do her work. . . ."

Mary's mother, too, took some managing: "I must say, Mother, thy letters rather disturb me. Here we are and in many ways much nearer the War than you and in many ways I believe we are in a more normal state than you are. Here and in all of France we all take things that come our way. If they are pleasant we give thanks and fully enjoy them, if very sad that too people bear with the grace given them and it is extraordinary how people can bear them and still have a good degree of happiness. You are so dreadfully serious that I fear you worry too much."

And her sister: "I am a little concerned about Kitty at Châlons. I wish I had sense enough to try to get them not to send her there. The English nurse has an awful idea of cold discipline and is about as much of an old maid as can well be imagined. . . . I do not want K to live long under too high tension."[67]

But in early spring real trouble befell the Duguids—so serious that they thought of returning to Philadelphia. While they were away on business their group "sprung an election" and ousted William as their head. Mary had, she said, learned how much mischief selfishness can make, and how much disloyalty lurks. "We neglected to do one thing," she wrote, "and that was to play politics." The Duguids transferred to Troyes, but after a short time there they "felt inclined to go to the south of France to assist in the care of refugees. . . ."[68]

Most of the time, though, the Friends' strong organization, shared beliefs, and respectful tolerance for the opinions of others kept morale high and relations among them peaceful. Mary Hoxie Jones caught their idealism—and their practicality—in an imaginary but factually based conversation among Friends relaxing in France on a Sunday afternoon: "I know I was sent here to take care of these old ladies. . . . I can speak French and I seem to be able to use my head, and what's more I can get along with the English, but twenty years from now what will my having done relief work in the war mean to me or any one else? We're all doing useful, practical jobs, like building houses, threshing grain, planting gardens, taking care of the sick, helping people who need us now. We're busy, we're fairly happy, and we're appreciated. . . . But it isn't enough. . . . We ought to be doing something that's more *vital*, more creative. We ought to be getting something of our own convictions over to these people."[69] But one condition of their presence in France stipulated that they not proselytize.

Besides all their work in France, which won general respect, the Friends Service Committee sent teams into Poland, Serbia, Germany, Austria. And Russia.

ЫЫЫ *I remember now what Mr. Yarros said before I left Hull House, that I would find the only amusements in Russia are talking, drinking weak tea, and smoking cigarettes, mostly done all together. They certainly are.*
—Lydia Lewis[70]

Politically the Friends accomplished miracles in their Russian service, for it required complicated and endlessly prolonged negotiations with the Kerensky and later the Bolshevik governments, who suspected even the American Red Cross of counterrevolutionary motives. Eventually the Friends outlasted most other foreign organizations who tried to meet the enormous human needs created or aggravated in Russia by the war and the revolution. At home support for the program faltered in the face of increasing American apprehension about what the Russians were doing.

Nonetheless, in July 1917, Nancy Babb, Emilie C. Bradbury, Amelia Farbiszewski (a Russian), Anna J. Haines, Lydia Lewis, and Esther White sailed for Russia. They went by way of Japan, since at that time Russia did not permit women to enter from Europe. It was quite a trip.

In Tokyo the women were delayed while the Russians checked yet once again on their motivation. In Vladivostock they boarded the Trans-Siberian Railway, where they eventually managed to get a first-class compartment. "The former inhabitants of it," Lewis wrote on August 23, "had spilled over from third class and objected violently (poor things!) to being ousted, but they were told that we were 'Americans with a mission,' and first-class, so they had to subside. . . . there are six of us, and only four beds; but the aisles of the express were full of people sitting on stools, with no place to sleep. . . . They swarmed over the couplings between cars to get in where doors were closed, dragging huge boxes and bags after them, and got pushed off again; the waiting-room floor was literally covered with men sleeping on it this morning, so the girls had to walk over them to get to the counter for hot water for our breakfast. . . . There was one compartment that contained two women and two men, all strangers to each other, and as . . . the back of each seat goes up at night for an upper berth, with no curtains or other protection, it is pretty awful. . . . Last night one of the men in this compartment got drunk, and when we went to bed the women were still uncertain what to do, and no one seemed at all concerned over them or the incident. Most of the people never made up their berths at all, simply leaving them as beds all day, and sitting or lolling on them in full view, visiting back and forth, men and women, and . . . smoking continuously all of them, girls of sixteen or women of seventy."[71]

Anna Haines described their housekeeping arrangements on the train (when they had already been on their way for two months). ". . . we visited the dining-car, which we found rather mussy; lots of flies and not any good food. We soon got into the habit of getting our own luncheons and even dinners, as the train (although an express) stopped at a great many stations, and each one had long covered sheds like a market, where all sorts of food could be bought as well as free boiling water. We would skip off the train with our covered kettles, yelling 'kiputok, kiputok' as loud as we could, and some obliging bystander would show us where the spigot was. . . . you could get roast chickens, still hot, for about sixty cents a piece. Bread, butter and fruit, with occasional tomatoes and cucumbers completed our diet. The bread was of many different colors and degrees of sourness; sometimes white and very good, sometimes black and very good, but often heavy. The butter is always unsalted, but I like it very much; we found good apples, some grapes, pears and plums. Nancy, who was our commissary department, had purchased cheese and crackers and jam, as well as tea, coffee, chocolate and condensed milk in Japan, so we fared sumptuously, and our housekeeping gave us something to do. Siberia was most interesting, great stretches of rich prairie land, just waiting for somebody to come farm it. All the generations of my ancestors rose up within me, and I fairly itched to get off the train and buy a farm. . . ."[72]

Finally they arrived in the Buzuluk District of Samara, just north of the Caspian Sea. Despite their preference for reconstruction work, the desperate conditions had forced the British Friends already

there to concentrate on emergency relief. Twenty thousand refugees—mostly women, old men, and children—in a population of
100,000 people had predictably roused hostility, which had forced
many refugees across the Caspian Sea into the deserts of Oriental
Turkestan; there, with their death rate at 55 percent, they turned
back to Samara.

Not one Russian doctor remained in Buzuluk. In their six centers, twenty to fifty miles apart, the Friends offered extensive medical
aid, distributed food and clothing, established workrooms for spinning, weaving, knitting, sewing, and embroidery for the refugee
women, and orphanages and trade schools which taught carpentry,
tailoring, shoemaking, and bookbinding to their children. Over time
the Friends sympathetically and ingeniously devised ways to help
the refugees: establishing a labor bureau for returning soldiers, loan-
ing money to the poorest peasants for seed, offering a bounty on the
suzlicks—muskratlike animals which were destroying the crops.

The American women, who each began in a different place, took
on whatever the situation demanded. One, after managing and closing two different workrooms (because of the refugees' shifts from
place to place), "began to believe there was something radically wrong
with me!" She filled in all winter at an outpatients' dispensary, even
learning to administer anesthetics. After closing that hospital in April
1918, she went to Buzuluk to start a workroom and help the Refugee
Committee with its orphanage. The Friends "found it in a terrible
condition. We agreed to contribute 10,000 roubles, provided we
could have our representatives living on the spot and could thoroughly reorganize it. . . . It was just like the orphan asylums you
read about. The children were dirty and ragged, and the boys worse
than reform-school boys. . . . Now we've started tailoring, boot-
making, carpentering and gardening classes, and it's like another
world. . . . We've gotten [the babies] fairly well cleaned up, their
diet improved, their bedrooms a little more decent, and at the end
of this week we shall have a kindergarten. . . ." Meanwhile Emilie
Bradbury was managing a workroom for a shifting population of
about 150 refugee women each day, and Amelia Farbiszewski with
an English nurse was starting a soup kitchen.[73]

Amidst all these shifts and hard work, Lydia Lewis consented

to marry the British Friend John Rickman. The young couple suffered a crisis of conscience over the required Russian civil ceremony.
For when they and their friends drove to Mogotovo for this ceremony
they found in the market square a mob lynching three soldiers who
had stolen from community stores; the Friends feared that the towns-
people would go on to lynch the sixty others in jail on the same
charge. Sadly, John and Lydia "came to the conclusion after much
discussion that we could not be married by a Tribunal that was
steeped in the butchery that we had seen in the market place. . . .
We therefore [decided] that we should have to give up the idea of
getting married in Russia. This blow came to us and settled our
minds to other affairs." The sad young couple, examining their consciences further, for a time thought it their duty to lodge a protest—
despite their "absurdly inadequate stock of Russian" and the dangers
of a hostile response. Then a happier thought struck, ". . . that the
best way we could show them that we really did have confidence in
them and that we did not go to them to criticize their action or to
get information, was to go to them to be married."[74] Best of all,
when the couple went to the tribunal, they found new authorities
superseding the old, and stopping the execution. Happy ending,
after all!

In many ways the Rickmans' reactions to the Russian brutality
and their struggles with their consciences to find their own right
course of conduct typified the Friends' reactions to the violence of
war and revolution in the country. As pacifists the Quakers thought
all exercise of military force wrong. They were quite clear-eyed about
the inadequacies of Russian officialdom, whatever party was in
power. They learned from repeated personal experience how unpracticed and volatile were the hordes of Russians who had had under
the tsar so little opportunity for self-reliance. Their work with refugees had taught the Quakers the cruelties that the Russians inflicted
on other peoples.

At the same time they recognized cultural differences and deeply
respected individual conscience. Like other Americans in Russia at
the time, like President Wilson, they hoped that out of the chaos of
revolution a better Russian nation would emerge—whether with the
Bolsheviks or with another party. The Friends would not lend them-

selves to actions they regarded as wrong, and they would try to stop
wrong if they could. But they were in Russia neither to criticize nor
to take over from the Russians. Rather their mission was to alleviate
suffering and to enable the Russian people to solve their own
problems.

>   ✌✌✌ *Then, of course, our position here in Russia is more
> or less of a delicate one besides. So we have been sometimes
> rather discouraged.*
>   —Esther White[75]

By October 1918, all the Friends had been forced to leave Buzuluk, knowing that the district would soon fall to the Bolsheviks,
and support from home cease. Some of the workers started home.
Theodore Rigg and Esther White managed to get to Moscow.

There they discovered a local Russian charity foundering. This
Russian society had established south of Moscow, in an area where
relatively cheap food abounded, three large children's colonies, to
which they moved starving Moscow children for the summer in an
effort to build them up to the point where they might make it through
another winter. But money failed, and White and Rigg undertook
the prolonged negotiations necessary for the Friends to take over the
colonies—while the children suffered from cold, scanty clothing, and
insufficient food. The Friends began constructing buildings to house
some of the children for the winter; others they took back to Moscow.
"We are hoping to have the children do the main part of the work
in the colony under supervision," White reported in October of 1918.
"Besides that, we shall of course have a school in each colony and
hope to teach some trades as well. . . . We should like very much
to have one English or American resident in each colony, but that
seems almost too much to be hoped for at present. We are trying to
find good enough Russians who can with some help run the colonies
themselves. I find it not so easy as it looks to find just the people
you want. . . . Just now it's impossible to contemplate what it's going
to be like through the winter. . . . At present I am not only cut off
from all communication with home, but even cut off from communication with the rest of our Unit in Samara."[76]

Other Friends in the fall of 1918 moved, in a boxcar which they later used as their home, from Buzuluk to Omsk, where they joined forces with a shorthanded American Red Cross unit for six months, establishing workrooms for women who had to support their families; cleaning up typhus, smallpox, typhoid, and scurvy among 3,000 of the most debilitated refugees; starting a milk station and a school.

Wherever they served, in Europe or in Russia, concern for the independence and self-esteem of the war victims distinguished the Friends' work. Letters from Lydia Lewis Rickman, winding up affairs in Buzuluk, and from Anna J. Haines, on the point of departure from Siberia, encapsulate their spirit: "Russia is going to improve from the bottom up," wrote Rickman, "and nothing superimposed on it from the top or the outside is going to be enduring. . . . our staying on now would simply relieve the Zemstvo [local government] of its obligation to develop the work, for which they have both funds and interest." Again, "We could sit here safely, where we are known, and take on one thing after another that *should* be the responsibility of some Russian committee. . . . I do not mean that we do not do these things infinitely better than they would, and that the things do not need to be done, only they are being run now just as everything in Russia is, and are a part of her general disorganization."[77] And Haines: "Our regret in leaving Omsk is due to the fact that the policy of the Red Cross . . . seems to centre more and more on medical and military work, and to evade the refugee problem as something too vague and not 'emergent' enough to be interesting. We have had to fight hard to establish some of the ideals which had been taught us in Buzuluk, such as workrooms and schools, which we feel to be necessities if the self-respect and general morale of the refugees are to be at all conserved."[78]

College Groups

Several women's colleges commissioned special college units of their graduates. Many of their alumnae, of course, served individually with other organizations: with their education and their status as "nice women," they were just the kind the Red Cross and the YMCA were looking for. And with their cultural and social ties with Europe, they were just the kind most likely to feel that they had a stake in the war.

An Intercollegiate Committee on European Reconstruction Service tried to work out a system through which both individual alumnae and college units could engage in reconstruction work overseas. Through it colleges that could not equip and send whole units could sponsor individual alumnae. In this way Mount Holyoke by January 1919 had four representatives in England and France.[79]

But three or four colleges each produced one entrepreneurial woman who saw to it that *her* alma mater did more, sponsored its own group of volunteers to serve as a unit in the name of the college. In the hierarchy of war work organizations that had emerged with the United States' entry into the war, each of these college units associated itself with a "mother" organization.

Wellesley, which by the end of the war numbered among its alumnae upwards of a hundred American women serving overseas, struggled valiantly but unavailingly against political odds and passport regulations to field its own unit. In late April 1918, five or six highly trained and professionally experienced women headed by Mary Whiting sailed as the "Wellesley Unit," only to be dispersed immediately upon arrival by the Red Cross, with the bland announcement: "A unit at home becomes individuals in France."[80] Although three or four other women joined the Wellesley Unit overseas during the summer of 1918, the group functioned as a unit only after the war, when Wellesley supported reconstruction efforts in France and the Near East.

Vassar sent overseas in 1918, under the direction of Margaret Lambie, five or six women, including a dietitian, a secretary, and a couple of social workers, who took charge of eight Red Cross Recreation Huts for convalescent soldiers in Savenay, France. After the war this Vassar group accepted the invitation of the city of Verdun to work with returning refugees, remaining there until September 1919.

The Radcliffe unit of seven women sailed only after the war, in April 1919, when Lucy Stockton returned from two years' work in France to recruit six other alumnae as motor drivers for Le Village Reconstitué, an association for the reconstruction of French villages.

But the Smith College Relief Unit, the first off the ground, and the largest, lived and labored through the most exciting and dangerous experiences of the college groups. Since this unit also managed to maintain the most independence, it afforded its women much scope for individual enterprise. The passion of one woman, Harriet Boyd Hawes, inspired the college to sponsor and the alumnae to fund and staff a unit for reconstruction work.

Hawes, Smith College '92, M.A. '01, wife and mother, had taught high school, had nursed in the Greco-Turkish War of 1897 and the Spanish-American War, had started relief work in 1914 in the Serbian Army. On April 10, 1917, she proposed the Smith College Relief Unit at an alumnae luncheon; incredibly, she and the other sixteen original members of the unit landed in France only four months later. In the interval, with the help and advice of Isabel Lathrop and Anne Morgan and of an alumnae committee, Hawes had circumvented the dislike of officialdom, particularly the American Red Cross, for privately financed groups, and had secured the protection of the American Fund for French Wounded. She had also recruited personnel, procured passports, bank credits, and steamship tickets, bought and shipped six portable houses, two motor trucks, and one Ford jitney, and chosen a uniform—"a difficulty which almost wrecked us."[81]

Yet the event proved the soundness of Hawes's preparations. Despite their haste, the committee had carefully selected the women workers—as they did the thirty others who joined or followed them, on the basis of character; health; ability to speak, read, and write French; and proficiency in driving, social service, or medicine. Each worker had to contribute $300 for travel, uniform, and incidentals (many continued to contribute $55 a month for their own support) and pledge her services for at least six months.

After a frustrating month in Paris waiting for their cars and putting them in running order, the unit settled in at Grécourt, where they crammed themselves into six rooms and plunged into their reconstruction work. ". . . the end of all our effort was to stimulate normal communal life and industry. If there was a blacksmith without a forge, and a continuous stream of travel bound to require repairs, it was our duty to get the forge. If a community entitled to a shack for a school was not receiving it, we called the attention of the proper authorities to this oversight. If there was a grocer by trade, without a stock and with no means of transportation, we bought for him and delivered. If there were supplies of fodder, or hay, or vegetables in storage in some barn, we paid for and consumed them, putting money in circulation. . . . in line with this was our introduction of livestock for the purpose of supplying the people, and our agricultural program which was of prime importance in this farming country. . . ."[82]

But they also responded to emergencies totally extraneous to their defined purpose of reconstruction work for French villagers. For example, when Dr. May Agnes Hopkins was working with the aged and children at Château-Thierry, "I found American boys and the Army found me, and they asked me if I could bring down [to Paris] a boat-load of wounded." On board she found no equipment, no food, and one woman aide. In their four-day journey on the Marne, they passed an American supply camp, hallooed, and the Americans rushed on board to bring supplies and to cook. When someone remarked that this voyage was not refugee work, Dr. Hopkins answered, "Of course not. But, over here, haven't you found out you do the thing you are not sent to do?"[83]

> ✂✂✂ . . . *one man wrote home that as they stood in line at the retreat and watched us, the private at his left said, "I wish they would send over a unit from Radcliffe," and the one at the right—"Gee, I wish they would send over a bunch from Gimbel's."*
>
> —Marie Wolfs[84]

The Smith College crew immediately attracted masculine attention and offers of help—from a camp of American Engineers, from Canadian Foresters, from the British and American Friends engaged in reconstruction work nearby, from French and British Army officers and enlisted men, many of whom frequently sent invitations and gifts. For instance: ". . . a French army camion drove up. The driver saluted and informed us that he had brought three pigs from the station at Noyon. . . . I was relieved when I saw that the soldier considered getting them out was part of his job. He cut a little stick for me and told me to keep the others in while he got one out. Such squeals I never heard in all my life and maybe you don't think I had a time keeping those beasts in." The women welcomed more eagerly a present from an English major of two loads of duckboards for a walk to cover the mud and men to put them down—along with an offer to buy the pigs. "I think," Marie Wolfs commented, "with the combined efforts of all the Allied armies we may be made comfortable for the Winter."[85]

The duckboards and rubber boots solved at least the pedestrian problems of coping with the mud, soft, slimy, and ankle deep, described by a man who had just come from Flanders as "the worst thing in Europe," which surrounded the women's barracks.[86] Those barracks, on the grounds of a bombed-out château at Grécourt, ". . . are made of thin boards, with an asbestos-like outside, single board floors right on the ground, and for cold and damp beat a leaky refrigerator all to hollow."[87] A woman writer for *The New York Evening Sun* briefly lived with the Smith College women: the barracks, she said, "are heated by stoves, which don't go unless some one stands by and feeds them with a spoon. . . . And you may take my word for it that it's cold up there—the kind of cold that gets through all the layers of clothes you wear. After your first day there you've discarded silk stockings and are wearing one, if not two, pairs of the heaviest made woolens, and you've borrowed every available woolie not in use; and you roll around more like a mechanical pillow than anything else. . . . The report one morning was that the alcohol in the dispensary had frozen, and one of the girls swears that she spilled some boiling hot water on the floor and a few minutes later her roommate nearly lost her life slipping on it."[88]

But amid the rains and cold which October had brought, ". . . we had a jolly time in spite of all our coats and mufflers worn at once. The men brought over a Victrola and we danced in rubber boots. . . ."[89] Despite, too, the war news: ". . . the French are absolutely *all in* & have been having bad reverses again. . . . last week we really thought we might have to evacuate—the Germans advanced twelve kilometres and the people at Ham were very much frightened—one night the cannonading was so heavy we couldn't sleep at all. . . ."[90]

The work increased as the unit's charge expanded from its original eleven villages to fifteen and as difficulties multiplied with bad roads and car breakdowns. Their transport had been supplemented by gifts of an English Ford touring car and a horse and high cart—though it took two to get the horse anywhere, "one to drive and one to poke him with a stick. No donkey could possibly be worse."[91]

But the women kept thinking up new schemes for their villagers. A library for the children, and games to loan them as well as books, to give families something interesting to do in the evenings by the light of their single candle. Classes in woodworking to train the boys and to replace the school benches the Germans had burned. Restocking farms with cows, pigs, goats, rabbits, and chickens. Christmas parties in their villages for all their 1,650 inhabitants, until "we are glad that Christmas comes only once a year even in the Somme, where most awful things happen oftener."[92] Replanting trees, especially fruit trees. Employing forty women in a cottage industry of sewing and knitting.

In the spring of 1918 they faced the tasks of bringing the fields back into productivity. They took orders for seeds, bought, packaged, and distributed them. Frances Valentine, who had worked in the U.S. Department of Agriculture, fought her way through the French bureaucracy and British military authorities to arrange for the land to be plowed. Not one to waste time, while she was in Paris she also bought chickens, and then found herself without a valid travel pass, forced to remain in her Paris hotel with her chickens. Finally she could no longer stand the remarks of the hotel guests, and decided to travel, pass or no pass. "The taxi driver swore roundly when he saw the three chicken crates but Anne [a Smith colleague] & Frances made him put one in front with him, one inside and one on the top. As they took the first corner on two wheels . . . the crate on the top not only fell off but broke open as well, the hens scattering in every direction in front of the Madeleine. . . . With the help of a number of people the girls finally . . . got them back into the box. . . . [when] the driver now madder than ever picked up the crate to replace it the bottom fell out and they had the same show to go over again. It was getting later and later so Frances just threw those chickens into the taxi as they were and used the time going to the station in getting them settled and tying up the crate with a string. At the station of course they check nothing but clothes but again they were firm so the crates were put on board."[93]

The "ladies of Grécourt," as the Smith College Unit was locally known, indeed frequently found it necessary to be firm with the French authorities. The inspector of education was firmly informed of "a lot of things he didn't know about the condition of schools in our district," and that the ladies would wait "while he went and got the proper papers," to liberate some much-needed school benches, but they ". . . really hadn't much time and would he please have the papers ready before lunch." They had to be firm with a railroad official who denied the existence of shipping space: "I told him if he would please write out the request in the proper form I would sign it but I had to have it back on Monday as my pass would expire. Again it couldn't be done but of course it was. . . . Monday he was obliged to rub out the 300 kilos [of weight allowance] and make it 2000, but it was only written in pencil so that wasn't hard."[94] Not even the traditionally immovable French bureaucracy was to interfere with the projects the women had initiated.

> *I decided the best thing to do was to advise people according to our best judgment and not bother the army.*
> —Elizabeth Bliss[95]

Then on March 21, 1918, a major German offensive began; a British officer brought the Smith College Unit orders to evacuate and the word that "they've broken through and are coming on, thousands and thousands of them; we can't hold them."[96] What followed made the Smith Unit legendary. For the members took upon themselves the task of warning their villagers and helping them to escape, making trip after trip over roads crowded with troops and refugees, transporting those who could not fend for themselves to hospitals and to a railroad station where trains evacuated them. In the intervals they found time to feed hungry troops and to evacuate their own livestock.

At first they tried to follow orders from the military and the Red Cross, but when as a result they almost lost two members of their unit, they used their own good judgment: "Nearly to Ercheu two French interpreters stopped us and told us not to go on, that the Boches were in Ercheu but there had been so much wind up that we were sure they were just a bit over scared and went along."[97]

Conflicting reports compounded the confusion, and the women had to make spur-of-the-moment decisions. "I gathered up a load of old people and just as I was ready, the R.C. camion came along loaded with mattresses and I transferred my load of people to the top of the mattresses with the aid of a stepladder produced from some lorry. Catherine Hooper had been on the lorry and now wanted to go with me. . . . Meantime Daisy and Marie made a trip to Marny to take out people there. . . . we went back again towards Ercheu and there the field artillery was drawn up for a stand. We didn't go into the town, for they were shelling the road now and an officer told us everyone was out. . . . So we turned around and picked up a load for Roye again. . . . Then the French asked us to go back to Marny which still had some people to take out. . . ."[98]

The Smith women were literally retreating with the British army, inch by inch. Their experience was all the more trying in that the women knew many of the soldiers along with whom they were retreating—most of whom were killed or taken prisoner.

Finally the order came to evacuate Montdidier, whence the refugee trains had been departing, for Amiens. ". . . after a night during which there was the worst air raid I ever knew, lasting from about 8:30 to 4 A.M., and bombs popping like cannoncrackers on every side, we decided to leave Amiens . . . and to go to Beauvais. . . . we have been here ever since. We fed refugees at first and the poor things came in here by thousands. Then we started feeding wounded soldiers as they entrained. . . . What the Unit will do eventually I don't know—certainly no more reconstruction work until the war is over."[99]

In fact the disruption had effectively ended the work of the group as a unit, though some of the members continued its work even after the war, still with strong alumnae support. Others redistributed themselves to ambulance units, refugee camps, and hospitals. Today reproductions of the Grécourt château gates stand on the Smith College campus as a memorial to the gallantry of the forty-seven women who served with the unit.

CHAPTER 4

Binding Up the Wounds

The Medical Needs

🖎🖎🖎 . . . *we stopped at several hospitals where the most serious cases are taken care of, not a woman nurse and that tells the tale, flies thick everywhere, the men [in charge] all smiles.*

—Elizabeth H. Ashe[1]

AT THE ONSET of World War I, despite Florence Nightingale, despite Clara Barton, European medical systems for contending with its ravages ranged from hopelessly inadequate, in France and Belgium, to nonexistent, in countries like Serbia. They lacked both the organization and the supplies to apply the relatively little that medical science knew about healing the human body. "Looking back," wrote Elisabeth Marbury, "I realize how extremely primitive and unhygienic were the resources which were then at hand [in France]. It is little wonder that eighty per cent of the first wounded died of gangrene. No modern equipment of any kind. The Generals were old, the Surgeons were old, the hospitals were old, the nurses were old, the material was old."[2]

Early in the war the American Red Cross asked the novelist and journalist Mary Roberts Rinehart, herself a graduate nurse, to tour hospitals near the front to evaluate their needs. Whatever else held fast during the first year of war, she reported, "the nursing system of France absolutely failed."[3] Hospitals, except those few affiliated with the Red Cross, were isolated and poverty-stricken. She told of a train unloading 400 wounded men on the station platform of a

79

small French village, all unannounced; the train went on and the villagers were left to cope as best they could.

Whether he fought for the Triple Entente or the Central Powers, the wounded soldier of World War I, with antibiotics and prompt treatment and evacuation still years away, suffered from the abysmal inadequacies of the medical services. American Red Cross nurses working in Europe in the early days of the war were appalled by the conditions they encountered. German soldiers traveling for five days in springless farm carts and freight cars to reach a hospital.[4] Shortages of supplies so acute that Austrians raveled old linen to use the threads as a substitute for absorbent cotton.[5] In Budapest, Katrina Herzer said: "Serbs, Albanians, Hungarians, Croatians, Austrians, Montenegrins and Russians began their long journey from the front on stretchers, ox-carts and hay wagons to the nearest railroad, where hospital trains brought them filthy, hungry, exhausted to us. Many of them had their faces blown away; pus flowed down their chests. . . . Hideous mutilation was the rule, not the exception. It was a frightful thing to take off foul dressings and see below the shattered, yellow flesh, the labored inspiration and expiration of the exposed lung."[6]

A wounded soldier's survival might depend on his own initiative, or on serendipity. "Poilus [French soldiers] would walk in when it seemed impossible they could even move," wrote the American Dr. Jean Pattison. "One of my patients walked thirty kilometers with a broken arm and scalp wound."[7] When the journalist Madeleine Doty volunteered in the American Ambulance in Paris, one of the patients she nursed was Maxim Gorki's adopted son, whom she had known in America as a boy. Wounded, he walked back past trenches of German prisoners, his plight, "so pitiful, his pluck so great, that instinctively these men saluted." At the dressing station, so crowded that he could get no attention, gangrene set in, but with the help of a lieutenant, Gorki made the twelve-hour trip to Paris by taxi and train; there an ambulance rushed him to a hospital, where his arm was amputated but his life saved.[8]

Even as late in the war as May 1918, correspondent Eunice Tietjens reported, "As usual the preparations were hasty and inadequate. There were only two or three nurses, and they were totally unable to take care of the situation. One of them, Maude Cleveland, had been trained, I believe, only as a nurse's aid; yet she had charge of two big wards of seriously wounded boys for seventy-two hours hand running during the worst of the rush."[9] And in July 1918, Major Theodore Roosevelt, Jr., startled his wife by suddenly appearing at their Paris house. Wounded that morning near Soissons, he could find no ambulances, so he hitchhiked his way to Paris, riding for several hours in the sidecar of a motorcycle, then borrowing a friend's car for the rest of the journey.[10]

Even in Paris, even well-equipped and well-financed hospitals like the American Ambulance lacked adequate staff in the big pushes. Juliet Goodrich, shelled out of canteen work at Épernay and transferred there in June 1918, wrote: "I knew nothing about nursing and had to learn on my patients, a painful process for all concerned, but . . . in this time of uncertainty and desperate fighting, there were not enough, even of such as I, to tend our wounded."[11]

And no one had taken thought at the beginning of the war for convalescent soldiers, discharged from the hospital, but unable to care for themselves. "On January 8 [1915]," wrote American-born Mme. Paul Hyacinthe Loyson, "I notified the military authorities that my house would be open and at their disposal on the 10th of the month. But before I left the office the secretary pointed out to me the pathetic figure of a young soldier of 22 with his arm amputated. 'Will you take him, he has nowhere to go?' . . . How often since then I have heard those heartbreaking words: 'Nowhere to go!' "[12]

The situation of the wounded or ill civilian was as parlous as that of the soldier, for the needs of the military drained the countryside of physicians even as wartime conditions endangered public health. Influxes of refugees in weakened health increased the risk of epidemic tuberculosis, meningitis, typhus, and cholera.

American Women in Foreign Medical Systems

From the outbreak of World War I, American women enterprisingly found niches for themselves in foreign medical systems. Even while the American Red Cross sent its Mercy Ship in 1914, and long before American hospitals began to send medical units overseas, individual American women began serving with, and supplementing, the hospitals of the belligerents.

They did all kinds of jobs, from scullery service with the British Voluntary Aid Detachment (VAD) to sculptor Gertrude Vanderbilt Whitney's hospital administration. Eleanor Saltonstall drove for "a volunteer group of American nurses attached to a French autochir . . . a hospital which moves on wheels and follows the troops. It is the first hospital after the *poste de secours* [first-aid station] and only receives the bad cases. . . . My life seems to hinge around choked carburetors, broken springs, long hours on the road, food snatched when you can get it, and sleep."[13] Elsie de Wolfe, noted actress and pioneer in the profession of interior decorator, learned the treatment of burns, "the celebrated ambrine cure, discovered by Dr. Barthe de Sandfort," which dramatically reduced both suffering and scarring.[14] Josephine Suwalska Jokaitis commanded forty women, mostly nurses' aids, with the Polish Army in France. The social worker Chloe Owings, willing to do anything and successful at everything she did, took charge of a kitchen for special diets for the seriously wounded and tubercular in a French military hospital, with such effect that she was assigned the task of establishing similar kitchens in other hospitals.

Even short-term American volunteers in foreign hospitals could contribute. Some gave an occasional day or week of service. Katharine Foote in January 1917 apparently was traveling in France; for three months she worked as an aide in a French hospital, then switched to a hospital in England, where, since her home folks felt uneasy about having her cross the Atlantic, she worked for nine months more—uncomplainingly ironing bandages, cooking, stoking fires, washing up, and endearing herself to her patients and coworkers. In her leisure time she visited nearby hospitals, to sing for the men, or just talk with them ("I now know all about the best way of getting a bayonet away from a Hun if mine gets broken!"). She wrote home about her patient Reilly, who under anesthesia relived his battlefield experience. "He fought us like a demon, and we all got some knocks. I expect he heard of his doings from the men, for the next morning when I was dusting his bed, he shyly produced a German penny. 'Take it, please, Nurse, I got it off a dead German in Belgium. I'm thinking I was over-rough with you yesterday, and I'm sorry.' *Amende Honorable!*"[15]

Other American women working in foreign hospitals committed themselves to longer service. With the support of a group of Massachusetts citizens, who designated her the "Edith Cavell Memorial Nurse," the American Alice Fitzgerald, a gifted, cosmopolitan, and astute woman who spoke both French and Italian, served with the British Expeditionary Force in France for almost two years, sometimes in casualty clearing stations near the front, where she wished she weren't so tall, since her patients lay on stretchers only six inches above the ground. Transferring to the American Red Cross in December 1917, she wound up with the touchy job of seeing that ARC nurses adjusted properly to their assignments in French hospitals, where the French did not always welcome them.

All kinds of adventures befell the American women working in foreign hospitals, civilian or military. Succumbing to "frontline fever," many women in their letters and memoirs emphasized, maybe sometimes exaggerated, their closeness to the fighting. What matters, though, is the overwhelming evidence that more women worked closer to the front and its hazards than histories of the period would have us believe. One woman nursing in Belgium just in back of the front-line trenches was briefly arrested by the invading Germans. Of her old Presbyterian Hospital mate Elizabeth Ashe wrote: "Miss Warner has charge of a large French military hospital. She has been bombarded several times and been obliged to flee with her patients, one of her nurses lost her hand during one of the bombardments."[16] Two or three American women, said Mary Dexter, served with the British "Dr. Hector Munro and his Corps of half a dozen men and four girls. . . . They are the *only women* allowed so near the firing line—and they go practically into the trenches to pick up wounded. . . ."[17]

Emily Simmonds, the prototype of the entrepreneurial woman, undertook on her own one rescue mission after another. A Red Cross nurse, of "English birth, but of New York rearing, a delicate, small-featured, curly-haired, pink-cheeked, soft-voiced slip of a girl, dressed in a covert khaki coat and a big Stetson hat, she came to Europe," wrote Inez Irwin, "the twelfth of August, after war was declared. . . . Since then she had been in Serbia, Athens, Salonika, and was, at the moment, engaged in bringing refugee Serbians, hundreds of them, from Corfu to Marseilles. She and a woman friend contracted typhus in Libia. Their illness lasted two months. Their only attendant was an Austrian prisoner. . . . Finally she had to perform operations although she had never operated before. The Serbians, their hands frost-bitten, would beg her to operate on them. On one of her trips from Corfu to Marseilles, an Austrian airplane followed them for two days dropping bombs. They never managed to hit the ship, although all about them the water geysered. On board she cooked for eighteen hundred."[18]

The legendary Simmonds left tracks everywhere. Ashe recognized her as the nurse "who found the Serbian boys and marched hundreds of miles with them. Thirty thousand of these boys between the ages of eight and eighteen were enrolled in an army and marched out of Serbia in order to save them. Only six thousand reached their destination, the rest died of starvation en route."[19] Simmonds also escorted escaping Serbian women and children across a Mediterranean teeming with hostile ships to safety in Italy, Corsica, and France. Whether she worked for the Red Cross, for the Serbian Relief Fund, or on her own, she seized the initiative: in Brindisi, when officialdom left 2,000 refugees foodless for two days, she reenacted the miracle of the loaves and fishes.[20]

Indeed, without American women the suffering of many injured and sick people all over Europe would have gone untreated and uncomforted. In her travels for the Red Cross, Elizabeth Ashe met and helped many American women struggling in obscure corners of Europe against odds and with insufficient resources: "I gave $30.00 the other day to a Presbyterian Hospital nurse who has given her services since the beginning of the war to a place for children in Evian and has never had any proper dispensary equipment. . . . the poor woman seemed so tired and discouraged."[21] Dr. Ethel Polk-Peters, a medical missionary in China, responded to a Siberian call for help by organizing an all-woman unit of two American doctors, two American nurses, and nine Chinese women with some medical training; arriving in Vladivostock in September 1918, they looked after refugees from the successive bases of a Pullman car, boxcars, and finally a Red Cross mess hall.[22]

The American-born Mme. d'Andigne demonstrated what a difference one woman could make. Having spent the fall of 1914 getting in the crops on her huge estate, she began a study of the French military medical system, a task for which an American Red Cross certificate and her experience in the Spanish-American War had helped to prepare her. Observing the critical need for ambulances, she cabled to family and friends in America—her father was the first to respond. After interludes assisting in an operating room in Paris and military hospitals at Amiens and Versailles, "to get my hand in," d'Andigne went to Champagne, where "I was asked to organize and superintend the Service of the Mussulman troops," with happy results. "One called me one day and asked me what my Allah was like. I told him I thought he was probably very much like his. Well! if my Allah was not good to me, theirs would take care of me, they would see to that." Then at the request of the French health service, d'Andigne helped to organize and presided over Le Bienêtre du Blessé.[23]

Another American, "Mademoiselle Miss" (as her French patients called her), after working in French and English hospitals and qualifying for a nurse's diploma in the French Red Cross in a two-and-a-half-hour examination conducted by nine doctors, was sent to the front with an army hospital and commissioned a lieutenant in the French Army. Constantly begging supplies from home, she "installed the whole place, from base-boards up, as a very up-to-date looking operating room, sterilized, ticketed, and in short very neat and complete. . . . I have made washcloths for every bed in my barracks, and there shall be a towel for each man, or I shall go undried. Also I asked the Head Surgeon for frames on which to tack burlap, for certain beds must be screened. He thought me rather exacting for the front, but will give me what I want." She reveled in occupying "perhaps the most important post in the hospital, requiring a head set square"—directing the sterilization, taking charge of the operating ward, working with celebrated French doctors. Work dominated her: "One works, and when that is over one sleeps enough to keep in condition, and that is absolutely *all*, except a cold sponge bath . . . and an eau de cologne rubdown in the morning, and the walk to and from the Hospital. In the morning now it is bitter cold and misty and half dark, and one gets weird glimpses of departing regiments, and white-capped old market-women, and pointed gables across the gloom; and at night the splendid stars, and now a great lustrous moon, and every day and night the boom, boom of the cannon."[24]

Ruth Holden, a graduate student at Cambridge University in 1914, roamed even farther afield. Having from the beginning of the war sought war work, and trained and served at a British hospital as an aide, in 1916 she set off for Russia with a British medical unit to establish maternity hospitals for Polish refugees. "In what capacity I go, remains to be seen, but probably a man of all work sort of thing. . . . Anyhow, it's all aboard for Archangel early in January. . . . They provide everything—camp bed, fur coat, sleeping bag, etc.—but I said go without salary. The uniform isn't yet chosen, but I hope it's trousers like that of the nurses in Serbia. . . . They are a weird lot of birds, these nurses; I think they're imbeciles, but at least they will never be taken for spies. The Drs. and Sec. aren't so bad, & it's bound to be awfully interesting, anyhow."[25]

Her letters show Holden assuming more and more responsibility: acting as an interpreter, with the Russian and Polish she learned as she worked; chivying workmen to complete the new hospitals which the unit was opening; traveling around Russia to procure equipment and supplies; wrestling with the Byzantine difficulties of the country's cumbersome and inefficient railroad system: "I've been here [in Moscow] 4 days, trying to arrange for a motor ambulance to get thru' customs duty free. . . . In the meantime our finances have gone bust, & we've got to sell the blooming auto anyhow so I'll never chauf. on the Galician front!"[26]

Repeatedly she assured her family and friends that she would soon return to Cambridge to resume her fellowship, but the plight of the thousands of refugees and the sheer adventure of her experiences held her. In February 1917 Holden wrote her father that she was recovering from an extended but light case of typhoid. "I wouldn't especially mind dying while doing something worthwhile—

at least I don't think I would," that letter said.[27] But the typhoid was followed by meningitis, and at twenty-seven this brilliant young woman died.

American Organizations

Not only did Americans volunteer in foreign medical services as individuals, but they also mobilized collectively, in existing or new organizations, to help the overstrained medical systems of the belligerents. The American Red Cross, for instance, managed by mid-September 1914 to launch its "Mercy Ship," carrying trained personnel and hospital supplies—not just absorbent cotton and bandages, but for some destinations everything needed for a 400-bed hospital. With twelve nurses and three surgeons in each, its units were neutrally assigned to France, England, Russia, Germany, Austria, and Hungary; eventually 126 other nurses either replaced or supplemented the original 129. The Red Cross also in the fall of 1914 sent three hospitals to Serbia, for which Mary E. Gladwin, the chief nurse, supervised fourteen American Red Cross nurses and many young Serbian nurses' aides.

These Mercy Ship units had to use whatever quarters offered themselves. One unit transformed a German theater into a hospital, setting up an operating room in the lobby, adapting theater properties and stage lighting to their purpose, and making the soubrette's dressing room into a dormitory for six nurses. In England a unit went to a splendid mansion, complete with marble staircases, tapestried walls, and a large park, borrowed by Jennie Churchill, the Duchess of Marlborough, and other American women married to Britishers, on condition that it be used as a hospital for enlisted men. At Christmastime this ladies' committee sent each patient there what every soldier needed—a silver cigarette case.

After a year the Red Cross withdrew the Mercy Ship units. But many of the nurses stayed on with other agencies.

In Paris the American community established, financed, and worked in the American Ambulance at Neuilly: a well-equipped hospital under the direction of Anne Vanderbilt when the war started, it became after the United States entered the war Red Cross Military Hospital #1. By 1916 it had 600 beds and three operating rooms, staffed by eighty-five American-trained nurses, and a corps of American, British, and French volunteers.

Some of these volunteers were leisured socialites, ". . . ladies almost all of them," according to the author Marie Van Vorst, and many "strikingly beautiful, with that distinction and grace that the American woman possesses to such a marked extent. . . . some of them have come from their homes and wear their own pretty blouses and their high-heeled slippers and their ear-rings, the rest being enveloped in the all-concealing apron. Many are in the full uniform of the hospital, that is in snow-white, with red crosses on their breasts and a little coif on their heads, medieval in its effect. . . ."[28]

Working at the American Ambulance was a chic way to volunteer, mainly because the business and social leaders in the American community had established it, and the women of that set were to be found there rolling bandages, serving tea, or nursing. But it doesn't do to assume that they worked only at their own convenience, or spent all their time in pretty uniforms soothing fevered brows. Florence Billings writes of working there for five hours every day for more than a year at the monotonous task of making surgical appliances and dressings: "I've developed a lively sympathy for factory girls, but it was absolutely necessary and I could do it better and faster than I could do anything else. My whole ambition concentrated into a simple: beat my own record each day."[29] Vera Arkwright, whom her friend Van Vorst had hesitated to introduce into the American Ambulance for fear that she would just flirt with the officers, did manage to look attractive, "with crimson cheeks and a floating veil," but she also carried "the vilest of linen and oilcloth— not to throw away, but to wash it herself with a scrubbing brush."[30] As for Van Vorst, she took charge of a machine for "electrical treatments," and became quite possessive about it, lugging it about Paris for repairs, and eventually learning to fix it herself.

Even before the United States entered the war, hospitals and medical schools from many parts of the United States began to organize units to go overseas. Julia Stimson, later the chief nurse of the ARC, first served overseas as chief nurse of the unit formed by the Barnes Hospital of St. Louis, assigned to the British Expeditionary Force. Mostly she loved it: being sent chocolates by Sir Thomas Lipton, entertained by the American ambassador's wife, and asked to tea by the Archbishop of Canterbury, as well as undergoing gas training. Gifted with a happy facility for supervision, she described her nurses as "bricks . . . loyal, affectionate, and entirely to be depended upon . . ." who "developed fine qualities that I really did not know they had in them." She fought for diversions, better food, and better equipment for them. "All of us who have large enough feet are getting our shoes from the quartermaster, and those with small feet are bewailing their fate. Our paths are all mud and sharp stones, and the ordinary sole of a woman's regular shoe lasts about two weeks, and even when new does not prevent the stones from hurting one's feet."[31] Stimson also bewailed her own fate as administrator—she never could cry, because she was there not to weep but to be wept upon, and, far worse, she couldn't join her nurses in temporary duty assignments to the casualty clearing stations near the front.

Some of the early-formed hospital units eventually served as U.S. Army base hospitals. Harvard and Peter Bent Brigham Hospital, for example, jointly organized the unit in which Base Hospital #5 originated. Besides its chief nurse Carrie Hall, the unit carried on its roster ninety nurses, a dietitian, and three secretaries—all women.

Our Government provided for the enlistment of nurses, but not for women physicians. This was a mistake. It is utterly impossible to leave a large number of well-trained women out of a service in which they belong, for the reason that they won't stay out.

—Esther Pohl Lovejoy[32]

Male doctors and female nurses worked together to form these American hospital units. But what of the almost 6,000 fully qualified American women doctors then in active practice? "The women of the medical profession," wrote Dr. Esther Lovejoy, "were not called to the colors, but they decided to go anyway."[33] Women doctors, who suffered the predictable rejections by the American military early on, took matters into their own hands, working through their established organizations to form hospitals for overseas service.

The New York Infirmary for Women and Children, backed by the National American Woman Suffrage Association, soon after the United States entered the war offered a mobile unit with a full staff of women physicians, to be called the Women's Overseas Hospital of the U.S.A. The United States War Department refused the offer; the French accepted it, but the group experienced delays and difficulties. At the end of November 1917, Dr. Caroline Finley, their director, was in France awaiting her staff, but not until May 1918, did a doctor first operate at the Women's Overseas Hospital (WOH). By midsummer 1918, WOH was taking care of 500 refugees, at Labouheyre, in southern France. Meanwhile Dr. Anna Von Skolly and several other doctors originally assigned to WOH had begun to work in French hospitals with French military surgeons, some of them caring for American soldiers; eventually Dr. Finley directed this unit, while Mrs. Raymond Brown became General Director in France of the Women's Overseas Hospital. Dr. Finley's "Medical unit in khaki and puttees . . . like real men . . . about thirty of them," a YWCA hostess observed, gave her dining room "a very military look."[34] In October WOH received from the United States a treatment unit for gassed soldiers, and in November the French military authorities asked them to install a hundred-bed hospital for a military unit, along with their work for repatriated French refugees. WOH carried on after the war, finally dissolving in 1920, and contributing their residual funds to the American Fund for French Wounded and the American Women's Hospitals (AWH).

More women doctors worked together under the aegis of the American Women's Hospitals formed by the War Service Committee of the Medical Women's National Association. This committee, established in June 1917, adopted, Dr. Esther Lovejoy recalled, "a naive resolution calling upon the War Department for a square deal regardless of sex, color, or previous condition of servitude . . . after which we probably sang 'We won't come back, till it's over, over there.' "[35]

Naive, indeed, but the women doctors backed the resolution by skillful fund-raising on a national scale, particularly among women's organizations.[36] They combined this fund-raising with enough political savvy that in July 1918 American Women's Hospital #1 opened under the direction of Dr. Barbara Hunt in Neufmoutiers in buildings assigned by the French army with the understanding that the hospital would serve both military personnel and civilians. "Within a few months, as the Germans evacuated territory, our hospital moved joyously toward the north, where the need was greater and facilities for work much better,"[37] wrote Lovejoy of a region of food scarcity, disease, unsanitary conditions, flu and typhoid epidemics, no medical supplies, and no doctors except for two women with the American Committee for Devastated France. "During the typhoid epidemic . . . our medical staff became emergency health officers. Double shod with supplementary sabots, they shuffled through barnyard filth from one hovel to another. Streets and courtyards were cleaned, decaying debris dug out of holes and corners, and these disease breeding spots liberally sprinkled with disinfectants."[38]

The AWH #1 staff also boasted three dentists, whose work, Lovejoy claimed, "will be a joy forever in France—at least as long as our fillings last. . . . A woman dentist had never been seen in that section of France. They were rare creatures, far more interesting than men dentists, their work was just as good, and they seemed to have a conscience regarding people's teeth."[39]

Like other medical women serving civilians, the staff of AWH #1 were pressed into service to soldiers in the big pushes. In the Allied offensive of the summer of 1918, physicians and nurses went to Meaux and later to Château-Thierry to treat French wounded. By war's end AWH #1 had been accepted as a military hospital for the French Sixth Army. Indeed the American Red Cross had cabled for six more units of the same kind, specifying, of course, that the Medical Women's National Association bear as much of the expense as possible; the Armistice apparently aborted these plans.

Meanwhile AWH #2, another group of Les Dames Américaines, as they were known in France, began work at La Ferte-Milon under Dr. Ethel Fraser. "This small hospital had a big dispensary route. With the help of one nurse, an ambulance and chauffeuse, Dr. Fraser cared for the sick in forty-eight villages, taking medical cases to her own hospital and sending the surgical cases" to AWH #1.[40]

By October 1918, seventy-eight physicians of the AWH were working in France with the Red Cross, as well as twenty-eight technicians and lay workers. They not only served in the AWH institutions, but also under different auspices (like the American Fund for French Wounded) took charge of contagious hospitals, managed clinics and crèches, gave psychiatric care, dispensed medicines and taught the principles of health, served as anesthetists in civilian and military hospitals, worked in evacuation hospitals, and headed laboratories.

The American Women's Hospitals continued and expanded their work in civilian relief long after the war—against male opposition. Evidently, Dr. Rosalie Slaughter Morton observed, male physicians could tolerate the idea of one unit of women on a temporary basis, but balked at more.[41]

After the United States entered the war, the Red Cross, in a familiar pattern, took over many functioning hospitals—but later endured the eye-opening experience of the Army's taking over Red Cross hospitals. A disconcerted Carrie Hall, by then chief nurse of the London branch of the Red Cross, who in May 1918 had complacently written home, "The American Red Cross has taken over all the hospitals in England that have been started and run during the past four years by American women . . . ," by August was writing, "My job is proving a disappointment to me. . . . it was supposed that the strictly Red Cross world would increase a good deal instead of which the army is taking over more and more of the hospitals which the Red Cross has established and from a hospital point of view the Red Cross is being permitted to do less and less work."[42]

As Hall notes, she was speaking only about *hospitals*. The Red Cross still carried a staggering and diverse medical load for both civilians and soldiers. Their concern reached everywhere and expressed itself in a multitude of services. In London the Red Cross even instituted a service whereby American volunteer women, notified of the arrival of American patients, visited the men in hospitals and communicated with their families.

Again, with typically acute sensitivity to the welfare of "our boys" (and correspondingly acute insensitivity to the probable French reaction), the ARC "loaned" its nurses and interpreters to French hospitals with American soldiers as patients, supplying the nurses with funds to buy special foods, tobacco, reading materials, and pajamas for their American patients. When they could, these nurses helped the French with other work. They had to be not only tactful but endlessly flexible and adaptable. One unit of these nurses found on their arrival that all the American wounded were already being taken care of at an American evacuation hospital, so they were assigned instead to escort a trainload of 1,500 American patients to Nantes, an eighteen-hour journey which kept them almost continuously on their feet. When they got back the next day they were sent to a triage hospital, where they worked for four weeks tending French wounded. Then the American evacuation hospital moved, leaving its most seriously ill patients in their care. At that point other American wounded began to arrive from the field. An onslaught of Spanish influenza increased their patient load by about a hundred French soldiers. Only after three months were they recalled to Paris.[43]

But the medical concerns of the American Red Cross extended far beyond fighting men. Their Children's Bureau alone was epic in its undertakings. It aided 519 childrens' institutions and societies and operated 25 hospitals and convalescent homes and 99 dispensaries.[44] Its spirit was epitomized in the woman who became its chief nurse, Elizabeth H. Ashe. Originally turned down by the Red Cross as too old for service abroad, Ashe accepted the invitation of Dr. William Palmer Lucas to organize the first pediatric unit to be sent to France, a privately supported group. Resisting with difficulty her own persistent impulses to roll up her sleeves and begin to care for the nearest impetigo-covered, lice-ridden refugee youngster, Ashe surveyed the needs for children's work. When in the ARC takeover all children's work in France was assigned to Dr. Lucas, Ashe was ready to act.

The Children's Bureau—besides their vast responsibilities in feeding and housing refugee and repatriated children—undertook their medical care. The bureau opened at Evian a hospital and dispensary for children too ill to travel. In Lyons the bureau ran a convalescent home in a palace, with fifty-six rooms, central heating, luxurious furnishings, and a beautifully kept farm. A series of dispensaries in cooperation with the American Fund for French Wounded; child health demonstrations, teaching centers, model playgrounds, and efforts to combat tuberculosis in cooperation with the Rockefeller Institute; a "baby house" in cooperation with the Society of Friends—the list is endless.[45]

All this, of course, was not without problems: "the nurses nearly go mad with the difficulties," Ashe wrote, "for instance, Dr. Baldwin at Nesle in the war zone has been running three dispensaries and a hospital for two months without gauze, alcohol, or night gowns. . . . Express simply never arrives in the war zone, except for the army." Illness and scarcity of personnel plagued the bureau. "We always have at least half a dozen nurses and aides ill with contagious diseases. It is most trying when they are so scarce. I am in terror now for fear an emergency will arise in the next few days before another steamer comes, as I haven't one nurse or aide to send." And when the German offensive threatened Paris in the spring of 1918, Ashe sent her Children's Bureau nurses and aides off to the front, and herself took a "vacation" to nurse American wounded. Certainly she earned her invitation from the French government to march with other nurses in the Fourth of July parade: "It was the first time women have ever marched in a parade in Paris. . . . I carried the flag, it was the proudest moment of my life, in fact don't think I ever had that proud feeling before. But when we fell in line behind the Marines, our band playing Dixie and I held that banner on high to the cheers of the crowd's 'Vive l'Amérique,' I really felt that I had reached the supreme moment of my life."[46]

American Medical Women: Who Did What

Whether within a foreign medical system, or for an American organization that dispensed medical aid, or on their own, many more American medical women served in many more capacities than history has recognized. They included doctors, ambulance drivers, clerks and interpreters, dietitians, occupational therapists, physical therapists, workers with the blind, and, in the largest numbers, nurses and nurses' aides.

> *Our ancestors and our experience provide us [women doctors] with two things: the capacity to meet emergencies and the energy to carry them through successfully.*
                                    —Dr. Rosalie Slaughter Morton[47]

Hard figures on the numbers of women doctors are impossible to come by—because some free-lanced, because they frequently moved from one assignment to another or were pressed into temporary service, because some worked with the French and Belgian armies and others as contract physicians with the American army, because agencies kept inadequate records, because the general disorganization generated incidents in which women doctors treating civilians were suddenly coopted by the military into treating wounded soldiers. The executive secretary of the American Women's Hospitals only slightly overstated reality when she wrote, ". . . unlike the Scottish women who have worked as units and made a splendid history, the American medical woman is working as an individual and is quite swallowed up, though the work that some of them are doing is nothing short of marvelous."[48]

Certainly American women doctors wanted to serve. When Dr. Rosalie Slaughter Morton officially represented women physicians and scientifically trained women in related health fields on the Medical Board of the National Council of Defense, she registered a total of 8,000 women—doctors (whether practicing or not), interns, anesthetists, and laboratory "experts." Of these an astonishing 40 percent of the physicians declared themselves ready to serve, a record surpassing "not only in percentage but in promptness, the men doctors."[49]

But the United States Army initially sniffed at the idea of employing them. Eventually it suffered their presence in military hospitals as "contract surgeons," a ploy that deprived the women of military pay, rank, and benefits, but gave the military the advantage of their services. These women minded most the lack of rank, which hampered them in the execution of their duties. Dr. Regina Flood Keyes, a surgeon who directed a hospital in Vodena, Greece, reported to the American Women's Hospital *Bulletin* a comment of a Serbian doctor: "So your country sends you so far away and gives you no rank, yet the British send all their women doctors out here with rank." The *Bulletin* editorialized: "This is a point all medical women accredited from this country to Europe emphasize. They meet British and Scottish women, on the same errand that engages them, with the rank of captain and major and they, having no rank, must take their place at the end of the line and twist their thumbs while their superiors are served."[50]

In the private sector, besides the jobs they created for themselves in the American Women's Hospitals, the women doctors found other opportunities in institutions like the Commission for the Prevention of Tuberculosis in France, the Rockefeller Foundation, and the Red Cross, which deployed fifty women physicians overseas in the first year the United States was in the war. Others found employment with smaller agencies like the American Committee for Devastated France, the college units, and refugee hospitals.

Once overseas, they didn't necessarily stay put. Sometimes the military coopted them. The third-year medical student Jean Pattison, spending her vacation with an American Women's Hospital, worked first for the French army at Meaux and then in an American field hospital at Château-Thierry. Dr. Clara M. Davis, according to the correspondent Eunice Tietjens, operated somewhere just behind the lines in France, taking care of civilians, "though occasionally the military pressed her into service."[51] Or the call came informally: A military surgeon asked Dr. Alfreda Withington "to go with him to the station to meet hospital trains. Oh, those long, long trains! Mostly they were made up of box cars of the same variety as the 'side door Pullmans,' as the dough boys called them, bearing the familiar legend, *'Quarante Hommes Huit Chevaux'* [Forty Men Eight Horses]. . . . The poor chaps had been fighting in the wheat fields only twenty-four hours before."[52]

Or one private agency might steal, beg, or borrow a woman physician from another—as, for instance, with Dr. Withington. At fifty-seven she was well past the age limit for women, but she managed to get herself accredited to the Red Cross. She didn't spell out just how, but she did write of asking a friend of equal age how she had managed to get overseas as a canteen worker. "Don't you suppose," her friend answered, "that I'd lie for my country?"[53]

Withington's expertise with tuberculosis prompted the Red Cross to appoint her chief physician of the Franco-American Dispensary at Dreux, which cared for both soldiers and civilians—but only on a temporary basis, because the ARC feared that the French would not accept a woman in so important a position. "I had been warned that I would not find the French physicians friends. However, the local doctor at Dreux, who had been appointed to cooperate with me did not bother to exercise supervision. . . . At first he was a trifle offish, but soon he took to beaming, often bringing his own private patients to me for a consultation. The military doctors seemed friendly from the first, inviting me to their wards to see special cases."[54] When the ARC reassigned her, the French physicians petitioned for her return. In the end the Red Cross and the Rockefeller Commission were vying for her services.

One just never knew. Dr. Withington tells of meeting ". . . a woman dressed in the same uniform as myself—older than any of us and somewhat bent—I accosted her as a fellow physician. 'I'm no doctor,' she said. 'Then why are you wearing the uniform?' 'I don't know myself. They just put me in it. I'm a research worker from Woods Hole. Dr. Alexander Lambert sent for me to come over here because he thought I knew something about lice.' "[55]

In still other cases, the women physicians themselves simply used an institutional affiliation to do what they wanted to do anyway. For example—Dr. Rosalie Slaughter Morton, already at forty heading her own clinic in the United States with five assistants, persuaded the ARC to appoint her a special commissioner to take sixty cases of medical supplies to the Serbian Army. She then seized the opportunity to volunteer for a short period (at her own expense) at a "large tent hospital under French direction with Serbian patients."[56]

Although we can document that both military and private organizations frequently utilized the services of American women doctors overseas, enough women physicians bob up in the records without any institutional affiliation that we can trace to suggest that many simply served and departed unsung. Repeatedly tantalizing glimpses appear of American women doctors working all over Europe and the Middle East. Dr. Ruth A. Parmelee arrived in Harpoot, Turkey, in June, 1914, where a missionary-run hospital for Turkish soldiers was subsidized by the Red Cross. Parmelee rode horseback to tend Turkish women in their homes, did relief work for Armenian refugees, trained Turkish women medical workers, and finally, when the United States broke off relations with Turkey, escaped after eighteen days' travel by wagon and three by train.[57] In Amsterdam in 1915 Lucy Biddle Lewis ran across two American ladies, one a doctor who with her assistant had been doing relief work in Belgium. And what of Dr. Mary L. Brown, described in a press release of the Committee on Public Information as a Howard University graduate commissioned to go to France? Did she actually manage to get to France, adding another to the minuscule number of black women allowed to serve there?[58] The faint traces of such women doctors as these remind us that we can now never know precisely how many American women actually went overseas in the Great War.

🙶🙶🙶 . . . *they were lithe, strong, and withal, fair to look upon. The appearance of our chauffeuses was a valuable asset for the reason that men are men the world around, and all the gasoline in France was controlled by poor, easy man. Surely it was wise to have chauffeuses who found favor in his eyes.*
—Dr. Esther Lovejoy[59]

Medical care depended not only upon women doctors, but also upon the many auxiliary women workers who staffed the clearing stations, the dispensaries, the supply depots, and the hospitals.

And the drivers. As a doctor with the American Women's Hospitals wrote, "While the doctors are in the dispensaries, diagnosing and prescribing, our chauffeurs are under the cars in the wind outside, at the same occupation, and when we see how they make the old, maimed machinery work, we see they are the better M.D.'s."[60]

The lives of these "chauffeuses" were demanding. "We were a strictly feminine institution," Mrs. P. D. Lamson reported of her motor unit. "Our daily job was first to see that the particular car entrusted to each one of us was kept in running order, then to take it over across the river to the headquarters of the committee . . . find out from the order book what our deliveries were to be, look up the hospitals, etc. on our maps of Paris, get our bales and bags into the cars and start away as quickly as we could. . . . Saturday afternoon . . . we had time in the garage to do any little odd repairs. . . ."[61] And Mrs. J. Borden Harriman always remembered "the times I saw the sun rise over the Place de la Concorde as I hastened forth to be present at roll call. How hard the cars were to crank after twelve hours in the freezing garage! Wartime motors had no self starters and more than one girl got a broken arm from a kicking Ford."[62]

Besides the critically important work of distributing hospital supplies, driving doctors on their rounds, transporting patients, and running innumerable errands for civilian hospitals, the chauffeuses took on all sorts of other jobs. During a German advance, with refugees pouring into Paris, Elizabeth Ayer's motor corps "served food and supplemented the trucks and ambulances transporting the refugees from one station to another."[63] Some of the chauffeuses drove ambulances, like Katherine Stinson, who with her sister Marjorie first ran a school to train Canadian and American military pilots, then went to France as an ambulance driver, and flew there for the Red Cross.[64]

Many faced danger, like Mrs. Guy Napier-Martin: "We had our first air-raid work last night. I was the night-driver on duty. . . . Some bombs fell very near just as I got to the H.O.E. [evacuation hospital]. . . . I had just

Motor corps uniform of Elizabeth Remsen Thompson. "Mother never was a nurse, but knew all about automobile engines. . . . She was born in 1894 and was known as Lightning Liz."

—Jane Darlington Irwin

stopped my engine, preparatory to beating it for cover, when shrapnel whizzed past my head and there was a tremendous crash close beside. . . . Then an ambulance call came and I tore off, taking one of the doctors along. There were soldiers wounded and killed. They filled my car with the worst cases. . . . By the time I had taken my first load to the hospital and got back, every one of our cars was there. . . . A good many of the drivers had gone to bed and the cars' radiators had to be filled—and they were on the road about eight minutes after the order came! . . . Shortly after, more bombs fell. . . . A doctor went with me, and we had to drive about from house to house and street to street before we could find where the wounded were. . . . People were huddled in their doorways, and we kept calling out, 'Où sont les blessés?' [Where are the wounded?] . . . the things I saw last night made me feel murderous—such suffering and all for nothing."[65]

The protean Mary Dexter, with war service as a driver, a probationer nurse, and a student psychoanalyst already behind her, became in September 1917 an ambulance driver with the British Hackett-Lowther unit, "officially attached to the French Army . . . the first women to be so attached"—and so much a part of the French Army that they even received the poilu's pay of five sous a day. But Miss Lowther, even though she ranked as second lieutenant, did not require them to salute her, "as she doesn't want it said, 'How absurd it is, women playing at being men!' "[66] Dexter, never one to understate the drama of her position, announced, "I am under martial law and tied for six months! If I left before, I should be shot at dawn for desertion!!! There are heaps of women driving for the English army, and for the French—an American woman spoke to me in the street yesterday who has been chauffing for the French near Amiens for some months. But there are none who are actually driving ambulances attached to an army, going up to the postes de secours, and under fire, as we shall be."[67]

Dexter thrilled over her silver ID bracelet—"quite a chic form of chain bracelet!"—and her big gray ambulance with its top speed of twenty-five miles per hour. In Paris the drivers ordered their *champignons de fer* (helmets): "The Army would give them to us, but we prefer to order an extra size, on account of our hair taking up room."[68] Whatever her frivolities, Dexter too took her chances and repeatedly drove under fire.

At Le Mans Ada Knowlton Chew, after a week's course in automobile maintenance, joined the demanding "Service des Automobiles." She drove ". . . a French doctor 140 km one night in a drenching rainstorm in an open car that broke down and had to be pushed up a hill. The car was a very, very small French Zebra, and the doctor was very, very large." And very upset. Only with difficulty could Chew persuade him to help push.[69]

Twenty-year-old Helen Douglas Mankin, having prepared herself by working as a mechanic in a Ford factory and in a garage, circumvented the minimum-age requirement by coolly joining the Passport Division of the State Department and writing her own passport. In France, in the intervals of driving and repairing her ambulance, she built from spare parts a little car, named it *L'Enfant*, and sold it before she returned Stateside. (Mankin later became an attorney and spent ten years in the Georgia legislature and three in Congress.)[70]

Number among the patient and the unsung the hundreds of medical secretaries and clerks, without whom no organization of any size could long function. Contemporary records reward the "paper shufflers" as seldom as our society today. Only occasionally a warm-hearted, empathetic administrator like Elizabeth Ashe mentions their vital work: "My secretary is a brilliant jewel—only twenty-one years old and so clever and attractive," she wrote of Helen Byrne, later the wife of Walter Lippmann.[71]

Sometimes the lives of these clerical workers exploded into adventure. During Ida Preston's fifteen months as a civilian secretary with a hospital unit at Rouen, often under air raids, she and her assistants were "pressed into operating room duty" during the Allied retreat of 1918. Transferred to the headquarters for surgical and medical consultants in the Vosges Mountains, she came under the big guns of the enemy. On to Amiens, where "lists of wounded grew longer and longer. The first day following an attack the men walked in for aid. The second day they were carried in on stretchers. The third day there was little we could do for them. . . . Pieces of shrapnel rained constantly on the tin roofs of the long wooden corridors. In many wards the only covering was the sky."[72]

Unseen and often unthanked, clerical workers did a myriad of jobs. Some took records from patients. Some interpreted for the medical staff. Others labored in the soul-destroying capacity of "searchers," going from ward to ward, trying to locate soldiers missing in action by questioning men from the same outfit.

> *What is the use . . . of my speaking glibly four languages, of having learned to read Braille with bound eyes, and to see things from the blind man's point of view unless I can now offer the expert knowledge which I possess?*
>
> —Winifred Holt (Mather)[73]

Trench warfare, in which the soldiers incurred so many terrible head wounds and were so often blinded, impelled advances in restorative techniques and the professions associated with them. Artists experimented with masks of galvanized copper, complete with moustaches of real hair and attached by spectacles, to conceal the dreadful facial disfigurements beyond the scope of plastic surgery. With the help of General Pétain, the sculptor Anna Coleman Ladd got around the restriction that forbade wives of men serving in Europe to go overseas. Landing in France in December 1917, she devoted herself to modeling and painting the "portrait masks" which made life and work possible for many *mutilés*.[74]

Fortunately Winifred Holt had already developed innovative techniques to train the blind and had molded an efficient supportive organization in the Lighthouse. In the spring of 1915 Mrs. Cooper Hewitt urged Holt to go to France, where the war blind were comforted and pitied, but left to sit hopeless and idle. Holt promptly went off to see M. Jusserand, the French ambassador: "In his quizzical fashion he asked, 'You are prepared to be torpedoed?' 'Perfectly,' I replied, 'I have a sea blue wrapper.' 'Perfect. In the sea blue wrapper you will sit on top of the periscope.' "

With her secretary Holt descended on France, where she formed Le Comité Franco-Américain pour les Aveugles de la Guerre (with its sister organization in the States the Committee for Men Blinded in Battle) and whence she pelted the New York Lighthouse with begging, demanding letters to the board by then in charge of the organization's finances: "Curtail, beg, steal, do anything, but let me stay over here and help."[75] She breezed through the startled French bureaucracy, who allowed her to "claim blind men wherever we please. This will probably mean that I start on a tour through France in my military motor before long. . . . We are having classes each morning in the hotel, teaching each day in the hospitals, training a corps of sighted aides, seeing diplomats and still, alas playing politics."[76]

She took a census of the French blind, experimented with a knitting department run by the mother of a blind soldier, opened a forty-four-room home for the blind complete with gymnasium and skating rink, started a printing plant, and gave lessons in agriculture and chicken raising. She took blind men to concerts, got pets for them, sold the dresses and sweaters they knitted to the designer Worth, and responded to the plea of the mother of her first French pupil to find a suitable wife for him.

In cooperation with the French government and with the American Expeditionary Force, Holt by the end of the war had opened seven Lighthouses in France, and was planning another in Italy. When after the Armistice, at forty-eight, she married for the first time, she asked that instead of sending wedding presents people contribute to a fund for the French blind, announcing her hope that it would amount to half a million dollars.

Other entrepreneurial American women also responded to the needs of the war blind. Dorothy Canfield Fisher founded and supported a press to print Braille books for them. Alice Getty intended only to respond to a 1915 request from two blinded French officers for English lessons. But when she could not lay her hands on an English grammar written in Braille, she wrote one. When that task showed her the lack of literature for the blind, she set up a Braille printing shop called La Roue (The Wheel, the Eastern symbol of wisdom), wrote a Braille French-Spanish grammar, and a book of instructions in massage, "a calling in which blinded soldiers have become particularly adept." When she had Braille books, she started a library to lend them. Eventually the work of the printing plant and the library became international in scope.[77]

Although a few practitioners in the then brand-new professions of occupational and physical therapy traveled to Europe in the spring of 1918, they went in numbers only in the late summer and fall; of course their reconstructive work extended far beyond the Armistice.

Lack of definition clouded their status with the United States Army. Clearly the pioneers among them began as civilian employees. But some time later the therapists were apparently included in the army's tables of organization as Reconstruction Aids. Woman after woman wrote of taking the oath of office, enlisting in the army, being mobilized. Were they, or were they not, in the army? As Mrs. Clyde McDowell Myres wrote, "To some of our fellow-travellers, we, the unclassified, may have seemed a little 'cobwebby in the ceiling,' as the French would say. We were nondescripts. We were pioneers going out with hardly the military status of scrubwomen."[78]

The therapists' uniform, they said, "was designed by a man who believed that women working in the hospitals were a menace to the men patients": navy blue serge with long, full skirt, Norfolk jacket, and a large cape sporting *136* buttons and which, unless carefully buttoned, pulled the wearer's head back uncomfortably—all topped with round beaver hats worn summer and winter, so large that "you could put both hands inside between your head and the crown." Oh yes: "square-toed boots that laced up the front, made of orange leather."[79]

The experience of the physical therapist Maude E. Cook may stand for that of many other "Re-aids." Having enlisted for service in August 1918, she sailed in September. Landing in Brest, she and her colleagues volunteered to help the nurses at Camp Kerhuon there. Then they went on to their individual stations, Cook with two others to Base 8, Savenay. "Here during the rush times we halted our work to help with plaster casts, secretarial work or anywhere the need was greatest, but for many weeks of long busy days we were working over cots in sometimes two or three wards." She served until April 1919.[80]

Some of the physical therapists were graduates of professional schools; others, like a teacher of manual training, were prepared only by a short course. More than one returned home with her health wrecked by illness or injury—like Harriet MacDonald who was wounded during an air raid. She postponed an urgent operation to continue with her work; as a result, she spent the rest of her life on crutches or in a wheelchair. Finally, in 1931, Congress voted her compensation.[81]

The occupational therapists too came from many different backgrounds. Like women in other jobs overseas, they had to improvise, making scrap baskets out of willows and rushes, looms from scrap lumber, vases and candlesticks from tin cans, and woven cloth from the dyed selvages of bandages. "The other day," wrote Alice DeFord, "we had one boy ripping up his 'issue' coat so that another, a tailor, could alter it; another, gluing up a broken violin; another, digging out his hob-nails from his shoes so that he could go to a dance; then in walked a boy to borrow some white paint. He had spilled some ink on the pillow and wanted to paint it over before the nurse saw it."[82]

Mrs. Clyde McDowell Myres and her small pioneering group of O.T.s, sailed in March 1918, taking with them their own tools and looms. Their workshop "was a barrack, twenty by a hundred feet, cracks in the floor, cracks in the wall, door off the hinges, windows flopping, dust flying everywhere. . . . No benches, no work-tables—a Quartermaster who demanded formal requisition for every box, nail, or tin can that we had begun to gather up on sight. There were no military strings tied to the water-faucets. We could at least live up to our status of scrub-women without fear of a summary court-martial. Up to the time of our arrival, there had been no women in the hospital. . . .

"The Quartermaster loaned us saw-horses, planks, and mess-tables—though he might send for them the next day. Some old French beds ('Kangaroo beds' they were called—oblong boxes on four broad legs, the two at the head longer than those at the foot) appeared overnight in our shop. Hammer and nails and boards spliced the short legs; and behold, we had fine, level work-benches. Boxes served as seats. Back went the saw-horses and mess-tables— the men had helped us to outwit the Quartermaster.

"Utilizing two large tin-cans, a little old rusty grate found in a

deserted blacksmith shop, and salvaged bricks, we soon had a char-
coal furnace for the heating of our soldering irons. From tin-cans,
we made drain pipes and lined three huge six-foot tubs for dish-
washing built by the patients; fashioned funnels, strainers, biscuit
and doughnut cutters, and soap dishes. The eyes of the harassed
Commanding Officer grew almost human. The kitchen sink had
won him.

"Furniture was needed everywhere. For the doctors rough boxes
were serving for chairs and desks. Wards were barren of everything
but beds; no bedside or ward tables, chairs or stools. The carpenter
found more volunteers than she could well manage. Orders came
from every corner. The doctors, as well as the Commanding Officer,
began to look upon the work-shop with a kindly eye—kindly or
calculating. . . .

"During that September and October, the men poured in from
the front. They lined up at the door of the workshop every morning
before opening hour. The[ir] work attracted buyers, a boon to men
who had sometimes been for months without receipt of pay."[83] The
obvious success of Myres and others like her in involving hospitalized
men in useful rehabilitative work impressed General Pershing, who
intervened to persuade the Surgeon General's officialdom to award
the reconstruction aides status in the Army.[84]

A different kind of restoration work is described by Mary Dexter, who in the fall of 1916 enrolled for a course of study at the
Medico-Psychological Clinic in London. Dexter received what was
apparently Freudian instruction until the early fall of 1917, when
she took off to become an ambulance driver for the French Army;
by the end of March 1918—and at the end of her memoirs—she was
back at the clinic, hoping when she had had more experience to work
with American doctors and American troops: "That would be a
realization of what I am beginning to dream of—war-shock work in
France!"[85]

In the traditional Freudian way, Dexter was required to undergo
psychoanalysis herself; what is startling, but perhaps explicable by
the war situation, is how quickly she was allowed patients of her
own, apparently about three months after she began her studies. "I
am to have a shell-shock case soon—loss of memory—three cheers!"

Dexter wrote in January 1917. By the end of January: "I have six patients now—an awful lot, more than any other student, but it is splendid, and I shall keep them all if I can. . . . One is a case of Gallipoli shell-shock—complete loss of memory—such a nice boy, only twenty-one."[86] Like the physical and occupational therapists, the psychotherapists were just getting started, strongly impelled by the terrible traumas inflicted by the "Great War."

👑👑👑 *It was a big responsibility sending [to the front] those aids who had come for children's work, but they were eager to go and I think it is their right to volunteer for such service just as their brothers do.*
                                                                —Elizabeth Ashe[87]

Just as the United States government initially rejected women doctors, so with nurses' aides. Eventually, however, common sense, the shortage of nurses, and the example of the British Volunteer Aide Detachments combined to send the much-needed American aides overseas. There they bore medical responsibilities far beyond what their formal training had prepared them for. Shirley Millard, for instance, when the surgical nurse in her unit collapsed, began working in surgery after two hours' study of the instruments.[88]

Often they acted as interpreters as well as assistants to the nurses. They endured long hours, sudden demands, hardship, and danger. As Frances Webster wrote in July 1918, "The night of the 28th was fearful in regard to bombs. After a second attack I went up stairs to bed but was no sooner in than . . . they wanted me at the hospital. . . . I will have to admit that I ran all the way there and kept my head more or less ducked as the shrapnel had only just stopped clattering on the street." It took Webster seven hours to do the admitting papers for the influx of wounded; the next day kept her busy interpreting as well as working in the gas ward. "I interpreted for patients, doctors and nurses, till I really didn't know whether I was speaking French or English. It was the greatest satisfaction, though, to be able to get them fixed up. Sometimes the smallest things which they wanted but couldn't explain seemed to make the boys perfectly contented."[89]

Olivia E. Hamilton wrote admiringly of the sixty-year-old aide "Mrs. Burkhead": "For 19 months she has come here every night and given her services to the hospital. She has charge of the diet kitchen and makes the cocoa and tilleul (a drink no Frenchman will sleep without). . . . There is no glory attached to staying up all night and fighting with unreasonable nurses who always want a little more than their share for their wards or their patients, but it slides right off her back. . . ."[90] Such women richly deserved Chief Nurse Elizabeth Ashe's description of the aides as "the flower of our civil army here."[91]

> ⊌⊌⊌   *Even during Miss Bullard's lunch-hour—if she takes a lunch-hour—there is a more restless spirit among the* blessés. *They talk of her from bed to bed. Her* drôle de français, *her funny French, which they delight in; her capacity; her sympathy; her well-earned* Croix de Guerre. *After all, they say, why should an American woman be nursing Frenchmen? There are no French nurses here.*
>
> —Elizabeth Shepley Sergeant[92]

American nurses, with the British, were recognized as the best in the world, thanks in part to the acceptance in both countries of nursing as a profession for respectable women. The French and the Belgians were caught at the beginning of the war without a sufficient cadre of trained nurses. Nursing had traditionally been left to nuns, and the divisions between church and state before the war had driven many of them away. Though it had become fashionable for society women to earn Red Cross certificates, nursing did not exist in France as a lay profession.

The United States Army had had ample evidence during the Civil War of the effectiveness of women nurses, 6,000 of whom were recruited and trained for service with Northern forces by Dorothea Dix. Nonetheless, the army struggled through the Spanish-American War with a hodgepodge of enlisted men, volunteer women, Red Cross women nurses, and civilian women and men army "contract nurses" as care givers. Thanks to the persuasive powers and Spanish-American War experience of Dr. Anita Newcomb McGee, Congress finally established the Army Nurse Corps in 1901—as an auxiliary, rather than an integral, part of the army. In 1908 the navy followed suit.

The excellence, dedication, and courage of American nurses did not, of course, win them fair treatment in World War I. The terms of their employment were not made clear. Few Red Cross nurses realized that by not joining the Army Nurse Corps they were rendering themselves ineligible for benefits should they become disabled, even though their work did not differ in arduousness, difficulty, or danger from that of the army nurses.[93] And few army nurses realized that they were committing themselves indefinitely, rather than for the two-year term common in the Red Cross.[94]

What's more, the army and navy nurses, despite strenuous efforts for regularization throughout World War I, held only a paramilitary status, since the military, even at the risk of hampering the nurses' efficiency, refused them the rank and benefits for which their responsibilities called: in its own hierarchical structure the military expected the nurses to exercise authority without rank.[95] The confusion about their status, as Alma Lutz observed, "sometimes held up their pay, and led to neglect and unfair treatment in matters of transportation and leave. It often interfered with discipline as regards corpsmen. . . . It tended to lessen the respect of Medical Corps officers for the nurses, and in general they were regarded as civilians rather than soldiers."[96] No wonder that Carrie Hall, coming from the prestigious position of chief nurse of Peter Bent Brigham Hospital, wrote: "I never should do army nursing from choice. . . . I feel much like the fly that has accepted the spider's invitation and finds he can't escape. . . . my authority [as chief nurse of Base Hospital #5] is limited."[97]

Yet nurses, some of them as young as twenty-one, bore responsibilities that far exceeded their expectations and sometimes their training. (The shortage of nurses caused the Red Cross in the last months of the war to recruit some of the youngest American women to serve overseas.) "I think you would sicken with fright," Mlle. Miss wrote her surgeon father, "if you could see the operations that a poor nurse is called upon to perform—the putting in of drains, the washing of wounds so huge and ghastly as to make one marvel at

Tributes to nurse from patient—from Ruth Stillman's autograph book

the endurance that is man's, the digging about for bits of shrapnel."[98] Reflecting on an experience common among nurses, Helen Homans wrote, "I have never learned so much in my life, but if I had known the responsibility I don't know that I would ever have come."[99]

American nurses frequently acted as anesthetists. The British, initially horrified at the idea, were eventually converted by experiences with women like Anne Penland. She was ordered out of her job by a profanely furious British colonel, deaf to the explanation that she had had more experience in anesthetics than any officer in the unit. But his attention was diverted by the arrival of 1,200 gassed casualties; Penland's display of skill that night so impressed other British officers that they asked her to instruct British nurses.[100] American nurses also served on the blood transfusion team sent to the British army to teach new techniques for saving wounded and shock victims.[101]

By no means did all nurses hold exciting front-line jobs. Women who had dreamed of heroism and glory found themselves instead absorbed by the French Sanitary Service and based in "lonely and remote villages where living conditions were primitive and social customs strange. . . . they were sent to the rear of the Armies and scrubbed floors in dirty and dilapidated French buildings or in rude wooden barracks, set up wards, made beds and nursed contagious cases." Their days were ruled by loneliness, monotony, and "the strain of endless inspections and criticisms of conditions beyond their power to remedy."[102]

But many of the American nurses served much closer to the front than reference to the regulations would suggest—not just in the frequent emergencies, but also in their regularly assigned duties. Chief Nurse Julia Stimson worried over the nurses she sent for temporary duty at casualty clearing stations toward the front. "What with the steam, the ether, and the filthy clothes of the men . . . the odor in the operating room was so terrible that it was all that any of them could do to keep from being sick. One of my nurses was sick at her stomach all night long the first night she worked there, and just ran in and out all night, but kept right on with her work. . . . no mere handing of instruments and sponges, but sewing and tying up and putting in drains while the doctor takes the next piece of shell out of another place. Then after fourteen hours of this, with freezing feet, to a meal of tea and bread and jam, and off to rest if you can in a wet bell tent in a damp bed without sheets, after a wash with a cupful of water. . . . One need never tell me that women can't do as much, stand as much, and be as brave as men."[103]

Many of the nurses moved in a kaleidoscopic world, never knowing where they would be sent next. Elmira Bears, for instance, rejoiced in her assignment to a flying squadron of medics with a French mobile surgical unit: Their small portable operating room "rocks and shakes like a boat when we are working there, but 'ça ne fait rien' [that doesn't matter]—for the boys are being rushed through with real American speed"—speed that averted the onset of gas gangrene.[104] American Mobile Hospital No. 2 traveled in fifty trucks, and could be set up in nine hours. One of its twenty-two nurses, Emily Clatworthy, wrote in her diary of the unit's "long trek over many battle-fields. . . . We were in the Argonne the day before that great offensive started, and we were there when the Armistice was signed."[105]

Other nurses received coveted orders to smaller emergency surgical, shock, and gas teams, which could move almost instantaneously to any part of the front. These teams led "a gypsy life. . . . The devastated country lying stark in the brilliant moonlight grew to have a natural aspect, town after town in ruins, fields plowed with shell holes, roadsides lined with ammunition and graves."[106] They worked in the open air or in tents often pitched in mud, with "the stick-to-it-iveness that French mud has. The most popular costume those days were raincoats over either a jersey or gray crepe uniform, rubber boots and sou'wester hat. Our boys told us that we looked like the advertisement of codliver oil. No wonder the mademoiselles asked our soldiers: 'Are all American women so homely?' "[107]

In German breakthroughs nurses and aides had to evacuate patients from their hospitals. The Red Cross might have to empty a maternity hospital in order to receive wounded soldiers. Sometimes nurses who had been routinely caring for civilians saw adventurous and dramatic service when they were suddenly reassigned to military hospitals. Florence Bullard, rushed to a French Army hospital in an evacuated village near the front in March 1918, found herself: ". . . installed in . . . a sort of coal-cellar, completely underground. . . . I have not seen daylight for eight days now and the stench in this cave is pretty bad: no air, artificial light, and the cots are so close together you can just get between them. Side by side I have Americans, English, Scotch, Irish, and French, and apart in the corners are Boche. They have to watch each other die side by side."[108]

Even navy nurses, regularly assigned to ports far behind the lines, in emergencies served as close as three miles from the front. "With high explosives whirring past us," one of them wrote of her trip forward, "we sped on past trench after trench, actually seeing our own boys, with guns to shoulder, ready for the words that would send them over the top."[109]

Navy nurses joined army nurses at Cohan, where, Mary El-derkins wrote, "We had air raids night after night. . . . When we were not operating at night, we spent the time from darkness to dawn in a cellar twenty feet under ground. It just held seven cots and thirteen nurses were supposed to sleep there. If we sat erect on the cot our head struck the rough stone above. Water dripped on us all night long. Huge black bugs crawled about and after we quieted down we could hear the rats. We, ourselves, felt like rats in some trap." Moving out of range of the shelling, they set up a crude operating room: "Packing boxes were used for instrument tables and seats for the anesthetist, a stretcher on two carpenter horses were the operating-table, while we had to put our solutions, etc, in tin cans, cooking utensils or stray bits of china ware."[110]

Nurses risked their lives well behind the lines as well as near the front. Some were wounded on duty, sheltering their patients, and others in their own beds. When the U.S. Army Base Hospital Unit of Harvard University came under air raid on September 4, 1917, one of the wounded was "Miss Parmelee," a Red Cross nurse who refused to be relieved of duty even when struck in the face by a bomb fragment.[111] A nurse from a Presbyterian Hospital unit lost an eye: "We had been asleep and were awakened by the humming of German motors . . ." wrote Helen Grace McClelland. "Then the bombs began to drop. We reached for our tin hats which we always kept hanging with our gas masks on the cot. I put mine on the side of my head and covered up again. Miss MacDonald was slightly raised on her elbow when two bombs struck the cook house nearby and a piece of shrapnel came through our tent wall and penetrated her eye; another piece struck her cheek." She later returned to duty with an artificial eye.[112]

Even worse than the dangers from air raids and artillery fire were the ravages of infection. Disease threatened not only in the more primitive areas—in Serbia, where typhus raged, in Russia, where malaria and typhoid were endemic—but also in France, where nurses giving civilian care were surrounded by the tubercular, where nurses worked to exhaustion in the Asian flu epidemic themselves succumbed. Everywhere meningitis hovered as a secondary, and fatal, infection.

Of all places women served in World War I, the Balkans and Russia must have been the most harrowing and the most perilous. Revolutions raged. Armies swept back and forth. Medical systems were rudimentary, and living conditions primitive. On all counts each could have been stamped with a warning: This country may be dangerous to your health.

Yet scores of American nurses worked even in their remote areas. Some helped to establish hospitals for Russian soldiers in a carpet factory in Hamadān, and at Khoi, Persia, in an adobe structure in which camel drivers had housed their caravans. Kurd tribesmen drove Eleanor Soukup's group back from the Russian front, where they had planned to do surgical work. Ten former Mercy Ship nurses joined a German-sponsored group to render relief to German and Austrian prisoners of war captured by the Russians. Helen Scott Hay and Rachel Torrance, at the request of Queen Eleanora, undertook to organize in Sofia a training school for nurses, with a projected two-year curriculum; they managed to give the Bulgarian women only a month's training before the students had to begin caring for soldiers. Hay and Torrance then worked for two years in cooperation with American missionaries caring for refugees.[113]

The Serbian government begged the Mercy Ship nurses to stay in their war-torn country—and some agreed. The Serbians were, after all, endearing: "Every time an Austrian bullet is removed from a Serbian's wound all the patients get around his bed and sing the Serbian national anthem."[114] But the nurses lived and worked on embattled ground: during an Austrian advance, for instance, the American nurse Anna Marie Hirschbrunner interpreted in negotiations for the hospital to continue to operate under the Austrian occupation, driving out to meet the invaders in an ancient buggy, with a white towel fastened to the whip handle.[115]

Other American nurses in Serbia served in an improvised hospital in a cigarette factory lacking "heat, water, or drainage. . . . Hospital equipment consisted of straw mattresses laid on the tobacco-littered floor. . . . All waste and excreta were carried to a cesspool several hundred rods from the building. The basement was filled with an accumulation of soiled clothes and linen over which thousands of body lice crawled. When Saints' Days did not forbid, three Turkish women came to wash a few sheets and pajamas in small crib-shaped tubs similar to American chopping-bowls. . . ."[116]

"Most tragic of all," wrote the American nurse Mathild Krueger, "was the meager and unsuitable food supply. Two meals a day consisting of vegetable soup and coarse brown bread was the allowance for all patients. They were fed on this diet and then treated for dysentery, typhoid and other intestinal diseases with a wisdom equal to that of the sage who dipped up water in a sieve."[117]

Masses of wounded overwhelmed skeleton staffs: "Twelve hundred patients and we were only two surgeons, eight nurses and some five hospital orderlies!"[118] Overworked nurses had to ignore the doomed. "I used to tumble into bed at two or three o'clock in the morning," wrote Mary E. Gladwin, "and hear those men [in the ward next to her room]. They begged and prayed in all languages for help. They swore, they tore their bandages and the nights when I got up (it took all my strength of mind to stay in bed), I knew exactly what I would find when I went in—the men in their agony tearing off the dressings, the dark streams of blood on the floor."[119]

In such conditions epidemics were inevitable, as Emily Louise Simmonds well understood: "Beds are often pushed together so that three men lie on two cots, with 200 in each barn, dying at the rate of forty a day. One of their buildings was on a steep hill and the orderly used to empty the dressing-cans over the wall where they would blow about in all directions. The Turks . . . used to pick these over, taking the cleanest ones to line their wadded waistcoats."[120] Typhus struck both patients and care givers.

All in all, service in Serbia demanded improbable quantities of courage, dedication, flexibility, and enterprise. The situation was so fluid that the all-women staff of a Red Cross maternity hospital established in August 1915 by mid-October had to abandon their assignment of caring for babies to function as a front-line field ambulance. "For ten days," Grace Utley wrote, "we were on the firing line, giving First Aid to the wounded on the field. This sometimes meant immediate amputation of a limb, operation on the brain, emergency surgery of all kinds. . . . We evacuated before the on-coming enemy; moving back a station, we set up our tents anew . . . so that our 'Front' was a constantly changing one. We now await here in Nish the arrival of the Bulgars, the Turks, the Germans. Many places around us have fallen; our turn comes soon. The Baby Hospital under the Stars and Stripes and the Red Cross flag goes on until we are called again to the front; or until the floods of wounded turn this into a military hospital; or until the Bulgars shall order us on our walk with thousands of other refugees to a port where a ship will take us home; or until we shall be taken prisoners of war."[121]

◥◣◥ *While we sat swathed in blankets around those miserable little French stoves . . . and waited for the monotonous hours to drag by, we nurses tried to puzzle out the meaning of war, of those sick boys on the wards, of our own ridiculous plight.*
                                                    —Bessie Baker[122]

Overwork, hardship, danger, and above all watching the suffering, disfigurement, crippling, and death of their patients collected their costs from the nurses in mind as well as body. Navy nurse Mary Elderkins reported: "I don't believe one of us had ever imagined men could be so absolutely 'shot to pieces.' Many of them were the Marines who had crossed with us on the U.S.S. *Henderson*. . . . I cannot describe those nights—the long hours spent at the sterile table, or in giving anesthetics or in doing the many tasks about the room; the intense suffering of the wounded; the ghastly sights and nauseating smells when gas gangrene was present."[123]

The journalist Ellen LaMotte, who had volunteered in 1915 to serve in a French field hospital, etched the nurse's ambivalences. "By expert surgery, by expert nursing, some of these were to be returned to their homes again, *réformés*, mutilated for life, a burden to themselves and to society; others were to be nursed back to health, to a point at which they could again shoulder eighty pounds of marching kit, and be torn to pieces again on the firing line."[124]

"Nursing at night was extremely difficult; few lights were permitted, owing to the frequent air raids," wrote Chief Nurse Grace

Allison. "The night nurse inspected the dressings, going from bed to bed with a lantern shaded. . . . One nurse detected eight hemorrhages in a single night. . . . the life of a Tommy was saved by a nurse who made constant pressure with her bare hand buried deeply in the wound until assistance arrived."[125] Chief Nurse Amy Florence Patmore: "Perhaps the most wearing work of all was night duty in the psychopathic department and in those wards where the patients were running high fevers. In their delirium, these men lived over again the battles they had fought, went over the top, killed the enemy or fell back wounded on the field. . . ."[126]

Alone on night duty, in an alien country, with groans, smells, and the sound of artillery bombarding her senses, sometimes worried for fear that she could not get her helpless patients into gas masks quickly enough in case of a raid, many a nurse experienced intense anger, frustration, or despair. As Olivia E. Hamilton wrote on April 16, 1916, "It is all very well for the men who sit comfortably in front of their warm fires, smoking a good cigar, to say that there are 'worse things than war, that to be held in disrepute and dishonor is worse.' . . . Do you think that a man who has lain wounded for five days in a trench without food, and at the end of that time has been picked up, the only one alive, from among heaps of dead men, could find anything very much worse than war? Then he has been brought into the hospital with a large sore on his back from having been in one position so long in the wet, and has had one leg amputated and the skin removed from the other to graft on his back, and in consequence has to lie day in and day out on his stomach . . . for what purpose? I cannot say that I want to see Germany 'crushed' at such a sacrifice. I would rather see the war end now, a tie. What ultimate good is it going to do to crush anyone, for doubtless in a hundred years or less, as it has always been, some new bugbear will arise, that the rest of the world will feel the need of vanquishing. Who knows but it may be one of the crushers of the present war."[127]

CHAPTER 5

Aid and Comfort

Canteening

THE UNITED STATES, a country which in the "Great War" spoke of its servicemen as "our boys" and sentimentally enshrined each of them as "some mother's son," quickly felt a need for someone to entertain them, sew on their buttons, cook treats for them, hand them cigarettes and sweets, and whenever possible provide them with a homelike atmosphere. How else were they to be kept in order, reminded of their mothers' teachings, and protected against evil influences? Unprecedented as it was, sending out virtuous women to "keep the boys straight" appealed to the American public.

At first the military balked. Blandly overlooking the existence of thousands of women nurses, they argued against subjecting women to the vicissitudes of war. But soon their opposition dwindled, gradually yielding to the argument that the presence of women improved morale, reduced the rate of venereal disease by diverting the men's attention from lighter ladies, and made the men easier to handle.[1]

I went about two kilometers on a large horse, lent me by a fat and perspiring Italian soldier acquaintance. I managed with his help to crawl up on the beast, and he led it. It was an awe-inspiring sight, as I had on a very short skirt, and a pocket full of raw eggs—which didn't break—and I was carrying a knapsack filled largely with onions, and a primus stove.

—Amelia Peabody Tileston[2]

118

Some women did not wait for the American entry into the war, organizational sponsorship, or official permission, but set about on their own brightening and easing the lot of soldiers. Of these no one could have furnished a more stellar example of independence and entrepreneurship than Amelia Peabody Tileston. As her mother commented, throughout her life "her methods were direct and forceful, shortcutting the devious paths of officialdom when possible (or even impossible)."[3] In her early forties when the war began, with a history of good works like day care for tuberculosis patients, she sailed in October 1914 for Europe, where she went from place to place—England, France, Italy, Greece—nursing, doing relief work, searching for the place and job in which she was most needed. She found it in Serbia. There she joined Emily Simmonds, an Anglo-American nurse who had been working for the Serbians since 1914, and successively nursed at a dressing station, managed a camp for about 500 children, women, and old men, and set up a series of soldiers' canteens.

Tileston's letters simmer with energy and impatience. In December 1917 she fretted about her inability to feed *all* the Serbian soldiers. Those to whom she served her hot soup "are much pleased, as it is the only hot meal they get on their way to the front, about six days in all. I should very much like, if . . . the Red Cross or Serbian Relief would supply funds, to start a canteen at one or two of the stations, to give soup to all soldiers going to the front. I could get it going in a few days and there would be no red tape, or money wasted, and I really think it would do a lot toward keeping the men from getting sick. Travelling for two days in unheated box-cars is no joke—and if you have no blanket! If I only had a lot of money, I could go ahead without waiting for anything."[4]

She scrounged money where she could, writing begging letters to her friends at home for supplies, and eventually receiving funds collected in England by the spectacular Flora Sandes, the English woman officer in the Serbian army. By March 1918 Tileston was arranging to open new canteens, handling transportation of clothing to troops at the front, and exulting in being busy. In April she reported a trip to the front to start "another soup place," complaining that "every one was absurdly slow, and I had to wait for permits,

and so forth. I also gave out about thirty thousand pieces of under-
clothing, stockings, and other things, sent by the Canadian Red
Cross. . . . Coming back, I walked thirty-seven kilometers, and
arrived at a station at half-past seven P.M., to find the train had left
ten minutes before, and I had to wait till one in the morning for the
next train, and travel all night in a boxcar that was usually given to
horses."[5] So she worked on, fuming, laughing, and absorbed. She
died of pneumonia in Serbia on February 22, 1920.

    △△△ *. . . canteen work is . . . a mixture of cook, waitress,*
and shop girl.
                                        —Edith Gratie Stedman[6]

Unlike such rugged individualists as Tileston, most canteeners
worked through organizations which sponsored recreational huts for
the troops, where soldiers could write letters, sing, play games, and
buy snacks and smokes. The Salvation Army, the Young Men's
Christian Association, and the Knights of Columbus—all religious
organizations—at the time recorded no theological qualms about this
kind of secondary participation in war, but the YM and the KCs did
debate the morality of letting women serve. These men's organizations pondered the responsibility of sending women thousands of
miles from home into the ultimate male sanctuary of the battlefield,
where in their version of history no woman save the professional
nurse had trod before.

    The Knights, a benevolent society of Roman Catholic men,
justified their decision to staff their wartime canteens only with males
with the courtly statement that a "scrupulous regard for the comfort
of young women would [not] warrant placing them to work in sur-
roundings which plainly demanded workers."[7] Not even the enterprise of the wife of a KC leader in France, Mrs. Walter M. Kernan,
swayed them, although she did ambulance work and set up a charming officers' club at Nice for almost nothing, scrounging in junk
shops and attics.[8] Ironically, the KCs did employ "young gentlewomen" as clerical workers in Paris, where they were bombarded
and shelled, and praised their work fulsomely, not to say conde-
scendingly: the young gentlewomen "scrupulously followed direc-

tions, carefully avoided mistakes and attained an efficiency which ought to make them very necessary in the technical and complex work of reconstruction. . . . The hazards of war did not frighten them from their work. On a certain day when Big Bertha succeeded in decapitating the statue of St. James in front of the church of the Madeleine, not twenty yards from the office of the Knights of Columbus, they went on with their work; this is only one instance, which they do not boast of, and which they would seriously object having chronicled here, of their fidelity to their duty."[9]

The YMCA found the situation more complex. They looked at the British example of using women in war. They heard the thousands of American women knocking on their doors to volunteer. They considered that "in our present American civilization women are the upholders of all the finer distinctions, the keepers of the amenities . . ." and therefore the natural guardians of servicemen's morals. And they noted the shortage of available men. Cautiously they announced their decision to allow women "to assist in the menial work, in the canteen, the kitchen and the cafe . . ." with "very limited opportunities in French and other educational classes, and in the entertainments . . . ," justifying their decision by a desire to free men for military service. Gradually women were used less for menial work and more for recreational work. A year and a half later the head of women workers in Paris rounded the circle with the decision to use only men in the Pavillon Hotel canteen "in order to set women free for social service."[10]

The YMCA also, like the other organizations, relied heavily on women clerks to write their letters and keep their records: In November 1918 they had already sent 164 office workers overseas, and were calling for 125 more.[11]

    Each Salvation Army hut in France has about four women and a man or two. . . . The women? Why, don't you know that our best men are the women?[12]

Beside the work of the Red Cross and the YMCA, that of the American Salvation Army was tiny—a small operation that almost everybody loved, for its openness to all and its loyalty to its own mission. The organization, patterned on a military model, sent abroad only about 250 regular officers and Salvationists (as the Salvation Army called its "soldiers" of lower rank), and secured additionally about 400 men and 150 women workers in Europe.[13] Unlike the YM, the Salvation Army refused the military offer to give its men officer rank, on the ground that such distinctions would create a gulf between them and the doughboys. Its very size contributed to the excellence of its reputation, for at its head Evangeline Booth could handpick her people; she "took no casual comers, even with offers of money to back them. . . . She sent only those whom she knew and had tried."[14]

The Salvation Army had always offered parity to women. In the "Great War" its Lieutenant Colonel W. S. Barker, pleading with the military to allow "lassies" in the canteen huts, argued that they "are different from the ordinary; that many of the follies and foibles of the outside world are entirely unknown to them, that they are by training amenable to military discipline and know how to serve and make themselves universally useful."[15]

Throughout the war the Salvation Army followed its slogan: "Soup, Soap, and Salvation." The soup and soap—in the form of doughnuts, banking services, and mending clothes—were but a means to the salvation. Famed for its work among the derelict, it approached soldiers as candidates for conversion, evaluating the success of its workers by their contributions to the religious life of the troops. Every doughboy knew where the organization and its people stood, for they clung to their peacetime principles, regularly holding religious services and preaching, opening their doors to all, regardless of race or creed, even refusing on moral grounds to sell cigarettes. (Ironically, the Salvation Army donated to the seriously wounded any cigarettes contributed to the organization.) Booth's charge to the people her Army was sending overseas—many of them already experienced in the Salvation Army's work—was unequivocal: they were to "remember that they were sent forth to help and save and love the souls of men as God loved them. . . . "[16]

By order of the United States Army the YMCA bore the major responsibility for the welfare of the American Expeditionary Force (AEF): it was to "provide for the amusement and recreation of the troops by means of its usual program of social, educational, physical, and religious activities," carrying on the work symbolized in the three sides of its red triangle logo, in religion, education, and athletics.[17]

The YM ran hundreds of canteens, ultimately employing about 3,500 American women, a fifth to a quarter of its total work force. The gigantic size of this undertaking forced the YM into weakening the quality of its male personnel. Struggling to recruit thousands of men in a manpower shortage, it inevitably enrolled some lazy men, some ignorant, some arrogant, whom soldiers sometimes accused of draft dodging. The constant need for people allowed little or no time for training. Some of the YM men antagonized the troops by swaggering about in Sam Browne belts to display their (simulated) military rank.

Under the stress of wartime pressures, the YM's critics thought, it compromised its principles as a Christian institution, laying itself open to the charge of "canting hypocrisy." It warned its workers not to proselytize. It offended conservative Christians by allowing dancing and smoking, and Christian pacifists by its enthusiastic support of the war. Its sales of cigarettes and food enmeshed it in misunderstandings, inviting the public to believe that the YM was profiting by selling cigarettes donated for soldiers.[18] "That damn Y," grumbled the soldiers.

But the records, official and individual, testify to the worth of the YM's efforts. Certainly their women workers earned lavish praise and appreciation. They served the AEF in cafeterias, enlisted men's huts, officers' clubs, and leave areas, most often in France, but also in Italy, in the Azores, even in Siberia. In Great Britain, American women worked in close alliance with British women, from the Orkneys—where Julia Coolidge operated a Y hut for 4,000 American and 500 English sailors who were clearing mines out of the North Sea—to Plymouth, from London to Bantry Bay. Seventy-nine American YM women worked with French women in the Foyers du Soldat (Soldiers' Recreational Rooms), providing some of the few such services available to French soldiers.

Their own identities and the different tasks imposed upon them governed the approaches of the YMCA, the Salvation Army, and the

American Red Cross to providing servicemen with refreshment and recreation. The Red Cross, focusing mainly on hospitals and civilian relief but keeping a finger in every volunteer pie, afforded relative luxury in a few canteens for soldiers. The Salvation Army undertook only what their own personnel, guided by their own principles, could accomplish; they remained what they had always been: an overtly religious organization with overtly religious goals of service and conversion, preaching and teaching. And the YM tried desperately to be all things to all servicemen, stretching their personnel, their funds—and their principles—to distortion.[19]

> ✄✄✄ *I am trying over here to . . . do rather hard and monotonous work in the right spirit, for I know it is worth doing and heaven only knows how I need disciplining. All this doesn't mean that I don't like my job for I do enormously.*
> —Edith Gratie Stedman[20]

The War Department set some of the personnel requirements for the women in canteens. Minimum age: twenty-five (lowered to twenty-three after the Armistice). No woman with brother, father, or husband in the army.[21] ("They say," wrote one YM worker, "that several anxious mothers who came over for the Y.M.C.A. ostensibly, have been so pestiferous in making applications to be constantly shifted near their sons they've had to be sent home."[22]) The individual organizations established their own additional limits, raising the minimum age to twenty-eight or thirty, or insisting that the woman worker have no dependents at home who required an allowance. On July 28, 1917, the military notified the workers that they were considered "militarized" and thus subject to the same regulations and orders that applied to soldiers.

Any personnel director today would describe most of the women canteeners as overqualified, certainly overqualified for the jobs to which they were originally assigned (for like their sisters in relief organizations they often created their own jobs). The women the YM accepted commonly added to the organization's requirements—physical stamina, good sense, a knowledge of life, an ability to mix, and high ideals—their own creativity, administrative ability, and broad experience. They brought to their jobs a lot more than the " 'Pep,' Personality and Persistence" that one newspaper headline described as necessary for success in a canteen.[23]

The YMCA consciously sought outstanding women, leaders in their communities, talented women with professional and social experience, good manners, and tact. Swamped in the summer of 1918 by 1,200 applications a week, Mrs. F. Louis Slade, recruiting for the YM, turned for help to the alumnae associations of the women's colleges, the Junior League, the Intercollegiate Committee, and the American Federation of Women's Clubs. In such ways the YM enlisted women like Margaret Deland, then sixty, an established author, with a career as a maverick behind her. With her sailed Edith Gratie Stedman, who had already done social work and managed a candy store; after the war she went to China as a missionary, and then to Radcliffe as head of the placement service. Bernetta Miller, who in October 1912 had flown the first monoplane demonstration flight before United States government officials, forbidden to fly at the front, got there instead as a canteen worker.[24] Such women were among those washing dishes and handing out doughnuts.

And who was to support all these volunteers? Many women workers, particularly those who enlisted with the Red Cross, never received a penny. ". . . when [the doughboys] learn that you are a volunteer and are paying for the privilege of being there," wrote Katherine Morse, "their amazement is so blank as to be positively ludicrous."[25] But other women quailed at the prospect of signing over their earning power, usually for at least a year, and preferably for the duration of the war. The Salvation Army apparently continued as in peacetime to allow each of its workers a pittance. The YMCA eventually worked out a democratic scheme by which each worker received a small salary, but the amount was frequently repaid to the YM either by the woman herself or by an American organization that sponsored her: the General Federation of Women's Clubs, for instance, funded two YM women from each state.

The Red Cross was first off the mark, opening canteens for the AEF in April of 1917. Later under the direction of Amy Vanderbilt it ran others, notably the Cantines au Front, staffed mostly by men, which from railway stations in the war zone sent out runners to the men at the front.

The Red Cross also operated the Cantines des Deux Drapeaux, designed to serve soldiers on the lines of communication. For these "Canteens Under Two Flags," the French furnished the buildings and utilities, and the ARC did the rest, selling hot meals, and providing rooms for rest and recreation, keeping open day and night. A "directress" bought supplies, kept accounts, looked after laundry, and weighed the garbage to be sold (for animal, or even human, consumption). Often the larger canteens served 5,000 men a day. For the Babel stream of Arabs, Italians, Russians, Portuguese, Americans black and white, English, and German POWs who flowed through her railroad station, Florence Billings not only superintended the canteen service but also coped with the unexpected: "I had an epileptic fit and a fainting woman going on together one evening for an hour."[26] And Mrs. Belmont Tiffany "personally drest and bandaged the frozen feet of twenty-three Senegalese in the last ten days, great huge blacks, they were, whose feet were swollen three times the usual size."[27]

In mid-August of 1917, the Salvation Army sent its first group of officers to France—six men, three women, and a married couple. They went at once to Paris to be fitted with uniforms, "as General Pershing had given them all the rank of military privates, and ordered that they should wear the regulation khaki uniforms with the addition of the red Salvation Army shield on the hats, red epaulets, and with skirts for the women."[28]

The YMCA got started a little earlier than the Salvation Army, thanks to two privileged and generous women. Mrs. Vincent Astor arrived in France in June 1917 to take charge of the first canteen for sailors at Brest. Mrs. Theodore Roosevelt, Jr., leaving behind her three children, hastened to France on July 24, 1917, to beat the regulation, imposed three weeks later, forbidding soldiers' wives from going to France. She volunteered her full-time services to the YM, conscientiously refusing an assignment from a French magazine which would have placed her closer to her husband. The YM put her to work running a canteen in Paris with the help of women from the American colony, and teaching elementary French to soldiers. In her spare time she managed a large house lent her by an aunt as a center for the family and responded to her husband's frequent telegrams to send at once for his battalion sports equipment, soft drinks, musical instruments, and a good saddle horse.

In August the YM asked Mrs. Roosevelt to design a uniform for its women: "I chose a gray whipcord jacket and skirt. The jacket had capacious pockets and a powder-blue collar with the Y.M.C.A. insignia embroidered in scarlet silk. The blue hat had a small brim and the same insignia. Instead of an overcoat we copied an Italian officer's cape which Prince d'Udine had given to Cobina Wright. . . . Long and circular, it proved far better than an overcoat, as we could roll up in it when sleeping in camp or on unheated trains. The uniform was successful except when some of the girls, unused to discipline, persisted in adding lace collars, strings of beads, and hats trimmed with flowers."[29] Not every woman who wore the uniform shared Mrs. Roosevelt's satisfaction with it.

Early in 1918 the YM set Mrs. Roosevelt to work organizing leave areas. The military had put Paris off-limits to enlisted men, because of their tendency to get into trouble, or cause it. Where to go? The leave areas, twenty-three of them by war's end, offered an answer. Mrs. Roosevelt and her coworkers looked for pleasant locations like resort towns, choosing Aix-les-Bains for the first. One attractive site they had to reject: the Prince of Monaco offered Monaco as a suitable location. "He said we could have his palace while he would live on his yacht, and he promised to pass any required laws about saloons and so forth within twenty-four hours after we asked for them. When it was pointed out that as Monaco was a neutral country no American soldiers could go there, he said quite seriously he would declare war on Germany."[30]

The YM staffed the leave centers mostly with women; in time twenty-seven women worked at Aix. Always outnumbered by the soldiers on leave at least fifty to one, the YM women acted as hostesses, chatting with the men, playing games, leading hikes, dancing. Not easy work, for the men were frequently unhappy and constantly changing—and shoes wore out fast.

"We have only twenty girls and there are always two thousand

or more men!" wrote Marian Baldwin. "[At the dances] Every time
the whistle blows they can 'cut in.' The consequence is that a girl is
literally hurled from one man to another while dozens of eager hands
try and snatch her away from him. Of course it is all pretty rough
and one comes out of it every night with black and blue spots, but
how the boys enjoy it!" The job required tact, too, as the men
competed for feminine favor: "I've had a very crowded week and
two young gentlemen to manage who, not having seen 'an honest-
to-God American girl' or anything like the U.S.A. for nine months,
promptly decided, on arriving here that I was the 'one and only' lady
for them! I had an awful time keeping them apart . . ."[31] Like other
women in the war, the workers in the leave areas had to be prepared
to rate at their true value the "inevitable proposals," for those who
took them seriously might well be pitied as "poor damsels."[32]

For all the ardors of the work in the leave areas, the women
who served there led relatively comfortable, stable lives, with more
than adequate living conditions. Mrs. Roosevelt described with rec-
ognizable administrative frustration her efforts to find quarters for
them at Aix: "While the great majority of women in the Y.M.C.A.
were conscientious, unselfish, thinking only of doing the best job
they could, and ready to work until they dropped, there were always
a few who were not content with clean comfortable quarters at reasonable prices, but demanded more. These were usually the shirkers
who arrived late and left early, leaving part of their work to be done
by someone else."[33]

The canteeners' lives elsewhere differed, often dramatically.
Some women had to shelter in the passages underneath Verdun constructed centuries before, or in chalk-rock wine caves. Others had
to settle for dirty German dugouts, which they did not dare to clean
up, for fear of booby traps. A woman who had lost her cot "crawled
into a sort of berth dug by the Germans in the wall, where some
German had slept. She found out from bitter experience what cooties
are like." Another group camped in the ruins of a shelled house,
where the walls slanted perilously: ". . . the [Salvation Army] lassies
took off their shoes, rolled up in their blankets, and were at once
oblivious. . . . One hour later . . . they were awakened by the arrival
of the truck. . . . The girls opened their eyes and looked about them,

and there all around the building were American soldiers, a head in every shell hole, watching them sleep."[34]

🐦🐦🐦 *We open the hut at 7; it is cleaned by some of the boys; then at 8 we commence to serve cocoa and coffee and . . . make all kinds of eats until it is all you see. Well, can you think of two women cooking in one day 2500 doughnuts, 8 dozen cup cakes, 50 pies, 800 pancakes and 225 gallons of cocoa, and one other girl serving it? That is a day's work in my last hut. Then [religious] meeting at night, and it lasts two hours.*
                                             —Salvation Army woman[35]

No matter where or how the canteen women lived, most of them worked hard. Their letters and diaries repeatedly record forty-eight-hour shifts, perhaps on a railroad station platform in a heavy rain, preparing and distributing hot chocolate, or in a dressing station helping surgeons, bathing patients, giving them lemonade to lower their fevers.

Sometimes before they could begin operations they first had to find space for the canteen, commandeering what they could, or negotiating with the military authorities for an unused room. Others had to settle for a tent, or a half-destroyed building. "We had our Y in a hall over a barn, the odors of which defied ten pounds of chloride of lime," wrote a YM canteener.[36]

Sometimes the women had to floor the hut themselves, certainly clean it thoroughly, and make it as homelike as they could, to lure the doughboys in. In time the YMCA enrolled decorators, but more often the canteeners themselves brightened their huts with whatever materials they could find, buy, or make. "The room is filled with folding wooden chairs and long, inkstained tables. . . . Opposite the door, at the far end, is the canteen counter, a shelf of books on one side, and a victrola and a bulletin board, to which cartoons and clippings are tacked, on the other. Back of the counter, on the wall, held in place by safety pins, are the hut's only decorations, four of the gorgeous French war posters brought with me from Paris. There are two stoves resembling umbrella stands for heating in the main

Cantine Americaine Epernay

part of the hut and behind the counter another about the size and shape of a man's derby hat, on which I must make my hot chocolate. . . . Our candlesticks form a quaint collection; some are real tin bourgeois, brought from Paris; some strips of wood; some chewing-gum boxes; while others are empty bottles. . . . For the rest, the hut is equipped with a wheezy old piano, a set of parlor billiards and a man secretary."[37]

While they waited for shipments of supplies from Paris, the women talked generals and mess sergeants out of tons of flour and fat, or bought their supplies on the local market. Juliet T. Goodrich "used to go off quite casually to the military *abattoir* in the next town, returning with two hundred pounds of meat, which would last us, perhaps two days. All our other supplies were laid in, on the same scale, bread, one hundred and twenty loaves a day, cheeses, as big as cartwheels and costing the equivalent of sixty five dollars each, great hampers of vegetables, which special women working day and night spent their whole time picking over, and eggs, in crates of one hundred and fifty dozen, which had always to be counted, upon delivery, because the 'egg woman' had been known to cheat. Their arrival at a busy hour was one of the calamities of canteen life, quite comparable with one of those air-raids, with which the *Boche* made hideous our moonlight nights. . . ."[38]

Alice Lord O'Brian wrote of her duties as purchasing agent, "They say I ought to get a medal for fighting with the French." Her spirits plummeted on the day her interpreter was sick, the chef was drunk, the garbage buyer complained about the insufficiency of garbage, the flour shipment was ten days late in arriving, she had no gasoline, her car broke down, and the carrots were spoiling for lack of sand to pack them in.[39]

The canteeners made hot biscuits, sandwiches, fudge, pies, doughnuts (lifesavers or life preservers, as the doughboys called them)—by the dozens, by the hundreds, by the thousands. For, as one woman commented, "I had had a great many things to learn since joining up with the A.E.F. One of them was . . . that young aviators cannot fly unless they have pancakes for breakfast."[40] Doughnut-frying and pie-baking contests produced incredible records, getting "the maximum of grace out of the minimum of grease."[41] "Aunt Mary" at Gondrecourt, whose oven held nine pies at a time, baked 316 pies in a day, only to be bested by "Ma" at Houdelainecourt, who with her helper baked 324, though *her* oven held only six pies. Even Mrs. Belmont Tiffany boasted of the cuisine: "We give them a whole meal for 15 cents, soup, meat, and vegetables, or meat and salad, bread and compote. It is really good too. I thought I had a good many occupations . . . but . . . I have been particularly proud of being a good cook."[42]

Canteeners cooked under difficulties: "It took three hours," one reported, "to boil our huge pots on the small stoves we had."[43] They contrived fireplaces out of stone, sheet iron, and sewer pipes. Or they baked in an oven constructed out of two tin cake boxes placed on a two-burner gasoline stove. They used grape-juice bottles for rolling pins, the tops of baking-powder cans and the tubes of percolators for doughnut cutters, and the tops of lard cans for cake pans.

"Besides the merely practical part of the work," wrote Juliet Goodrich, "we were expected to talk to the *poilus*, to cheer up the low spirited, sympathize with the bereaved. . . ."[44] The canteeners heard over and over again, "You look exactly like my wife/sweetheart/mother," and many of them thought of themselves as representing those absent women. They listened to confidences. They sewed on buttons and badges and altered ill-fitting uniforms and mended, some of them even carrying sewing machines with them. In the Salvation Army huts they operated banks to transmit servicemen's funds back home. Twenty-four young women jerked sodas in the only ice-cream-soda canteen in France, founded by Georgia Toler.[45] YM canteeners danced hundreds of miles. Indeed the strain produced on the relatively few women available by the requests of so many men for dances roused considerable concern in the YM administration, which tried limiting the number of dances canteeners were allowed to attend, and devised "flying squadrons" of chaperoned groups of women to go from hut to hut dancing with the men.

Canteeners answered the doughboys' requests to bake a short-cake for a man who had found some wild berries, to fry eggs bought on the local market, to write a letter assuring a mother that her particular doughboy was behaving himself, to teach him the Bible, to wear his mother's ring as his pledge of sobriety. They invited men to tea. They helped them shop for gifts for the home folks. They testified for men enmeshed in the military justice system. They kept money and mementos for men going over the top—to be sent home in case they did not return. And they looked at photographs "of most of the women of the United States of America."[46]

They did first aid, especially in chiropody—everyone's feet hurt in a war. When flu broke out, they nursed. They visited hospitals and in emergencies worked in them. At graveside services "the girls sang at the graves, and prayed. There would be just the grave digger, a few people, and some of the boys. Off to one side the Germans were buried. When the simple services over our own dead were complete one of the girls would say: 'Now, friends, let us go and say a prayer beside our enemy's graves. They are some mother's boys, and some woman is waiting for them to come home!' "[47]

Many a woman invented her own way to serve—like Mabel Otis, who recognized boredom when she heard it, and dispelled it with classes in whatever interested the men, from arithmetic to architecture, getting teachers where she could. When she found a pianist driving a truck, she arranged for him and other musicians to practice on instruments in local music shops. "I was sitting under a counter undoing parcels of cookies and gently going mad," testified a lawyer, "when she came and salvaged me. If I ever get home I'll write a book called 'Rescued by a Woman.' "[48]

Because of the general disorganization that war inflicts, the canteeners who did best could and did take charge. Lila F. Kurtz, who worked in the YM's Eagle Hut in London, reported with amusement her struggle during a riot between American sailors and English police "to retain the billiard cues belonging to the Hut. They were fine clubs for fighting, and I no doubt saved many a policeman a broken head."[49] Elizabeth Potter wrote of having to "dash out at midnight to give coffee to fifteen hundred men, and handle the whole bunch because the officers are generally helpless and act as if they have never seen a coffee station before. So Elizabeth lifts up her voice: 'I want double lines here—double lines, do you hear me? Tha-a-t's the stuff. Now make it snappy, men, make it snappy; don't hang back. Here, is this what you call a line? Straighten up there, come on now, hold your cups low,' et da capo, while all the fifteen hundred are tremendously tickled at having a girl ordering them about, and all call out, 'Here's a girl from God's own country. Hey, sister, what state are you from?' If there isn't time for embarrassing explanations, sister is from any state in the union, just to oblige."[50]

The merry of heart among the canteeners had a lot of fun. Even a hospital visit to friends recovering from tonsillectomies turned into a party for one YM woman. She got to the hospital "about six, only to be told that ladies were allowed to call only between two and four. It is a big hospital full of Americans, built on three sides of a large court yard, with hundreds of windows. Some lad that knew me saw me there in the court yard and pretty soon the windows were full of heads in all stages of convalescence, some in pajamas and some in bath robes, with the nurses and orderlies trying to get them back to bed from behind, and all talking and whistling and sending messages, and letting down strings so that I could tie the flowers I had brought on them. I had a big bunch of jonquils that went up in a minute. My, but it was funny! Pretty soon a few doctors came along and decided to let me in to see my friends in order to stop the general riot."[51]

True to their assigned roles as the guardians of morality, can-teeners tried to lure servicemen away from the wicked wicked ways of the wine shops and the ladies of the night. With astonishing success, to hear them tell it, especially considering their limited resources: their pitchers of lemonade and pots of hot chocolate. "You know I am beginning to think that the Paris canteens are quite as well worth while as those out in the field," wrote Edith Stedman, "for the temptations here are awful and every cup of cocoa served to a man after ten o'clock at night is worth a dozen in the daytime."[52] And an older YM woman told a young volunteer, "American girls in the camps were the greatest deterrents to immorality that the men had. . . . the health of the American troops as they landed was the best of any in the world, but . . . already [by December of 1917] 18% of the men over here had some venereal disease contracted over here! The percent is so high that they think it must be in some way due to German influence (in the women)." *Toujours, cherchez les femmes.*[53]

The YM women's most extraordinary effort of this sort took them to the streets of London and other cities, where they joined with British women in the night "Street Patrols," to steer soldiers away from the temptations of bars and prostitutes. All the volunteers "were mature women, especially chosen for this type of work. Don-ning their uniforms shortly after supper they patrolled the main thoroughfares, in pairs, until the small hours of the morning."[54] Much as we have sought, we have never found a first-hand account from a member of a street patrol. The closest we have come is a report on Sara Frances Jones: as part of her duties in the Eagle Hut in London "she did street work (and she said, If none of you know about this, it is something we shouldn't discuss here.)"[55]

Of course what the canteeners offered in their huts did not appeal to every serviceman. Laurence Stallings wrote of roistering aviators who longed for quite different kinds of ladies: "There were only a Red Cross hut with some nice girls quick to serve hot chocolate and a Y.M.C.A. canteen with well-to-do American ladies selling chewing gum and cigarettes. In fact, it would have been a paradise to any of the foot-sloggers these aviators frequently died to serve; but none of the Y.M.C.A. matrons or the Red Cross workers wanted to drink champagne out of a slipper, or even so much as dance barefoot on a table to an orchestra accompaniment of soup-plate cymbals."[56] But for men who chose to frequent them, the huts were a refuge.

Often what the women did mattered less than their presence, for they reminded servicemen of home. Men came out of the nightmare of the trenches and No Man's Land not merely to more mud and destruction, but to familiar associations, to women who clearly represented the warmth and values of the world they had known in peacetime. The women in some degree kept the men's monstrous, Dadaistic experiences from overwhelming their sense of the past and of possibility.

Stories abound of the men's gratitude and their pleas for more "honest-to-God American girls," not to work so much as to listen and to smile what one woman described as "the eternal canteen smile."[57] "Yesterday morning," wrote a YM worker stationed at an airfield, "the cadets had doughnuts for breakfast for the first time in the history of the camp and *fourteen* of them saved their doughnuts for me."[58] "The boys" cleaned up their language for the women, tried to make their rooms comfortable, took up a collection to buy a Salvation Army woman a new uniform, brought the women flowers, eagerly volunteered to do in the canteens the kitchen police work they detested in army kitchens, and half-masted their flags when the women had to leave.

🚩🚩🚩 *Colonel, we can die with the men, but we cannot leave them.*
—Salvation Army woman[59]

The best efforts of the United States Army and the welfare organizations to keep the women canteeners out of danger failed. The military ordered women to stay behind brigade headquarters, but at the front brigade headquarters was easy to lose—even if the women had wanted to find it. Women kept ignoring orders to leave the troops they were looking after, and bobbing up again after they had been sent to the rear. Inevitably the chaotic situation, the women's determination, and the real need for their help eroded the regulations designed to keep them well behind the front. So highly did the military come to regard the women's work that the authorities ultimately permitted them to stay with divisions at Soissons and St. Mihiel, and in the Meuse-Argonne.

"We could not serve hot drinks here," wrote a YM woman, "because the Germans could see the smoke. . . . We had a pocket edition of the movies and used to run them ourselves, having three sets of films a week. We operated a tent there, but had to move it because they bombed it once. Next time we camouflaged it more thoroughly. We slept in dugouts most of the time. We used to feed the men coming back from the front. The relief would come up at 10:30 when it became dark and the men coming from the trenches would be served hot chocolate from 2 til 3:30 in the morning. We would get to bed about 4 o'clock and had to be up at 8 to be at the hut."[60]

In Tartigny one Salvation Army lassie under her first bombardment started for her dugout carrying a tray of lemon pies in one hand and a pair of new boots in the other. As she fought for her balance on a twelve-inch plank bridging a little gully, the soldier detailed to help her "registered deep agitation. 'Drop the shoes!' he shouted. 'I can clean the shoes, but for heaven's sake don't drop them pies!' "[61]

Three other Salvation Army women battled to rejoin their own outfit at the Field Hospital in Cheppy, hitching rides on reel carts, mule teams, and wagons over roads the engineers were constructing ahead of them. The hospital welcomed them when they reported for work. Five days later, with shells coming in every twenty minutes, the women helped evacuate the wounded into a cave; at the last minute they rushed to take cover themselves, but the first one into the cave fell across a pile of blankets, shutting out the other two, and a bursting shell buried her, wounding her slightly in the leg— an incident she concealed from the authorities, for fear they would send her and her companions to the rear.[62]

Alice O'Connor established a YM canteen in an area that was gassed three days a week and bombed every other night. When the division that had been holding the area was ordered to join the St. Mihiel and Argonne drives, O'Connor moved with her regiment, traveling in a camouflaged Ford camion and setting up canteens at every stop, often in the shelter of a broken wall. At St. Mihiel she walked over open roads in range of German guns and in sight of their lines to get supplies. When gatherings of soldiers were forbidden, she operated a canteen from a high horse-drawn covered wagon, which she drove from post to post.[63]

Among the most riveting accounts of journeys at the front, particularly because of her low-keyed style, is Marian Baldwin's narrative of her trip to rejoin her regiment during the battle of the Argonne Forest. In September 1918 she and her friend Alice, with a YM man to drive their truck, had been advancing with their regiment, dashing ahead each day to set up their canteen for "the boys' " arrival. Truck and driver were sometimes recalcitrant—he got testy when he got hungry, and the truck had to be unloaded and backed up hills, to keep the gasoline from draining out of the engine. But "As we passed each motor truck, naturally we smiled and waved. Instantly the whole truck came to life, a great shout went up and the boys tore their caps off their heads and waved them in the air, shouting 'Honest-to-God, American girls!' " Then a two-star general, with a daughter at home just their age, spoiled it all by ordering Baldwin and her friend back to YM headquarters.

But with the battle of the Argonne starting, they champed, fretted, and with two other YM women ". . . finally revolted, took our bedding rolls and musette bags and started off on 'our own.' We knew approximately where our Divisional Headquarters were situated and decided that some women ought to be there when the boys came out, orders or no orders." At the station they slipped past the MPs. French soldiers on the train fed them bread, cheese, and red wine—the best breakfast ever. At the end of the line they stayed overnight in the house of the village "groceress" and ate with charming Southern troops who filled them full of beaten biscuits and begged them to attach themselves to the Southerners' regiment. But they walked on for most of a day, the sound of the guns growing louder, and finally, "a weather-beaten, muddy quartet," they caught a ride with friends to their own divisional headquarters, where they learned that their regiment was expected back from the front soon. "After that we knew the Y men *must* let us stay and help and they did. . . .

we picked out a nice little ruin and put up our four cots in what was left of the second story," running the canteen in the story below. So they labored, and on the sixth day the whole division came out of the lines.

". . . we stood at the entrance to the town waiting, our hearts in our mouths. . . . Suddenly there was a stir. Around a bend in the road came the first column of troops. Hundreds, thousands of men passed us. Some we recognized and some we never would know again as the young lads who had marched so gayly into their first fight. Their faces were lined and their eyes glazed with fatigue and the horrors they had seen. Some wore bandages about their heads or hands, and others limped painfully as they tried to keep in step. Finally some one murmured 'Here comes the 148th.' It was so dark one could scarcely see but the regiment came to a stop close to where we were standing and we had a few hurried words with some of the men and officers we knew best. Only a few words, but enough to hear of scores who had 'gone West' in the great drive and many more who at that moment were being rushed over the cruelly bumpy roads to dressing stations. Our hearts were pretty heavy as we crept into our blankets that night."

Then on toward the St. Mihiel front. "The process of 'getting there,' suggested by our Y chief, would have taken weeks, and so we had thought it best to take the direct route and surprise him." An engineers' truck picked them up; they perched on the rocks with which it was loaded, and dropped off at a Red Cross canteen, where they fortuitously found in the road a map which showed the exact location of their unit. A damp, dismal ride by ambulance brought them to their YM chief, who brusquely ordered them back—but changed his mind when he learned that the quartermaster's trucks were bogged down miles away and the YM must feed the men; he needed all the help he could get. Hurrah!

But the women still worried about their own regiment farther forward, so they set out on foot to find them, dropping newspapers on the heads of the men in camouflaged ditches along the way. When they reached St. Benoît and the regimental headquarters several hours later, the adjutant greeted them enthusiastically, said that in a few days the regiment would be settled and ready for the YM, and told them where help was needed most. By hitching rides they got back before anyone had missed them, and their useful information saved them a scolding. "One old bird raised his voice to say that he thought it outrageous for women to be at the front and to take it upon themselves to travel on roads in the daytime that sensible people didn't risk even at night. However, he was hushed up and we were told we could leave for our regiment and their woods early the next morning, which was all we wanted." Soon, after almost a week on the road, Baldwin and "Alice" were back with their own company, comfortably ensconced in a German-built log cabin.

When in mid-October the division marched off to the Flanders front, the women were "cut up," for the English intransigently allowed no women on their front, "but we cannot help realizing that we have been fortunate beyond our wildest dreams in staying with one Division on three different fronts."[64]

In Service to Women—The YWCA

The immediate protection and assistance of women and girls affected by the war is the task undertaken by the Young Women's Christian Association.
— *War Work Bulletin*[65]

The Young Women's Christian Association, in the face of the general concentration on serving "our boys," throughout the "Great War" clung to its mission of meeting the needs of women, at home and abroad. Its desire to serve women war workers strained against— and temporarily overwhelmed—its historic pacifism. But by defining its war work precisely in terms of its original purpose, the YWCA was able to recruit competent, highly trained and educated women, employing them in tasks worthy of them, in causes to which they had already dedicated themselves. With its small force of about 350 women overseas, that women's organization discovered and imaginatively met the wartime needs of all sorts of women, American and foreign.

In its overseas work the YWCA applied what it had learned

both before World War I and in its extensive efforts for women in the United States from 1914 to 1917. The hostess houses created for women visiting their soldiers in Stateside training camps provided models for hostess houses for American women workers overseas. What had served women working in American factories was adapted to serve French women munitions workers. Techniques developed to teach young American women job skills and physical fitness were exported with the YW workers who went to Russia. Thus when the United States entered the war, the YW women could quickly establish services in Europe both for the American women flocking there, and for Europeans.

For thousands of American women workers overseas they provided transient and permanent living quarters, restaurants and recreational facilities. In the heart of Paris, the YW operated for American women its 250-room Hotel Petrograd, with its luxuries of steam heat and hot baths, opening its restaurant, tea room, and social rooms to women of all nationalities—a home away from home. The YWCA also developed services specific to the needs of particular groups of women. All over France American nurses, Signal Corps women, Ordnance women, Quartermaster women, YM and Red Cross women lived a little more comfortably and functioned a little better for the care and forethought of the YW.

For the nurses, for instance, the YW provided rooms, made homelike with pretty curtains and rugs, and equipped with tea tables, books and magazines, sewing corners, easy chairs, writing tables, and pianos and Victrolas. These "Sunshine Rooms" near their hospitals gave the nurses not only a place to relax, but also a modicum of privacy: women who slept in sixty-room dorms were otherwise hard-pressed to find a place even to cry.[66]

YW women acted as hostesses, housemothers, and chaperones for the telephone operators of the Signal Corps. When the first group arrived in Paris amid severe air raids, a YW woman soothed one operator with a snoring roommate and another who had lost her hairpins—trivial complaints, but "*most* upsetting at the end of a long, hard trip. . . ."[67] YW women tried to justify to the disgruntled French chefs who cooked for the operators the United States Army's order for them to soak their hands in disinfectants for three minutes. And the YW's Miss Russell found quarters in a devastated village at the front where the operators could stay while they handled the communications work for the St. Mihiel advance—a feat that the army had regarded as impossible.[68]

For at least one group of Quartermaster stenographers, the YW bore even more responsibility. The YW's War Work Council actually recruited the stenographers, and a YW worker escorted them to Paris. They conscientiously chose "women old enough and of sufficient character to stand the strain of the abnormal conditions here," women who came to work, not just for the thrills; women old enough to withstand the "tendency to weaken moral standards."[69]

The YW extended its concern to foreign as well as to American women. A Swiss soldier in the French Foreign Legion appealed to Mary McKibben to help his fiancée, who was working long hours in a munitions factory for inadequate pay: "Please help me, mademoiselle. The Americans always have a plan and I've no one else to ask for advice." If one woman needed job counseling, McKibben asked herself, what about others? Not only did she find the lady another job; she subsequently opened a labor bureau for American, English, and French women.[70]

French women munitions workers had been leading lives at once dangerous and dull. Many had "known what it was to sleep several in a room and sometimes three in a bed with one shift coming as another went out."[71] Under the leadership of American women experienced in labor problems, institutional management, dietetics, and physical education, the YWCA provided dormitories, canteens, gymnasiums, and social rooms. They ran kindergartens and nurseries for the Frenchwomen's children: "Yesterday a woman's face fairly beamed as she brought her little four months' old boy from the *pouponière* [nursery] for us to see. . . . The father is in Salonica and the mother here is struggling alone."[72] They started classes in dressmaking, stenography, typewriting, and singing. English classes proved particularly popular: as Mary Dingman wryly commented, "Because of the presence of large numbers of Americans, the whole feminine population is stirred to take English."[73] The YWCA tried not only to ease the munition workers' present but also to plan for their future, discussing with the French the possibilities of a follow-up in reconstructive work, and developing French leadership.

In all their endeavors, the YW workers tried hard to instill in the people they served the egalitarian principles of American democracy. In St. Étienne, for instance, they responded to a call for leadership from twenty willing but inexperienced Frenchwomen of all sects, "an unheard-of mingling in France," struggling to feed and house munitions workers. "When we started," wrote Emma L. Romeyn, "there were two things that every Frenchwoman we met was assured of. We could never run a restaurant without wine and we could never put different classes of women into the same dining room. We have accomplished both without a word of protest from anyone. . . . It was tried out only yesterday. Two richly dressed women came in and asked if we had a dining room separate from the factory girls. When we said that we had not, they came in just the same. Before leaving, they bought two tickets in advance. Our most picturesque guest that day was a coal picker, covered with soot, her bag of coal with her."[74]

Other American influences happened by chance, not by design: "Tuesday evening at our 'sew' so many of them were working on those awkward, cumbersome French 'pantalons' that I produced a pair of very simply made muslin 'envelope' chemises. They created quite a furor and immediately there was a rush for paper to cut a pattern from. And now there is a perfect epidemic of 'chemises américaines' raging."[75]

As the capabilities of the YW women in furnishing women's housing became recognized, the authorities turned to them in one exigency after another. "I had never before tried to imagine what would be the form of procedure," wrote a YW worker, "if one were suddenly dropped on a foreign city of 70,000 inhabitants plus its 10,000 refugees, and expected to find cheap, safe, and comfortable quarters for half a hundred French stenographers . . . over whom one had no leverage of military authority or personal friendship."[76] Perrie Jones reported from Tours a request to house "a rather uncertain number of office girls, typists, dactylographs, and interpreters . . . the next day. . . . The number of girls varied, anywhere from

25 to 60." Jones "happened" to hear of a pension, wrested it away from the army, and "appropriated it as a receiving station for the 25 girls who arrived during the next two or three days. English, Irish, Australian, American, French, Belgian, and even Welsh, Spanish and Italian, a very interesting, alive lot of girls."[77]

When the United States Army, floundering in the unmapped territory of unanticipated marriages, finally admitted that someone had to cope with war brides, it asked the YWCA for help in feeding them. Husbands and wives often could not communicate, and the YWCA furnished interpreters and started English classes. Babies came, and the YWCA rented apartments for mothers and babies. The wives needed authorization to go Stateside, and the YWCA helped them to negotiate the paper work. "In my own barracks of fifty [war brides] I have the most interesting variety of personalities," wrote a YW worker, "women of different ages, nationality, training, ability and standards. There are eight Russian girls, one Egyptian, one Algerian, one Alsatian, and others from every part of France. They come from all walks of life. One woman of 22 worked in a munitions factory fifteen months during the war on night shift and as a result was blind for one month and even yet has difficulty with her eyes. The woman next her is the only child of a French titled family . . . who found Army barracks a great contrast to her château and yet who was much more game than many others. No more than ten percent of women speak or understand English. Many are having their first lessons in homemaking . . . some their first lessons in the value of fresh air. Many are learning lessons in self-control."[78]

No wonder Marion F. Allchin asked, "Is there any phase of war work that we have not been called upon to tackle?"[79] Mary McKibben of the YW even ran an impromptu, but thoroughly proper, dating bureau. "A colonel came in the other evening with a note of introduction from a Red Cross worker in Limoges, asking for the companionship of an American woman for an evening at the theatre. He was rather apologetic and seemed to think he was asking a good deal and appeared the next day and thanked me profusely for the pleasant evening. One Sunday we had five such requests."[80] Marion Allchin heard a somewhat different plea from a dozen American soldiers whom an unknown lady at the railroad station had directed to the YWCA hotel, with the promise that they would be well taken care of there. They were, though the services provided were not what their lascivious imaginations had anticipated.[81]

By war's end, the YWCA estimate, they were serving 20,000 French, British, and American women in France, with eighteen hostess houses for soldiers, American women, and war brides; fifteen Signal Corps houses for "hello girls"; three Army Service Corps centers; forty-four nurses' clubs; thirty-one *foyers* for Frenchwomen; six recreation centers; five summer camps; a summer conference; an emergency training school; five refuges for port and transport workers; four cemetery huts, where they offered lodgings, food, and kindness to visitors to remote cemeteries; and three British/American cooperative undertakings.

By the Armistice the organization was also working or planning to work in Russia, Finland, Italy, Poland, Czechoslovakia, Turkey, Belgium, and Rumania. Among the earliest of these efforts was the YWCA mission to Russia, where YW workers, along with many another American, saw the future as "throbbing with possibilities."[82] It throbbed also with danger and difficulty.

In 1917, after the March revolution, in response to a request for help from Russian women, the YWCA sent Elizabeth Boies and Clarissa Spencer to study the situation. Boies, educated at Smith College and the University of Chicago, had behind her experience on the Mexican border, where she had enlisted upper- and middle-class American women to help factory workers; she was to distinguish herself by her unwavering dedication to the cause of international sisterhood.[83]

She and Spencer, arriving in Petrograd in late May 1917, faced formidable odds. Normally the YW would have turned for support to wealthy Russian women, but the revolution had rendered these women uncertain of their own futures, and alienated them by the class hatred so vigorously finding expression. The Russian authorities, often with good reason, suspected the motives of all foreigners. The American ambassador was not helpful. Revolutionary turmoil in Russia had not ended; the YW women had to slog through constantly shifting political sands.

The Americans found the health of the Russian women poor

and the moral conditions "deplorable"—and cabled for seven more YW women: "send them over like cannon balls." For, like some journalists and some Quakers then in Russia, the YW women found amidst the revolution an extraordinary need and an extraordinary spirit. As Marcia Dunham later reported: "We have an abiding faith that through all these growing pains, Russia—true Russia—will find herself. With all the awful things one hears daily, there are many beautiful things—the spirit, of the women who have lost their big estates, and who yet can say, 'If through my loss Russia will grow strong and good, I am happy,' is remarkable."[84] The YWCA had found in Russia work worth doing.

By August 1917 they had begun classes in Petrograd in English, French, bookkeeping, commercial arithmetic, stenography, choral singing, and gym, to which the Russian girls responded eagerly— "And this meant loyalty through times of revolution and blood-shed. . . ."[85] As in France, the American YW workers refused to kowtow to class distinctions. They persuaded girls of all classes to play games together—an unprecedented practice in Russia.

Having well begun their work in Petrograd, the YW women went on to Moscow, even as the political situation heated up in both cities and dangers to the women they served and to the YW workers themselves heightened. Nonetheless Boies found a Muscovite woman factory owner to lend a hall, the walls of which "unfortunately are hung with a very valuable collection of hundreds of ikons. . . . before basket ball is started in the beautiful salon, with all of these windows, breakable lighting, mammoth paintings of past Empresses and arch-bishops and ikons, we shall have to do some screening. . . ."[86]

By December 1917 the YWCA workers were not only giving regular classes, but even managing to serve tea before them to the very young and minimally educated girls from the poorer sections of Moscow, mostly department store messengers, who came to the Y directly from work, hungry, tired, and often frightened.

They had reason to be. In the same month Helen Ogden wrote her family from Moscow (in what she evidently thought reassuring terms): "When we reached Moscow all seemed peaceful and quiet at the station, though soon we began to hear the rifle shooting and the larger guns of the revolution in the distance . . . The next day was quite exciting in the city. Guns were popping everywhere. . . . Trolley wires were down, thousands of windows smashed and the Hotel Metropole absolutely riddled. Some of the Inner City's gates were very much battered. Streets were torn up for barricades, and some buildings were burned. . . . It is thrilling to have been right in a real revolution but I don't want my friends and family to worry about me. . . . P.S. Please send candy."[87]

Elizabeth Boies described a routine marketing trip: "Then from the houses in front of us, other shots came. We backed into an open stall and I was meditating getting into a big empty barrel, but the old peasant shopkeeper decided it was too hot for her and began closing up things. . . . So we had to get out into the boulevard and run for it. Bent half double, we tore along, stumbling over sleds and bumping into everybody and everybody tumbling into us. I took a tumble and rolled into a large puddle of water. . . . There is no knowing when or where these things are going to happen, so one can't very well keep out of it unless one wishes to go into a retreat."[88]

But although neither Russian revolutions nor Russian winters kept these women from their appointed rounds, the machinations of the Allies generally and the United States specifically in Russian affairs soon made the YWCA workers unwelcome. By February 1918, the American women in Petrograd had to evacuate, leaving their work in the hands of two Russian women, while they themselves went on to work in Vladivostok. Spencer returned to the States to raise support for the Russian project. The American women in Moscow went to Samara.

Except Elizabeth Boies. For the life of her, she couldn't understand YW women who left: she described them as " 'malcontents'; goodness, just look at their opportunity for work here, and they want to get home."[89] She talked the Russians into letting her stay in Moscow along with a few YMCA men. There, in the face of the food shortage ("just a small cake of hard dog biscuit, and today it is hay again. The only way we could eat it was to fry it in bacon grease."[90]) and a maximum heat allowance of forty-five degrees, she carried on classes and tried to alleviate the enervation and mental suffering that led some young Russian women to suicide. In April she even managed a trip to Petrograd, where she found the Russian women still carrying on YWCA activities.

By mid-April 1918, triumphantly back in Moscow, her co-workers there returned from Samara, and more YW women already launched from the States, Boies devised an elaborate and ambitious strategy. The YWCA would hold Petrograd and Moscow. (Clara Taylor, an industrial expert, was already visiting 225 factories in Moscow to see what was happening to women workers; she found them in poor health and poorly educated, being displaced by returning soldiers.) Also the YWCA would begin operations in Samara, with Elizabeth Dickerson, a physical-education director, surveying playgrounds, reorganizing Boy Scouts and Girl Scouts, and training supervisors.[91] And the YW would cooperate with the World Student Christian Association in student work and with the YMCA in summer work on the Volga.

On the Volga River trip, designed in conjunction with the YM, the Red Cross, and the Soviet government to teach people along the river about advances in agriculture and home economics, Boies and other YW women took charge of women's work and (inevitably) the commissary. The eagerly received boat stopped at eighty towns, particularly attracting teachers, who often followed it to the next town to see its exhibits a second time. By July 1918, Boies found herself more at home on the Volga than on the Hudson.

But at that juncture, the United States sent troops to Archangel and Vladivostok. In reaction the Soviets ordered the YWCA and the YMCA personnel out of Russia. The YW perforce closed their Moscow operation, though Russian women carried on in Petrograd. Once again the indomitable Boies fought to remain: she considered her enterprise not an American undertaking, but a woman-to-woman compact. The Russians permitted her to return to the Volga Exhibition—but fighting prevented the boat from moving. Finally, in late August 1918, the insistence of both the American and the Russian governments forced Boies to leave. Thoroughly disgusted, she "renounced her own government's policy in the spirit of international sisterhood."[92]

In early October she moved to Archangel, which she dubbed

"a black hole" because she was deprived of her work for women.[93] Settling for second best, she set out to improve the morale of the American troops stationed along a 400-mile front on the railway by informing them about the Russian people and society.

As usual, the authorities doubted and the troops welcomed the women—Boies and her coworker Marcia Dunham. As usual, the women soon proved their worth. Boies and Dunham established and ran a hostess house and a boxcar canteen attached to a car operated by the YMCA. ". . . wherever we go the men look at us as if we were too good to be true," Boies and Dunham found. The troops called Boies "the girl who stood on the burning deck." No wonder. The soldiers were living "in boxcars like animals . . . in days of 20-hour darkness and temperatures of 30 to 40 below zero."[94]

Boies's frustrations increased. ". . . as allies we are having to do such overbearing things," she wrote, "I just hate myself."[95] The long-suffering YWCA, despite requests of the American authorities and Boies's passionate pleas, was finally refusing to send more workers. Only after the war, though, did Boies return to the States. Even then she pled, successfully, for more workers to be sent to Russia, and ultimately herself assumed charge of the YWCA's extensive postwar foreign operations.

Meanwhile, as the "Great War" drew to its weary end, the YWCA was vigorously undertaking new enterprises throughout Europe and the Middle East. In June 1918, it was invited to Italy to serve American women there with a nurses' club and a hostess house; to care for Italian women munitions workers; and to train Italian YW workers. In October 1918 the YW, in cooperation with the American-born Countess Turczynowicz, opened a school in the States for Gray Samaritans, Polish-speaking Americans who planned to work as nurses' aides with the Polish Army during the war and in reconstruction work later.[96] In the Near East, the YWCA began work in the spring of 1918, planning support systems for civilian workers, helping Armenian Christians.

A dramatic contribution, that of the YWCA, which found its significant place in the "Great War" by remembering its mission of service to women.

Books for Sammies

In the "Great War" professional men and the military alike strongly resisted the efforts of women, no matter how highly qualified, to serve in "men's jobs." Nurses, hostesses, typists, telephone operators, yes! Women doctors and women war correspondents, a thousand times no! Particularly ironic was the situation of women librarians, who numerically dominated their profession, but had made the mistake of allowing men to officer their professional organization. Not only did their War Service Committee not want women overseas; they even tried to bar them from service in Stateside military libraries.

The annals of the American Library Association (ALA) record a gender war so intriguing as to endanger recognition of the genuine services that librarians rendered to American troops during World War I in the United States and overseas. These services are beyond question. Librarians collected millions of books for the troops on a wide range of subjects—technical, literary, inspirational, and escapist. Against odds and the competition for shipping space, they delivered them to servicemen, who found in them information and solace. In Europe, librarians allowed soldiers to borrow the books they wanted, with little prospect of their being able to return them. In the trenches, the canteens, the hospitals, books passed from soldier to soldier, often disappearing completely, sometimes turning up again at some distant point in the army library system. The ALA instituted in Paris a mail service of books for soldiers in remote areas or with special requests. "Orders for books ranged in variety from French history to detective stories," wrote librarian Louise Prouty. "We even had calls from lawyers and architects who were continuing their education between bombardments. One day we received a letter asking for a copy of Plato's Philosophy, and if we could not send that, then a book on farming. I've often wondered about that boy."[97]

All the same, it's hard to look away from the battle of the sexes that raged within the ALA—in part because it damaged the efficiency of their wartime efforts. Against the vigorous opposition of men like

Dr. Herbert Putnam, Librarian of Congress and General Director of the ALA's War Service Committee, women members had to struggle to share in the war work.

It didn't help that a public image of wimpishness afflicted male librarians, challenging them to prove their masculinity.[98] Like some YMCA men, some male librarians flexed their muscles in the cause of militarism, and vaunted their "patriotism" in such absurdities as suggesting that the only reason for offering servicemen a moment of escape or consolation through a book was to win the war; or defending books as the "best antidote" (or prophylactic?) for the danger of contracting venereal disease.[99]

Putnam alleged that military library work was simply too demanding for women, exceeding their endurance and their physical strength. The military authorities, he said, neither would nor should authorize women in the camp libraries: "Every person on the staff thus far has been a man who was willing and able not only to do library work, but also to handle 200-pound bags of magazines and large boxes of books, to shovel coal and to drive and care for an automobile. Most of these things women librarians could not do."[100] Some hardy men even had to walk perhaps a mile from the bus stop to the camp library.

Women librarians were outraged. Beatrice Winser of the Newark Free Public Library on February 20, 1918, wrote Secretary of War Newton D. Baker: "May I venture to ask the Secretary of War himself to decide what still seems not a settled question, namely, the employment of women in the cantonments? I understand that women nurses are employed in the camp hospitals and that women have charge of 'hostess houses' but that they are absolutely barred from the camp libraries. Is this true? . . . Also, may we know why women librarians are not allowed to take the place of the men librarians, many of whom could be released for work not now within the scope of women. There are 662 men in the library profession and 2,185 women. . . . I have been a librarian for twenty-eight years, and may be pardoned for the interest I take in this matter." Again on April 28, 1918, Winser wrote to the War Service Committee, "The fundamental mistake made by you, Dr. Putnam, and your confreres, seems to have been the very usual one of thinking that men are better qualified than women for work in the world. I trust someday the examples of English, French and perhaps German women will bring about a change in this attitude. While we are 'making the world safe for Democracy' let us not forget that women form a half of all Democracies.''[101]

At the 1918 annual meeting of the ALA, Annie Carroll Moore and six other women formally inquired what role women were to be allowed, warning that young women were leaving library work to go to volunteer organizations.[102] The men at the head of the ALA answered by assuring the women that children's librarians were making an unparalleled contribution to the war effort. (Rock the cradle, not the boat.)

The protests against confining library war service to men came from male librarians also. On May 15, 1918, Herbert Putnam wrote an appeal asking men librarians to volunteer for library War Service. In the top margin of the copy of his letter in the ALA archives is a penned comment "Why not ask all *women* also?" signed by J. C. Dana, librarian of the Newark Free Public Library—a man who also distinguished himself by resisting wartime censorship.[103]

Meanwhile the ALA officers were simultaneously fighting the Red Cross and the YMCA for control of the distribution of books. Even though they started rather late, the ALA officers managed to extract from Pershing an allotment of fifty tons of shipping space a month and a rather cautious statement that though they must cooperate with organizations already on the ground, the library work should be centralized in the ALA.[104] (Like other organizations, the ALA suffered from a shortage of shipping space throughout the war. They supplemented this allotment as best they could: Mrs. Greensfield Watson, an army nurse, told of taking with her to France as many books collected for soldiers as she could carry from their storage place in the basement of the New York Public Library.[105])

But what with the ALA's apparent failure to anticipate the United States' entry into the war, the time consumed by their power struggle with other organizations, and the male officers' single-minded determination to recruit only men, relatively few librarians of either gender got to Europe before the Armistice. Luckily for the sanity of literate soldiers, books did arrive sooner. Often it was the very organizations with whom the ALA officials were contending that got the books to the troops. The YMCA maintained libraries of sorts in their huts, and Salvation Army lassies "served books as well as doughnuts."[106]

Some women librarians, as Annie Carroll Moore had warned, resolved their frustrations by offering their services to other organizations; the YMCA enrolled fifty-eight, often sensibly employing them as librarians in the Y huts. Asa Don Dickinson, arriving in Bordeaux in September 1918, found "a phenomenon with which I was soon to become increasingly familiar. I found an accomplished librarian in the uniform and on the payroll of the Y.M.C.A. and giving her whole time to the conduct of A.L.A. work, and ordering about several hulking and cowed-looking Y secretaries [male administrators]."[107] Florence A. Huxley, formerly the office editor of the *Library Journal*, worked for the American Red Cross, eventually transferring to the ALA, for whom she did office work at LeMans, dealing with a printer's strike, entertaining French officials, telegraphing for books, and generally showing herself invaluable.[108] Esther Johnston, a librarian in a YMCA hut serving nearly 8,000 soldiers, distinguished herself by her work with black troops and her efforts to teach illiterates to read.[109]

The few women librarians who did get overseas during the war under the aegis of the ALA immediately demonstrated their competence and their willingness to endure discomfort and danger. Alida M. Stephens of the Library of Congress cataloged and classified the collection of the ALA headquarters library in Paris, which opened in August 1918, with bookshelves made of packing cases and seats of rough boards set on soap boxes.[110]

Mary Frances Isom, a prominent and dynamic librarian in the Northwest, undertook the organization of hospital libraries overseas. Despite ill health, she spent six strenuous months overseas, and died soon afterward. Her biographer in *Notable American Women* suggests that Isom may have volunteered out of a feeling that her own patriotism had been challenged by her defense of a pacifist assistant librarian's refusal to buy war bonds. Possibly too she may have been motivated by the need to demonstrate that a woman could indeed work effectively in establishing libraries overseas. In any case, she ably performed an arduous and complex task. She added thousands of books to each hospital library's holdings. She set up operational systems. And she offered her expertise to the workers of other organizations who were actually operating most of these libraries.[111]

But neither the fulminations of women like Winser and Moore nor women's eagerness to serve, their demonstrated competence, and their actual presence swayed the director of the ALA War Service Committee. Putnam lamented that too few men volunteered and professed his willingness to accept men who were not trained librarians, but he wanted no women (nor, for that matter, any black men). As late as the spring of 1919 he was writing of his difficulties in getting men who could assist in general administration and field-work: "The War Service have produced too few such men. It was difficult to secure them even for service at home. None could be thought of for our Paris Headquarters whose transfers would not have embarrassed the still more important headquarters at Washington. (If I say 'men' rather than 'men and women' it is because the peculiar conditions at Paris and in France rendered men alone effective for the particular need I refer to.)"[112]

The measure of women librarians' determination to serve is that in spite of male forebodings, women were proportionally well represented in the military libraries both at home and overseas. In fact, according to the "Preliminary Historical Statement" of November 1919 in the ALA Library War Service Reports, "From the beginning to January 1, 1919, there served from time to time at headquarters, in the camps, at the dispatch offices and overseas, seven hundred and seventeen persons, three hundred and fifty women, three hundred and sixty-seven men." Overseas the women may actually have outnumbered the men. The *Handbook of ALA War Service Personnel*, corrected to December 10, 1918, shows sixteen women and only eight men, but the figures are soft, apparently including people who had been appointed but had not yet sailed.

Too bad that the ALA really did not get rolling overseas until almost the end of the war—though it did effectively serve the army of occupation and the troops waiting for transport home. Until World War I, no one had thought much about troops' need for books, so the United States' entry into the "Great War" caught the organization unprepared. The seven million books it then collected for the four and a half million American troops were simply not enough. And its officers, without plans or precedents to guide them, enmeshed the organization in futile efforts to recruit only men and in squabbles about which organizations and which sex were actually to distribute the books.

Trouping for the Troops

🎵🎵🎵 . . . *it's really splendid playing under shellfire. . . . not knowing which song may be your last makes you do your best, spurred on by the ambition that fills every performer's heart to make a good exit.*

—Elsie Janis[113]

The accounts of the American troupers who went to Europe during World War I crackle with pride and good spirits. All sorts of entertainers went, from little-known vaudevillians to the likes of Loie Fuller, Ruth Draper, and Tex Guinan. By and large, they enjoyed themselves, the soldiers, and their work.

They loved good stories, and told a lot of them—doubtless with embellishments—starting with their shipboard stories, like Mary Sample's tale of crossing on the same ship as Irene Castle: "We were nearing the submarine zone, and lookouts were constantly watching the horizon. Imagine our amusement when we glanced up one day to see their binoculars converging upon the shapely ankles of Irene as she reclined on a deck chair below, as the irresistible apex of an isosceles triangle—and to hell with submarines!"[114]

And Margaret Mayo's: "On the first Sunday morning of the voyage . . . I heard a monotonous mumbling. I followed the direction of the sound and soon looked down on hundreds of red coats on the backs of kneeling Polish soldiers. Against a background of ally flags a priest in white vestments officiated at an emergency altar made up of packing cases. . . . The next night I stood at the door of the saloon after dinner with Parker Nevin. . . . a dance was now starting in which there was no small sprinkling of 'Y' and Red Cross uniforms.

At the far end of the corridor through a cloud of smoke, one could see other members of these two organizations sipping light wines, smoking, and playing bridge. . . . I heard Parker Nevin's sigh. I turned to see him shaking his head sadly. . . . the world was all upside down, 'The Y.M.C.A. dancing and the Red Cross drinking and the soldiers praying.' "[115]

To their own surprise, the entertainers tolerated, even liked, working with the YMCA, which sponsored most of them. The magnitude of the YM's operation and their refusal "to take advantage of a world crisis to thrust their personal creeds or propaganda down the throats of the defenceless. . . ." impressed the entertainers.[116] Elsie Janis at first "was not too keen on being with the Y.M.C.A. It sounds rather like it might cramp my speed—and I asked them quite frankly if my friends could come to the shows whether they were Young Christians or not? They explained that they had only one idea, that was to make the boys happy. . . . I must say for the Christian Association they have some speed."[117]

They also had a tremendous job on their hands, for 828 professional entertainers, of whom 561 were women, went overseas either for the associated Overseas Theatre League or under the direct aegis of the YMCA.[118] Altogether the American stage and lyceum sent 1,064 people to France. War conditions and the entertainers' own entrepreneurial ways defied the efforts of Paris director A. M. Beatty to keep track of them, but, he said, ". . . fortunately we had two 'Y' girls who could, and these women handled all our actors' expenses with a finesse that was another modern miracle. They conserved the funds and yet hurt no one's feelings, which was a delicate task. Another 'Y' girl ran our complex card-indexing system, by means of which we knew the movements of every unit and the records and affairs of every individual actor."[119]

As the entertainers generously acknowledged, their eventful travels spared them the monotony and drudgery of such paperwork— and of other unglamorous jobs. Time and again they praised other war workers. Those "who for the good of the cause had forced themselves to fit into dull obscure niches over here and work for eighteen hours a day at secretarial jobs which they had outgrown at home in their youth."[120] The nurses, "those stout-hearted American girls who braved the privations of the front and the deprivation of feminine clothes for many long months."[121] The telephone operators "who are here saving the time and temper of the A.E.F. I loved seeing them," wrote Elsie Janis, "such a nice crowd of girls. . . . our boys all claim that these 'hello girls' are the best-looking girls in France."[122] One evening Janis "stumbled upstairs [at her hotel] by the light of a match and found that the very nice Y.M.C.A. girls had put hot water bottles in our otherwise Labradorian beds. . . . —and what credit those girls deserve! We think we are doing something staying here one night—they stay here all the time—in a plethora of the finest mud I've ever seen."[123]

Janis, a star famed on both sides of the Atlantic for her one-woman show, came on stage for the British and French troops in France in 1914. All through the war this buoyant, breezy all-American girl sang, did imitations, told stories, danced a little, cartwheeled across the stage, and achieved instant rapport with her audiences. Here, as she would have put it, is her speed: "A big Baldwin locomotive puffs up one of the tracks [in a shed at an American railway repair shop where 4,000 doughboys waited]. The men make way on either side, cheering madly, for there on the cowcatcher, her famous fluted skirt streaming in the breeze, her hand waving the usual breezy salute to everybody, is 'the girl.' Up to the very platform she proceeds, jumps nimbly off, turns a handspring, and shouts: 'Boys, are we down-hearted?' There comes a thunderous ear-splitting answer: 'Hell, no!' "[124]

Janis anticipated Bob Hope in her devotion to entertaining the soldiery. Throughout the war years she—and her mother—traveled in France, pausing only for intermittent trips to the United States and England to recruit, play benefits, entertain soldiers, and "grab as much money as the income tax collectors would allow and go back to the Big Show! . . . War had me and still has me, and my life really began when I set my foot or rather both my feet, and Mother's feet, in France. . . . We were in the BIG SHOW!"[125] As an American colonel proudly remarked, "The British give their men rum when they go over the top, and the French hand out cognac, but we give ours 'Janis straight.' "[126]

Other entertainers followed Janis to Europe—particularly after the United States entered the war. Some fended for themselves, like the grand opera contralto Mme. Cobbina Johnson, the first woman to appear with the AEF. (Like many a singer who followed, Mme. Johnson lost her voice in her country's service; she couldn't speak for two months. Fatigue, dampness, cold, and catch-as-catch-can living made touring the front particularly hard on singers.)

The group effort began as a small lecture bureau tasked with explaining the issues of the war to the AEF and reassuring the French about the American presence. Gradually the YMCA added small troupes. Like the threesome of a baritone, an accompanist, and Cornelia Barnes, an elocutionist who enjoyed great success with the poems of R. W. Service and her own "Now That My Boy Has Gone to France." Like the Liberty Quartet, with the church choir singers Beulah Dodge and Kate Horisberg, who boarded American transports arriving in France to sing operatic arias, hymns, spirituals, and comedy songs, and to lead singsongs. Like the Shakespearean troupe in which Mary Anderson appeared with E. H. Sothern in *Macbeth*, their props reduced to "Two blood-stained daggers, a saucer of blood (or rather, two saucers in case one got spilled or lost), a bell, and the mechanism for producing 'the dull ominous knocking at the gate.' "[127] Like Mary Rochester, the "Nightingale in the Trenches," who sang and played the piano, solo and in duet with a male singer; in her late twenties, teetering on the brink of a musical career of considerable promise, she went to France in February 1918 and enjoyed her war: "Being the only girl is really fun," she wrote. "I have been spending two days A.W.O.L. in this lovely château with three charming men and a middle aged French woman housekeeper. . . . My hosts treat me like a queen. . . . Tonight the four of us danced in the spacious rooms, on beautifully waxed floors, to music furnished by a five-piece soldier orchestra."[128]

Others joined the earliest entertainers. Margaret Wilson, the President's daughter, finally overcame his opposition to her going overseas.[129] Tsianina, daughter of a Cherokee Indian chief and sister of two soldiers, sang and danced in the traditional Indian modes. The Hoyt sisters, "Smiling Sue and Silly Sally," featured the song "Kaiser Bill's a Bum"; as one of them reported in July: "Last week we gave a performance for about 2,000 men who had been in the trenches since February. Our stage was a boxing platform in a beautiful grove. The piano was two tones below pitch. My sister sat on a soap box to play and the army mules broke loose during one of our songs. The men sat and stood in mud at least three inches deep—all who were not festooned in the trees."[130]

The entertainment effort exploded spectacularly with a huge meeting of the theatrical community in April of 1918 at the Palace Theatre in New York called to recruit performers for overseas service. "Elsie Janis cabled from London making a date with the whole audience in France." Winthrop Ames eased the supposed qualms of the women in the audience by telling them how Mrs. Ames had stayed alone with 200 doughboys in a canteen just back of the lines. When Ames asked his wife how she had felt, she said, "If I had a daughter of sixteen, I'd leave her there alone. And if any man touched her with his finger, these boys would tear him into a thousand pieces."[131]

That night at the Palace entertainers created the Over There Theatre League. Actors, singers, playwrights, vaudevillians, and artists signed up with the league, which offered them uniforms and living expenses from the YMCA, and a salary of two dollars a day from the league, in return for a promise to obey orders from the military authorities and from the Y secretary to whom they reported, and to remain in the Entertainment Service abroad for not less than three months. They suffered through screenings which sometimes—though not always—disqualified them if one of their parents had been born in an enemy country, or if they had brothers in the services, or if they were married to spouses also serving in Europe—a real catch-22 for those entertainers whose spouses were their stage partners. They donned the Y uniforms, remarking "I am willing to do this for my country, but for no one else," and "I should say the boys will certainly be heroes to face us now."[132] They struggled through the "long drawn fatigue of getting passports and standing in line for days in badly ventilated offices only to be told that *whatever* one had done or *wherever* one had come . . . one was all wrong and must start over again. . . ."[133] Players who had given up bookings waited weeks and months for shipping space.

In France the entertainers performed wherever they found sol-

diers. Mary Young and her husband, John Craig, themselves the
parents of two sons in service, gave Margaret Mayo's Broadway hit
Baby Mine, which the author donated to the war effort. Their company of six with all their props traveled in a Ford. They played in
railroad stations, their audiences diminishing and increasing as trains
moved in and out. They played in barns, the stage lit by the soldiers'
flashlights. They played in quarantine camps for patients with spinal
meningitis and diphtheria. They played in Y huts and on the drill
grounds of Napoleon's old barracks.

Elsie Janis often gave her shows in a prizefight ring: "Had an
enormous crowd on all four sides which made it rather difficult. I
asked them to please close in on three sides, for though I knew the
back was the best part of a goose I was rather scared of an attack
from the rear!"[134]

Mary Young played Joan of Arc before the cathedral at Dom-
rémy. Trouble with an inadequate fire at the first performance led
the company to ask the Camouflage Corps for help, with the result
that "Joan was concealed so completely and apparently consumed
so rapidly that she was unable to read her final lines."[135]

Some entertainers performed in the underground citadel at Verdun, and others gave a concert from a flatcar, with the audience lined
up along the tracks. Overtaking an ammunition convoy of fifty-eight
motor trucks, the Broadway Bunch gave their vaudeville show in the
road. And Eunice Prossor Crain performed one day on a stage made
of boxes of ammunition and decorated with hand grenades. "We
received something of a shock when we saw it, but ended by earning
the distinction of giving a program on 800,000 rounds of ammunition."[136] A surefire hit, no doubt.

Neysa McMein—painter, illustrator, and famous party-giver—
in France became an actress and playwright, traveling in a little car
with Anita Parkhurst Wilcox and Jane Bulley. McMein entertained
the troops by sketching—by flashlight, candlelight, or searchlight.
On a movie screen tacked to barn walls the company presented a
farcical cartoon of Gertie the Dinosaur, at the end of which Gertie
strafed the Hun and "returned to her dinosauric nest chortling in
Jabberwockian glee." They put on an original show, *Orlando Slum,
a Man of Mystery*, choosing soldiers in the audience to play Harold

the Hero and Orlando the Man of Mystery; at the end "the vamping villainous lady spy" played by McMein "eats corn willy [a much contemned army dish] and dies." "In my whole life I have never worked so hard nor been so happy . . . ," wrote McMein. "I used to be rather fussy about my work, but here I've made pictures in cow-pastures, on manure wagons, on the walls of hospitals, on operating tables—and usually a barn door or a canteen table—and while this war may have put the jinx on my career as an artist, it has made me a first-class roustabout. I can build an easel or push a piano around with equal ease."[137]

The impromptu life- and work-styles didn't dismay the entertainers, who often simply took matters into their own hands. Marian Chase Schaeffer, Marian Dana, and Hazel Bartlett went over on a leaky old ship; they sang in ankle-deep water for the soldiers in the hold: "If He Can Fight Like He Can Love, Then Good-By, Germany."[138]

When Irene Franklin and Corinne Francis and their husbands arrived in port in August of 1918, Franklin told her husband that she was going to give some shows, and rented a theater for the purpose. "Then I asked the captain [of the S.S. *Quilpue*] if he would wigwag to the captains of all the boats in the harbor and ask if their men could come to the show. I guess that was the first time that a program with all the acts and names of the performance was announced in real shipshape sailor fashion. All the captains except one agreed. That one commanded a special mother ship to submarines or something of the kind and everybody was strictly kept off her mysterious decks. Everybody? Well, now listen. That afternoon I hired a tug, and Mr. Green [Franklin's husband] and several of the other entertainers went out to that ship. The stern captain came to the side and said nobody could come aboard. He looked so sorry, that I thought I might take a chance, so, standing on the rope ladder, we started one of the strangest shows that you ever saw on sea or land. I don't know what watch it was, but before we finished everybody was watching us. Finally, just as I had thought, the stern captain relented and I led a troop of boys to the back deck, where I shut my eyes and said I wouldn't tell what I'd seen, and then for about a half an hour we gave a regular show."[139]

Besides concerts, vaudeville acts, recitations, singsongs, and dramatic productions, the Over There Theatre League and the YMCA offered speakers. Rheta Childe Dorr, on her way back from Russia, and the journalist Eunice Tietjens lectured for them. Euphemia Bakewell talked on *Joan of Arc* and *The Streets of Paris*. Mrs. August Belmont, formerly the actress Eleanor Robson, gave dramatic readings. Troops clamored for Ella Wheeler Wilcox's readings of her own sentimental poems—and she earnestly cautioned them to keep sexually clean: "I may lie in the mud of the trenches,/I may reek with blood and mire,/But I will control, by the God in my soul,/The might of my man's desire."[140]

Coaches and producers trained soldier-actors, who trained others, and helped soldiers put on shows—like the popular *Oui, Oui, Marie*. Marian Baldwin, a YM canteen worker, wrote home about how some of the YM women and soldiers got up a movie, a takeoff on the usual plot between country lad and lassie, where the lad goes to the big city and gets involved with a siren. ". . . it was the most 'professional' thing I have done and every one is suggesting that I leave the Y.M.C.A. for the movies. The part was the usual tiresome one which is always shoved on me, the part of sweet innocence, with curls, etc. . . . [I] acted like a foolish little nut without an ounce of brains, but that's all I seem capable of doing, as I have such an expressionless countenance."[141] The movie was a smash success with "the boys."

Movies, lots of them, carried from place to place by devoted couriers, supplemented the personal appearances: "I had promised Verneuil, 130 kilometers from Bourges, that I would take them three films on a certain Friday," wrote one woman. "I left Bourges in the flivver at 1:15 and twelve miles out the car refused to go. I walked on to St. Just where I phoned to the Motor Transport Department, but the French central cut us off, and it took two hours and a half to get the call through the second time. By this time only a motorcycle could possibly get the films to Verneuil in time for the boys."[142] She didn't disappoint them. One movie producer made it her business to search out and film unadvertised heroes, like the company whose guns had fired America's first shot in the war.

The entertainers could count only on what they carried with

them—and it got heavy: "Can you imagine," asked her husband, "Rita Walker [a dancer with the unit "Some Pep"] loaded down with a blanket roll, five blankets, a grip, banjo, musette bag, canteen, tin kelly [helmet], and a gas mask?"[143] And Margaret Mayo wrote: "How we came to detest those blankets and cots . . . when we staggered under them by day and tried to cling to them by night! And how we longed to throw away our gas masks and helmets and all the rest of our cursed paraphernalia and how weary we grew always having to go back for one or the other of these that some one in the party had always forgotten."[144] They worked with whatever came to hand. The Liberty Quartet "used a piano that had been hit only a few days before by a German shell—not to speak of the many pianos which, Miss [Lillian] Jackson said, should have perished in this way."[145]

The women entertainers, despite the detested Y uniforms, the difficult travel, and the omnipresent mud, tried hard to look nice. As the lyric soprano Amparito Farrar said, "It never fails to bring a throb to my heart to hear Americans on the street when they catch sight of us. . . . They always say 'American girls! Gee those American girls look good to me!' "[146] So they struggled to live up to expectations. Elsie Janis, whom the YM excused from wearing a uniform because of the theatrical contracts that frequently interrupted her war service, prided herself that "I was just a girl in a blue serge suit—very thin silk stockings—a silver fox fur and rather a smart hat. . . ."[147] A young woman with the "Mayo Shock Unit" (so named because at one point they had been closer to the front than any other players) on the way to a performance lost one of the satin slippers she was carrying. "She was tired and depressed by the long pull through the mud and she fell onto a camp stool inside the big truck that had been rolled inside the hangar to serve as a dressing room and began to cry. Her street shoes were caked in mud to their tops and she refused to try to play in them. Three aviators immediately shot off into the darkness . . . to search the muddy field. . . . At last the missing slipper was recovered and on the lady's small foot."[148] And the show went on.

Sarah Willmer of Chicago rode ten miles through a storm to perform before 5,000 men, soaking her white dress until it looked,

a soldier said, "like a last year's nightdress left out in the rain."
Months later in a rear-echelon hospital an Illinois soldier, not rec-
ognizing her, told Willmer: " 'The last "Y" girl I saw was up in
———— the night before the St. Mihiel drive. Her name was Sarah
Willmer—I remember her because she came from my state. I shall
never forget as long as I live the blessed white dress she had on the
night she recited to us. We had not seen a white dress, it seemed to
us, in years. There we were with all our gas masks at alert, all ready
to go into the line, and there she was talking to us just like a girl
from home. It sure was a great sight, you bet; and don't forget to
tell her if you ever see her.' "[149]

Officialdom—though it often helped—sometimes complicated
the entertainers' travels. In the early days, not yet accustomed to
American ways, the French questioned Elsie Janis: "We stayed in
Paris ten days. About eight of them were spent in trying to explain
to the French Government what right we had to leave. . . . they
could not see where I got on or off in the War. I was not an '*infir-
mière*'—I did not deal out chocolate and terrible smelling smokes in
a canteen—I did not even drive an ambulance—and yet I wanted to
go to the Front. *Pourquoi?* To amuse the soldiers. *Mon Dieu!* was
not the War amusement enough? I was a well-known actress—ah!
well, that they began to understand, and draw their most French
conclusions! But *sapristi!* no! she has a Mother with her, who is
always with her! *Quel blague!* poor girl, we will do her a favor and
get her a little freedom. Mlle. Janis may go, but the French Military
do not wish any more women than necessary in the danger zone.
Whereupon Miss Janis threatened to turn all of France into a danger
zone if they tried to cut into a combination that experts have tried
to wreck. . . ."[150]

Much later in the war, Janis's car was stopped and she and her
mother sent back to Paris by train under suspicion of spying. "The
next morning the Y.M.C.A. called up to say that they were so sorry—
it had all been a misunderstanding. We knew that, but we felt we
were more misunderstood than misunderstanding. . . . So we decided
to tell our troubles to a policeman and told them to the one who had
some *force* under him, our Boss General [Pershing], who from that
time took us under his very splendid American eagle wings and made

the rest of our stay in France one long winding French road of roses."[151] (Janis evidently enjoyed this protection a good bit. She could be crisp enough about generals—"Some day I know I will find a General who has only a house [rather than a château]!"—but when "Black Jack" asked to share the enlisted men's privilege of using her first name, "I wanted to say, 'Call me anything you like, Jack, I will come at top speed,' but I only said, 'Oh yes, sir.' "[152])

Eunice Prossor Crain, in a troupe which consisted of the three Hearons sisters and Ruth Bush: ". . . got lost. In a strange country, during a war and unable to speak the language. . . . And if you wander around in a war where you're not supposed to be, you can just take the consequences. . . . we were duly arrested as the French thought we were German spies. And when they heard Ruth's last name [*Bush*—which reminded the French of German beer] they were prepared to shoot us on the spot. As we were the first organized company to go over they were not accustomed to our uniforms which were surprisingly like the German in color. After a series of conversations in the sign language and all the red tape on the calendar, we were given tickets to Troyes and went meekly off."[153]

Margaret Mayo too had her spy story: "On our way out from the camp . . . a soldier jumped on the running board of our car as we passed one of the sentry posts, refused to accept our countersign and ordered our chauffeur to take us to the guard-house. We were haled before a sleepy-looking officer who pronounced us suspicious characters, said he had heard of no entertainment being permitted that night in the camp and gave orders that we be locked up for trial in the morning. Tommy Gray . . . produced his false whiskers and other stage 'props' . . . Will Morrisey offered to play his violin . . . Lois Meredith, our ingénue went into giggling hysterics to prove her right to the title, Elizabeth Brill our leading chanteuse became properly temperamental and I argued as calmly as my bad disposition would permit, but all to no avail, we were about to be led forth to a night of torture when a captain . . . appeared in the doorway and 'gave us the laugh' and we realised for the first time that we had been the victims of a clever practical joke. The story went the rounds . . . the next day and for some reason or other seemed to add to our popularity."[154]

The demands on the entertainers' time—particularly the women's time—never stopped. No privacy existed: they were constantly surrounded by "our 'camp followers' . . . young lieutenants who had attached themselves to our party without consulting us, who insisted upon carrying our coats and usually ended by losing them, who frisked about like gay young puppies regardless of what mood one might be in."[155] Neysa McMein captioned one of her drawings, "When for weeks you've had performances morning, noon, and night, and at last comes an afternoon with nothing to do but three weeks' laundry, a few letters, a bit of mending, some socks to darn and maybe wash your hair and file a nail or two—and along comes Jimmy something-or-other, aged nineteen, from Tulamasoo, Idaho, to pay you a call (knowing you must be lonesome!) and he stays and stays and stays and tells you of all his love affairs (oh what a devil with the ladies he is!) of the last sixteen years, but vows no girl holds a candle to you!—wouldn't you just like to forget you're a nice 'Y' lady and say something in 'shavetail' language?"[156]

Often the entertainers were pushed beyond exhaustion. Margaret Mayo tells how "One of the 'Y' women and a Red Cross nurse came back to the dressing room of the hut to tell me confidentially that the men had worked until seven that night decorating a new hall that they themselves had renovated and painted and that they had been scheming for days to 'get up' a supper after the show and would be heart broken unless we came. We all looked at each other in despair for . . . we were so tired, as one of the girls put it, that our very souls ached. The men of our unit tried to explain this for us but the inevitable answer came back—'Just come for a few minutes. They haven't seen any girls for so long. It will do them so much good.' We knew the speech by heart and we had often responded to it when we were longing and aching for our beds, and to-night on the way out we had pledged ourselves to each other not to give in to it again, and now we were all ashamed to refuse them and also ashamed to go back on our word to ourselves and to each other." The women gave in, of course, and "When we saw how hard the boys must have worked to decorate the barracks and with what pleasure they watched each course of the supper come onto the long tables we were glad that we had not disappointed them but, Ye gods, there were hundreds of them and they had a band waiting to play dance music and there were only three of us. . . . When we were about half-way home one of the girls said wearily—'Well, I've only *one* life to give for my country, thank God!' "[157]

▶▶▶ *I'll never get away from the consciousness of that side of war again no matter how funny the stories round the supper table. . . . there will always be that dark, gaping, subterranean passage underneath all the flow of chatter and chaff and art.*
—Margaret Mayo[158]

With all the zest, with all the excitement, with all the fun went heartache. The emotion that the underlying tragedy of the war evoked was never quite subdued. Her hospital experiences sobered even the ebullient Janis: "One day I found an Italian trying to make his nurse understand that he wanted an orange. I have always wondered why I took up that language; I thought it was because of a handsome dark-eyed Latin I had met . . . —but now I know it was to talk to that dying boy. . . ."[159]

Mayo described an incident that troubled her: A Y secretary failed to notify an audience of doughboys that the sickness of the ingénue necessitated the cancellation of the second show. "When the 'Y' man told them I was there—it was so dark they couldn't see me—they were quiet and attentive but when I explained that we could not give a second 'show' they booed and protested. I told them that if they would only come again the next night we would play all night for them. . . . 'We'll not be *here* tomorrow night,' came a voice out of the darkness. 'You needn't trouble. We'll be in the trenches tomorrow night,' was another bitter answer, and I knew it was the truth. . . ." Mayo's desperate efforts to recall the rest of the cast to piece some kind of show together failed. ". . . at last I fumbled my way back through the dark street to tell the boys waiting at the theatre that there was no hope of another show. But they had evidently divined this and had slipped away into the night, no doubt cursing us in their hearts. I went back to our desolate little room and sat by the few remaining embers with my head in my hands so tired and so depressed and so sorry for the bitter thoughts that those boys would carry away with them that I didn't care a whoop whether I lived or died."[160]

"It has been hard for me to sing today," wrote Mary Rochester Roderick, "realizing that many of these boys will be killed before this time tomorrow. Tears would come and the only way I managed to sing was to look over their heads and not into their faces. The hard life of trench warfare will leave an effect on our men which they will never lose. How futile it all seems. If only I knew just the helpful things to say (or sing) to give them courage. I have felt so inadequate."[161]

CHAPTER 6

The Black Record

✄✄✄ *Lady, I just want to look at you, if you charge any-thing for it I'll pay you—it takes me back home.*
    —A black soldier to a black woman YMCA worker[1]

WHILE THE UNITED STATES seethed with anger against the Germans, its meanest actions and cruelest words were directed against its own minorities. Even as the country availed itself of the services of Chinese-Americans and black labor battalions and the protection of fighting black soldiers, whites ignored their contributions, denied them comforts and services, maligned them to other nations, and finally excluded them from the victory parade.[2] Yet 200,000 black American men served abroad, about half of them as combat troops.

"We think you might be able to tell some of the Y men about our condition here, and they could help change it. We find the French villagers here have been told we are an aggregation of diseased men, sent to dig these graves and bury the dead as a punishment!"[3] Black soldiers addressed this plea to Addie Hunton and Kathryn Johnson, two remarkable black women who succeeded in getting to France under the aegis of the YMCA. ". . . the story of the roughness of the colored men," Hunton and Johnson later wrote, "was being told to the [French] civilians in order that all possible association between them might be avoided. They had been systematically informed that their dark-skinned allies were not only unworthy of any courtesies from their homes, but that they were so brutal and vicious as to be absolutely dangerous. They were even told that they belonged to a semi-human species who only a few years ago had been caught in the American forests, and only been tamed enough to work under the white Americans' direction. . . . Literature [created by Americans] was gotten out through the French Military Mission and sent to French villages explaining how Americans desired the colored officers [and troops] to be treated; that they desired them to receive no more attention than was required in the performance of their military duties; that to show them social courtesies not only would be dangerous, but that it would be an insult to the American people. The literature was finally collected and ordered destroyed by the French ministry."[4]

Ironically, even in the face of such American barbarities, black American soldiers sometimes preferred their situation in France to that in the United States. "The many ports of France were particularly the home of the colored soldiers [working as stevedores]," wrote Hunton and Johnson, "so that landing at Bordeaux it did not seem strange to be greeted first of all by our own men. But it did seem passing strange that we should see them guarding German prisoners! Somehow we felt that colored soldiers found it rather refreshing—even enjoyable for a change—having come from a country where it seemed everybody's business to guard them."[5] And many, perhaps most French people chose to believe the evidence before their eyes rather than the propaganda disseminated by white Americans: "The colored soldiers were greatly loved by the French people, and while passing through the town of Laon, which had been in the hands of the Germans for four years, the French civilians knelt by the roadside and kissed the hands of the [black] boys of the 370th Infantry, so grateful were they for their deliverance."[6]

Most of the 200,000 black men who served in Europe never saw an American black woman there. Black women struggled in vain to get to Europe. During all the years of the war only five or six succeeded. The YMCA sponsored four. In the last months of the war, Helen Hagan, a professional black pianist, was permitted to entertain soldiers overseas. Just possibly, a black woman doctor went.[7]

The Red Cross needed nurses, and qualified, registered black nurses were available. "Press and pulpit, organizations and individuals were beseeching and demanding in 1918 that the Red Cross add some of our well-trained and experienced [black] nurses to their 'overseas' contingent, but no favorable response could be obtained"—though, according to Alice Dunbar-Nelson, "Rumor, more or less authentic, states that over 300 colored nurses were on the battlefields, though their complexion disguised their racial identity."[8] Nor, with one exception, did the service organizations contemplate sending black women to Europe to work in canteens and huts: the YMCA alone sponsored black welfare workers overseas—mostly men.

Not many, absolutely or proportionally: eighty-seven black workers altogether; hardly ever more than seventy-five at one time. Among them were three black women, Mrs. James Curtis (widow of a United States ambassador to Liberia), Miss Kathryn Johnson, and Mrs. William A. Hunton—all women of distinction. Take, for instance, Addie Waites Hunton. Born June 11, 1870, in Norfolk, Virginia, she was educated at the Boston Latin School, at the Spencerian College of Commerce in Philadelphia, of which she was the first black woman graduate, and later at the City College of New York. After teaching for a year in Portsmouth, Virginia, she was appointed lady principal (dean) of the State Normal and Agricultural College of Alabama, where she served for several years. She began her association with the YMCA by proxy with her marriage in 1893 to William Alphaeus Hunton, the first black secretary of the International YMCA; she herself did pioneering work among black women for the national board of the YMCA. In 1895 she became secretary and bursar of Clark College, and from 1907 to 1915 advisory secretary of the national board of the YMCA, as well as an organizer for the National Association of Colored Women. She traveled extensively in Europe, studying at the Kaiser Wilhelm University at Strasbourg.[9] Despite all these achievements and her long relationship with the organization, the YMCA had turned down her first request to go overseas.

Apparently the YM had planned to follow these three black women, who sailed in the spring of 1918, with more. But when Hunton, Johnson, and Curtis arrived in Paris, they found that the first black woman, then on the staff of Matthew Bullock, "had been ordered home [with a group of black men administrators] as persona non grata to the army; this was done on recommendation of army officials in Bordeaux, who had brought from our southland their full measure of sectional prejudice. This incident resulted in the detention of many secretaries [administrators], both men and women, from sailing for quite a period of time."[10] The newly arrived black women workers, thus greeted, "questioned the wisdom of our adventure. . . . Would blind prejudice follow us even to France where men were dying by the thousands for the principles of truth and justice?"[11]

In all too many cases, the absence of black women completely denied services to black soldiers. Even if they gained admittance to the canteens, white women workers often ignored them.

The three black women canteeners struggled to meet the desperate needs as they encountered them. ". . . we had fitted out the first reading and reception room for the soldiers in our area. . . . this room became best known for its Chat Hour that came to fill it to overflow on Sundays at the twilight hour. Somehow it came to us that this was a lonely time for men. . . . [we] began with just informal talks on current topics—apart from the war or army. The interest grew. Men were there from Howard, Union, Hampton, Tuskegee, Morehouse, Atlanta, Clark, and other schools, so we had talks about their institutions and their founders. We had talks on race leaders, on work after the war—music, art, religion and every conceivable subject."[12]

Of course not all black troops had attended college; some indeed were illiterate. To meet their varying needs, the black canteeners developed a range of educational activities, from teaching soldiers to write their names to enabling a handful of black soldiers to attend French universities after the war. For those who came from the many Southern cities without libraries for blacks, the women instituted and taught book-lending systems.[13]

When need arose, the black YMCA women served white as well as black troops. In the influenza epidemic, with hospitals and barracks crowded, they converted their hut into an infirmary. "Sick men could hardly be left in 'pup' tents in the deep mud and constant rain of that season. That night another change comes over our hut. On all the benches, in all the corners and in what had been our cheerful reading room are sick men, many of them ill unto death. . . .

It is a sad time—graves can hardly be dug rapidly enough—nurses are scarce—every one is doing the best he knows. True, these are not colored boys we are serving, but what matters that. . . ."[14]

The black women were sharply disappointed in their hope—which they shared with thousands of white women—of working near the front. But unlike white women, they were not permitted during the war to serve their own combat troops, though "one of us had come from Illinois, and had already been adopted as the daughter of the 370th Regiment."[15] With one exception: In the last weeks of the war, the black women did serve some black Pioneer Regiments, hastily created and sent to France after three to six weeks' training, with the intention of putting them in combat. They arrived so late, however, that though they came under fire few of them had the opportunity to fight. For the most part, though, the black women's service was confined to the 100,000 or so black noncombatants, most of whom worked as stevedores or engineers, or in labor battalions.

The men's gratitude for the presence of the few black women was touching. "I just want to thank you for the way you entertained us soldiers last evening and say that you really did bring sunshine to us all," a soldier wrote the musician Helen Hagan. "To-day it seems that a burden has been lifted off us, and we wish you could stay in our camp forever. I feel better than I have felt in the whole eleven months that I have been overseas. All the soldiers are talking of you to-day; it has been a year since some of them saw a colored woman."[16] And Hunton and Johnson reported, "One man came to us saying, 'Lady, do you want to get rich over in France?' We gave an affirmative reply and questioned how. He said, 'Just get a tent and go in there and charge five cents a peep. These fellows would just be glad for even a peep at you.' . . . Hundreds of incidents gave evidence of the love of these men for their women. Sometimes they shed tears at their first sight of a colored woman in France."[17]

But the black women received quite different treatment from many whites, who were clearly threatened in the more liberal atmosphere of France by the difficulties of condescending to and dehumanizing black people as they always had in the United States. Charles Williams tells of "A noted divine from Atlanta, Ga., [who] was for a time in charge of one of the three-day conferences for new

[YMCA] secretaries in France. At the close of one of the sessions a colored canteen worker told him she had enjoyed the discussion. 'I am glad you enjoyed it,' he said, 'but we don't mix in the States and you must not expect to here.' "[18]

Even the YWCA, which had specifically elected to serve women in Europe—particularly the women of other organizations, seldom "gave any attention to this little colored group, notwithstanding the fact that they were women, and Americans, just like the others," wrote Hunton and Johnson. A YWCA woman so deeply insulted one of the black women on the street that thereafter she kept to places where their paths wouldn't cross. The black women's experience overseas "was more or less clouded at all times with that biting and stinging thing which is ever shadowing us in our own country. . . ."[19] But they solaced themselves with the friendship of the French: Mrs. Hunton speaks of a "lovely French family—*Monsieur et madame, les deux tantes, la chat blanc et le bon jardin*—with whom she had lived for seven months. She had been worshipped into feeling a part of all their charming life."[20]

Perhaps hardest of all, these women had to watch the suffering inflicted on the black men. "Always they were aware of some case of cruel injustice for which there seemed absolutely no redress. We found in our camp a young college student, who, believing that war spelled opportunity, was among the first to enlist. His education placed him at once in the office of his company, and he went to France a sergeant. He did not find that war meant for him what he had dreamed it would, but he kept loyal; his work commanded respect, and, for a time, all went well. But a company commander came who resented the pride of the colored boy, and then began a series of humiliations that took away rank, sent him to the guard-house and dock. . . . his face hurt us as often as we looked upon it, so full it was of the endurance of an outraged manhood."[21]

In the unfriendly American military, the black women offered black soldiers honor and respect: soldiers who "still kept their faith" even though "subjected to a stern discipline; with discriminations, cruel in their intent and execution; long hours of toil; scant recognition for service or hope of promotion. . . ."[22]

The indignities inflicted on black soldiers and workers (and on other minorities) came all too naturally to citizens of the American society, which assumed the inferiority of other races to whites. In such an environment a young white woman YMCA canteen worker, otherwise unfailingly kind, could unself-consciously write home: "There are a lot of Chinese French Colonials here, ditch diggers, etc. Some of them from Annam. They are about the lowest down people in the world, I think, especially the Annamites, who are a grade lower than the 'Chinois.' The boys call them 'Dynamites' and 'Carbides,' the latter from the odour in their vicinity. They seem almost like mere animals, far less human and with much less personality than the most degraded blacks. They come into the canteen to try to buy tobacco and we aren't allowed to sell them a thing. They drop their money on the counter, grab the cigarettes and dash for the door, pursued by Americans, who lead them back, return the cigarettes, give them back their money and turn them out."[23]

From the leave area at Aix Marian Baldwin wrote of the much-admired 15th Infantry band's performance: "These niggers play in a way that would lead the worst slacker to battle. There are about thirty of them and of course since they have been here they have been the wonder and the admiration of the townsfolk. . . . This adulation has caused these ridiculous niggers to put on the most screaming airs and graces."[24]

Even some of the white entertainers, though they thoroughly enjoyed performing for and with the black soldiers, used the same offensive language and told the same condescending jokes as the rest of America. Elsie Janis, for instance, exulted over a London night when a general "had a real jazz band of chocolate hue brought up to London, and I sang my song about taking my jazz band to the Fatherland and then led them out. Oh! boy, what a night! I went wild leading them. . . . We certainly jarred the roof of the Palace. . . . After the show they marched down the streets playing 'Over There' as if they were walking down the Unter den Linden. If you have never been in London on Sunday; if you don't know that Philadelphia on Sunday is a wide-open mining-town compared to London on that same day, then you will never understand the super-joy of seeing and *hearing* fifty black-faced, white-hearted sons of Southern salubrity hoofing it down Shaftesbury Avenue, London, England, Sunday night and getting away with it. . . ."[25]

Ella Wheeler Wilcox is a happy exception. Under instruction, she said, from the spirit of her dead husband, she went on tour in France reading her poetry, lecturing on sex, and urging "the boys" to "come back clean." She openly professed "a growing appreciation and love for the colored people, and I have seen nothing in France finer than the work of the stevedores. I have written and dedicated a poem to them." It's quite a poem, beginning with the assertion "We are the army stevedores, lusty and virile and strong./We are given the hardest work of the war and the hours are long," and ending resoundingly, "Somebody has to do this work, be glad that it isn't you,/We are the army stevedores—give us our due!"[26]

🖐🖐🖐 *The colored women who served overseas had a tremendous strain placed upon their Christian ideals, but [a few] officials . . . helped them to keep their faith in the democracy of real Christian service. . . .*
> —Addie Hunton and Kathryn Johnson[27]

Hunton, Johnson, and Curtis served in Europe at bitter cost. They were repeatedly subjected to indignities, from the original struggle to get overseas to discrimination on the trip back home, when "All the Negro women were placed on a deck below the white women. At mealtime, they were given a secluded, poorly-ventilated part of the dining room. . . . When Kathryn Johnson protested, she was told that Southern workers on board the ship would feel insulted if the Negro workers ate in the same section as they, and that the Negroes 'need not expect any such treatment as had been given them by the French.' "[28] They knew loneliness and isolation, for each of them worked as "a lone woman in her hut. There might be a dozen Y women in her camp—but she worked absolutely alone, often her hours stretching from 9 in the morning to 9 at night—but always it was a work of love." Only generosity of spirit enabled these proud and independent women to rise above fatigue, isolation, and pitiless inhumanity to evaluate their war experience as "the greatest opportunity for service that we have ever known; service that was constructive, and prolific with wonderful and satisfying results."[29]

Hunton and Johnson's book stands out among the hundreds of World War I memoirs, distinguished by the authors' strong compulsion not to tell their own adventures but to describe the accomplishments and contributions of the black soldier—and some of the injustices inflicted on him. Hunton and Johnson wanted readers to know how much he had been honored by the French, how often decorated, how recognized by being invited by the French to lead the way to the Rhine. They wanted readers to understand how much difference the French environment had meant to him—and to them: "The relationship between the colored soldiers, the colored welfare workers, and the French people was most cordial and friendly and grew in sympathy and understanding, as their association brought about a closer acquaintance. . . . the first ten days in France, though filled with duties and harassed with visits from German bombing planes, were nevertheless a delight, in that they furnished to some of us the first full breath of freedom that had ever come into our limited experience."[30]

YWCA promotional poster

Back our girls over there
Y.W.C.A.
United War Work Campaign

Journalist-lawyer Madeleine Doty sorting American women's peace petitions, November 1915

Motor corps women of the American Fund for French Wounded

Signal Corps telephone operators'
quarters, Neufchâteau

RIGHT: Mrs. Burden Turner in her
"nursing uniform"—a do-it-yourself
design, France, 1917

Salvation Army "lassies" making pies

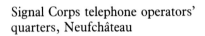

Tailoring for the troops:
a Salvation Army woman and
her portable sewing machine

A railroad station platform
somewhere in France

"This is that famous scene 'over there.' Arriving in a strange town, preferably late at night, and finding nary a 'Y' representative or an army man to meet us."

"When all the fellows had a friend . . ."

Original drawings and captions from
Entertaining the American Army:
The American Stage and Lyceum in the
World War (1921) by James W. Evans
and Gardner L. Harding.
Illustrations by Neysa McMein,
Anita Parkhurst, and Ethel Rundquist.

"The sore-throated and wet-footed soprano, ruining her voice for the sake of her country, while the young gallant shields her with his marvelous find—yes, an umbrella."

"To come back from the front for the three-day rest and see a regular girl again—one who could 'parlez Americaine'— was the height of many an ambition."

" 'Sleeping cars! Insomnia!' Words not in the entertainer's vocabulary. After a few months, one could travel atop a supply truck and sleep as soundly as in one's own trundle bed."

"The Performance de Luxe. Aided by a pin or two, a much-appreciated dishpan 'mirror,' and a lot of chatter, one can (even in a six-by-ten room) make oneself a wondrous sight for the boys who have seen naught but uniforms for many a month."

"Dancing is generally conceded to be a pleasure, but when one has, in the space of a few months, danced 78,571 miles—or three times the distance around the earth—it ceases to be such. With smiling faces and aching limbs, in heavy shoes and hot uniforms, before breakfast, through lunch hours, on stone, on wood, on cinder floors, or on no floors at all, they danced."

BEWARE

—OF—

FEMALE SPIES

Women are being employed by the enemy to secure information from Navy men, on the theory that they are less liable to be suspected than male spies. Beware of inquisitive women as well as prying men.

SEE EVERYTHING
HEAR EVERYTHING
SAY NOTHING
Concerning any matter bearing upon the work of the Navy

SILENCE IS SAFETY

Louise Bryant, correspondent, who spent *Six Red Months* in the Russian Revolution

"Madame, identify yourself!"

LEFT: Elsie Janis
does her Will Rogers act

Ruth Law, who flew
over the Western Front

Dust jacket for Mary McAuley's
Germany in War Time

Amusing—Inspiring—Tragic

BUTTER—EIER—KASE

The Butter Line

Germany in War Time
Personal experiences of an American woman in Germany
By Mary Ethel McAuley

"In Germany before the butter card was introduced,
we had to stand in line for hours to get one-half pound
of butter."

"The German frontier is the easiest in Europe to cross,
because if the Germans suspect you, you never get as far
as the frontier."

"In June in my room at my boarding house in Berlin,
was hung this notice, 'After July first all people coming to
this boarding-house must bring their own bedding with
them. The bedding will be washed every four weeks.' It
was signed by the Berlin Boarding-House Keepers
Union."

THE OPEN COURT PUBLISHING CO., CHICAGO.

A Red Cross nurse joins the
Armistice celebration, Paris,
November 11, 1918

CHAPTER 7

The Hello Girls

Uncle Sam Presents "Hello Girls" A Melodious, Mirthful Extravaganza in Three Coils, Produced for the First Time in France, under the auspices of the A.E.F. Protective and Benevolent Society for the Suppression of Huns, in the Théâtre de Guerre. Performances in both French and English. Assisted by a chorus of 33—COUNT 'EM—33 Real American Telephone Girls, representing half the States in the Union, and able to get anybody's number the first time—including the Kaiser's.
—"Telephone Review" of the New York Telephone Company[1]

IN THE SPRING OF 1918 a small group of women each dressed in what the Army Signal Corps described as chic blue serge suits and fashionable wide-brimmed hats posed for a picture on the roof of the AT&T building in New York City. They were proudly wearing a uniform prescribed by the Army for the Woman's Telephone Unit and adorned with U.S. Army Signal Corps insignia and badges of rank and function. These thirty-three bilingual women sailed for Europe early in March 1918 aboard the troop ship *Celtic*; from Southampton a channel steamer transported them to France, where they took up their duties of running army telephone switchboards for the American Expeditionary Force, and coping with the operators of the French telephone system, who rarely spoke English. Before the Armistice five more units of American operators followed the first, bringing their numbers to 233.

General Pershing himself had fought the War Department to get them there. Initially, some of his staff had opposed bringing

American women to France to serve so closely with army troops. But necessity overcame male reluctance. With the United States ill-prepared to fight, General Pershing's problems were exacerbated by the vagaries of a telephone system where the operators spoke a foreign language and seemed to have adopted the infamous obstructionism of French bureaucrats. Two-hour delays and abrupt cutoffs roused American denunciations of French operators that rivaled attacks on the Hun. Every long-distance call required the cooperation of tele-phone exchanges in all the cities and towns along the line, a process complicated, muttered General Harbord, by "all the delays that could be born of French curiosity, conservatism and cupidity."[2] Misun-derstandings pyramided. The United States Army needed telephone operators who could also interpret, often on matters of vital impor-tance where a misconstrued message could spell disaster. Bilingual operators were particularly crucial in the early days before the Signal Corps could string its own lines and install its own equipment; but afterwards also reliable communication with the French military had to be maintained.

Even in the unlikely event that the Signal Corps could muster enough trained bilingual soldiers to provide good service, was this the most efficient use of its manpower? The British had already employed women behind the lines, releasing male troops for more dangerous duties. So when the correspondent Rheta Childe Dorr told General Pershing of her distress at seeing American "men in uniform working at card indexes, sorting mail, pounding typewriters and attending the telephone," Pershing assured her that "we shall have to have women telephone operators."[3]

It probably helped that Americans expected to hear a pleasant woman's voice—widely advertised as the "Voice with the Smile"—when they picked up a phone. The morale-building effect of their presence upon nostalgic American officers and troops may not have inspired General Pershing's request for the women telephone oper-ators, but it provided a fringe benefit. "It broke up the blues," wrote a war correspondent. "I wanted to give three cheers. . . . I breathed a silent prayer that all the hello girls in the world might prosper and marry well. I reckon that the well-modulated, courteous and very American accents of a hello girl dripping in at the left ear have much the same effect on a homesick American as the soothing hand of a nurse on a sick soldier."[4]

    ♚♚♚ *Oftentimes, during the early days, after saying "number please," there would be a silence, broken by an awed, "Oh!" Sometimes it would be, "Thank heaven, you're here at last!"*
                                 —Signal Corps telephone operator[5]

The War Department assigned responsibility for selecting and training the operators to the American Telephone and Telegraph Company. Ma Bell sought recruits among her own daughters, but could not find enough bilingual operators. The first call to the public for French-speaking volunteers went out on November 13, 1917— and evoked 7,000 responses. Eliminating women insufficiently fluent in French, women with male relatives overseas, and women with German connections, AT&T chose from the many fully qualified women the hundred Pershing had requested for the first contingent.

All the women selected for the first several units spoke fluent French, but most had little or no telephone experience. At camp switchboards and in toll offices at seven training centers, AT&T provided intensive instruction in switchboard operation. Signal Corps indoctrination and daily "military drill" rounded out the preparation.[6]

The women of the first group, the trailblazers, ranged in age from nineteen to thirty-five; four came from Canada and the other twenty-nine from twelve states. Grace Banker, leader of the group with the rank of Chief Operator, a Barnard College graduate and a veteran of AT&T's Long Lines (long distance) Division, boasted about them: "What good sports the girls were in that First Unit! They took everything in their stride. They were the pioneers."[7] By war's end, six units had gone to France, with volunteers from thirty-two states and four foreign countries (Belgium, Canada, France, Switzerland).

Some were college graduates, some came from public schools, some from private schools; some had been educated in French convents. Among them were seven pairs of sisters, at least two married

women, some French-born girls who had learned English while employed in the United States as maids, and "gentlewomen who laid
aside home duties to master the switchboard."[8] "Go to any one of
our switchboards in France," said a military historian, "and you can
see a Wellesley graduate seated alongside a girl who had to make her
way from childhood."[9] Visions of the colonel's lady and Judy
O'Grady, patriots under the skin, spring to mind, but the women
accepted into the telephone service had qualifications that distinguished them from the Judy O'Gradys of Kipling's imagination.

Louise Barbour, chief instructor in the Long Lines New York
office "knew many of the members personally, supervised the training of some, and heard accounts of their selection and outfitting
every evening from my apartment mate, Miss Helen Cook, who . . .
attended to the thousand and one details incident to preparing the
groups for embarkation." Barbour's own interest in joining
". . . grew until . . . One hot noon . . . Miss Cook and I walked
into the office of Mr. Frederick S. Robinson, then with our [AT&T's]
Legal Department, and, with right hands raised, took the oath of
enlistment." Did Barbour and Cook—and Robinson, for that matter—believe that the women were enlisting in the army? And if not,
in what? The record is silent.

The two went overseas with the fifth unit, which sailed from
New York on the S.S. *Aquitania* on August 5, 1918, Barbour to
become district chief operator, the highest-ranking woman in the
group.[10]

All reports agree that the trip was exciting, though some stressed
the fun and others the danger. "There were some seven or eight
thousand troops on board," Barbour wrote her mother, "and with
the exception of nineteen quartermaster girls we were the only women
so you may imagine that the girls had a gay time . . . we soon became
acquainted with a number of officers who helped to make the days
pass pleasantly. All were obliged to wear life belts during the day
and it was an amusing sight to see couples trying to dance in them."
The Signal Corps women had their own tables in the dining room
"to which we marched thrice daily in columns of two headed by
Lieutenant Hill [their official escort], through a labyrinth of carefully

canvassed corridors and decks."[11] Banker wrote of "Twelve days of life-boat drills. . . . Three nights obeying orders and sleeping in our clothes. Stuck on a sandbar at the harbor of the Mersey River just outside of Liverpool, a target for German submarines all one moonlight night. . . ."[12]

The strong odor of Lifebuoy soap—a smell supposed to persuade customers of the soap's vaunted utility in overcoming "B.O., body odor"—aggravated the operators' seasickness. "This soap was a part of our required equipment but its presence in our luggage became so offensive that with one accord we opened wide the port hole and dumped our entire supply into the Atlantic Ocean," Louise Barbour remembered. "Nor do I recall ever having felt the lack of it during my year in France."[13]

All the units landed in England (where they encountered short rations) and then crossed the Channel to France—an experience with memorable moments: "Two days on a little channel packet caught in a dense fog between Southampton and Le Havre. Running into a submarine net and narrowly missing being rammed by a French cruiser."[14] "The hospital ship [on which we were transported] was fitted with hammocks slung in a large saloon. Beside each hammock was a disagreeably suggestive basin supported on a movable arm. The whole place smelled horribly of disinfectants and we were immediately assigned to life boats, given a drill, and advised on no account to remove our clothing during the night. . . . the boat's officers entertained us with stories of what had happened on similar crossings to boats torpedoed in the channel."[15]

On the train to Paris: "We snatched what sleep we could sitting up wrapped in our army overcoats. . . . Soon we heard the staccato rattle of anti-aircraft guns punctuated at intervals by the deeper note of an exploding bomb. . . . There was no more sleep for us that night and a rather subdued unit climbed into the Signal Corps truck at the Gare St. Lazare in the morning and stood clinging to side posts as we jolted across the cobblestones of Paris in the glorious sunshine of another day."[16] "I'm sure," wrote Berthe Adel Carrel, "I was the only one who fell out of bed when the Big Bertha went off at six o'clock on the morning after we arrived in Paris."[17]

🏵🏵🏵 *Never a word about the Signal Corps Unit of 250 girls who plug from morning until night, who scream their lungs out to trenches over lines that are tied to trees, to fence-posts, and along the ground. Not that we care. We came over here to do our work and to give quick service and to help the boys a few miles ahead of us to get what they want and what we need to get, the Kaiser.*

—A Signal Corps telephone operator[18]

Ultimately, the telephone operators were assigned to American military installations in some seventy-five French cities and towns. Some photographs show them before their barracks in Tours: "In spite of those ankle-length skirts and high button shoes, we were the glamour girls of the AEF," commented Merle Egan Anderson. "Under no other circumstances could we have been induced to wear shoes that didn't fit, long woolen underwear, and those hideous sateen bloomers. . . ."[19] Others picture them working the switchboards at duty stations like the First Army Headquarters during the St. Mihiel offensive, with gas masks and steel helmets ready for use at a moment's notice. "The largest telephone exchange was located in Tours, where about thirty-five women worked the switchboards at the Headquarters of the Service of Supply. We handle 100 more long distance calls a day than Chaumont [Pershing's headquarters]," Barbour wrote from Tours, "and almost twice as much as Paris. . . . Of course we were terribly busy in Sept and Oct [1918] and our traffic went up more than 30% a month but the girls are a picked lot and not one of us would have changed places for worlds."[20] Women operators also worked the switchboards at Pershing's headquarters, and at the headquarters of the First and Second Armies. As these headquarters moved, the women moved with them.

Often they were billeted in hotels presided over by a YWCA "hostess" responsible for the facility and its management. By army dicta the Signal Corps women were not to visit navy and army huts or barracks, nor the docks, and they were required to tell their YWCA hostess where they were going in their free time. Any disciplinary matters were handled by the Chief Operators—a responsibility for which one of them, a Miss March, thought herself too young.[21]

Their living arrangements varied. At Neufchâteau the government built a barracks with a recreation room and ten bedrooms, each shared by two women, on the grounds of a large house which accommodated their kitchen, dining room, and bedrooms for their YW hostess, their chief operator, and servants.[22] At Tours, Barbour reminisced, they stayed in a large hotel where "Our rooms were comfortable, our beds were very high, and hot water was brought to our doors night and morning in shining brass pitchers. There were no bath rooms!"[23] Not all the women were so fortunate. At First Army Headquarters in Ligny, Banker lived in a room over a barn used to store herbs and old furniture. There she slept in a canopy bed, over which "hung, like a sword of Damocles, a cross of dried flowers at least a foot high."[24]

Accommodations worsened when the First Army Headquarters moved to Souilly. "The barracks were flimsy things that had been lined with old newspapers and maps to keep out the cold," wrote Berthe Hunt. "The Y.W.C.A. helped us out by giving us a blanket each, a rug, oilcloth and other comforts. In fact, our sitting room (which we acquired later) was furnished with a piano and other things taken from Boche dugouts in the vicinity. Everyone assisted in making us as comfortable as possible, considering the fact that we were in the advance area, where we could see the red and yellow glare from the shelling and feel the reverberations caused by the booming of the big guns. The 27th Engineers helped us get settled and made us shelves for our various belongings, wash stands, wooden tables and benches, etc."[25]

All the same, said Grace Banker, "the barracks roof leaked in the autumn rains. The weather was cold, for winter comes early in the hills about Verdun. By October there was ice on the water pails in the morning. Once I froze my feet badly without even going out of the barracks. I had been working long hours with very little sleep. Before a drive [military offensive] I seldom had more than two or three hours of rest. Consequently, when I tumbled into bed at night, I never noticed anything until my feet began to swell and then I discovered that the bed covers were soaking wet from a leak in the roof overhead. It was a long time before I could wear shoes again. Of course I moved the bed, but, although I moved it several times,

I never found a place where there wasn't at least one leak. I kept
thinking of the boys in the trenches. They were so much worse off.
We didn't really suffer; we had plenty of warm food; were happy in
our work; and we had fine officers to work for."[26]

    ♬♬♬ *For making you feel that you are a real part of the*
army I recommend the long distance telephone service. When
Pershing can't talk to Col. House or Lloyd George unless you
make the connection you naturally feel that you are helping a
bit. My! But it was fun!
                                   —Louise Barbour[27]

The operators gloried in their work—at times onerous, at times
dangerous, but always filled with a sense of historic usefulness. Wherever they were posted they worked with the management and direction of the armies in the field. And of course, close as they were to
the centers of military command, they were privy to much sensitive
information. In this respect their responsibilities were perhaps
unique among those of all the American women in France.

They also instructed soldiers—a situation threatening to the
male ego. ". . . with the increasing need for men to operate the front
line switchboards which were of the magneto type found in small
Montana towns with which I was familiar," Merle Anderson reminisced, "I was soon teaching classes of a dozen or more soldiers
whose disgusted remark, 'Where's my skirt?' was their standard
greeting. However, when I reminded them that any soldier could
carry a gun but the safety of a whole division might depend on the
switchboard one of them was operating, I had no more trouble.
Except for one hardboiled sergeant who refused to report to a woman
until he spent a week on K.P. duty and decided I was the lesser of
two evils. In the end he was my prize student."[28]

Like other women, the telephone operators clamored to get to
the front. Everyone envied the six women who worked the switchboards for the First Army during the St. Mihiel and the Argonne-
Meuse offensives. Colonel Parker Hitt, Chief Signal Officer, who had
from the start urged the use of women operators in France, wanted
some of them to work at an advanced army post of command. His

call for volunteers produced a unanimous response, but ". . . the mean things would let only six of us go"[29]—six selected for their competence in French and at the switchboard and their good physical condition. The YWCA's Julia Russel arranged for their billeting and meals at the front and accompanied the six lucky operators.

The work fascinated them: ". . . much of it was in codes changed frequently. Ligny was 'Waterfall.' Toul might be 'Podunk' one day and 'Wabash' the next. The Fourth Corps was known as 'Nemo,' etc. Once in the mad rush of work I heard one of the girls say desperately, 'Can't I get Uncle?' and another, 'No, I didn't get Jam.' It all sounded like the Mad Hatter in *Alice in Wonderland*." Doughboy French further exercised the operators' linguistic abilities: " 'Benoity Vox' was the average American soldier's way of asking for the French town of Benoîte Vaux."[30]

In these offensives operators worked at the top of their powers, as Esther Fresnel wrote her parents: "We worked day and night, six hours at a stretch, and then ran home to snatch a few hours' sleep, then go back to work. . . . officers were all on edge, and it was rather hard to keep our tempers at times because everything came at once, and *des faits* the lines would go out of order, bombs or thunderstorms up a way. . . . men would ask for places we had never heard of and wanted them immediately. Sometimes it would take us over an hour to complete a call." Berthe Hunt found it "most thrilling to sit at that board and feel the importance of it—at first it gave me a sort of 'gone' feeling for fear the connection would not be made in time and a few seconds would be lost. . . ."[31] The women couldn't keep away from their jobs: "Soon after 2:00 A.M. I was back in the office with the girls who had left on the earlier shift the night before," wrote Grace Banker. "No one could tell what might happen next; it was like an exciting game—and I couldn't leave."[32]

Despite forty-eight-hour stints with only short intervals of sleep, Helen Hill "found it quite entertaining to sit through the night until dawn. There was always a Wire Chief and soldier-operator on duty in case we needed help. I amused myself, also, by swapping stories over the wire with different soldier-operators when they would call in to test the lines. . . . The officers were getting no sleep and were sometimes impatient to us, but we kept our tempers fairly well and gave every ounce of endeavour that was in us. Nor did it have a marked effect on any of the girls. One could see the dark hollows under their eyes, but not a change in their usual happy voices. . . . I have gained a whole lot of self-control and patience, and am awfully proud of having had such a real part to play in this great salient of St. Mihiel."[33]

The six operators who served so well at St. Mihiel accompanied the First Army Headquarters to Souilly where, reinforced by seven others, they did their part in the Argonne drive. "At first we had charge of the operating boards only. You know with our advance units there were two types of board—that used for the ordinary routine of local and long distance calls, in regard to supplies, transportations, etc.; and that which carried all the messages between the fighting units and the commanding officers directing their movements. Every order for an infantry advance, a barrage preparatory to the taking of a new objective and, in fact, for every troop movement, came over these 'fighting lines,' as we called them. These wires connected the front up with the generals and made it possible for the latter to know exactly what was going on at any moment and to direct operations accordingly."[34] Soon the women were proudly handling the entire exchange.

During the battle of the Argonne, fire spread through the barracks housing the First Army switchboard. In the grand tradition, the women refused a direct military order to leave their post. When they finally yielded, they returned after an hour and resumed their work with the one-third of the lines the fire had not ruined.

A number of operators extended their service to work with the Army of Occupation in Germany. A select few were recalled from post-Armistice leave to operate the switchboards for the Americans in Paris for the peace negotiations—among them Grace Banker, who took charge of the telephone system in the residence of President Wilson, and Louise Barbour, who became chief operator for the Paris District. "Oh Boy!" wrote Barbour, ecstatically anticipating this opportunity to attend on history in the making. "Aint it a grand and glorious feeling! I can hardly wait to get there. . . ."[35]

Grace Banker found the realities of the new assignment less thrilling: "Hotel life in Paris and all the comforts again, but we

didn't appreciate it at all! We missed the First Army with its code
of loyalty and hard work. We were back in the petty squabbles of
civilian life where even chief operators [a reference to Louise Barbour, perhaps?] had 'tantrums,' and where the wives of civilians
attached to the Peace Conference spilled all over Paris in army cars."[36]

Affectionately known as "Hello Girls" or "Soldiers of the
Switchboard," the Signal Corps women caught the public's imagination. They were widely praised for their courage, dedication to
duty, and efficiency, as glowing examples of American womanhood
at its finest, rising to the emergency, standing shoulder to shoulder
with their brothers-in-arms. Everything they did amazed. "Girls"
transmitting battle orders! Journalists wrote story after story about
them; servicemen stood in line to dance with them; an Army unit
sent them horses to ride; generals commended and decorated them;
and civilians and military alike waxed lyrical about them. Brigadier
General Fox Connor rhapsodized about "the superiority of American
womanhood." And at a special Christmas dinner in their honor in
1918, Brigadier General George Van Horn Moseley, praising them
as "better disciplined than the army itself," said, "You have nobly
performed your duty as part of the Advance Guard of the women of
America—the strongest force for good in the world today."[37]

But when after the war some of them tried to claim their state
bonuses as veterans, adulation turned to rejection. Those of them
who courageously undertook a postwar battle for recognition won
for all of them their rights to veterans' benefits only in 1977, when
the youngest was nearing eighty.

CHAPTER 8

The Reporters

Amateurs and Chance Observers

A NUMBER OF PROFESSIONAL American women journalists went to Europe to report various aspects of World War I. In that writing generation, other American women also recorded their observations and impressions and often published them. The wartime American public, so publishers and propagandists clearly believed, thirsted for the minutiae of any experience overseas.

Many of these amateur reporters and chance observers, moved by the same curiosity that draws people to gape at the site of any catastrophe, succeeded in visiting a battlefield—the more recently active, the better. Book after book records pointless ventures into trenches, "fairly well-behaved trenches, but real ones nevertheless,"[1] peeks into operating rooms and tours through hospitals, thrills at the sound of gunfire and the sight of red drops falling from ambulances, and cozy dinners complete with flowers and written menus in officers' dugouts. So standardized did these trips become that Mrs. J. Borden Harriman was asked, "Which trip do you want to take, Verdun or Noyon?"[2] Often women returned to write sentimental claptrap that jibed with the conventional morality of the times: "Upstairs in the convalescent ward a boy, to cheer his comrades, was banging the jolliest kind of music on an old tin piano, impatiently waiting the day when he would be declared well enough to go back to be wounded again."[3]

More interesting by far, both psychologically and experientially, are the reports of women in enemy territory. As late as 1916 American women were still going abroad to study. One of them, who at nineteen went to Germany to study opera, published a description of her sojourn there under the pen name Josephine Therese. She knew some German; a cousin resident in Europe conducted her to Berlin; and she lived with the family of her father's old friend Joachim Miller, a naturalized American of German birth. But for all these advantages she made heavy weather of her thirteen months in Germany.

She cried when Germans alleged that Wilson was in the pay of the British. The German reverence for titles and rank, particularly their idolatry of the kaiser, disgusted her. So did the trappings of Prussian militarism, embodied in (and on) her suitor Leutnant von Luben, with his monocle, silver bracelet, and pompadoured blond hair. All the same when her conservatory class went to sing for wounded German soldiers, she went along: "I suppose that I was giving 'aid and comfort to the enemy,' but I am not ashamed. *We* do not make war upon the sick and wounded."[4]

The American breaking off of diplomatic relations with Germany in February 1917 frightened Therese—but not too much to keep her from going to a concert that afternoon with a young American man who "breezily insisted upon talking in our native tongue until a darkly scowling German leaned over, and said in an angry whisper, 'You fool, this is no day to talk English.' For a few moments my escort was more cautious, but . . . he must have lapsed into our mother tongue again, unconsciously, for suddenly I heard a voice behind me saying in a ludicrously guttural accent, 'I only vish dot I vas in der goot old Choonided Stades myself, today.' "[5]

When Ambassador Gerard left Berlin with a large party of Americans, she pondered going home, but was reassured by promises of protection from her German friends. What's more, she had paid her tuition. But—"Then came the day when I was first to feel the iron grip of Prussianism," which expressed itself in a demand for her to appear with her papers at the local police station. When she got there "a grim-visaged, pompous policeman" said "Ho, another damned Yankee!" but relaxed when he heard that she lived with the Millers. He ordered her to report to the police station once a day and stay in the house between 10 P.M. and 6 A.M. " . . . it nearly made me ill to have to visit that police station each day, and I had to force myself with all my will power. Being thus in the grip of the law, like any felon, was to my soul as bitter as gall to my tongue."⁶

Worse still, on a later occasion when she had let her passport expire, a policeman was rude to her—by this time Therese seemed to regard men's manicures as symbols of Prussian bestiality: "Suddenly he leaned over the desk and shook his manicured finger in my face. 'Well, you listen to me. If we haven't won this war by ten years from now, those brothers of yours will probably be coming over and bombing Berlin from airplanes, *and I hope that the first bomb hits you . . . !*' " She was getting no news from home, and the misinformation and jeers in German papers often reduced her to tears. However, "the feeling against us was rather impersonal, and directed principally against the Government. This fact, coupled with the one that I was under the protection of an exceedingly popular household, made my friends and acquaintances tacitly forget that we were really enemies and, although my mind was troubled, my person was not. I continued to live, to study and to go about socially much as before. . . ."⁷ She was even allowed to travel.

But she did have trouble now and then with some of the young men, like Leutnant von Luben, ". . . whose attentions had by this time become rather alarming. He gave me my cue one day when we were walking alone together, for I refused to be bound by German customs [like having a chaperone]. 'If I'm willing to give you the privilege of walking with me like this,' I said rather sharply, as he tried to put his arm about me, 'you should be gentleman enough not to abuse it.' 'All's fair in love,' he quoted, sententiously. 'And in war,' answered my thoughts." And she had to repulse another young man, crying, "If there was an *American* man here he would smash your face, you beast." The Herr Leutnant's influence proved quite useful, though, in getting all the permissions necessary for Therese to leave Germany in the winter of 1917. "I told him that, if he wanted to win my full forgiveness, he might do so by helping me a little." Indeed, so besotted was he that he defended her to a German official who growled, as he tossed her papers to her, " 'Another damned American going back home to knock us!' That was more than Lieutenant von Luben could stand and he stepped forward with, 'She is

going to do no such thing! I can vouch for the fact that she is a friend
of Germany's, and will tell the truth about us.' "⁸

The American nurse Glenna Lindsley Bigelow was tending a
private patient in his château situated amid Belgian fortifications
when the Germans invaded in 1914. She was a virtual prisoner from
August to November 1914, while the Germans fought through the
Belgian fortifications toward France. ". . . one gets inured to danger
(particularly if one has not so far been hit)," Bigelow wrote on
August 13, 1914, "and after a week of the bombardment, we have
a distinct feeling of annoyance at being disturbed at an unearthly
hour every morning by the screeching and bursting of shells." During
the German occupation, she nursed wounded soldiers hospitalized
at a nearby convent, and tried to avoid controversy with the Prussian
officers billeted at the château. Coming home from the hospital bone
tired, she dined with the Germans in "a veritable playworld of the
Middle Ages with the most beautiful setting . . ." in which the
Prussians were "a vision of shining buttons, polished boots, gleaming
swords and a military salute accompanied by clinking spurs."⁹

Early in September, Bigelow was delighted by "a possibility of
our going to Brussels. Oh, the joy of it! That may find me the means,
through the American Ambassador, of getting back to my beloved
France." But despite a passport from the military governor, their
cavalcade of three automobiles, "packed and jammed full inside and
crowned on the roof with an overhanging cornice of every sort of
bundle," could not get through because of the fighting, and had to
return to Liège, forlorn. Bigelow despaired, particularly with the
news of fighting near Paris. Her occupation was gone, since no more
wounded soldiers were arriving, the fighting having swept past Liège.
She and her Belgian hosts spent their time playing Patience. Their
liberties were more and more curtailed; neighbors were arrested as
spies.

The American consul was not helpful. When she proposed to
escape to Paris, he asked, "In the first place what would you go in,
and in the second, why should you want to go, with Paris surrounded
by 2,000,000 [German] soldiers?" Even when friends invited her to
go with them, he dawdled. "For what other reason," she cogently
inquired, "is an American Consul if he is not to protect his people,

particularly in wartime?"[10] If he wouldn't go to the Germans for a travel permit, she would. And so she did. Her righteous indignation untangled even German red tape and carried her successfully first to England, then to Paris to nurse for the Red Cross; ultimately she joined the American Army Nurse Corps.

     ⚑⚑⚑ *. . . it was a queer twist in the order of my life, that, hunting in all directions for a quiet retreat in which to rest my weary spirit, I should have ended by deliberately sitting myself down on the edge of a battlefield—even though it was on the safe edge—*and stranger still, that there I forgot that my spirit was weary.

                                        —Mildred Aldrich[11]

In France, Mildred Aldrich, startled to find herself living close to battle, reported in a series of books her wartime life in a small village on the Marne. In her early sixties in 1914, Aldrich had retired there after a career as a journalist, manuscript reader, and theatrical critic on both sides of the Atlantic. She began her reports in September 1914, nine days after the Battle of the Marne. The population of her hamlet before mobilization had been twenty-nine; now it was down to thirteen, seven of whom were children. "There is no doctor if one should be so silly as to fall ill. There are no civil authorities to make out a death certificate if one had the bad taste to die—and one can't die informally in France. If anyone should, as far as I can see, he would have to walk to his grave, dig it, and lie down in it himself . . . and I am positive it would lead to a *procès*. The French love lawsuits, you know. No respectable family is ever without one."[12]

By late September engineers had repaired bridges and telegraph wires; the post office had reopened; the newspapers had arrived. The dead were buried; roads were being repaired; and woodcutters were working on the battle-broken trees. But the shops were still closed, and few of those who had fled had returned. ". . . the devastation of the German occupation, with its deliberate and filthy defilement of the houses . . . defies words. . . . The deliberate ingenuity of the nastiness is its most debasing feature. . . . Your imagination, at its most active, cannot do any wrong to the race which in this war seems determined to offend where it cannot terrorize."[13]

Much of the time she lived quietly, with little news of the battle, though she could hear the cannon and, "when the wind was right, the sharp repeating fire of rifles as well as *mitrailleuses* [machine guns] . . . ," could see the trucks going to the front with provisions and the smoke from the battlefield. Although her food was limited, cold was her great enemy: she kept one small fire in the kitchen, and the rest of the house hovered around zero (Celsius). Undaunted, Aldrich refused self-pity: "Don't you imagine that I am a bit down. I am not. I am cold. But, when I think of the discomfort in the hurriedly constructed trenches, where the men are in the water to their ankles, what does my being cold in a house mean? . . . But oh, the monotony and boredom of it! Do you wonder that I want to hibernate?"[14]

Often more interesting than Aldrich's accounts of what was happening around her are her reports of what was going on in her mind. By April 1916, she was wondering, heretically, "if some of the women are not better off than in the days before the war. They do about the same work, only they are not bothered by the men. . . . Here are the women of the class to which I refer working very little harder than in the days before the war. Only, for nearly two years they have had no drinking man to come home at midnight either quarrelsome or sulky; no man's big appetite to cook for; no man to wash for or to mend for. They have lived in absolute peace, gone to bed early to a long, unbroken sleep, and get twenty-five cents a day government aid, plus ten cents for each child. . . . under my breath, I can assure you that there is many a woman of that class a widow to-day who is better off for it, and so are her children. The husband who died 'en héro,' the father dead for his country, is a finer figure in the family life than the living man ever was or could have been."[15] Aldrich here sounded a discordant note in the chorus of praise for the gallantry of French soldiers and the stoic suffering of French women then resounding throughout the American popular press.

Her reflections on war testify to what its depredations can do to the human spirit—including hers. She came to a point where she felt that "if the world cannot stop war, if organized governments cannot arrive at a code of morals which applies to nations the same law of right and wrong which is enforced on individuals, why, the world and humanity must . . . reconcile themselves to the belief that such wars as this are as necessary as surgical operations." She was actually "sorry to feel that our own country is evidently going to avoid a movement which might have been at once healthy and uplifting."[16] America's break with Germany made glorious summer of her winters of discontent: "I feel as if I had never had an ache or a pain, and Time and Age were not. What with the English advance, the Russian Revolution, and Zeppelins tumbling out of the heavens, every day has been just a little more thrilling than the day before."[17]

Like Aldrich, the twenty-nine-year old American Frances W. Huard lived near the Marne. The very prototype of the entrepreneurial American woman, she experienced a series of wartime adventures, with which she regaled readers in one book after another. Married to a French artist who went off to fight, in the summer of 1914 she promptly converted her château into a hospital. The Red Cross sent supplies and an excellent nurse, who trained twenty local volunteers whom Huard had recruited; they hoisted the Red Cross flag, and the wounded began to flow in. About the same time, Huard began to feed and lodge the Belgian refugees streaming by her doors. In fact, the decisive and competent Mme. Huard, it's quite clear, would accomplish whatever needed doing.

A good thing, too, for the village people looked to their chatelaine for decisions. When she learned of fighting at Château-Thierry, seven miles away, she packed her husband's drawings in a trunk, his paintings being too large and heavy to carry. She sealed her own desk with her private papers inside and the American flag outside, with a note asking that her privacy be respected. A message came from her husband, saying to evacuate, head south. Twelve people traveled with her, including one sick woman who had to be transported in a cart pulled by an old lame horse. She herself rode a bicycle. All of them slept in the fields. The Red Cross arm band she wore helped Huard to get her people past checkpoints and barriers.

At Rebais she was ordered to the hospital to work, but after one night the town officials told her to flee. Leaving the nurse to tend the wounded, Huard took the rest of her people onward, the retreating French army surging around them, while Huard looked for a place to stop and wait out the battle until they could return to the château. At a railroad crossing they saw French soldiers preparing to ambush Germans from freight cars. With her binoculars she watched a great battle on ground over which she and her people had passed a few hours before. At one place where they stopped to rest the horses an elegant funeral was being conducted; she thought she ought to warn the people attending of the German approach, so she told an altar boy in a discreet whisper—only to have him shout, *"Vite, vite, M. le Curé! Voilà les Prussiens!"*

Huard rode ahead with one man to Jouy-le-Châtel, south of Paris, to arrange to stay there until they could go back home. But the next morning a soldier was brought in with a terrible wound—and, she learned, he had been wounded only a mile and a half away. So off they set again on a journey of seventy kilometers to Melun, taking wounded soldiers on a cart Huard commandeered. The Germans were actually in sight, firing at them. Huard stopped a British army car at gunpoint and forced its driver to take one of her wounded who needed immediate help to a hospital. When she herself arrived there, she assisted the doctor in the operating room, having falsely assured him that yes, she had seen operations before. Then she spent a day translating for the English.

When she and her party finally got together again, they learned that the Germans were retreating. Huard decided that she and the others must go back to her château immediately behind the French Army, before controls were set up, since they had no papers. They found the countryside ravaged. A couple of French soldiers arrested her as a spy because she was foolish enough to speak a few words of English—and as far as they were concerned any foreign language was German; an officer finally rescued her. Since many of the bridges were blown, she had to take a roundabout course home, seeing horrible sights, piles of dead, hearing stories of torture and rape. One night they slept in the forest at an abandoned hermitage, and mistook horse chestnuts falling on the roof for bullets.

At last she reached home to find her château only a shell of what she had left fourteen days before. Her possessions were looted and destroyed. The Germans had killed her animals, bayoneted her furniture, defecated everywhere, poured two hundred pots of jam into her piano. But a week later she got good news of her husband. And she set about reestablishing her hospital.[18]

The records of women like these, the direction of whose lives the war changed, add immediacy and intensity to the observations of the professional women correspondents who chose, rather than chanced, to see war and war's victims.

Journalists on the Western Front

The military establishment suspects journalists, and periodically tries to do without them. If it must put up with them, it prefers to keep them strictly under control, and to attract their allegiance to the military's point of view. Accordingly in World War I, the military tried first to ban journalists from the front, then permitted them occasional visits on carefully designed itineraries, and—when it had finally to allow them in the trenches—attached them to specific units, in the often-fulfilled hope that the journalists would loyally sympathize with their units. Male journalists, that is.

Male journalists were nuisance enough—but women journalists? Never. The military shut them out from areas under bombardment and categorically refused to accredit them, thereby denying them billeting, transport, and access to military briefings. Only Peggy Hull breached this barrier, and then only after World War I, when she was accredited to report on American troops in Siberia. Hull did go to France during the war, at her own expense, for the *El Paso Times*— but unaccredited by the military. She did publish a series of articles in the Paris edition of the *Chicago Tribune,* the success of which prompted some male journalists to protest against her presence near the front. Neither her popularity with the troops nor the friendship of General Pershing, who had known her when she covered his border skirmishes with Pancho Villa, could save her from their jealousy, or persuade the military to accredit her.[19]

Certainly there were lots of qualified women journalists around.

In the post–Civil War era, women had moved into the offices of family and women's magazines, and had begun to conduct women's departments of newspapers. Gradually they began to comment on politics, labor, and public affairs generally, as well as the social scene. By 1914 they had made their way not only into newsrooms but also into editorial offices.

But women journalists had to dodge and finagle to get to the front. Gertrude Atherton, a well-established novelist and magazine writer, found the military mind "like a steel mask with the key lost." She had to cover her journalistic errands by arguing that she needed to get to the war zone to observe the operations of Le Bienêtre du Blessé, for whom she had promised to do publicity. She worked through friends of friends, squeezing out permissions, sometimes one city at a time. Now and then the French Ministry of War would suggest that perhaps she "might persuade some General to take me closer to the front," or furnish her with a letter asking the local military authorities to show her every civility, or insist that she find an American officer to escort her.[20] Rheta Dorr of the New York *Evening Mail* and the New York *Evening Post* cleverly circumvented restrictions by signing up with the YMCA's entertainment bureau as a lecturer, and making a deal with the director to schedule her wherever her journalistic tasks took her.

Some well-established women writers gave up professional reporting of the war in the face of such difficulties. Sophie Treadwell, a reporter for the San Francisco *Bulletin*, frustrated by repeated refusals to let her get to the front "because you are a woman," went to nurse in a hospital. So did Ellen LaMotte, who wrote for *The Masses*—but her reflections on what she saw produced one of the strongest and most truthful accounts of World War I in her book *The Backwash of War*. Oddly enough, her very retreat from active reporting to hospital duty furnished her both the material and the time for thought without which she could not have produced her remarkable book. "Much ugliness is churned up in the wake of mighty, moving forces, and this is the backwash of war," LaMotte wrote to explain her title. "Many little lives foam up in this backwash, loosened by the sweeping current, and detached from their environment."[21]

Of this backwash, these little lives made "weak, hideous, or repellent" by the war, LaMotte wrote. "There was much talk of home, and much of it was longing, and much of it was pathetic, and much of it was resigned. And always the little, ugly wives, the stupid, ordinary wives, represented home. And the words home and wife were interchangeable and stood for the same thing. . . . You know, they won't let wives come to the Front. Women can come into the War Zone, on various pretexts, but wives cannot. Wives, it appears, are bad for the morale of the Army. They come with their troubles, to talk of how business is failing, of how things are going to the bad at home, because of the war; of how great the struggle, how bitter the trials and the poverty and hardship."[22]

Her most pointed irony she hurled at war's victimization of women. Propaganda always insisted that the Germans raped women, whereas the innocent Allied soldiers were seduced by women, who "cajoled the men till they gave in. . . . Anyway, [these women] are all ruined and not fit for any decent man to mate with, after the war."[23] No wonder the French, British, and American governments all banned LaMotte's book.

But other women journalists persisted as newspaperwomen and correspondents for magazines. Though they rarely sent daily dispatches or described battles, they did report the war from many perspectives and in many places. No one can say how many or who they were. Skimpy and oblique references to them litter the records. "A New York newspaper woman brought tragic word of Serbia [to a Red Cross unit in Budapest]."[24] On a German-sponsored tour for foreign correspondents in 1916 Madeleine Doty ran across "a woman who lives in Germany and writes for the 'New York Journal.' "[25] In the war zone Ruth Wright Kaufman represented the Vigilantes, an organization of writers formed just before the United States declared war to "awaken" Americans to "their duty." The Hearst feature writer Winifred Sweet Black went to Europe in 1917 to report the war. Helen Johns Kirtland worked as staff correspondent and photographer for *Leslie's Weekly*, taking pictures of airplane manufacture and war wreckage, working her way to the Italian front after Caparetto.

Several women correspondents got in trouble. Inez Milholland

Boissevain in 1915 was requested to leave Italy after writing a series of pacifist articles. Carolyn Wilson was arrested in Europe for espionage. Sigrid Schultz, manager of the *Chicago Tribune*'s Berlin office, "incurred the displeasure of the Berlin government [because] she gave utterance to many plain truths about the way the Kaiser was running his end of the war."[26]

Other women besides Schultz held down responsible administrative jobs on newspapers. Consider Alice Rohe, who worked in Rome as correspondent and bureau manager for the United Press, whom Roy Howard described as "the best newspaperman in America who never wore pants." She coped successfully, despite her ignorance of Italian, with such major events as Italy's entrance into the war. She also contributed photographs of Italy at war to *Leslie's Weekly*.[27] Consider Ruth Hale, cofounder of the Lucy Stone League, who in 1917 edited the Paris-based *Chicago Tribune*. As her son speculated, "It must have been a tremendous job to put together a paper in wartime Paris, even a weekly as this was. . . . Given the handicap of the English language with its baffling spelling, the French typographers must have given Mlle Ele a difficult time." Alexander Woollcott, then on the staff of the AEF's *Stars and Stripes*, wrote a friend that Hale "has been far nearer the front than I and can tell you many things I have never seen. . . ."[28]

But perhaps the ultimate example of a woman correspondent's determination to report the war was that of Clara Savage Littledale of *Good Housekeeping*—who spiritedly refused her magazine's orders to return Stateside with the cable "Resigning and remaining," to free-lance and interview political prisoners in Bolshevist Hungary.

Many of the women reporters sent overseas were commissioned by their papers or their magazines, to write from the "woman's angle." Often editors prescribed not only approach but also style. Littledale, asking a friend's opinion of one of her stories, noted that "Mr. Big complained that it didn't have enough 'heart kick.' "[29] Under such pressures some women, like many a male reporter, descended into straight propaganda. Even the suffragist Rheta Childe Dorr of the New York *Evening Mail* bathed in sloppy sentimentality her account of her behind-the-lines tour, deliberately choosing to emphasize her role as a mother. "My letter of credentials to the

French Foreign Office said that I had reported the Russian revolution for my paper and that I was now assigned to France with the view of informing readers in the United States as to participation of the United States troops in war and the political situation of the allied countries in the war." But "I discovered that try as I might to think of armies, strategies and diplomacies, the only thing that vitally concerned me in France was to find out how my son was faring, and in doing so I was finding out the things that other mothers wanted to know about their boys."[30] She gushed about the courageous Frenchwomen, the stalwart American doughboys, the paternal care exercised by the military in keeping the boys pure, and the improvements in the boys' physiques and spirits wrought by the war.

Anna Steese Richardson wrote amusingly but sentimentally for *McCall's* about one of the several "mutinies of the upper deck" which occurred on ships bound for Europe. Women workers, traveling first class while the soldiers went steerage, redeemed their pledge to serve the troops by demanding the destruction of the barriers between decks and improvement in the soldiers' food, raiding their own state-rooms for edibles, and organizing French lessons, boxing matches, and songfests for the men's entertainment. ". . . etiquette on high seas notwithstanding . . . America resents any insinuation that her enlisted men are not the equal of kings, and this goes whether the enlisted man is the son of a multi-millionaire or of a day-laborer."[31]

Other journalists assigned to "women's stories" made the most of them, sending back invaluable records of what women were accomplishing in England and France. Gertrude Atherton, in France for three months in 1916 to study "the war-time work of its women and to make them better known to the women of America," reported from the inside out the war work of both French and American women in France—not the senseless knitting which a contemptuous American government tried to foist on its women, but critical undertakings, like caring for refugees when they overwhelmed the resources and powers of the French authorities, and nursing soldiers and civilians when the French medical system had broken down. But Atherton's eagerness to propel the United States into the war sometimes led her to exaggerate and distort. She insisted, for instance, that munitions work had been good for women—most of whom had before the war "looked on the verge of decline," but now had "high chests and brawny arms . . . ," clear skin, ruddy cheeks, bright eyes. Never sick a day. Men remaining in factories "never dreamed of disobeying those Amazons whose foot the Kaiser of all the Boches had placed on their necks."[32]

Jessica Lozier Payne in a series of letters on "What I Saw in England and France" for the *Brooklyn Eagle* described some of the wartime occupations of British women, particularly those jobs traditionally male. English- and Scotswomen were drill and lathe operators, riveters, hearse drivers, streetlighters, streetcleaners. "It is interesting to see a mason, who two years ago would have scorned to work next to a woman, now co-operating with the Government and teaching a group of girls the cherished tricks of the trade. . . ." In a hospital staffed completely by British women, an amputee praised the women doctors: ". . . they are just splendid, and many of the men ask to be sent here. . . ." But, he complained, the women doctors were too anxious to prevent amputations, whereas in his opinion they might as well lop off the limb "and then you'll get your pension."[33]

Payne and other correspondents also broadened their horizons, reporting not just on women but on what it was like to live in wartime England and France. Corra May White Harris described conditions behind the battle lines for the *Saturday Evening Post*. Inez Irwin, an established writer when she accompanied her journalist husband William Irwin to France in early 1916, wrote stories based on the material she gathered during their prolonged stays in England, Switzerland, France, and Italy. She heard all sorts of anecdotes, like the experience of Eleanor Egan, whose ship was stopped by an Italian submarine when she was crossing from Piraeus to Alexandria. The submarine commander ordered the ship cleared; boats were lowered, some passengers jumped, and others, Egan among them, were pushed by the surge of the crowd into the water, where she swam for some time, avoiding the clutching hands of the drowning. Finally the submarine commander declared that he and his crew were not murderers, and permitted the survivors to reboard the ship—those who were still alive. "I asked E. E. if this terrible experience had affected her nerves. She said not especially, but that for several days, she did not enjoy getting into her bath."[34]

ϠϠϠ *It must be so disappointing to these gentlemen [German spies] to find me vibrating between the German Red Cross, the poor, and plans for feeding German babies. But before I [left] Germany the spies [got] on my nerves.*
                                              —Madeleine Zabriskie Doty[35]

Accounts of life among the Central Powers are scarcer. But two American women journalists, Madeleine Zabriskie Doty and Mary McAuley, described wartime life-styles in Germany.

Doty reported on two trips to Germany in *Short Rations*. A convinced pacifist, she went on to Germany, against the advice of the American embassy, after reporting the Women's International Congress of 1915 in The Hague for the New York *Evening Post*. In Germany "I was seized upon as the missionary seizes the cannibal. . . . My host is a university professor, his wife an American. . . . I am the heathen whose soul must be saved. . . . From the day of my arrival to the moment of my departure, we have but one topic of conversation—Germany's virtues and America's sins." But she found friends among "rebel women, *whose love for the Fatherland is so great that they dare protest* [against the war]!" They met secretly in out-of-the-way places, conscious of being spied upon. "My life in Berlin was a double one. I ate and slept and was unregenerate in one part of town, and really lived only when I escaped from 'respectability,' and, strange contradiction of terms, became—a 'criminal' fighting for peace!"[36]

On a second trip to Germany, about a year later, Doty, in the face of appalling "tales of hunger and imprisonment, the fate of all foreigners in Germany,"[37] destroyed all her papers except her credentials from the *Chicago Tribune*, since that paper was tolerated in Germany, while her other paper, the *New York Tribune*, was despised. She carried with her also $500 for German war orphans and starving babies, and the promise of more to come, given her by the New York Church Peace Union.

In Hamburg she found women, children, and old people suffering, but concluded that the Allies could not conquer by starving out Germany, as some hoped, since rich and powerful Germans continued to live well. Doty saw German women at hard labor all around her, a phenomenon which she interpreted differently from the American women correspondents enthusing over British and French women in traditionally male jobs. German women were cleaning sewers, relaying railroad tracks, acting as subway train starters, and "in the munitions factories, working for about sixty-two percent of men's pay."[38] What many an American woman correspondent praised as the patriotism of British and French women, Doty called the exploitation of German women. Her terminology often reflects the influence of her socialist friends on her perceptions.

Ignorant of the language and therefore dependent for information on those friends, Doty saw her own passionate desire for peace mirrored all around her. "Everywhere people are signing a petition for peace, on the basis of *status quo* before the war." Her pacifist informants quoted unwilling soldiers, like one who said: "Thank God, I'm near-sighted. Naturally, I will never kill any one, and my failure to land a bullet may be mistaken for bad eyesight. . . ."[39] At a peace meeting in Munich, one of her German friends, already under surveillance because of her plea to women not to have children unless men would guarantee that they would not be cannon fodder (shades of *Lysistrata*), defied the authorities by speaking out again. Doty echoed this defiance by a secret and illegal trip to see the veteran peace fighter Clara Zetkin. "In the morning I might be arrested, but for the moment I didn't care. It had been splendid to see what I had seen—Germany's awakening. If all this passionate energy breaks through Prussian organization, what a Germany it will be."[40]

🏵🏵🏵 *Whatever is printed in the German newspapers is the truth as far as it goes, but not everything that is known is printed.*
—Mary Ethel McAuley[41]

Mary McAuley, a columnist for the *Pittsburgh Dispatch*, who stayed longer and later in Germany than Doty, reported on *Germany*

in War Time: What an American Girl Saw and Heard. McAuley, on
the surface (only) an engaging flibbertigibbet, was determined to give
Americans all the information she could about conditions in Germany. She brought to this task an objectivity denied to the ideological
Doty—as well as a knowledge of the German language. Doty concerned herself with cosmic issues; McAuley recorded the details of
daily life.

McAuley went to Germany as an art student (though in her book
she almost never mentioned art), in October 1915; she stayed on well
after the United States and Germany were at war. She lived in Berlin,
which she described as a city of soldiers. "One day on the street car
I heard a common German soldier say, 'What difference does it make
to us common people whether Germany wins the war or not, in these
three years we folks have lost everything.' But every German soldier
is willing to do his duty. . . . To believe that Germany has exhausted
her supply of men is a mistake. Personally, I know lots of young
Germans that have never been drafted."[42]

Like Doty, she felt for "The poor German working women! No
one in all the war has suffered like these poor creatures. Their men
have been taken from them, they are paid only a few pfennigs a day
by the government, and now they must work, work like a man, work
like a horse. . . . Most of the women seem to like the familiarity
which working on the streets brings them, and they find it much
more exciting than doing housework at home."[43] German women,
McAuley alleged, were even being drafted for the munitions factories.

McAuley described poignantly the state to which the rationing
of household linens and clothes had reduced German women: "The
[ration] ticket is very hard on girls about to be married, as a German
girl must furnish the house and have at least two dozen sets of sheets
and pillow cases and about one hundred towels. As one person can
get only two sheets a year on the ticket, it would at that rate take a
girl twelve years before she could be properly married. So the scheming of getting things without a ticket was as great as the scheming
of getting food without a card."[44]

Worse still was the officially advocated "rational dress": "They
dug up a lot of fashion plates from the styles fifty years back, and
had fashion plates printed from them and model dresses made, and

they tried to convince the modern German girl that this was what she should wear. . . . the German girls I know said that they would die before they would wear them. . . . a woman's patriotism ceases where styles are concerned. . . . All the German women will be glad when they can have Paris fashions again, and most German men try to dress like Englishmen."[45]

Most of the German people, in McAuley's observation, did not hate Americans—although she did not pretend to speak for "the high officials and the big *Militär*." The boarding house maid, for instance, astonished McAuley by asking if America was in the war, and if so, on which side. The maid's reaction: "*Donnerwetter*, we have so many enemies, I can't keep track of them. But I want to go to America, and I am going there after the war." Understandably, McAuley entertained mixed emotions: "Of course one has the feeling that one is in an enemy's land when one has to go to the police every week, and it did get on my nerves. And yet, every one was nice to me, and I was there five months after the break [between the United States and Germany]."[46]

McAuley interspersed her observations about wartime life in Germany with accounts of her own adventures. Her willingness to adapt to German customs and the country's wartime rules and regulations, she said, left her free to live in a reasonably relaxed way, even to speak casually and openly about her situation. When a youngster of thirteen politely solicited a donation for the families of German submariners, she asked: " 'Why should I give to this? I am a *feindliche Ausländerin* [an enemy foreigner] and if I give you any money it encourages you Germans to go on sinking American ships. I must save my money for the wives and the children of the men who have lost their lives by the U-boats.' The boy blushed deeply. 'That is true,' he said. 'I beg your pardon. I feel for those people too. And if you will allow me I would like to donate something for your charity,' and the little fellow pulled a mark out of his pocket and handed it to me."[47]

On a Christmas 1916 trip to Hamburg McAuley and another American woman talked their way onto the ferry in the harbor, even though they knew that "strangers are absolutely forbidden near the docks, and foreigners poking around are arrested." But a ferry ride would be such fun, and besides, they would come right back without leaving the ferry on the other side. ". . . the old man [the ticket seller] escorted us to the ferry and talked to us until the boat was ready to start. He said that night and day 15,000 men were employed on the docks, and that besides all the men coming over on the boats many more came over through a tunnel that ran under the water. He said that they were building many boats, and that the 'Bismarck' would be the largest boat afloat—55,000 tons—and that the 'Tirpitz' would be 32,000 tons, and that so far during the war there had been made a total tonnage of new boats of 740,000 tons and that 100,000 tons were under construction." A young boy working on the ferry told the young women: ". . . the old boss on the docks doesn't allow foreigners out here. But I suppose he saw that you were girls and you wouldn't know much. We have got to be careful of spies. . . . I can tell you nothing gets by me. I can see you two are harmless.' "[48] So much for German efficiency.

McAuley left Germany July 1, 1917. The United States government seized her book upon publication. Although today it reads as an unvarnished account, even potentially useful in its detail to the American government, it could not survive in the hysterical America of 1918, when people saw German spies everywhere, and banished the German language from the classrooms of their schools and universities.[49]

In that fevered atmosphere, any writer who questioned atrocity stories or deviated from the line laid down by the virulent propagandists might subject herself (or himself) to the accusation of being pro-German. Margaret Deland, who wanted nothing so much as to rouse America to join the Allies, was so accused, largely because of the inevitable time lapse between her writing and the publication of one of her articles. The alarm she sought to raise about the parlous condition of the Allies *before* the entry into the war of the United States read as defeatism *afterward*.[50]

Among the American women journalists who successfully evaded restriction to "women's stories" by the breadth of their reporting was Eunice Tietjens, who simply disregarded her editor's mechanical assumption that women write only about women's affairs. Tietjens, who had worked for the magazine *Poetry*, maneuvered her way to France as war correspondent for the *Chicago Daily News*, whose managing editor "said, as though it settled the matter, 'We have never had a woman correspondent.' 'No,' I said, 'but never before has the heart of every woman in the United States been in France.' . . . I wrote of the American soldiers on leave and in hospital, the French civilian population, refugees and children, color stories about war-time Paris. . . . I never was really good at the strictly women's stories I was supposed to write. In particular there was one story about what became of all the socks knitted by the women at home which I was told in Chicago to write, but which I never could bring myself to do. . . . Mowrer [her bureau chief] understood this perfectly and never pressed me. Indeed he left me almost entirely to find my own stories. . . ."[51]

Wherever she went in search of a story, she found ways to help, organizing a toy drive for 10,000 French children, assisting an over-burdened nurse's aide, scavenging bread, cheese, and *vin ordinaire* for exhausted soldiers in a bombed-out village. Once, when she was asked to accompany a sick nurse to the rear, her efforts were frustrated: "Periodically I would alight, open the door at the back, and ask her if there was anything I could do for her; but I was always met with such a stream of savage profanity and a request to 'get the hell out of here!' that I could only retreat."[52] In October, 1918, ordered home by her paper as the war neared its end, Tietjens instead signed up with the Red Cross.

But through the paper she arranged a final, and disastrous, trip to the front. Accompanied by a French friend, Mlle. de la Vallette; an American officer's wife; Elizabeth Shepley Sergeant, who wrote for *The New Republic* and also worked for the Red Cross information section; and [Miss] Cecil Dorrian, correspondent for the *Newark Evening News;* and escorted by a French lieutenant, Tietjens visited a battlefield near Rheims. Ignoring the lieutenant's cautions, Mlle. de la Vallette picked up a hand grenade, which exploded. Before Tietjens's eyes, her friend was disemboweled, the French lieutenant's arm blown off, and Sergeant so severely wounded in the legs that she had to spend the next two years in hospitals.

(The miracle, what with the number of curiosity seekers visiting the front, was that this sort of accident did not occur more frequently.

Mary Dexter blithely reported finding a hand grenade in No Man's Land: "It is probably not exploded, but I have tied it up in a cushion, in my tool box, and am going to see if I can get it démonté [defused] by some artilleryman. I should like to keep it, having found it myself just there. . . . I have the percussion fuse of a French 75—which we found on an old dump heap among a lot of empty shells. But I'm afraid it is still explosive, and that I shan't be able to keep it."[53])

Sergeant herself wrote a journal of her reflections during her slow recovery, for part of which she was treated in military hospitals—the record of a professional writer, from a patient's point of view. Alone among so many soldiers, she felt out of place, solitary and superfluous: "Perhaps I am the only woman in the world." Often a feeling of unreality afflicted her: "Can it be that only forty or fifty miles from here people are discussing, over partridge and *fraise des bois*, whether it would be better for Foch to accept an armistice or to push the Germans to a complete *débâcle*? . . . Can it be that in Paris I, too, believed in the end of the war?"[54]

> ✄✄✄ *I could claim . . . that I wanted to see this war so that I could write against war; that I was flaming with indignation; that as a mother I felt the brutal and wanton waste of sons, and that at least one other mother should see this war and tell the truth about it. But it would not be true. Not then. I had at that time no hatred of war, only a great interest and a great curiosity. All my suppressed sense of adventure, my desire to discover what physical courage I had, my instincts as a writer, had been aroused by what was going on in Europe.*
> —Mary Roberts Rinehart[55]

Of all the women who reported professionally in wartime Europe, Mary Roberts Rinehart has left the most startling record. In late 1914 Rinehart, already a best-selling writer, defied rumors that all war correspondents near the Allied front were to be thrown in jail and arranged with the *Saturday Evening Post* to go to Europe as their correspondent. No one but her thought she would get farther than London. But she confidently took along "a full equipment for the trenches," including a fur coat. "I rather imagine that I am the only woman in the world for whom the Curtis Publishing Company, as an organization, ever purchased a fur coat."[56] (What apparently troubled the *Saturday Evening Post* more, though, was that she eventually returned $1,200 in expense-account money, and they had no bookkeeping procedure to accept it.)

Within a week of her arrival in England, working through the Belgian Red Cross and arguing that "Of invaded Belgium we knew a great deal; of the small Belgian army, of the Belgian refugees pushed ahead of the army and still trying to subsist behind the Allied lines, we knew nothing," Rinehart persuaded the Belgians to credential her—at a time when access was being denied to all other correspondents of neutral nations, regardless of gender.[57]

So she set out, "elegantly attired in a black taffeta dress under the fur coat, carrying roses, wearing a money belt around my waist," and equipped with a trench periscope: "A long square arrangement of khaki-colored tin, with reflecting mirrors so that one might peer over the parapet of the trench and not be killed. Never did I see one in use, but London shop windows were filled with them, and unlucky soldiers were laden with them as they started for the war."[58]

Arriving in Dunkirk only sixteen days after she left America, she spent each night for the next three weeks at the Belgian front. "I am still somewhat puzzled by the ease with which I got about, and by the privilege later of getting to both British and French fronts. There is no doubt that it had been arranged for me to secure all possible facts, and the Belgian purpose was clear enough. But later on I was to believe that having escaped the network in London or Paris [by her ploy of getting Belgian accreditation through the Belgian Red Cross] my presence at the front was largely overlooked." She owed a great deal, she felt, to a mysterious man who helped her interpret what she saw. "I would go to him after a series of excursions, into the trenches, into shelled towns, once even into No Man's Land, and he would check over my notes. After two months of sporadic but expert explanation, I began to know a great deal about the war. But I knew nothing about him."[59]

Every night a staff car with a Belgian officer would come for her, drive without lights as near the trenches as advisable; then they would go forward on foot, stumbling over communication wires and shell craters, through ruined towns and cemeteries torn up by shells as the enemy fired at Belgian observers in church steeples. "If the night was quiet one kept on to the trenches, warned in advance of their nearness by the odors. Not only the odors of death, but the odors inevitable when men are confined in wet and miserable ditches for days and weeks. . . . these men who had done nothing to deserve it were now living lower than the beasts. . . . Sometimes there would be shelling, and I would have to turn back. Once I sat in the car and watched a little village which was our destination being altered as to skyline by one explosion after another. Again I went into a shelled town, to have a final shell drop at the end of the street and blow to pieces an old woman, the sole inhabitant left, as she was bending over her stove."[60]

One night she went into No Man's Land, through bodies afloat in the water with which the Belgians had flooded the country, with a group of male correspondents brought up for the occasion. "I was not, I think, greatly popular. It annoyed them to realize that I was there for an indefinite stay, and I did not blame them." In rain, wind, and dark, they walked a mile parallel to the German trenches only a thousand feet away, fully exposed when the moon came out, to a ruined church tower where an observer was stationed. They were instructed if a flare went up to hold still; otherwise the Germans would fire. At the church they could see the sandbags which made the German parapet; down the line rifle firing had begun. "This was the first official trip into No Man's Land allowed to any correspondents by the Allies, and as the men represented many newspapers, including the Scandinavian, the story was widely reported. But I have yet to learn that any one of them reported that a woman had accompanied them!"[61]

After a quick trip back to England to interview Queen Mary, Rinehart encountered difficulties in returning to the Continent, for in the interim new restrictions had been put on travel, the Germans had announced a new submarine policy under which any boat leaving the coast of England was to be sunk, and the fear of spies was rampant, with women particularly suspect. Her Belgian sponsors expected her at Calais, but at Folkestone Rinehart was told that the

Calais boat would take no passengers that night. Suffering from flu but desperate, she sneaked aboard the Calais boat, found an empty cabin, and dozed the night away in the dark; in the morning, undetected, she walked off the boat, only to find Calais under military law. "It required twenty-four hours of intensive explanation to get me out of Calais, and I do not yet know how the officer sent to meet me engineered it. I rather think that those Frenchmen found a little humor in the situation. I had undeniably put something into the eye of the British. . . . A year or two later I told that story to a British admiral, and he was divided between astonishment and alarm."[62]

Back at the front, this time with the French, Rinehart interviewed General Foch, who showed her maps and explained the Battle of the Marne. Next, in the British zone, "in the early dawn I would have coffee and rolls, with a thin curl of butter. Then a staff car would pick me up, whirl me hither and yon. One moment I was inspecting an anti-aircraft battery. . . . Again I would be in dressing stations, and for the third time I found myself one day in Ypres, still under fire. . . . At one place I stopped to talk to Canadians, at another to the East Indians, shivering and cold, and unhappy in a warfare they did not understand."[63]

Rinehart had scored a scoop. But the experience had changed her thinking: "I had now a new and different viewpoint as to the war. Not only did I hate war, with a terrible hatred; but I was dissatisfied with my own position as an observer. The place of a woman in war is service, and what had I done? A bit of work here and there, sitting by the dying, lending a hand with dressings. What was that?"[64] An interesting commentary on Rinehart's conditioning into the ideal of woman as nurturer. Despite the brilliance of her reportorial feat, Rinehart never tried to return to the front, undertaking instead such womanly tasks as surveying conditions in French hospitals and, at the behest of the United States government, writing stories to tell families how their sons were trained into soldiers.

Reporting the Russian Revolution

▨▨▨ *I saw the world has been turned upside down. The cooks and waiters had become the aristocrats; the lawyers, bankers, and professors, the riff-raff.*
                                        —Madeleine Zabriskie Doty[65]

The revolution in Russia which in March 1917 overthrew the tsarist regime did indeed turn the world upside down.[66] Russian society had come apart; bonds of trust and confidence had disintegrated; clashing factions plotted to control events and govern the country. For months they couldn't. The Provisional Government based on a shaky coalition of parties in the Duma (the Russian parliament) tottered along, struggling against impossible odds to keep the country at war with the Central Powers, long after the people's will to war was sapped. The power and authority of the Provisional Government were challenged by the Petrograd Soviet of Workers and Soldiers, representing an assortment of socialist factions, including the Bolsheviks. In November 1917, the Bolsheviks seized power, promising bread, land, and peace. Soon thereafter, in the face of the panicky opposition of the other Allies, the Bolsheviks took Russia out of World War I. They still had a long struggle ahead of them to consolidate their power.

Revolutionary groups were still battling when four American women journalists appeared on the scene in the spring, summer, and winter of 1917. The four, often at odds in their assumptions and conclusions, but all professionals, sought the telling story and the illuminating interview. They wanted to see for themselves, and they traveled widely in Russia interviewing revolutionary leaders and reactionaries, aristocrats, businessmen, professionals, rich people and poor, generals and enlisted troops. They dodged bullets in unpredictable street battles and went to the front with the all-woman Battalion of Death. In Russia they, like male journalists, faced well-nigh insuperable difficulties in relaying their reports to the States; under these conditions, they—like John Reed—turned to writing books as a means of reporting and interpreting the revolution to the American public.

Rheta Childe Dorr had cut a wide swath as post-office worker, insurance underwriter, writer of fiction and verse, reformer, and journalist. Her colorful and adventurous career had been built on public-relations work for the suffragist movement and investigations of the conditions under which women worked: she herself had labored as laundress, seamstress, and factory hand in a sweatshop to obtain information. But in 1916 she had become a Republican, increasingly scorning pacifists and reformers. In 1917 she was reporting for the New York *Daily Mail*. The instant she heard about the Russian Revolution, she "caught hold of the city editor's arm and said: 'I'm going. I'm going to Russia.' . . . Nobody else was so well fitted for the job. I had been there twice, I had followed the revolutionary movement for ten years, and I could write about it now against a background of knowledge and experience."[67] She lived in Russia from the end of May until the end of August. She published her book, *Inside the Russian Revolution*, in 1917.

Bessie Beatty, war correspondent of the San Francisco *Bulletin*, set out for Russia almost immediately after the overthrow of the tsar on her two-month trip, which culminated in twelve days on the Trans-Siberian Express. For more than seven months she lived, breathed, and wrote about the revolution, using Petrograd as her base, ranging far into the countryside. On one trip, for instance, with a Miss Smith, an expert in peasant art who spoke Russian, she went to Moscow, from there to Nizhni Novgorod by rail, then up the Volga in a river steamer. She left Russia in January 1918 amid the long-drawn-out struggle between the Bolsheviks and their opponents, on one of the last trains to pass safely through war-torn Finland. In 1919 she published *The Red Heart of Russia*.[68]

Louise Bryant sailed for Russia by way of Stockholm in mid-August of 1917 with her husband, John Reed. Born in 1885, Bryant had left the husband of an early marriage to go to New York City, where she participated in the intellectual ferment of Greenwich Village. For her trip to Russia she was accredited by the Bell Syndicate (which had earlier sent her to Paris); by *Metropolitan* magazine; and by *Seven Arts* and *Every Week*.[69] She left Russia with Beatty in early

1918, though she was to return in 1920 and again in 1922. She published the observations garnered during her first visit in *Six Red Months in Russia*, issued in October 1918.[70] By 1923 she was a top writer for Hearst.

Madeleine Zabriskie Doty, a lawyer by training, had built a career as a writer and social reformer with particular interests in prison conditions, women's suffrage, and the peace movement. She helped form the Women's Peace Party in 1914, and was a delegate to the International Congress for Women at The Hague in 1915, reporting it for the New York *Evening Post*. In 1917 she had published her book *Short Rations: Experiences of an American Woman in Germany*, in which she described two wartime trips through Europe. A year later on a trip for *Good Housekeeping* to survey the conditions of women throughout the world, "the Russian revolution . . . descended upon me." The situation was still wildly in flux—a "maelstrom. . . . Russia had swung clean out of the Twentieth Century." But she found it all "thrillingly interesting. You could not be bored. Every day the Bolsheviki issued some new decree. One day all titles were abolished, the next judges and lawyers were eliminated. . . . I confess to a wicked delight on that occasion. I am a lawyer and know how little justice there often is in the law." In such a world she could only disregard her editor's instructions to interview the czarina: "To associate with the Czarina in Russia was like talking to a member of the I.W.W. on Rockefeller's front lawn." Her book, *Behind the Battle Line, Around the World in 1918*, appeared that year.[71]

All these women understood the horrors of the tsarist regime the Russian Revolution displaced. Some of them thought the revolution a disaster, while others ardently supported it. Their reports, supplying a substantial portion of the contemporary information available to the American public, reflected their individual biases.

Louise Bryant, with a fiery radical of a husband, admiring the good intentions she saw manifested, elated by glimpses of possibilities, more and more identified with the revolution. Her passion sometimes made her credulous to the point of euphoria. "I who saw the dawn of a new world," she exulted in her introduction to *Six Red Months*, "feel as one who went forth to gather pebbles and found pearls. . . . Socialism is here, whether we like it or not—just as woman suffrage is here. . . . In Russia the socialist state is an accomplished fact. . . . if it must fail because it is premature, it is nevertheless real."[72]

Madeleine Doty, sensitive to the excitement of the situation, but with a briefer experience of Russia and more skimpy evidence, stood farther back from events. She recognized that shifts in power did not bring spiritual regeneration or political sophistication: ". . . each group assumed the character and faults of its predecessor." Though she found it hard to judge the revolution, one thing was apparent: ". . . in a *bloody* revolution . . . everything fine gets pushed to the wall. . . . The working class . . . became dictators. They ruled not by the vote, but by force. They pulled existence down to the conditions of the poorest workingman." But in the long run, she concluded, Russians were democrats with no taint of German militarism. "It is with them America belongs."[73]

Bessie Beatty, who stayed longest in Russia, strikes the modern reader as the most professional of the four in her reportage. She breathed the heady air of revolution without losing her balance. She saw that the overthrow of the tsar was "beautifully logical, gloriously unanimous,"[74] but she regretfully observed the clefts among classes, the manacles of ignorance and inexperience in governing, the obduracy of the true believers. She remained a witness—sympathetic, but always apart.

Rheta Childe Dorr? Well, at fifty-one she had come a long way from her early life as a reformer and radical. She listened more than the others to factory owners and aristocrats, she had practical experience which cast doubt on the possibility of solving problems by committee, and she interpreted her observations more skeptically. "I went to Russia," she wrote, "a socialist by conviction, an ardent sympathizer with revolution, having known personally some of the brave men and women who suffered imprisonment and exile after the failure of the uprising in 1905–6. I returned from Russia with the very clear conviction that the world will have to wait awhile before it can establish any cooperative millenniums, or before it can safely hand over the work of government to the man in the street."[75]

But, she insisted, she had faith in the future of the Russian people. Given time and empty bellies, they would opt for "a sane, practical democracy," to which the United States would show the way. Russia urgently needed, she said, plumbers and moving pictures. "Another thing Russia needs is the soda fountain. A cold soft drink in summer and a hot chocolate in winter . . . would do more to take Ivan's mind off moonshining vodka than all the laws in the world." (Why can't the Russians be more like US?) But if these frivolous recommendations reflect more of the traveler's longing for home than of sense, Dorr was nonetheless no fool. Grasping the danger of tyranny at the heart of anarchy, she ended: ". . . I am just as much of a socialist as when I went to Russia . . . and just as little of an anarchist."[76]

Living on short rations, in dirt and danger, the women reporters shared a keen sense of the ludicrous. They passed around stories about the commonplace street-robberies. Bryant told of robbers who let an American keep his money because they "decided that it was unsportsmanlike to hold up a man who could not speak the language. So one of them said: 'Well, go along, old fellow; we will get another one.' "[77] Doty described another holdup man who returned a ruble to his victim for carfare, instructing her, "If any soldiers start to rob you again just tell them that Comrade So-and-so has already robbed you, but has left you a rouble to get home with." And Doty learned to fend off trouble: "Often I was on the street until midnight, but no one molested me; I had only to smile and say 'Amerikanski Bolshevik Tavarish' (American Bolshevik Comrade) to have a hundred hands stretched out in aid. . . ."[78]

The women reporters made their personal arrangements casually, as best they could, living in a hotel near the center of the action, or with a working-class family: "When you are under a working class government," Doty pronounced, "live like the workers."[79] Bryant ate many of her meals "in the great mess hall [of Smolny Institute, Bolshevik Headquarters, where Trotsky had his office] . . . with the soldiers. There were long, rough wooden tables and wooden benches and a great air of friendliness pervaded everywhere. You were always welcome at Smolny if you were poor and you were hungry. We ate with wooden spoons, the kind the Russian soldiers carry in their big boots, and all we had to eat was cabbage soup and black bread. . . . 'So you are an American, Tavarishe, well, how does it go now in America?' they would say to me."[80]

Most of their energy the women correspondents devoted to strenuous efforts at finding out what was happening, reporting it, and assessing its effects. No one of them rivaled John Reed in his classic analysis of the political intricacies, chronological succession, and factional subtleties of the Russian Revolution. But time and again they sketched unforgettable scenes, like Doty's riveting account of the conditions surrounding the negotiations for the treaty of Brest-Litovsk. They picked out incidents that illumined the actualities of the revolution, like Beatty's account of helping to translate the Bolshevik decree of peace: "Here was this new government of the People's Commissaries preparing a document that they confidently hoped would revolutionize the status of the struggling world, and there was no one to translate it but a Lett who had not been to bed for three days, and an American war correspondent [Beatty herself]."[81] Their style, instinct with telling details, immediate in its observations, carried the impact of primitive painting.

They lived in the thick of the events they wrote about. Beatty woke one morning at 5 A.M. to knocking and looked out on a sea of cutlasses. No one knew what was happening: the women reporters feared a bloodbath of Russians killing Russians in an effort by the Provisional Government to put down the radicals. But as it turned out, Beatty wrote, the troops "had taken things into their own hands and were settling them in their own way. They were using the new Russian method of liquidation—they were fraternizing. . . . The soldiers turned the bloody civil war into a fiasco."[82]

In just as human terms, catching the naïveté of the participants and the ironies of the situation, Bryant reported the successful Bolshevik attack of November 1917 on the Winter Palace, the seat of the Provisional Government. Bryant and Reed found the Winter Palace defended by 1,500 Junkers, and about 200 women troops, equipped with little ammunition, no food. "For three hours we were there," wrote Bryant. "I shall never forget those poor, uncomfortable, unhappy boys [the Junkers]. They had been reared and trained in officers' schools, and now they found themselves without a court,

without a Tsar, without all the traditions they believed in. The Mi-
liukov government was bad enough, the Provisional government was
worse and now this terrible proletarian dictatorship. . . . It was too
much; they couldn't stand it."[83] While they awaited the Bolshevik
attack, the Junkers asked questions about the United States, and
exchanged keepsakes with Bryant. The women soldiers were building
a barricade out of firewood. Now and then a shot caused wild
confusion.

Beatty arrived with a truckload of sailors, who had picked her
up on the way: "Two strong hands came over the side to pull me
up," Beatty wrote, "and two sailors sitting on a board across the
body of the truck arose to give us their seats. . . . [But] they decided
that this exposed position would be too dangerous for women. The
Cossack lad in the shaggy cape spread some proclamations on the
floor of the car. 'Sit here,' he said, 'and when the shooting begins
you can lie flat on your backs and keep your heads low.' "[84]

In the crowd around the Winter Palace, Beatty reported, "were
many of the men and women who had been the firebrands of
Russia . . . who were quietly walking forth to oppose themselves
unarmed to the force of these new revolutionists [Bolsheviks] who,
to their way of thinking, were murdering the cause of Russian freedom for which most of them had suffered years of imprisonment and
the unspeakable hardships of exile in Siberia." The Americans
watched Bolshevik rifle shots break the glass of the Winter Palace—
then its quick surrender. "The attacking force had gone about its
work, determined to take the palace, but to take it with as little
bloodshed as possible, and in the lulls between storms they had made
frequent attempts to break the resistance by fraternization. None of
the defenders had been killed, but six of the soldiers who had fought
in the open square had paid with their lives for their revolutionary
ardor. . . ."[85]

Beatty captured the instability of the situation and its extraordinary spirit when she reported the story she later heard from the
women soldiers defending the Winter Palace: "As they marched them
away in the dark, some of the [Bolshevik] men . . . took [the women]
by the arms and shook them, shouting: 'Why do you fight us? Why
do you go against your own class? You are working-women. Why

do you fight with the bourgeoisie and the counter-revolutionists?' So effective was their propaganda that then, for the first time, a class breach was made in the ranks of the women soldiers, and some of them went over to the radicals. . . ."[86]

Meanwhile inside the Winter Palace, the Junkers were being disarmed, given their freedom. "They looked relieved that it was all over," Bryant reported; "they had forgotten about the 'one bullet' they were keeping for themselves."[87]

Repeatedly the women correspondents watched riots erupt, came under gunfire, reported warfare. Doty one midnight heard gunfire up ahead and was told by her sleigh driver that soldiers were looting the tsar's wine cellar. Next morning she learned of their orgy, in which "tempers rose higher and higher and a small battle ensued. In the end the hose of a fire engine was turned on, all the bottles in the wine cellar were smashed, and the place flooded. Three soldiers were drowned in the wine, and between twenty and thirty killed and many wounded. But with daylight order came and shame and re-pentance. The Russian is always very repentant. He may murder a man, but afterwards he will feed and clothe the child of the man he has murdered."[88]

"I will never forget the first time I saw the [Bolshevik] Red Guards going out to battle," wrote Bryant. "A cruel wind swept the wide streets and hurled the snow against the bleak buildings. It was 25 degrees below zero; I felt ill with cold under my fur coat. And there they came, an amazing, inspired mass in thin, tattered coats and their pinched white faces—thousands and thousands of them! The Cossacks were marching on Petrograd and Petrograd rose to repel them. They came pouring out of the factories in a mighty, spontaneous *people's army*—men, women and children. I saw boys in that army not over ten years of age." Bryant was reminded of Washington's derelict army at Valley Forge. "I wish every one in America could have seen that army as I saw it—all out of step, in odds and ends of clothing, with all sorts of old-fashioned fighting implements—some only armed with spades. . . . All of them expected to die. Suddenly they broke into a wailing, melancholy revolutionary song. . . . they were so unused to warfare that they forgot to fire off their guns. But they did not know the meaning of defeat. When one line was mowed down another took its place. Women ran straight into the fire without any weapons at all. . . . The Cossacks seemed to be superstitious about it. They began to retreat. The retreat grew into a rout. They abandoned their artillery, their fine horses, they ran back miles. . . ."[89]

Besides riots and battles the journalists reported political meetings and maneuvers; the daily life of the Russian people caught in the maelstrom; the functioning—and failure to function—of the courts, the farms, the factories. They lived amid contrasts and contradictions, and recorded them all.

In Moscow, taking a night walk, Bryant watched soldiers digging a "brotherhood grave" in front of the Kremlin for 500 "martyrs of the revolution," while women cut and sewed red banners. The next morning the Executive Committee of the Soviet invited her to march with them while ". . . young giants of soldiers wearing towering grey chapkies bore the rough wooden coffins, which were stained red as if in blood. After them came girls with shawls over their heads and round peasant faces, holding large wreaths of artificial flowers that rattled metallically as they walked. Then there were bent old men and bent old women and little children."[90]

That night Bryant was invited to dinner by a family of merchants turned speculators. All three of the sons had bribed their way out of the military and were conducting illegal businesses. "The warmth and light of the room stunned me after the thin bitterness of the Red Square. . . . while people starved just around the corner, they had an abundance of everything. And they were charming and cultured and very pleasant to their friends. . . ."[91] Meanwhile they laughed at the plight of the soldiers at the front, and spoke in favor of a German invasion, which they preferred to the dominance of the Bolsheviks.

     "There is a Turkish saying," said Marya, "that it is no good for the world to be wide if my shoes are too narrow"; and the women say: "It is no good for the government to be Socialist if the queues grow longer every day."

                             —Bessie Beatty[92]

Whether they leaned more to admiration or to revulsion, the American women acutely recognized the many characteristics and forces arbitrating against efforts to establish a new order: the inability of the politically inexperienced populace to compromise; their costly lack of managerial experience; their disagreement about whether or not to continue the war.

Beatty, heading one of her chapters "On the Rocks of Uncompromise," observed: "Each man translated revolution into the terms of his own life. . . . Revolution was to every man the sum of his desires."[93] And Bryant described clashes in the Constituent Assembly, where men coming straight from the trenches, the fields, and the factories voiced their own hopes and fears. A soldier, in the first speech of his life, cried: " *'I come from the place where men are digging their graves and calling them trenches! . . . We are forgotten while you sit here and discuss politics! . . .'* Then the peasants would get up and plead for their land. . . . *If it was not given to them now they would go out and take it.* And the factory workers told of the sabotage of the bourgeoisie, how they were ruining the delicate machinery so that the workmen could not run the factories; they were shutting down the mills so they would starve. . . ."[94]

The revolutionaries lacked enough experienced people to operate the government, the factories, the transportation system. The revolution transferred power from the tyrannical but experienced officer corps to unpracticed soldier committees, throwing the army into chaos. From inside Russia, it looked as if whichever group temporarily prevailed, its officials failed to run the country.

Dorr, vibrating between incredulity and indignation, recorded incident after incident of disastrous inefficiency. An engineer and a stoker quarreled, stopped their train, and fought. Authority finally arrived, arrested one of them, unhitched the engine as evidence, and sent it back to Moscow. "The train all this time, with its hundreds of passengers, stood on the tracks waiting for a new engine and crew, and if it was not run into and wrecked it was because it was lucky." In every region to which she traveled, in every aspect of life, Dorr found irresponsibility, ignorance, civil disorder, chaos. "The death penalty having been abolished, and the police force having been reduced to an absurdity, murder has been made a safe and pleasant diversion."[95]

Revolutionary theories about government by the workers and peasants meant government by committees—and more confusion, more disorder. After the Provisional Government ordered committee regulation of the army, election of officers by soldiers, and the limitation of the death penalty to desertion under fire, the murder of officers became common. Soldiers' committees decided which orders to obey. Desertions became epidemic. Idle soldiers in Petrograd and Moscow harassed the populace.

Civilian undertakings as well were run by committees elected, in Dorr's observation, for their political views: no one respected them, no one would accept their orders, yet no decision could be taken without their consent. Men in hospitals refused medication until they had consulted the elected committee. Dorr, the erstwhile labor reformer, was horrified by the egocentric and inconsistent performance of labor committees: ". . . in no instance of which I could learn," she wrote, ". . . have they used their great opportunity wisely or unselfishly for the common good. They have used it to get all the money possible out of the employers and to render back the minimum of service."[96]

The American women saw Russia bedeviled not only by inability to compromise, inefficiency, and near-anarchy, but also by fundamental disagreement about whether or not to continue Russian participation in the war against the Central Powers. "War and revolution are irreconcilable bedfellows," wrote Beatty. "Out in that nebulous land . . . 'the front'—I came close, very close, to the staggering reality of war. I came to know how revolution wars on war, and war on revolution, and both on freedom and democracy."[97] The Bolsheviks were winning popular support away from the Provisional Government, which labored under Allied pressure to continue the war. The egregiously mismanaged war with its 7,000,000 Russian casualties, the correspondents observed, had exhausted the substance and will to fight of the country; the revolutionary vision had allowed the people to glimpse an earthly paradise of peace and equality. Millions yielded to the belief that the German workers would rise, revolt, and end the war. ". . . the dream of the Russian revolutionist," as Beatty saw it, "was not only to stop Russia from fighting, but to put an end to all wars. . . . Internationalism was at the bottom of their creed. . . ."[98]

The sentiment for peace, Beatty saw, extended to the front, where eventually Russian gunners were confronted by other Russian soldiers who ordered them to stop shooting Germans because "Those are our brothers over there. . . . They don't want to fight us; we don't want to fight them."[99] A general's nightmare come true, in which his soldiers have found more in common with the enemy soldiers than with him.

> ▚▚▚ *In Russia woman . . . did not seek to express herself but instead adopted man's methods in the fight for freedom. . . .*
>
> —Rheta Childe Dorr[100]

In some ways their gender advantaged the four American women—particularly in talking to Russian women and discovering what was happening to them during the revolution. Yet passionate feminist hopes sometimes made the Americans credulously optimistic. All four agreed that no feminist movement as such existed in Russia. "Russia's struggle was the struggle of human beings as human beings, rather than human beings as males or females," wrote Beatty. "Instead of becoming feminists, they became Cadets, Social Revolutionists, Mensheviki, Maximalists, Bolsheviki, Internationalists, or attached themselves to one or another of the parties and shadows of parties."[101]

But Beatty brushed past the almost complete absence of women from the seats of power to write, "When freedom came to Russia, no one questioned the right of women to share it."[102] Although she interviewed her, Bryant seemed unaware of Alexandra Kollontai's frustration as the token woman in the government after the Bolshevik Revolution. Bryant did ask Maria Spiridonova why more women did not hold public office, since, said Bryant, "Russia is the only place in the world where there is absolute sex equality." Spiridonova, whom Dorr termed the Charlotte Corday of the Russian Revolution, after ten years in solitary confinement in Siberia had refused to leave until all the other women in the prison were freed. But she only suggested that Russian women, unlike Russian men, were too conscientious to take responsibilities for which they were not fitted. Bryant commented skeptically that she herself could "never see any spiritual difference between men and women inside or outside of politics. They act and react very much alike; they certainly did in the Russian revolution."[103]

Dorr applauded Mrs. Pankhurst's efforts to get Russian women "to storm the soviets all over Russia and force the men to support Kerensky and the Provisional Government in their effort to rally the army and defeat the Germans." But when Kerensky responded by saying that women would not be allowed to demonstrate, Dorr seemed more bewildered than disillusioned, and she kept hoping for future improvement, for after all, hadn't Russian women shown themselves to be "at least as ready for citizenship as the men"? Hadn't the telephone girls proved their loyalty during the March revolution by refusing "to connect the headquarters of the Bolsheviki . . ."?[104]

Doty, too, pinned her faith to the evidence of the past and the hope of the future. She cited past glories: in March 1917 when the men of the Provisional Government were silent on the issue of women's suffrage, 40,000 women marched to tell the men of the Council of Workingmen and Soldiers' Deputies: "*We will not leave this place until we have received the answer that women as well as men shall have the right to vote in the Constituent Assembly.*" Capitulating, the men formally declared that universal suffrage meant women as well as men. "When a feminist movement does arise," Doty prophesied, "nothing can stop such women."[105]

Hollow as these hopes may sound now, they evidently rang true to these four American journalists, who could still believe that all women had to do was to prove their loyalty, their energy, their devotion to duty, and their competence to gain not only the responsibilities but also the rewards of men.

✄✄✄ *Destiny was preparing the most amazing single phenomenon of the war—the woman soldier.*

—Madeleine Zabriskie Doty[106]

Russia had no feminist movement, but it alone had women soldiers. No wonder that the women correspondents were impressed by them. Their accounts sparkle with admiration and intense sympathy. "One of them walked a little way with me into the night," wrote Louise Bryant. "It was painfully cold. . . . I looked down and suddenly I realised that her feet were bare. . . . When I think back now she personifies Russia to me, Russia hungry and cold and barefoot—forgetting it all—planning new battles, new roads to freedom."[107]

Bryant saw the deep commitment of the women soldiers to Mother Russia, and their deep confusion about revolutionary factions. Knowing nothing of the revolution, most of them volunteered to help their menfolks fight Germans. But, they learned, many of those men no longer wanted to fight Germans. Fresh from the farms and workplaces, hurled into the maelstrom of class struggle and disagreements about whether or not to continue Russian participation in World War I, how were the women to know where to stand, on which side to fight? One of them, Anna Shub, explained to Bryant: " 'We are working girls, and traitors have been trying to persuade us to fight our own people. We were fooled and we almost did it. I left home. . . . I left everything because I thought the poor soldiers of Russia were tired after fighting so many years, and I thought we ought to help them. When I arrived in Petrograd I began to see the truth; we were supposed to be shaming the soldiers. . . . When you go back to America, tell them I am a woman soldier, and I fight only imperialistic invaders.' "[108]

Beatty confronted the idea of woman as soldier with mixed feelings. "Against the fervid faith of the Pacifist—that 'women, who pay such a terrible price to give life will never be able to take it away'—[Destiny] was preparing to drive her saddest and bitterest blow." But, she knew, "The issue is no longer a question of whether Vera can fight. . . . She will fight whenever and wherever she feels she must. She is a potential soldier, and will continue to be until the muddled old world is remade upon a basis of human freedom and safety."[109]

Dorr, who knew three regiments of women soldiers in Moscow and Petrograd, saw them as heroes, combating the demoralization of the troops and rallying men to fight against the Germans. She knew best the regiment commanded by Maria Botchkareva, who in an earlier incarnation had fought with a men's regiment. Dorr wrote of how she "shared Botchkareva's soup and kasha, and drank hot tea out of her other tin cup. I slept beside her on the plank bed. I saw her and her women off to the firing line, and . . . I sat beside their hospital beds and heard their own stories of the fight."[110]

Botchkareva's regiment was a "Battalion of Death," a term applied to any unit whose members meant to fight to the death for Russia against Germany. In it she enlisted former Red Cross nurses, a woman doctor of forty-eight, clerks, office workers, factory girls, servants, farm women, and ten other women who had fought in men's regiments—even, Dorr said, one Nina, the regimental clown and a bundle of contradictions, who had been in an Austrian prison for six months, and who professed love for her rifle "Because it carries death. I love my bayonet, too. I love all arms. I love all things that carry death to the enemies of my country."[111] The women soldiers carried poison, having no intention of being taken prisoner.

Dorr, failing to win permission to accompany Botchkareva's unit to the front, finally went without papers. At the station the women soldiers pushed their way through Bolsheviks to the train. "As for me," said Dorr, "a mixture of indignation, healthy muscle and rare good luck carried me through and landed me in a somewhat battered condition next to Adjutant Skridlova." When an official asked for Dorr's papers, Botchkareva shoved him away, and took Dorr into her own second-class compartment with Skridlova and the peasant girl standard bearer. "Our luxury consisted of cushioned shelves without bedding . . . which served as seats by day and beds by night. . . . As for food, we all fared alike, and we fared well, friends of the regiment having loaded the train. . . ." As they traveled toward the front, the attitudes of the people at the stations changed from applause to sneers and personal insults from soldiers who shouted their own refusal to fight. The women flung back, "That is the reason why we do. Go home, you cowards, and let women fight for Russia."

At their destination, Botchkareva, with sword and revolver at her side, waded into a mob of soldiers and shouted an order in a voice that reminded Dorr "of that extra awful motor car siren that infuriates the pedestrian, but lifts him out of the road in one quick jump . . . : 'You get to hell out of here and let my regiment pass.' " That night the women threatened to fire on men who attempted to enter their barracks. From then on the men confined themselves to following the women everywhere, jeering at them when they made a mistake or fell down. "Some of that laughter," Dorr wrote, "I feel pretty certain, hid hurt pride, for every decent soldier I talked to expressed his sorrow and humiliation that the women had felt the necessity of enlisting."[112]

The women lived in a crude but new and clean building about a hundred feet long, said Beatty, who also accompanied Botchkareva's Battalion of Death, ". . . with steep roofs sloping to the floor, and just enough width to allow for two shelves eight feet deep [on which the soldiers slept] with an aisle between. . . . Above my head, hanging from the rafters, was a jungle of gas-masks and wet laundry, boots, water-bottles, and kit-bags. Beside each girl lay her rifle."[113] The women soldiers went into battle after less than two months' training.

Dorr and Beatty were not permitted to witness the battle in which the women fought, and the contemporary evidence about it is muddled and contradictory. Beatty wrote: "All the world knows how they went into battle shouting a challenge to the deserting Russian troops. All the world knows that six of them stayed behind in the forest, with wooden crosses to mark their soldier graves. Ten were decorated for bravery in action with the Order of St. George, and twenty others received medals. Twenty-one were seriously wounded, and many more than that received contusions. Only fifty remained to take their places with the men in the trenches when the battle was over."[114] In the two-day battle, she said, the women and forty men became separated from the main body, took four rows of trenches, but finally had to retreat for lack of reenforcements.

Botchkareva's version, as told to Dorr: "The Russian men hid in a little wood while the officers swore at them and begged them to advance. Then they sent us forward, and we called to the men that we would lead them if they would only follow. Some of them said they would follow, and we went forward on a run, still shouting to the men. About two-thirds of them went with us, and we easily put the Germans to flight. We killed a lot of Germans and took almost a hundred prisoners, including two officers."[115]

Later Beatty heard a woman officer admit that "war is not easy for a woman," especially when she knew that she might kill a German relative, or was ordered to fire on German wounded.[116] But some of Dorr's sources claimed that fighting was "less arduous if a little more dangerous" for them than the work they had done before in field or factory.[117]

The reports of the American women journalists conflict over the contemporary conditions and the future of women soldiers. Bryant wrote: "In all Russia less than three thousand were gathered into the recruiting stations. . . . many more have since taken part in the Red Guard Army. . . . In my opinion the chief reason for the failure of the woman's regiment was segregation. There will always be fighting women in Russia, but they will fight side by side with men, and not as a sex."[118] Beatty, however, found that "There were nearly five thousand women soldiers in Russia at the beginning of the fall of 1917. . . . They had their own transport and medical service, signal corps, machine-gun company, mitrailleuses, and a scouting detachment of twenty Cossack women."[119] And Dorr reported that many women who had served in men's regiments were leaving them for one of the women's regiments, and that the Russians intended to enlist ten to twenty thousand women and spread their regiments through the front lines to lead the men into battle against the Germans. Frustrating though their contradictions are, these first-hand reports allow us to glimpse the lives and personalities of a group of women on the cutting edge of history.

The books of the American women are distinguished also by their stories of the notable women of the revolution, like the tsar-defying Babushka, the Grandmother of the Revolution—Katherine Breshkovsky. Bryant tells a charming anecdote about the loyalty of Mme. Kerensky to her husband, from whom she lived apart. After his government fell, she was arrested for tearing the opposing Bolshevik party's posters from walls with her bare hands, but when the arresting soldier discovered her identity he repented and begged the officials to let her off—they did.

And the Countess Panina entertained Bryant with a story of her imprisonment. An official in Kerensky's government famous even in tsarist days for her charities, she was imprisoned by the Bolsheviks. When she was finally freed, she said to a Bolshevik officer as she picked up a book: ". . . that's what you get for imprisoning the bourgeoisie—we immediately begin to collect property." Oh no, said the officer—Bolshevik prisoners left with far more property than Panina. And Panina had never had a moon. A moon? "Yes," he explained, a Bolshevik had "fitted her cell up with pink satin and wore pink satin robes and lace covers on her cot. In one corner she had specially arranged a shaded electric light that looked like a stage moon. In the evening she would lie back among the satin cushions and the soldiers and guards would come in and she would discourse cleverly on literature and art—just like a courtesan in the time of the Louis."[120] Stories like this of good-humored relationships between prisoners and their guards, as well as between political opponents *during the revolution* run through the accounts of the American women correspondents.

Minister of Warfare Alexandra Kollontai had moments of black humor. Describing to Bryant her accomplishments in improving maternal care, public education, and veterans' benefits, Kollontai remarked that residents in old people's homes made their own decisions, even chose their own menus. " 'What would that consist of in the present day?' I asked. Kollontai burst out laughing. 'Surely,' she said, 'you must understand that there is a great deal of moral satisfaction in deciding whether you want thick cabbage soup or thin cabbage soup!' "[121]

> ▰▰▰ *I was followed by spies, I was in battles. . . . A few days ago I read with some amazement about a brave reporter who travelled all the way from Petrograd to Moscow and back to Petrograd again. It was the first time that I realised it was a brave thing. I did it many times. . . .*
> —Louise Bryant[122]

The four American women journalists were intrepid. But, although they revealed a professional interest in presenting their stories as exclusives—none of them gives the others any credit—they did not dwell on the hardships and dangers they underwent. Of course they were often hungry and tired and achingly cold. Of course when they slept they might be awakened by gunfire. Of course when they went out they might encounter street fighting. When they traveled the conditions were grueling. Often to get their stories they had to travel without papers, maneuver around officialdom, serve as Bolshevik couriers. But after Doty left Russia, she commented, "No longer should I have to sleep in my clothes; go without baths; be covered with fleas, and hear rifle shots and machine guns in the street below. . . . [But] I grew hungry for the dirty Bolsheviki. They could think and talk."[123]

The American women correspondents were, after all, at the center of the action, privy to secret governmental meetings, helping to translate and publish government edicts. They were *engagé* with the events whirling around them. Bessie Beatty spoke for all of them when she wrote, "I had been alive at a great moment, and knew that it was great."[124]

CHAPTER 9

The Novelists

MORE THAN MOST WOMEN who wrote about World War I, the novelists undertook the distinctive task of interpretation, judgment, and a search for significance. Diarists and letter writers as a rule simply furnish the raw materials of incident and immediate human reaction; they tell us what happened, how they felt about it, and, now and then, what they thought about it. While Elizabeth Shepley Sergeant and even more Ellen LaMotte out of their violent encounters with the horror and terror illuminate war's landscape with flashes of insight, novelists try in the clear light of recall and reflection to order experience, and, however desperately, to fit it into a meaningful universe and worldview. It's a process that usually requires time and distance from the propaganda and passion that all too often skew the thinking of even the most sophisticated in wartime.

During the war, of course, most novelists wrote in the terms of the times. Often the plot fails to shore up the propaganda. Consider Edith Wharton's story line in *The Marne* (1919): A young American ambulance driver who picks up a rifle to fight in the second battle of the Marne is rescued by the ghost of his former tutor, a Frenchman. Excuse enough for Wharton to argue for the chivalry of war, attacking "the odd belief that life-in-itself—just the mere raw fact of being alive—was the one thing that mattered, and getting killed the one thing to be avoided. . . ." Such a belief, Wharton wrote, "did away at a stroke with all that gave any interest to the fact of living. It killed romance, it killed poetry and adventure, it took all the meaning out of history and conduct and civilization. There had never been anything worth while in the world that had not had to be died for, and it was as clear as day that a world which no one

231

would die for could never be a world worth being alive in."[1] Mary
Roberts Rinehart's plot in *The Amazing Interlude* holds up better,
largely because her own adventures at the front which she here fic-
tionalized were so dramatic, but also because even in 1918 she was
able to concentrate more on the impact of war on her heroine than
on the glories and virtues of the war itself.

Even long after the war, hundreds of popular short stories and
novels continued to glorify war or at least to justify it, to treat it as
inevitable, to offer its exploits as entertainment, or simply to use it
as a conveniently dramatic setting.[2] American women as well as
American men contributed their share of these. They wrote adventure stories, melodramas, spy stories, and romances. But most of
these authors have vanished from public recognition. To read their
books today (when one can find them) is to adventure in another
world, a world with different ideas and habits of thought, a different
morality. They tell us little about the actualities of war, but much
about its psychology and appeal.

For despite the many works on World War I in this popular
vein, it is the perception of war of the Lost Generation writers that
has infiltrated and now dominates our ethos. Love of peace and
recognition of the horror and futility of war shape our speech—if
not our actions. The disenchantment of the American public stopped
the Vietnam War; even our most ardent militants proclaim their
detestation of war; and our Air Force emblazons its gates with the
motto "Peace Is Our Profession."

All in all, it strains our understanding to grasp that seventy-five
years ago many gently bred American women thought of and publicly
described war as salutary, healthy both for the society engaged in it
and for the individuals who waged it. Mary Raymond Shipman Andrews, for example, an author with an unparalleled capacity for
bathos, subtitled her 1915 book *The Forge in Which the Soul of a
Man Was Tested* and attributed to the war the elimination of class
pride, race prejudice, and atheism.

A more sophisticated and less blatantly propagandistic work,
Anna Robeson Burr's *The House on Charles Street* (1921), commented
on British society and conduct of the war through its protagonist,
Sydney, an American woman who becomes secretary to a member

of Parliament. Sydney writes home, ". . . don't waste any more paper asking me to be neutral—I go in for righteous wrath. You and your busy ladies and your Belgian Relief are all very well, but the only relief for Belgium that I can see is to kill the Germans."[3]

Far better writers than either Andrews or Burr set forth notions about war as redemptive. Consider Willa Cather's *One of Ours* (1922), a novel largely based—since Cather did not go to Europe during the war—on the letters of a soldier-son of a pioneer woman. Cather, disillusioned with the materialism which had settled over the prairie frontier and emotionally attached to France, presented her protagonist as a gallant idealist. Claude Wheeler is a sensitive boy sickened by the money-grubbing of his father and brothers, his farm community, and early-twentieth-century America generally. Ensnared in a miserably ill-matched marriage (to a woman frustrated by the lack of any opportunity for the exercise of her managerial powers) and in a job he detests, Claude sees no future worth wanting. War comes to him as an occasion for redemptive action. "He believed that he was going abroad with an expeditionary force that would make war without rage, with uncompromising generosity and chivalry."[4] The war reveals new worlds, literally and symbolically, as Claude sails to Europe and forms a friendship with the cultured, decent David Gerhardt, a concert violinist whose values Claude adopts. That friendship sustains in Claude a self-image as a leader of men. "That was one of the things about this war; it took a little fellow from a little town, gave him an air and a swagger, a life like a movie-film—and then a death like the rebel angels."[5]

Gerhardt believes that "The war was put up to our generation. I don't know what for; the sins of our fathers, probably. Certainly not to make the world safe for Democracy, or any rhetoric of that sort. . . . I've sometimes wondered whether the young men of our time had to die to bring a new idea into the world . . . something Olympian."[6] To Claude the guns said "that men could still die for an idea; and would burn all they had made to keep their dreams. He knew the future of the world was safe; the careful planners would never be able to put it into a straight-jacket—cunning and prudence would never have it to themselves. . . . Ideals were not archaic things, beautiful and impotent; they were the real sources of power among men. As long as that was true . . . he had no quarrel with Destiny . . . he would give his own adventure for no man's. On the edge of sleep it seemed to glimmer, like the clear column of the fountain, like the new moon—alluring, half-averted, the bright face of danger."[7]

Claude's death—a scene in which he looms cinematically above the trenches, urging the troops forward—becomes his protection against disillusionment and lesser modes of being. As his mother reflects, "He died believing his own country better than it is, and France better than any country can ever be. . . . Perhaps it was as well to see that vision, and then to see no more. She would have dreaded the awakening—she sometimes even doubts whether he could have borne at all that last, desolating disappointment. One by one the heroes of that war, the men of dazzling soldiership, leave prematurely the world they have come back to. Airmen whose deeds were tales of wonder, officers whose names made the blood of youth beat faster, survivors of incredible dangers—one by one they quietly die by their own hand. . . . as she reads, she thinks those slayers of themselves were all so like him; they were the ones who had hoped extravagantly—who in order to do what they did had to hope extravagantly, and to believe passionately. And they found they had hoped and believed too much. But one she knew, who could ill bear disillusion . . . safe, safe."[8] Claude's mother does not bitterly excoriate the war. Rather than repudiating the war, Cather blamed what society failed to do after the war.

The many approving letters her book evoked from veterans suggest that Cather had authentically described what the war and its aftermath had meant to at least some of the men who fought it. Today her treatment of the war as redemptive rings strangely in our ears, even while we are stirred by the accuracy and power of her description of its impact. One wonders what kind of book Cather might have written had she directly experienced the war.

But direct experience, alas, is no guarantee of a good book, even from so admirable a writer as Edith Wharton. Her biographers understandably tend almost to ignore the nauseatingly sentimental *The Marne* (1919) and the chauvinistic *A Son at the Front* (1923).[9] Yet Wharton, already living abroad when war broke out, traveled extensively in France during the war years, with several trips to the front, and from her war work knew all too well the terrible costs of the war. Material teemed around her. But even in 1923, it seems, she was still too close, still trapped in the maze of wartime reactions. After all, her investment of time, energy, and emotional commitment to the war had been extraordinarily heavy; in addition to the many agencies she instituted she wrote reams of straight-out propaganda under the guise of travel books and books on life in France. Evidently she could not put the war aside until she had rehashed yet again the evil of the Boche, the lethargy and selfishness of the Americans in not entering the war sooner, and the wrongheadedness of the pacifists. This is not the Wharton of *Ethan Frome*.

A Son at the Front reflects a major concern of the war years: the generation gap in attitudes toward the war. But nothing works. Only one character assumes any reality: the artist father, Campton. The others are stick figures: the knight's effigy of a son; the tart-tongued "old maid" devoted to good deeds; the empty-headed wife; the older woman with a young lover. With only one real character, there can be no significant interaction, so the plot jerks along mechanically, as Campton moves from trying to protect his son George with a cushy job back of the lines to the belief that George's duty (with his inevitable death) is at the front.

Although it's hard to find out what George thinks, since his character is nailed closed, his idea of war is apparently built on *dulce et decorum* and "Loved I not honour more," modified by some sense that war in general is bad, though this particular one is necessary to end war, and by his recognition that this war has been mismanaged from its inception by statesmen and generals; in any case there is no honorable way for young men to escape it. "War's rot; but to get rid of war forever we've got to fight this one first." But the German invasion of Belgium enrages George: "The howling blackguards! The brigands! This isn't war—it's simple murder!" So he and his fellow-soldiers become knights, *sans peur et sans reproche*, crusading against the powers of darkness. The saintly young soldiers fear only being sold short by their own country: how dreadful if "political blunders, inertia, tolerance, perhaps even evil ambitions and connivances, should at last outweigh the effort of the front"![10]

In the novel Wharton worked off some of her irritation at America's long neutrality and her frustration at the Red Cross takeover of her charities by lambasting the pacifists and those relief workers who offered their services only after the United States entered the war. She zeroed in on Mayhew, who represents both of these detestable groups. Mayhew sails to attend a peace congress, is captured by Germans, and feels victimized by the "atrocities" they commit against him, like confining him to house arrest in a good hotel. His experiences turn him into a gung-ho advocate of destroying the Huns. He then becomes a worker for war relief, raising money by regaling people with stories of his suffering, firing all the capable workers and hiring the incompetent. "The speciousness of Mr. Mayhew's arguments, the sleight-of-hand by which he had dislodged the real workers and replaced them by his satellites, reminded the painter [Campton] of the neutrals who were beginning to say that there were two sides to every question, that war was always cruel, and how about the Russian atrocities in Silesia? As the months dragged on a breath of lukewarmness had begun to blow through the world, damping men's souls, confusing plain issues, casting a doubt on the worth of everything. . . . No one seemed to feel any longer that life is something more than being alive; apparently the only people not tired of the thought of death were the young men still pouring out to it in their thousands."[11]

Five years after the Armistice was signed Wharton still felt impelled to fight all these battles. Suffice it to say that *A Son at the Front* was eminently a novel of wartime emotions, interesting today primarily to demonstrate one of the terrible effects of war: how even intelligent and highly gifted artists can be betrayed by the passions of their times.

But if time and distance are necessary to separate the novelist from war's passions, what are we to make of Atherton and Rutledge, both of whom were in France during the war, both of whom published antiwar novels during the war years? Gertrude Atherton, who earned the Legion of Honor for her war work in France, published in 1918 (when she was sixty-one) *The White Morning: A Novel of the Power of the German Women in Wartime*, in which German women defy the Prussian system and end the war. This hotly feminist melodrama of a novel argues that in Germany a "slow secret revolt against the insolent and inconsiderate attitude of the German male . . . had been growing among its women for some fifteen years before the outbreak of the war." The novel is not to be missed by students of feminism. Often hilariously witty, it benefits from Atherton's experience of living in prewar Germany to satirize the German male: "Their father, the Herr Graf, a fine-looking Junker of sixty-odd, with a roving eye and a martial air despite a corpulence which annoyed him excessively, had transferred his lost authority over his regiment to his household. . . . His brain, a fine, concentrated Teutonic organ, strove to grapple with two ideas at once."[12]

Atherton supplies an aristocratic German Joan of Arc to lead the German women in a successful revolution in which they seize all the railroads, destroy all the ammunition, and inform "Wilhelm Hohenzollern" that the war he fomented is over. What's more, Atherton follows the novel with an essay propounding the likelihood of such a finish to the war which the men who had started it could not end.

Atherton's novel may well have seemed less improbable when it was published than it does now. People were searching for some way, any way, to end the fighting. As Barbara Tuchman observes in *The Zimmermann Telegram*, the generals themselves had run out of ideas: ". . . regiments of lives spent like water, half a million at Verdun alone, without either side's winning a strategic advantage, but only being riveted together like two fighting elks who have locked horns."[13] And the mutiny of half its troops had already shaken the French Army. Reports often circulated within the peace movement of the pleas of soldiers on both sides for women to stop the war. Partly desperation, partly a reassertion of women's traditional role as custodian of hearth, home, and tranquillity raised these cries for women to do something, anything, to end the horror.

Marice Rutledge passionately called on not just German women but all women to end war. Her novel *Children of Fate* (1917) debates where to place the blame for war: on men, with their hormones running amok, or on women, who fail to exercise their powers to restrain men.[14] Rutledge recounted the torment of Natalie, an American girl, who has sent her French fiancé off to war professing to accept the justice and morality of the Allied cause. Instead, she believes, she should have trumpeted the truth: "Why not tell our people of the men cooped in the trenches through days of sweltering heat . . . soon through days of cold and driving rains . . . to be trapped like dumb animals, murdered by an unseen enemy? . . . The democracy of the trenches? A democracy of prisoners! . . . Why not tell our people that the men are filled with rum and ether before the bayonet charges? . . . filled with madness to make the killing easier! . . . Why not tell our people of the disease that hides its ugly face behind the paid woman's smile; such few women as are smuggled inside the lines where wives may not go, to appease a lusting regiment?" In the end, bedraggled with guilt over her own assent to Pierre's fighting, Natalie confronts him: "The peoples to-day are fighting to enrich further capitalists and munition makers. . . . *They are your real enemies.*"[15]

Strong language, indeed, for 1917. Rutledge dared even to reject the sentimental adoration of the soldier which most Americans accepted as an article of faith: "The women knitted. They knitted like Destinies bending fatefully over their everlasting skeins . . . chattering of their absent heroes, boasting in watchful rivalry of the wounded and the dead, trading exploits that warranted their relationship to the defenders of France. They had achieved a cult which permitted, in noblest form, the expression of lives stunted or envious, yearning or vain, passionate, sentimental or fanatical. Their men, who only a short while ago were perfect or faulty sons or mates, had with one sublime gesture of parting become mysterious factors in a mighty struggle. The man and the rascal shared the same superhuman virtues. In the armies they were mere units; in the hearts of the tragic, rapturous women they were the determining elements of victory. Had they beaten their wives in peace times, they were now beating an enemy; had they loved indiscriminately, they were now vowed to one cause; had they shirked their duties as citizens, they were now accomplishing a supreme duty."[16]

Dorothy Canfield Fisher's *The Deepening Stream* did not emerge until years later, in 1930, when styles of novel writing and popular attitudes toward the war had both changed drastically.[17] This story of a woman's coming to terms with her war experiences is based on

Fisher's own life. Deeply sympathetic with France, a country in which she had lived and in whose literature she had her doctorate, Fisher in 1916 went there with her husband, who became an ambulance driver, and her two children. There she worked continually for the relief of the war's victims and wrote incessantly, trying to explain to people in America what was happening.

The Deepening Stream traces the course of Matey's life from childhood, with many and extended visits to France, through marriage and the birth of two children. When war is declared, both Matey and Adrian, her husband, suffer from a conflict between their desire to help and their Quaker-bred pacifism. Adrian, though, is astonished that Matey feels as stifled as he: after all, what could she, a woman, do to help, and what about her responsibility to her children? *Their* children, she reminds him, and what does he plan to do that she can't? The couple go to France, he as an ambulance driver, she to share the life of her adoptive French family and to give aid and comfort to soldiers and war victims.

Fisher packs her novel with observations and judgments on people she knew and worked with in France. For instance, of the *poilus:* "a strange mixture of personalities, castes, and abilities, but with a few never-varying traits in common, such as their intense dislike of people who called them 'defenders of civilization,' their profound silence on the subject of exploding shells, bayonet attacks, trench life—war in general—and their deep concern over the state of their underwear. . . ." The Breton farmhand: "His particular grudge against the world was the language of the newspaper reporters. . . . 'I'd like to have one of those pen-pushers in the trenches! He'd see how hard it is to restrain us from going into an attack ahead of time. . . .' " A hard-bitten, swaggering front-line fighter, "recklessly outspoken in his detestation of the war and its makers: 'There'll be a strike if this business goes on another year . . . a strike of soldiers. . . . And we'll drive the Cabinet Ministers and the people who write books about war up to the front to take our places.' "[18]

The war and the book end with Matey's struggle to make sense of the war, of the betrayals incorporated in the peace, and indeed of the human condition. For she was among the women crying out "in horror at the implication that their sons and husbands and brothers had died to win material advantages," women who fixed their hopes on Wilson, the seer, so soon to be defeated by the failure of Wilson, the politician.[19] Ultimately Matey comes to believe that war is not a fault in the universe, but a mistake men make. What she must concentrate on instead is the sum of the efforts of human beings toward the good, the true, and the beautiful.

Of all novels, the most direct testament of an American woman war worker's reactions is Mary Lee's ironically titled *"It's a Great War!"* She ran into problems in publishing it—problems so severe that she refused ever to write another book.[20] For two years she peddled it from publisher to publisher. It won a prepublication prize from the American Legion—a prize about which the Legion had second thoughts on the discovery that the book was written by a woman: she finally had to divide it with a male author.[21] When *"It's a Great War!"* finally appeared in 1929, it evoked attacks: ". . . the American Legion and the D.A.R.," the *Boston Herald* reported on January 12, 1930, "are discussing it officially, for complaints have been made to these two organizations that the book is not patriotic because it does not always depict the legionnaires as heroes."

Lee, educated at Miss Winsor's school and Radcliffe (Phi Beta Kappa, 1917), went to France as a civilian secretary with units of the United States Army, in Bordeaux and Paris. Later she served in a YMCA canteen in the zone of advance, and eventually with the army of occupation in Germany. On her return she worked on the city staff of the New York *Evening Post* and then as special correspondent of the Sunday magazine and special feature section of *The New York Times*.

Lee's novel, like Fisher's, fictionalizes autobiography, but it's darker, less affirmative than *The Deepening Stream*. When Anne Wentworth sails for France, she enters a world of "people, bouncing in and bouncing out of one another's lives. People, thrown together, growing to know each other better in a week than in a year at home. People thrown apart again, forgetting about each other in the next week . . . People keeping on the surface of things, for fear that if they dive below they may be drowned there . . . lives, like bits of confetti, tossed from a high place, fluttering downward, downward. . . ."[22] A chaotic, tense, artificial, temporary world, where the characters learn to live with and on an excitement which becomes essential to them. To project this world, Lee adopted a stream-of-consciousness style, full of ellipses and broken thoughts.

Lee endows her protagonist with intelligence, energy, and, above all, honesty. Anne's honesty makes her recognize and acknowledge the "moral slumping" that war brings to its participants. Women and men are unfaithful to one another. Some of the women workers lose their reputations, some their chastity, some their jobs. Soldiers curse, get drunk, roister, rape, consort with prostitutes. Enlisted men are shot for refusing to leave the trenches; officers lie to escape danger. Ministers of God lose their faith, seize rifles, join in an orgy of fighting.

Anne even turns her honesty against herself: "There was a place left in the First Class, no one except American officers. . . . The American officers were negroes. They were polite, and quiet. They helped Anne with her bags. One of them moved, gave her his seat by the window. The officers sat, quiet. They had got into the train early, on purpose to get a compartment by themselves, careful not to offend." Yet Anne, hating herself, makes an excuse to leave, and stands on the platform debating. "Anne believed in Justice for the Negro. Her grandfathers had fought for the north in the Civil War. At college she had always championed the negroes. Used to ask them to sit with her at lunch. . . . This car had no corridor . . . The train might stop and stand on the track for hours. Might spend the night there . . . So, she was a coward. So ideals weren't, after all, worth anything."[23]

But Anne's honesty does not extend to telling the truth to the folks back home. Neither in her letters nor after the war does she talk about its mismanagement: the American army's continuing to order Nieuports after their pilots report that their wings fall off and a gasoline connection works loose, so that pilots are burned alive. The failure to provide American pilots with parachutes. The gassing of American soldiers by their own artillery, in defiance of warnings. A friend tells her: "What I object to is that the people at home have to be guarded from it. . . . First thing you know people will be teaching children all over again that War is noble. . . . I'd like to see them stop saying 'Johnny, this is your father's sword!' and begin saying, 'Johnny, this is a photograph of the French girl that your father lived with. Your dear father was so thoroughly bored by the Great War that he got pleasure from a woman like that.'. . . it would make Johnny's wife and Johnny's mother twice as determined to keep him at home.''[24] But Anne cannot bring herself to tell her elders what the war was really like, partly because the elders won't listen or believe her, partly because she loves her parents and wants to spare them the truth—and partly, one assumes, because her upbringing dooms Anne to follow the code to which she no longer intellectually subscribes.

As protagonist Anne is reflective, constantly evaluating her experiences, to the point of questioning her own mission—the YMCA, for instance. She knows that many of the male secretaries are hypocritical layabouts, crude, ill-spoken, repeatedly proclaiming that they didn't come to Europe to do menial tasks. But are the women Y employees, herself included, any more effective? Maybe they're only messing up, making the soldiers jealous, not bettering their lives. The soldiers still engage in immoralities, only under cover. A coworker argues with her: a town with a Y woman in it is a better town. Some of the nicest soldiers fall a little bit in love with the Y girls—it's good for them. In the end Anne concludes: "What we do is to remind them just a little of the past and of the future, the things they're going through all this mess for. If we're any good, we keep a vision just a little bit, before them. We make them respect themselves.''[25]

Anne and the other idealists who went to World War I because they bought Wilson's credo that it was the war to end wars, see their sacrifice sold out by the people who initially urged them to it: their elders, who oppose the League of Nations. In the end Anne, after going through the war, after living in occupied Germany, after working to secure the United States' endorsement of the League of Nations, concludes that "the whole War was just a farce."[26] She—and the book—end in despair. Anne and, one suspects, Mary Lee despair not because they think nothing is worth working and fighting for, but because they come to believe that nothing can be achieved by working and fighting.

Lee attempted to "see through the heterogeneous, chaotic

stream of separate events of War toward the Truth." And indeed
what compensates for the difficulties of her stylistically experimental
novel is her honesty, her attempt to make a book "built up of Truth."
She tried hard and with a good bit of success not to romanticize war,
nor the reactions of those who experienced it. Her technique of
maximizing observations and minimizing reactions lends credibility
to what she records. In the long run Anne Wentworth is a lot more
believable than Hemingway's fantasies of Lady Brett or Catherine
Barkley. Anne is an educated young American woman of her period
moving through the deepest involvement and commitment toward
alienation. A woman of her time liberating herself from her corsets
and her long hair and skirts, but unable to deny her upbringing.
Lee's novel is impressive as a serious attempt to come to grips with
the question that bedeviled so many soldiers and war workers: What
was it all about?

Throughout the more serious of these war novels, several themes
recur: The generation gap between the young, who learn the realities
of war, and their elders, who sentimentalize it or profiteer by it at
the expense of the young. The differences between Europeans and
Americans, often with an emphasis on the greater suffering endured
by Europeans. The mismanagement of the war by the statesmen and
generals responsible for its conduct. The impact of the war on the
individual survivors.

All these themes are developed in the novel *Three Daughters,* by
Ruth Eleanor McKee and her collaborator and researcher, Alice
Fleenor Sturgis.[27] Published on the brink of World War II, when
the failures of the Great War had become all too apparent, this
remarkable book undertakes to record fictionally the achievements
of American women in Europe in World War I. McKee and Sturgis
had access to the oral and written evidence of nine or ten women
who had worked in various capacities overseas: Sturgis herself
worked for the Department of Public Information of the ARC in
England and France and later with the Graves Registration Service
of the American Expeditionary Force. McKee was a professional
writer. The book is admirably accurate; detail after detail can be
verified from other evidence.

On their separate paths the three daughters of an ammunitions

manufacturer, Elizabeth, Candida, and Camilla Huntington, meet
other American women engaged in all sorts of war work. Elizabeth,
in Europe when the war starts, becomes a canteen worker, and then
a nurse who eventually works with a mobile hospital unit. Candy,
though trained as a nurse's aide, goes to Europe with the YMCA.
Packing her trunks with evening gowns, she frivolously dreams of
dancing through the war, but the actuality bores her and she moves
away from Paris to help set up a canteen, working for roughneck
enlisted men instead of taking tea with elegant flying officers. Then
she switches to the Signal Corps as a telephone operator, moving
ever closer to the front. Camilla, who has raised money at home for
the Red Cross by telling stories embellished by her imagination and
unblemished by fact, goes to England and France on a six-month
tour to collect information and work in public affairs.

The lively plot makes the book a good read. Sometimes it verges
on melodrama. But the evidence of the participants McKee consulted
continually imbues her book with realism. The intervention of two
decades doubtless helped too; decreased public gullibility about the
chastity of American troops permitted greater frankness about sexual
behavior. A YMCA-secretary husband is faithless to his YM wife at
the very instant of her giving birth to his child. Candy chances to
read "an official warning to the men against venereal disease, cau-
tioning them against relations with French prostitutes and acknowl-
edging the futility of that caution by demanding that they report to
a prophylaxis station within a given period after intimacy with a
woman. That must mean, reasons Candy, that a large number of the
men, "these same ones who seemed so much like children to her,
went with the prostitutes. . . ."[28] A more sophisticated friend rages
against women's ignorance about protecting themselves in sexual
encounters, an ignorance that the military establishment, so concerned about distributing prophylactics to men, would not for worlds
dispel.

Most saliently of all, *Three Daughters* affords insight into what
the war did to the American women who worked in it overseas.
Camilla is killed in a senseless accident directly attributable to the
war. Two nurses commit suicide on the boat home. During Elizabeth's dreadful nervous breakdown, Candy, searching for help for

her sister, discovers that the government offers none. For a time "not even the nurses may be admitted to the government homes or hospitals."[29]

Even the pragmatic, lighthearted Candy suffers from terrible dreams and visions: "Why, now that the war was over, should she remember in those moments before she slept each separate distressing sight and experience she had known? And why, asleep, should she be forced to endure again and again the angry drone of besieging planes, the sight of walls crumbling about her, the roof tumbling in upon her, the horror of dying people crying beneath the wreckage."[30]

No better evidence of the impact of World War I on the women who worked in it exists than in the novels of Mary Lee and Ruth McKee. Factually based, they demonstrate that the women of World War I, like the women of the Vietnam War, were subject to what we have come to call post-traumatic stress disorder. Mary Lee's Anne suffers from aching teeth and falling hair, from an inability to make decisions, from an unwillingness to settle down, to adapt to dull routine, from the impossibility of reconciling the inconsistencies of the establishment which will "send the whole generation to war, and then fuss about a person's morals!"[31]

CHAPTER 10

The Women's War Against War

I took my power in my hand,
And went against the world;
'Twas not so much as David had
But I was twice as bold.

I aimed my pebble, but myself
Was all the one that fell.
Was it Goliath was too large,
Or only I too small?
—Emily Dickinson

EMILY BALCH, evaluating in 1946 women's efforts for peace in World War I, quoted this poem. Probably Goliath was too large. Despite the growing vigor of the peace movement from the mid-nineteenth century to 1914, an ancient concept of war still attracted the support of Americans as different as Teddy Roosevelt and the social reformer Vida Dutton Scudder: war as an exercise of strength, virility, and chivalry, periodically necessary for the health of the country and its individual citizens. Scudder, later to become an absolute pacifist, during World War I found herself ". . . unwilling to cast on the scrap heap the ancient record of the glorious virtues engendered by war. . . . My apologia for war was contained in one word: chivalry. That word connotes heroism raised to the nth degree of sacrifice; it connotes the defense of the weak, and it implies a world which is a battlefield. Fighting is the condition of real living. . . ."[1]

Besides, this particular war roused the sympathies of the many

American Anglophiles and Francophiles, disillusioned the adherents of German *Kultur* through actual atrocities like the burning of the library at Louvain and alleged atrocities assiduously publicized by Allied propaganda, appealed to the idealism of the true believers in a war to end wars and make the world safe for democracy, and swelled the pocketbooks of the industrialists and workers who benefited by American arms sales.

But the declaration of war in Europe appalled the millions of Americans who believed that Western civilization had evolved beyond war. Jane Addams described "that basic sense of desolation, of suicide, of anachronism, which that first news of the war brought to thousands of men and women who had come to consider war as a throwback in the scientific sense."[2] And Emily Balch: "My formative years were passed in the long Victorian peace and war seemed as obsolete as chain armor."[3]

Women felt a special urgency to stop the war, partly because they had long been prominent in the peace movement, partly because of the close connections between the suffrage and the peace movements, but most of all, perhaps, because of the still-honored tradition that women were morally superior to men and responsible for restraining men's passions—whether of love or of war. The appeal to women to stop the war that men had started met a response among many different kinds of women. As the famed social worker Lillian Wald wrote, "The voices of free women rise above the sounds of battle in behalf of those women and children abroad, for it is against women and children that war has ever been really waged."[4]

Women at once imaginatively and ingeniously, entrepreneurially, set about rallying for peace and seeking means to halt the war. Ready to help were huge numbers of American women whose organizations—from the YWCA to the DAR—had committed themselves to preserving the peace. To coordinate their efforts, in January of 1915 Carrie Chapman Catt, with the encouragement of the British suffragist Emmeline Pethick-Lawrence and the Hungarian journalist Rosika Schwimmer, convoked the Woman's Peace Party, a group of eighty-eight leaders, who besides their many Stateside activities formulated a plan for an international conference of neutrals. They found support among European women whom they knew from their work in such organizations as the International Woman Suffrage Alliance (IWSA).

In mid-February 1915, Dr. Aletta Jacobs, a Dutch physician, with a group of fellow-workers in the IWSA from Holland, Belgium, Germany, and Britain, issued invitations to an International Congress of Women at The Hague *and* agreed to support it financially. They asked Jane Addams as a prominent neutral to preside. Despite the opposition of several governments, some 2,000 women attended the sessions, of whom 1,136 were voting members, representing 150 organizations in twelve countries. No Russian women attended, and no French—although the French were the first to form a national organization to support the programs the Congress worked out. But there were British women, and Germans, Austrians, Hungarians, Italians, Poles, Belgians, Dutch, Americans, Danes, Norwegians, and Swedes.

The forty-seven American delegates were an impressive group, built around a nucleus of Hull House residents, uniting women from the American Federation of Labor with the Daughters of the American Revolution. They were, Balch wrote, "a very heterogeneous group of mostly highly individualized women used to being leaders and playing a conspicuous role, 'rebels' by temperament in many cases. . . ."[5] Yet "Every woman on board was tense with the desire to serve to her utmost capacity in the cause of peace."[6]

Their own accomplishments distinguished many—among them Sophonisba Breckinridge, dean of the Chicago School of Civics and Philanthropy; Grace Abbott, director of the Immigrants' Protective League; Dr. Alice Hamilton, expert on industrial health; Emily Balch, professor of labor and economics at Wellesley; Mary Heaton Vorse, godmother of the Provincetown Players and labor reporter; Madeleine Doty, lawyer, social reformer, and journalist; Annie Molloy, president of the Telephone Operators Union of Boston; Elizabeth Glendower Evans, social reformer and contributing editor of *La Follette's Magazine;* Belle La Follette, progressivist leader; Mabel Hyde Kittredge, founder of the Association of Practical Housekeeping Centers; and Alice Thacher Post, editor, and vice president of the American Anti-Imperialist League and the Women's Peace Party.

Among them, too, was the Canadian-born Julia Grace Wales, author of a remarkable plan for "Arbitration without Armistice," calling for the immediate appointment by their governments of a commission of experts from neutral countries to mediate continuously, offering to all the belligerents a series of proposals to end the war. The commission's activities were to be publicized, both to give hope of peace and to preclude the secret diplomacy that many believed had cast the world into war. Ultimately Wales proposed a supranational organization. The Wisconsin State Legislature had already endorsed this plan and recommended it to the United States Congress. On shipboard Wales familiarized the delegates with it, and the delegates decided to advocate it in the International Congress of Women.

Rosika Schwimmer also sailed with the delegation. This daring, gifted, exasperating ideologue fatefully changed the course of the work for peace. By 1914 she already had behind her a career in Hungary as a social reformer and feminist, organizing women agricultural laborers and office workers. She had published her own mediation plan, and worked in England as a correspondent for European newspapers and press secretary for the International Woman Suffrage Alliance. In the United States she cooperated with Catt, saw Wilson, lectured widely, fomented many a peace initiative. She charismatically inspired the pacifists to extraordinary efforts, but almost no one could work with her. As events demonstrated, only Jane Addams, with all her political skills and the power derived from her soaring reputation, could (sometimes) check Schwimmer and, ironically, enable her to function productively.

Do you think there is a ghost of a chance of bringing peace on earth or anything lastingly useful by going? If so, I'll go if they blow me to atoms. . . ."

—Leonora O'Reilly[7]

The delegation, who sailed on the *Noordam* April 12, 1915, conscientiously applied themselves to preparations for the Congress, an experience, Alice Hamilton observed, "like a perpetual meeting of the Woman's City Club. . . . It is interesting to see the party

evolve from a chaotic lot of half-informed people, and muddled en-
thusiasts, and sentimentalists, with a few really informed ones, into
a docile, teachable, coherent body. . . . We have long passed the
stage of poems and impassioned appeals and 'messages from wom-
ankind' and willingness to die in the cause, and now we are discussing
whether it is more dangerous to insist on democratic control of diplomacy than it is to insist on the neutralization of the seas."[8]

These women recognized all too well the improbability of success
for their unique enterprise. "We know we are ridiculous," said Emily
Balch, "but even being ridiculous is useful sometimes and so too are
enfants terribles that say out what needs to be said but what it is not
discreet or 'the thing' to say and which important people will not
say in consequence."[9] Or, as Leonora O'Reilly more earthily put it,
". . . the reason women succeed in doing new things while men stay
put in ways that are old, is that the women are such darn fools they
don't know the thing can't be done. . . . maybe . . . the future will
show how the God of War was vanquished forever by the Goddess
of Peace."[10]

When the *Noordam* had almost reached Europe, it was inter-
cepted and detained incommunicado for four days by the British—
no one knows just why. But it was difficult for the women not to
wonder whether the British were trying to keep them from attending
the conference, particularly when the British press labeled them
"Pro-Hun Peacettes," the American ambassador to England, Walter
Hines Page, contemptuously dubbed their ship "The Palace of
Doves," and the main body of the British delegation to the congress
were prevented from attending. At any rate the situation was trying
for the Americans, forced to lie at anchor surrounded by the booming
of cannon, the comings and goings of vessels of war, and the occasional explosion of a loose mine. Fortunately their eventual release
allowed them to reach The Hague in time for the opening of the
congress on April 28, 1915.

In the four days of the congress the delegates' indomitable commitment to peace overrode their natural antagonisms as citizens of
the belligerent nations and their disagreements about the means by
which to end the fighting and prevent future wars. Their unexampled
self-discipline is highlighted in Margaret Sanger's account of her

encounter elsewhere with five German delegates to the congress. "Unable to comprehend how those towards whom they felt such friendliness could return this sentiment with hatred, the women said to me in bewilderment, 'Tell us really why people who do not know us hate us as they do.' The dignity of their sorrow, the heavy burden of grief under which they labored, the very calmness and fairness with which they bore it, had a quieting effect."[11]

At the congress the delegates faced down the jeers of the press, most of whom, Balch wrote, "apparently had been sent to get an amusing story of an international peace gathering of women—'base and silly' enough to try to meet in war time—breaking up in quarrel. Day by day they went away with faces long with disappointment. In England the congress was reported to be managed in the interest of Germany; in Germany the delegates were threatened with social boycott for attending a pro-British meeting; and in many countries the meetings were reported to have been either practically unattended or to have closed in a row. Nothing could be further from the truth. . . ."[12]

Of course the delegates sometimes disagreed, vigorously and energetically. Rosika Schwimmer denounced Alice Post for suggesting the acceptability of some wars. Some delegates wanted immediate peace; others wanted only a peace accompanied by justice! Delegates differed on procedures: as Lucy Biddle Lewis observed, "The foreigners are not able to understand our American democratic ideas and debate and discussion are almost stifled by their rules governing the Congress. It is very galling to Miss Addams, who fights bravely for more freedom . . . but has to obey the rules in her capacity as chairman: she lets off steam when with us alone, and it is fun to hear her."[13]

But the participants avoided discussing responsibility for the war and methods of conducting it. They avoided clashing along national lines. The feeling of the assembly was epitomized on the second day with the arrival of five Belgian women who had wangled from the German occupation authorities permission to attend: a German delegate rose to welcome them, and asked that they be seated on the platform. That spirit expressed itself conclusively in the accomplishments of the congress.

Notably, the congress constructed a series of principles as conditions of a permanent peace, among them:

1. No territory should be transferred without the consent of the men and women in it. The right of conquest should not be recognized.
2. Autonomy and a democratic parliament should not be refused to any people.
3. The governments of all nations should agree to refer future international disputes to arbitration or conciliation and to bring social, moral, and economic pressure to bear upon any country which resorts to arms.
4. Foreign policies should be subject to democratic control.
5. Women should be granted equal political rights with men.[14]

President Wilson later told Addams, "I consider [these proposals] by far the best formulation which up to the moment has been put out by any body," and borrowed many of them for his Fourteen Points.[15]

The congress also created the International Committee of Women for Permanent Peace, today known as the Women's International League for Peace and Freedom. This organization planned to meet after the war when and where peace terms were being negotiated, intending that women should thus have input into the treaty making.

And, most controversially, the magic oratory of Rosika Schwimmer persuaded the congress to send two delegations to hand-deliver to the prime ministers and foreign ministers of the neutral and belligerent countries its resolutions and plans. This extraordinary scheme originally struck Addams as "hopelessly melodramatic and absurd," and Hamilton as "a singularly fool performance."[16] But Schwimmer sold it to the delegates as a first step toward implementing Wales's plan for continuous mediation.

Reluctantly, when she saw how much this unorthodox venture meant to some of the European delegates, Addams yielded. She felt it barely possibly that by undertaking this mission the women might improve the chances of adoption of continuous mediation. How were those people in the belligerent countries who wanted peace to communicate otherwise, with the newspapers under the control of the war parties? How else could a politician who wanted peace build a base of popular support? How else, indeed, could anyone even make an informed judgment, absent the information that the press was not printing? Obviously governments presently incommunicado needed channels of communication.

"We believed," Hamilton cogently wrote in 1943, "that while offers of mediation by a single nation might be rejected because one side might feel doubts of the impartiality of that nation, the same objection would not be felt toward a conference which would include nations of different sympathies. . . . We believed also that placing conditional proposals simultaneously before both sides would bring out into the open the real attitudes of governments and strengthen the hands of the pacifically inclined ministers who were struggling against the militarists and who, in the absence of any such strengthening, were destined . . . to go down before the bitter-enders. Governments at war cannot ask for negotiations . . . lest this be at once construed . . . as a sign of weakness. But if neutral people commanding the respect of those ministers should study the situation and make proposals over and over again if necessary, something might be found upon which negotiations might start." And, looking back twenty-five years later Hamilton asked, "Can anyone believe that soldiers could have been held in the trenches through 1916 and 1917, if they had known that their governments were refusing peace terms which were fair and reasonable?"[17] An interesting question, given the mutiny of the French army in 1917.

So Addams set off with Rosa Genoni, Aletta Jacobs, and Alice Hamilton to visit the officials of Austria-Hungary, Belgium, France, Germany, Italy, Switzerland, and Great Britain. A second group— Rosika Schwimmer, Cora Ramondt-Hirschmann, Christal Macmillan, and Emily Balch, with Julia Wales as secretary—went to the Scandinavian countries and Russia. Since each had to pay her own expenses, and only neutrals and allies could go to warring countries, the delegations were hard to arrange. Among them they interviewed twenty-two prime ministers and foreign ministers, two presidents, a king, and the pope—all in five weeks.

Hamilton, who downplayed her role as that of a "confidante [to Addams] in white linen," and a "lady's maid," reflected the sense of unreality that enveloped these women as they made their way through a Europe at war. In Belgium "it was all so new as to be unbelievable: the search at the border when the German woman passed her hands all over my body and ran her fingers through my hair and cut the 'Marshall Field' label from my hat and confiscated my Baedeker because it had maps . . . the visit to the [American] Legation . . . to receive many warnings about spies and pitfalls which might mean confiscation of our passports and indefinite delays. And a surreptitious trip . . . to ruined Louvain."[18]

But even in such circumstances, Hamilton recognized the ridiculous: "Our Italiana friends were much excited when they heard we were to have a private interview [with the Pope] and they saw to it that we were properly dressed, in long-sleeved and high-necked dresses . . . and veils of black Spanish lace on our heads. We were ushered in past the gorgeous Swiss guards . . . to the inner part of the palace where they were replaced by still more impressive figures, men in beautiful suits of ecclesiastical red brocaded silk, or of black velvet faced with blue satin and trimmed with silver. As we sat waiting in the antechamber in a crowd of somber-clad women, I could not help speculating on this striking contrast between the sexes which was evidently planned deliberately. We women must so dress ourselves as to obscure all our charms—if any—lest we seduce the thoughts of the men, but they, on the contrary, might make themselves into figures so beautiful that we could not help being fascinated. It seemed to imply a much greater spiritual resistance on the part of the weaker sex, and it was certainly an indirect tribute to our charms—an undeserved one, I thought, for as I looked around the room I did not see one woman who could disturb the thoughts even of Saint Anthony the Hermit."[19]

🏵🏵🏵 *One official "said that he had wondered many times since the war began why women had remained silent so long,*

adding that as women are not expected to fight they might easily
have made a protest against war which is denied to men."
                                        —Jane Addams[20]

Throughout the trip the delegates strove conscientiously to record and accurately interpret the official responses, listening carefully
to tone as well as content—and to off-the-record comments. "The
delegation," Emily Balch wrote, "did not find a general desire to
fight to the bitter end."[21] Except in France, they heard unequivocally
that repeated submissions of peace terms by respected neutral nations
might discover grounds on which to begin negotiations.

Besides the reactions of officialdom, the women in the delegations were also forming impressions of the war's impact on other
people. In general, Hamilton observed, Germans "were absolutely
sure that Germany was fighting in self-defense, they reverenced the
military so deeply that to them the actions of Belgian francs-tireurs
[sharpshooting guerrillas] was a horrible crime, and even the very
best of them accepted the *Lusitania* incident without questioning.
She was carrying munitions, the passengers had been warned, she
was rightly doomed. One really lovely young married woman told
us that the day the news came she declared a holiday and took her
children on a picnic to the country to celebrate."[22]

But also everywhere they went the delegations were meeting
pacifists, sometimes individually, sometimes—especially in the Scandinavian countries—by the thousands at peace rallies. Even in the
kaiser's Germany workers conducted mass demonstrations to demand
peace. What the delegates heard from the pacifists and the war weary
contradicted the official line.

To counterbalance the ubiquitous jingoistic press reports, the
women gave voice to the protests against the war they heard among
both the Allies and the Central Powers. "It was hard to see my boy
go," a German soldier's mother told them, "because he did not
believe in war; he did not belong to a generation that believes in
war." And Addams saw a letter from a young Englishman who
"congratulated himself upon the loss of a leg because it enabled him
to resume reasonable living with an undivided mind. He had responded to his country's call in deference to the opinion of older

men. He would now return to the ideas of his own generation." At one hospital she heard of five German soldiers who killed themselves because "they would not be put into a position where they would have to kill others."[23]

Addams and the other women knew that most soldiers did not share such sentiments. "It would be impossible of course," Addams wrote, "from one type of man to make any generalizations in regard to the 'average' soldier." Similarly, they discerned among civilians "two bodies of enthusiasm: one, and by far the larger, believes that the war can be settled only upon a military basis after a series of smashing victories; the other, a civil party, very much deprecates the exaltation of militarism and contends that the longer the war is carried on, the longer the military continues censoring the press and exercising other powers not ordinarily accorded to it . . . the more difficult it will be for normal civil life to reestablish itself."[24]

The hope of civilization lay in the voices of peace. What more appropriate task for women than to carry their message to the officials who could negotiate to end the war and to the public? Who else would, could, do it? "We were told," Jane Addams wrote, "of soldiers who say to their hospital nurses: 'We can do nothing for ourselves but go back to the trenches so long as we are able. Cannot the women do something about this war? Are you kind to us only when we are wounded?' "[25]

Well, they tried. The women themselves modestly claimed little for their efforts. "We do not wish to overestimate a very slight achievement," Addams wrote, "nor to take too seriously the kindness with which the delegation was received, but we do wish to record ourselves as being quite sure that at least a few citizens in these various countries, some of them officials in high places, were grateful for the effort we made."[26] Looking back from 1943 the brilliant Hamilton wrote: "It still seems to me the wisest and most practical scheme put forward by any group during the World War and I believe had President Wilson (or Colonel House) been willing to try it, success might have followed instead of failure. . . ."[27]

Certainly the women had enabled communication among enemy countries. They had introduced the possibility of a neutral conference for mediation to officials and to the public. They had offered alternatives where none had existed before. Wilson, of course, did not back their efforts. Politically he wanted the support of the pacifists. But, as he was to say, "My heart is with them, but my mind has a contempt for them. I want peace, but I know how to get it, and they do not."[28] They failed, and he failed.

On their return from Europe in the early summer of 1915, the delegates rejoined the vigorous ongoing domestic campaign for peace. As they had to abandon their expectations of governmental mediation, they began to consider the advantages of nongovernmental mediators.

At this juncture, the peace efforts moved into the realm of mysticism and melodrama, spinning out of the control of the responsible women who had heretofore directed them. In dramatic contrast with the careful, broad-based planning for the International Congress of Women, serendipity and impulse, with a touch of mysticism, initiated the Peace Ship and the Neutral Conference for Continuous Mediation.

As the pacifists cast about for financial support of nongovernmental mediation, in the ears of ex-delegate Rebecca Shelley, she said, rang the voice of God, with the message "Go to Ford." Off she went to Detroit, where persistence and a chance encounter enabled her to set up a meeting between Henry Ford and Rosika Schwimmer.[29] Schwimmer and Ford—what a bizarre combination! She a sophisticated, educated, radical European Jewish woman; he the quintessential self-made, ignorant, anti-Semitic American man. Both were brilliantly entrepreneurial. Both wanted to end the war.

Once committed, Ford wasted no time. In late November of 1915 he visited Wilson to offer him unlimited financial backing for a neutral commission—an offer that Wilson refused on the grounds that a better plan might come along later. Ford pushed: he had chartered a ship; Wilson could use it if he chose to transport delegates to Europe; if he wouldn't, Ford would.[30]

Upon Wilson's refusal, Ford announced to the press, on November 24, that he would have the boys in the trenches home by Christmas. He and Schwimmer between them loosed pandemonium. Schwimmer spent Ford's money wildly. Ford rattled on to the press: "I have all faith that on Christmas Day the world will see a general strike—that on that day of days war-worn men will climb down from the trenches, throw down their arms and start home. . . . A general strike on Christmas Day, that is what we want."[31]

The press, as skeptical as at the International Congress of Women, found a plethora of material to exploit. One of the reporters on the Peace Ship, Burnet Hershey, admitted that their "cynicism helped to wreck the 'Peace Chase' with a cruelty and levity that was unique in American newspaper reporting." More than a decade later the *Chicago Tribune* was still sneering, in a biographical note on its reporter Sara Moore: "Her last big assignment was the Ford Peace ship story. That meant sixty days in Europe with the peace delegates! A peace banquet and luncheon every day, with speeches in four languages, completely broke her spirit, so she came back and got married, and settled down. . . ."[32]

Wales, Balch, Addams, all the patient, painstaking, responsible workers for peace, were aghast. The serious purpose of implementing the Wales mediation plan was foundering. Yet what could they do but cooperate in the Schwimmer/Ford undertaking, even though they could not control it? As Addams said, "I was fifty-five years old in 1915; I had already 'learned from life' that moral results are often obtained through the most unexpected agencies."[33]

The invitations were issued just a week before the *Oscar II* sailed. Many refused, including all of the socialists, and the entire executive board of the Women's Peace Party. The group that sailed on December 4, 1915, included forty-four members of the press. Fifty-five passengers, about half women and half men, were delegates. The eleven members of the staff under general secretary Louis Lochner and expert advisor Schwimmer were called working delegates. Rebecca Shelley took charge of the twenty-five students who went along as observers.

Though few on the Peace Ship were well known outside their own fields, the passenger list did include a governor, a lieutenant governor, and six gubernatorial representatives; Grace DeGraff, from the Oregon State Federation of Women's Clubs; Katherine Devereux Blake, of the New York Peace Society; Mary Fels, heir to a soap fortune and charter member of the Women's Peace Party; Helen Ring Robinson, the first woman elected to a state senate; septu-

agenarian May Wright Sewall, suffragist organizer; Henrietta Neu-
haus, founding member of the absolute pacifist Fellowship of
Reconciliation; Julia Grace Wales; and the colorful Inez Milholland
Boissevain, lawyer, feminist, pacifist, and war correspondent, no-
torious for leading a suffragist parade down Fifth Avenue in a Grecian
gown on a white charger, with her hair down her back. Inevitably,
the hastily collected group also attracted a few adventurers only too
pleased to travel to Europe at the expense of Mr. Ford.[34]

It did *not* include Jane Addams, who at the last moment had to
withdraw because of illness. She had reluctantly agreed to go, but
only as an individual. She warned the Woman's Peace Party in the
United States and the International Committee of Women in Europe
to dissociate themselves from the venture. ". . . if she had gone,"
Ida M. Tarbell insightfully wrote, "things would have been different
on the Peace Ship, for she and not Madame Schwimmer would have
been in command. . . . But she did not go."[35]

The breathless, off-the-cuff atmosphere of the enterprise is
caught in Lella Secor Florence's account. "Pretty, piquant, blessed
with a mop of golden red curls and total self-confidence," she was
sent by the *Seattle Post-Intelligencer* to cover the Peace Ship.[36] She
boarded the ship with a faked passport on "the heels of William
Jennings Bryan who had come along to wish the venture God-speed.
. . . I hadn't the slightest idea what the Ford Peace Ship was designed
to do—they seemed to want the war to stop and that was sensible
enough. . . . The whole scheme had been organised in such haste
that many of its details had to be worked out after the *Oscatwo*, as
the ship came to be known, had got under way." Ford, accustomed
to factory autocracy rather than participatory democracy or international anarchy, could not see the problem: "I doubt if he ever gave
much thought to the plans and purposes of the Neutral Conference
once he had decided to support the venture. It seemed a silly thing
for the war to go on, and he felt that people would be reasonable
and stop it if you got hold of them and talked it over."[37]

Bickering and shipboard politicking disrupted the harmony,
purpose, earnest conversations, and well-attended meetings of the
early part of the voyage. Schwimmer, clutching a black bag of "secret
documents," quarreled with the press, temporarily locking them out

of the wireless room, and split the delegates on the issue of what answer to make to Wilson's advocacy of military preparedness. "A sincere attempt at democratic control," said Florence, "was often frustrated by the strange atmosphere of critical mistrust which seemed early to develop on board the peace ship, and which was fostered and encouraged at every turn by the newspaper contingent."[38]

Once on the Continent the delegates met wariness, mistrust, and resentment at American interference in European affairs—even though Ford's money flowed for meetings, nightly dinners, and at each stop a $10,000 contribution to a worthy local cause. Schwimmer's maneuvers alienated many Scandinavian and Dutch pacifists. On December 21 Ford, plagued by minor illness, decided to go home. He would continue his financial support, but he himself effectively washed his hands of the enterprise. By mid-January 1916, six weeks after they had left, most of the party had followed him back to the States.

Ford dubbed the enterprise a success. And in a sense it was. For, despite the political machinations in which the Americans indulged and the sorry spectacle they presented to the European pacifists, they did manage to start up the Neutral Conference for Continuous Mediation.

The Neutral Conference had as stormy a passage as the Peace Ship. Its constitution provided for five delegates from each of the six neutral countries; the United States never mustered more than two—one of whom, fortunately, was the competent and well-informed Emily Balch, whom Jane Addams, still sick, sent as her surrogate. Only a third of the delegates were women, half of whom had attended the International Congress of Women, and many of whom later worked in the League of Nations. Chaos, crises, and Louis Lochner finally forced Schwimmer's resignation, but the convulsions continued. Chance or design prevented the assumption of leadership by the able women who had guided the International Congress, and the members of the conference as they maneuvered for power showed little of the forbearance which had characterized the women at the congress.

Worst of all, the stresses and strains eroded the principle of continuous mediation which was the reason the conference existed. Julia Grace Wales, a tactful, gentle woman, who persevered on the staff despite disappointments and insults, watched the conference pummel and finally abandon her plan. The delegates disagreed about their mission: to concentrate on ending the war as soon as possible by continuous mediation, or to focus on helping to construct a just peace. Whatever chance they had of a successful compromise vanished as Ford's representatives repeatedly cut back funds. The delegates did, however, manage to formulate, submit to the belligerent powers, and publicize tentative peace proposals.

By the summer of 1916 the conference had effectively ceased to exist. In its final agonies Ford ordered Lochner to get the women out. He officially disbanded the conference on February 1, 1917. Emily Balch, a woman worth listening to, always regarded "it as a terrible pity that Mr. Ford abruptly ended his experiment."[39] Julia Grace Wales bravely said that they had offered their "mite . . . to a great world movement." And Jane Addams commented wryly: "I suppose we ought to be grateful for having had a chance for fifteen months."[40]

🗡🗡🗡 *Never again must women dare to believe that they are without responsibility because they are without power. Public opinion is power; strong and reasonable feeling is power; determination, which is a twin sister of faith or vision, is power.*
                                                            —Emily Balch[41]

But how hard American and European pacifist women tried to end World War I—soon, and with a just peace. How well, all things considered, they worked together—particularly when women controlled the effort, as in the International Congress of Women. How much they achieved, in communicating among the belligerents and in initiating a process of continuous mediation. Where in history, before or since, can one find a parallel for what these remarkable women created and accomplished? Merely to conceive the idea, as Wales did, let alone to implement it, as the International Congress of Women and the Neutral Conference (in some sense an offspring, however frail, of the congress) tried to do, was a breakthrough without precedent in international relations.

Such enterprises are expensive to the human spirit—though the women who led were not ones to count the cost. Julia Grace Wales was to continue teaching at the University of Wisconsin, and Dr. Alice Hamilton after the congress resumed her distinguished career as a pioneer in industrial medicine. Emily Balch went on working with peace groups; in the spring of 1919 while she was attending the second Women's Congress she learned of the decision of the Wellesley trustees not to reappoint her. But her work in pacifism, which she continued in the Women's International League for Peace and Freedom, eventually won her the Nobel Prize.

Jane Addams in an address at Carnegie Hall in 1915 reported what she had learned in her wartime travels, adding incidentally, "We heard in all countries . . . statements in regard to the necessity for the use of stimulant before men would engage in bayonet charges—that they have a regular formula [ether, Hamilton said] in Germany, that they give them rum in England and absinthe in France; that they have to give them the 'dope' before the bayonet charge is possible."[42] This interjection, despite its accuracy, precipitated a widespread and virulent attack on Addams. She who had built a reputation approaching that of a saint was castigated as "a silly, vain, impertinent old maid." And of course some men extended the attack to women in general; a letter to the Rochester *Herald* argued, "If the woman conceded by her sisters to be the ablest of her sex, is so readily duped, so little informed, men wonder what degree of intelligence is to be secured by adding the female vote to the electorate."[43] Addams went courageously on with her work for peace, but never did she regain the reputation and influence that she had won earlier.

Rosika Schwimmer, born for conflict, after the war was appointed by the Karolyi government of Hungary as minister to Switzerland. But foreign friends had to smuggle her out of Hungary when the Communists took power, and she spent bitter years homeless, stateless, in broken health. In the United States she was accused of being alternatively a Bolshevik agent and a German spy, and in 1929 was denied citizenship because she would not take an oath to bear arms in the defense of the country—a moot point, it would seem, for one of her age, sex, and condition of health. Supported by the charity of friends, she fought on, originating a plan for a world center for women's archives, and trying to instigate an appeal to lock up Mussolini in an insane asylum. A woman of ideas.

CHAPTER 11

The Front as Frontier

THE DIARIES, memoirs, and letters of American women overseas in World War I overflow with accounts of what they did. But what of the quality of their lives? It's hard to discover how they came to feel about their own experiences in particular and about the war in general. And it's even harder to judge the impact of their experiences on their personalities, their value systems, and the rest of their lives, particularly since after the war no one thought much about these women; certainly no one studied them.

The women themselves did, of course, sometimes describe their reactions. But the conventions of the day inhibited them. Nice women—and these were almost all thoroughly nice women—did not gossip, did not openly criticize men, did not say anything that might damage another woman's reputation, did not worry their families unnecessarily, and did not talk about certain areas of experience, particularly sexual experience. Not, it should by now be clear, that these were self-effacing namby-pambies afraid to speak, but rather that concern for others was the hallmark of their good manners. And that, as with all of us, the mythos of the time colored their perceptions and influenced their behavior. Given this societally ordered conspiracy of silence, or at least of polite understatement, what were the women not saying?

♦♦♦ *Was there ever an army where a girl could live alone in a tent in the middle of an enormous Aviation camp and feel as safe as a church and be treated with the utmost respect and consideration by everyone? I think not. . . . Sometimes I get a little discouraged with men and their ways over here, but when*

I see how they treat American girls, I can see that we are a lap ahead of the others in civilization.

—Mary Lee[1]

Did the women, for instance, suffer from sexual harassment? Did they have affairs, get pregnant, get sent home in disgrace?

American society allowed its young women an independence unusual or even forbidden elsewhere, because it regarded friendship, asexual relationships, as possible between them and young American men. "Even the young Frenchmen are impressed by our strange ways," an American soldier confided to Elizabeth Shepley Sergeant. "At first, of course, they simply couldn't 'get' us at all—us and our Y girls. They thought it was all some sort of a hypocritical fake. But now they believe and rather admire, though some of them simply can't understand how it is possible for a man and a woman to go off for a day's excursion on mere comradely terms, or for a man like myself to have so many close friends among women and still care for only one."[2]

Theoretically such friendship was a camaraderie of peers—but it rested on a "separate but equal" doctrine that blandly concealed inequities of power and privilege: men were superior in and responsible for political and financial affairs, women in and for the domestic and moral spheres. The omnipresent chitchat about the powers of mothers to change the world originated in the fallacy so attractive to the male mind: that a society that denied women the vote, control over their own bodies, and economic independence still somehow vested its "real" power in women, was still miraculously matriarchal. The power ascribed to American women was only moral, with about as much force as a moral victory. But it carried with it the assignment to women of moral responsibility. Women bore the onus of guarding not only their own virtue but also that of men. Whatever else she did, the American woman must be pure, and she must strive to keep the American man pure as well.

But the presumption was in her favor—and his. "Our boys were so much cleaner physically and morally than the average European, so free from drunkenness and vice, lewdness and debauchery, that they stood out in comparison with the soldiers of the other allied nations, excepting the Canadians . . . as a great tall lone pine tree stands out in a clearing in the wilderness," ran one paean to this inane myth.[3] Clara Savage Littledale, correspondent for *Good House-keeping*, straightfacedly reported the reaction of American troops accosted by a French prostitute. "Disgust was written all over their faces. She was repulsive to them. They were just three typical American boys, young and clean and decent, and instinctively they loathed the horrible commercial vulgarity of this street woman of France."[4] Why? In his heart the doughboy "has kept an ideal [of American womanhood]," Katherine Morse asserted. "It has stood between him and utter darkness. In this ideal he put all his faith. If he loses it, he loses everything."[5]

Therefore "our boys" always protected the pure American woman: "Say! There are twenty fellows just standing around [the YMCA canteen worker], hoping that some one will say something she doesn't like, so that they can knock his block off. If I ever want to get in the hospital quick, I'll just go up and look crosseyed at her. The next day they would be sending me flowers and walking slow behind me. When it comes to having body guards, the Kaiser is a piker compared to her."[6]

Meanwhile, in Piccadilly Circus and Pigalle, the doughboy found his playmates. In fact, of course, the whole myth rested on a cultural double standard. As the librarian Samuel H. Ranck commented, "The number of boys in that barbed wire and guarded enclosure [of the Venereal Disease Stockade in just one camp] equaled the total attendance at an annual meeting of the ALA [American Library Association]."[7] Doughboys differentiated between "nice" American girls and other women, and treated them differently. American troops behaved so badly in Paris as to cause the United States Army to close the city to them and create leave areas in its place—while, at the same time the "boys" approached the American women in the YMCA canteens with respectful deference.

Ruth McKee in her novel *Three Daughters* sketches the doughboy ethic: "Always there were American soldiers going up to the front, young, clean, hilarious. They leaned out to yell and cheer and throw kisses. One boy gestured in a more primitive fashion, then, hearing a 'Hello, Yanks!' from the girls, was so overcome that he dropped off the slow-moving truck and ran back to beg them to forgive him for being 'fresh.' He thought they were French girls! He didn't know there were any honest-to-God American girls up there!"[8] Elsie Janis too identified this double standard: ". . . one of the most wonderful things in the A.E.F. was the absolute and undying respect the American soldiers had for the American girl. They put them on a pedestal that grew and grew with each succeeding day the boys spent in France. The more he saw of other women, the more he boosted the girl at home, until she was almost too high to be human."[9]

The contemporary records' repetition of the story of the protective ring of fire around the American woman and the consistent gallantry of the American doughboy testifies to the power of the myth. Officialdom assiduously propagated it: Secretary of War Newton D. Baker remarked that he had never seen a doughboy who was not "living a life which he would not be willing to have mother see him live."[10]

And, no doubt, the age, class, and character of most of the women who served overseas decreased the probability of sexual relationships with the men they nurtured. Not only were these women handpicked, but most of them were older, more privileged, and better educated than at least the enlisted men they catered to. Hear a YMCA canteener stationed at an airfield, where she repeatedly remarked that she liked the mechanics (enlisted men) *as well as* the cadets (officers): "Some of the mechanics here say the most delightful things. . . . They give us such subtle compliments. Like this: 'Which is the nut choc-lits, ma'am?' 'This in the blue wrapper. Do you like that kind?' 'Yas'm, I like blue wrappers and I like blue eyes, too!' Then embarrassment and blushes for fear he has said the wrong thing."[11]

At any rate, with these thousands of women living among hundreds of thousands of men, cases of sexual assault, affairs, and romance are almost completely missing from the record. Why? The sense that women's lives should mostly be anonymous, certainly as far as their intimate relationships were concerned? The fear of loss of reputation and censure? Strict discipline? Some women at least regarded skeptically romances that sprang up in such circumstances, like Adriana Studebaker, who found amusing "the inevitable proposals—and those who took them seriously, poor damsels!"[12] Women like that knew how to head off trouble before it arose: Henry S. Villard ruefully told a story of a date with a stunning Red Cross nurse in Italy: ". . . the wind suddenly went out of my sails when Agnes approached, for to my consternation she had Elsie Macdonald in tow. 'We have to travel in pairs, you know,' she said disingenuously."[13]

For whatever reason, only a handful of instances even of weddings turn up in the contemporary records—for instance, that of Ethel Harriman to a young American officer, a wedding complete with gown by Worth and Cole Porter at the piano, with the bride's mother conveniently in attendance on a trip to Europe for labor leader Samuel Gompers and the American Red Cross! Only at the end of the twenties did stories of wartime love affairs begin to surface in women's writings, usually in novels—like those of Mary Lee and Ruth McKee.

Obviously, American women and men overseas in World War I sometimes consorted with one another sexually. But, all things considered, it is improbable that American women were subjected to severe sexual harassment, though they did of course hear considerable grumbling from men, usually older or with at least some slight authority, who thought women didn't belong in the war zone at all, or who disliked the idea of women's doing "man's work." Certainly they never underwent anything like what the WACs and WAVES had to take from their male colleagues in World War II, or what military women experience from military men in today's armed forces.

> ❧❧❧ We were subject to court martial same as any other soldier.
> —Oleda Joure Christedes, telephone operator[14]

But if Americans in World War I agreed almost to a woman on their freedom from sexual harassment, they found other conditions of their work and life overseas trying: most of all, one would think, the underutilization of their abilities, skills, and training. For men too, of course: the inefficiencies of war transcend gender. Virginia Armistead Nelson's "first choice was sculpture as part of plastic surgery," but "like so many others she was assigned to an entirely different branch" of the YMCA.[15] The paleobotanist Ruth Holden, working in a British hospital, wrote on February 7, 1915: ". . . you said you hoped I had an orderly. No—I am the orderly—it's me that makes the beds, empties the slops, sweeps, dusts, etc. I'll admit I'm mighty sick of it, but the work has got to be done & lots busier people than I are doing such jobs."[16] Nelson's and Holden's cases strike a familiar note as instances of the kind of thing that happens in wartime to male and female alike.

But male aviators were not shoved aside, like the pilots Orra Heald Blackmore and Bernetta Miller, to do relief or canteen work or act as searchers.[17] And male doctors were not denied rank and sometimes forbidden to use their skills, whereas the resistance against women doctors and sometimes even women nurses was widespread. The physician Eleanor B. Kilham, for example, reported that a new chief surgeon of a big French military hospital near Bordeaux "announced that he did not want women in the Hospital. The Doctors protested; finally he said that they could not dress wounds, but could cook, make beds, etc."[18] Even in 1918 Harriot Stanton Blatch was cogently complaining of Red Cross underutilization of women in management positions, and the subordination of women nurses to male orderlies.[19]

Many women worked under rigid discipline—particularly those whose employing organizations had been militarized. Its severity depended, as always, upon who was running the show. Chief Operator Louise Barbour might describe the regulations in the YWCA hostess houses where the telephone operators lived as "similar in kind to those in the more liberal colleges for women," but other operators thought of office discipline as strict, paramilitary.[20] Louise Maxwell, warned that whenever General Pershing's light showed red on her switchboard she must "drop everything, disconnect anyone, and answer it within a half second," was so excited by his first call that after it she blurted loudly, " 'Gen. Pershing just asked me for the time!' Well, if a bomb had fallen in the office there couldn't have been more of a commotion. CO [Chief Operator Grace Banker] and supervisors came running, my headset was removed, and with a 'follow me' I was taken to our restroom where I was sternly reprimanded for disturbing the office in such a manner, and told that if Gen. Pershing were in residence, our office would have been notified . . . in other words, she didn't believe me. . . . With, 'You are confined to quarters for 30 days,' she walked out, very angry." The next day Pershing congratulated Banker on Maxwell's efficiency in giving him the time. Banker "admitted she had been hasty, but I was still confined to quarters for a week. Military discipline had to be maintained."[21] Oleda Joure Christedes too reported that discipline was "Strict! Which we accepted without question. War was serious business and not to be prolonged. Life was precious and so was our country."[22]

YMCA discipline sometimes competed in severity. One of their regulations specified that no woman might stay alone in a town without civilians. Mrs. Theodore Roosevelt, Jr., and Edith Stedman flouted the YMCA ban on smoking by putting their heads up a chimney and puffing away. A technicality triggered dishonorable discharges for canteeners Letitia W. Norris and Emma Claire Jones: they had not informed their superiors of their plans for a perfectly respectable postwar two-week vacation. AWOL! Even such infractions were rare, though; for all its strictness, the YMCA at war's end found cause to deny honorable discharges to only 2 percent of its women—none for "serious moral offenses."[23]

Women, like men, did have problems adjusting to military life and regulations. Experienced nurses resented the authority exercised over them by young doctors—of the Mercy Ship lot, seven nurses were relieved from duty for insubordination.[24] And throughout the war the refusal to give military rank to nurses exacerbated the difficulties—and rankled.

The overwhelming majority of war workers, self-disciplined women, seldom caused problems because of sloth or selfishness, but occasionally because of their independence. It was hard to convince a woman who daily fed thousands of men with supplies bargained from French peasants that she couldn't travel without permission.

Besides, in the still-patriarchal mode of the times, women workers were often subordinated to less-well-qualified men, particularly in the YMCA. A questionable decision, indeed. Consider the facts: the YMCA was recruiting four, five, even six times as many men as women, and competing for the men against the military and industry, inevitably under these conditions accepting some lazy, pietistic, self-righteous, and almost illiterate rednecks. At the same time, in its concern about introducing women into the war zone, the organization exercised extreme caution in the quality of its women.

Publicly the women voiced few complaints, but here and there the records whisper. Now and then a woman canteener commented on the refusal of a YMCA man to sell or serve food: he had been sent to France for higher, spiritual duties. Again a woman might mention her annoyance at having to stop making cocoa and frying doughnuts to cook breakfast for a YM man. Usually the women criticized only indirectly: one praised a male secretary by commenting on his delightful sense of humor, "a quality," she observed, "sometimes lacking in men secretaries."[25] Margaret Deland, in her sixties during her war service and perhaps privileged by her age, was more explicit: "There are arrogant, small-minded men who squabble about creeds, men who can see the religion of Jesus at a prayer meeting, but cannot see it in a dance or a football game, men who ought themselves to be in the trenches . . . men who ought to be put on the *Lusitania*. . . . mentally and temperamentally there seems to be a great gulf fixed between the men and the women workers."[26] And in a postwar letter to her erstwhile colleague Edith Stedman, Deland reminisced: "For my own part, I had no views about Mr. Cate [of the YMCA], but I remembered that you loathed him."[27]

卐卐卐 . . . *many even felt that their days were definitely numbered. This seemed to make people feel that they should cram everything possible into the short period left to them, and of course this attitude brought out the very worst in some, while in others it brought out all their good points.*

—Rhuie D. Caster[28]

Women reacted variously to the dangers, the hardships, and the exhaustion. Sometimes tempers flared, and jealousies eroded good intentions. Sometimes a nurse resigned when her candidate for head nurse was displaced by a Stateside appointee. The small American colony in Petrograd split into factions, perhaps over disagreements

about the administration of an orphan asylum the Americans supported.[29] Vira B. Whitehouse, on a quick trip back home in 1917,
remarked that on her ship "the greater number of passengers were
members of the Red Cross and the Y.M.C.A. who had not liked
their work or their superiors."[30]

Some women grew disillusioned, surrendering bit by bit their
idealistic hopes that this "Great War" might bring a millennial peace
to the world, convinced that nothing was worth the suffering they
watched. Others succumbed to the battering of the atrocity stories
constantly disseminated by the British and French and circulated by
American media. As if the harsh realities of war weren't bad enough,
some people—American women who should have known better included—assiduously passed on rumors, especially early in the war.
In their turn the atrocity stories combined with all the other tensions
to evoke some horrifyingly bloodthirsty outbursts from American
women overseas, at least the true believers among them. Marie Van
Vorst in October 1914: "My maid came to me the other day and
said, with a smile of positive joy, 'Isn't it perfectly lovely, Miss,
another son of the "Kayser" has been killed.' I have not seen a
woman who would not tear the War Lord to pieces with her own
hands, and I could begin it with joy."[31]

Even the flippant Elsie Janis indulged in such vituperations. She
enjoyed "a most wonderful dinner with the officers of a famous
regiment of engineers who specialize in putting on 'hours of hate'
for the Boche—that is, they travel about from sector to sector, and
when our people want some especially deadly gas these fellows arrive
and put on a Dillingham production of 'poison gas' assorted." But
her red-letter day came when she "personally killed a German and
maybe three or four" by firing a cannon. "They told me I was the
only woman who had fired regular hundred and fifty-five power hate
into Germany."[32]

Mrs. James T. Anderson of the YMCA, much admired for her
motherly relationship with the doughboys, received a parcel containing "a lot of Boche buttons, an iron cross, and the spurs, belt,
and rank insignia of a German captain. 'Dear Madam,' ran the note
enclosed, 'when we said good-bye, I asked you if there was anything
I could do for you. You said, 'Yes, get me a German.' Here is all I

can mail of him. I'm in hospital myself.' "[33] Repeatedly sentiments like "I feel that I would LIKE to kill a Prussian" crop up in the letters of "gentlewomen."[34] Often, of course, they followed an experience of horror, of seeing the suffering inflicted by the Germans—as when Chief Nurse Julia Stimson wrote in July 1917, "Our nurses don't need any 'Hate Lecture' after what we have seen in the past few days."[35]

Amid all these stresses and tensions of war hovered always the ultimate risks of ruined health and death, from bombardments, from air raids, most of all from tuberculosis, pneumonia, blood poisoning, meningitis, typhus, and the flu epidemic. Accounts of American women's deaths stud the records. Meningitis killed nurse Margaret Hamilton in October 1915. Winona C. Martin died in a Paris air raid. A shell killed Ruth Landon in a St.-Germain church. The sisters Viola and Ruth Lundholm died within days of each other in different Army hospitals. Rose Buckingham Selfridge died in England at her country house, from "suddenly contracted pneumonia as a result of overwork and exposure in caring for wounded soldiers. . . ."[36] Three hundred forty-eight American women died overseas, according to the records of the Women's Overseas Service League—the best available estimate, but probably an understatement.[37]

Other women who served overseas in World War I suffered long-term damage to their health. To Adriana Studebaker of the Smith College Relief Unit it seemed that "most of the girls 'up front' in mud and cold lost their health."[38] Army nurse Mildred B. Byers "was very ill after returning home for three years after discharge," and Mary Gruetzman reported "an intestinal disturbance which gave me a *bad time*."[39] Dr. Rosalie Slaughter Morton "While traveling in a box-car crowded with a company of soldiers [in Serbia] . . . had been gassed when the train was wrecked in a tunnel. Much scar tissue was still in my lungs. . . . Pneumonia, therefore, was a hazard which made future winters in New York a virtual impossibility."[40]

Elizabeth Campbell Bickford remembered that in France "One of our gentle, beautiful nurses escaped from reality; wandering aimlessly about, with part of her face covered." Bickford had heard that she had never returned to reality. Bickford herself for years after the war woke up at night screaming and hallucinating.[41] After her death her mother wrote of Harriette May Dilla: "Her impressions of the war period were most horrible, as she was a Hospital Searcher in large hospitals. Was greatly loved by soldiers and families. Came home in 1919 wrecked in health because of the trying duties of searching the stretchers of wounded and dying as they cleared from battlefields."[42]

No reliable figure exists for the women impaired during their World War I service overseas. However, the Women's Overseas Service League, struggling after the war to secure medical treatment for them, in 1923 found 200 absolutely disabled women in California alone. Certainly far more American women war workers suffered physical and mental damage overseas than are remembered.

᭛᭛᭛ *I had great expectation of a bright future. Instead there was a severe and long depression.*
                                                    —Marian V. Dunn Adams[43]

All in all, the American women who went overseas during World War I, like their brothers-in-arms, lived at high tension, at the top of their bent. They suffered the hardships, the dangers, the alien environment, and the horrors in the expectation of ending war, preserving democracy, creating a better society. And then, letdown: Letdown from the excitement of war to the routines of peace. Letdown of expectations, as society struggled to "return to normalcy."

The postwar depression which crippled a minority of the women who went to Europe in World War I was an extreme form of a common affliction. With the doughboys, these women had farther to fall than the women and men of World War II, most of whom had grown up with the possibility of war always looming over their shoulders, and approached their war as a disagreeable duty rather than as a crusade. "If we had not believed in the ideal of the war for the establishment of international peace," wrote Dr. Rosalie Slaughter Morton, "we could not have gone forward, planning, organizing, so strenuously."[44] The many idealists of the "Great War," pacifists and war workers alike, shocked that a war could be fought at all, had been buoyed up through its horrors by the hypnotic

Wilsonian rhetoric, only to be cast down by the American rejection of the League of Nations and the self-destructing Treaty of Versailles.

The evolution of Alice Lord O'Brian's thinking traced a course followed by many other women. At the beginning of her service, in 1917, she wrote, "No one seemed to know what it all meant but we all started out with high ideals to do our share in this war, which they tell us is to mean peace and safety to all who are to come after us." Her experience abroad further obscured the war's purpose: ". . . after being right up here almost at the front line, watching men tramp day and night in rain and mud, only to come back a few days later shot to pieces, patched up temporarily, then sent to a base hospital, I cannot understand what it is all about or what has been accomplished by all this waste of youth. . . ." The peace terms shocked her: "Oh, you can never understand my feeling. It all seems so ignominious—that all the pain and suffering, the labor and work and horrors, have all been for such a peace. The whole thing seems to have petered out so—it began over nothing and so it ends, where it all began." Yet "peace at any cost is worthwhile." Eighteen years later, watching with horror the approach of another world war, she published her letters from France under the title *No Glory*, in the vain hope that they might help to avoid similar suffering for her nieces and nephews.[45]

The experiences of the women and men in World War I resembled those of the Americans in the Vietnam War in that so many of them came to consider it futile. "Every doughboy, every Tommy, every poilu, every Wop that I talked with didn't want to fight," wrote Adda Frances Goodwin. "Even the seven Boche prisoners who did all the menial labor around our canteen didn't know what it was all about."[46] And Dulcie Hummel: ". . . we were hurled dizzily into the depths of war, and sailed over the sea singing 'I don't know what the war's about, But I guess, by heck, I'll soon find out!' but I guess there were some of us who never did find out."[47] Some of the participants came to believe the war a cruel trick played upon them by the older generation: an old man's war which killed off the young; a war in which superannuated generals with hardened hearts and hardened arteries in their brains resorted to a strategy of attrition.

Others believed that greedy businessmen at home fat with the profits
of war destroyed the League of Nations, which alone might have
given the "Great War" significance and worth.

> 🗡🗡🗡 *Maybe it was adventure, maybe love, maybe the some-*
> *thing big, beyond ourselves, we all hoped for. And now they're*
> *just women nearing thirty, coming home to little towns and jobs*
> *and the ladies' missionary society, and husbands if they can get*
> *them.*[48]

What, after all, were the women coming home to? These women,
so strongly impelled in the war by the ideal of service and sustained
by the intensity of wartime life, so greatly daring, so accustomed to
responsibility, returned to a country still ruled by the concept of
woman as nurturant homemaker. Men were eager to claim or reclaim
jobs, to thrust women out of the marketplace and back into the
home. Parents still assumed that their own age and experience entitled them to the respect and obedience of the young, and the devotion of their dutiful daughters.

Certainly returning women could expect little understanding
from family and friends. Gertrude Stein told a story about Louise
Hayden; when Hayden went home to Seattle a friend said, "My dear
Louise, you do not know anything about the real hardships of war,
over there you were in it you were busy every minute in the midst
of it but over here we had the real nervousness and anxiety of war
we were not in it we could only suffer about it."[49] What a contrast
to the sixty-year-old Margaret Deland's sober observation: "Over in
America we thought we knew something about the war and conditions in France, but when you get here the difference is as the difference between studying the laws of electricity and being struck by
lightning. The only way I can keep sane and steady is to look very
closely at my own immediate little, trivial, foolish job . . . for if I
dare to lift my eyes to the black horizons I lose my balance."[50] After
the war the war workers had no alternative but to lift their eyes to
the black horizons.

The folks at home had little idea of what their women and men
had experienced overseas, that they had looked at evil so directly as

to make them question their own values, the "truths" that their society had tried to pass on to them. The war workers' families had not taken their roads, nor had they any reliable maps for them. Even with World War II and Korea in many a living memory, we did not treat our workers and soldiers returning from Vietnam decently, and for years we refused to listen to them. Stateside folks after World War I had little to guide them in relating to their returning veterans. They hailed the conquering heroes, but faltered in ignorance and dismay before the traumatized and disillusioned.

After all, women and men overseas alike had consistently failed to describe accurately what was happening in the war, consistently minimized its horrors. Who knows why? Did they wish to protect the sensibilities of their families and friends? Did they not dare tell the truth because of censorship or censure? Did they fear a reaction in the hysterical atmosphere of a United States where newspapers filled their columns with blatant propaganda; universities closed German courses; women, at the prompting of the government, handed out white feathers to men not in uniform; and the Association of Collegiate Alumnae enrolled college women to inform Americans of the "peril of a premature peace"?[51] "The trouble is, of course," wrote Clara Savage Littledale, "that you can't see this war—I mean you *couldn't*, it was too colossal to see, and you couldn't tell much of what you did see because of censorship. . . ."[52] And Edith Gratie Stedman: ". . . over here it looks sometimes as if the end of the civilized world as we know it was close at hand with a complete overthrow of our present social and moral organization. . . . That is why it is so stupid writing home to people—from the objective point of view there is nothing to say."[53]

Whatever their reasons, the women wrote, in Carrie May Hall's phrase, only about the "edges of things."[54] The differences between the articles and books published during the war and those of a decade later are dramatic. So are the differences between the letters women wrote home during the war and the evaluations of their experiences they wrote from the late twenties on.

Accordingly, when the women war workers and the troops returned Stateside, more often than not they found their families still romanticizing the war, and ready to embrace the same daughters and sons they had sent off to war, who were no more. Parents were having a hard time. As Dr. Morton observed, "They missed the stimulus of all they had fed themselves about heroism. Now they had misgivings about the behaviour of their sons and daughters, many of whom had returned from foreign service. As parents, they would not have kept them at home, for they were proud of the wish to go. The girls had been able to take care of themselves, to be trusted in unusual and untried positions. The war had helped the advancement of women in comradely endeavor with men. But somehow, somewhere, now that the emergencies no longer existed, the code of good society was broken, the pattern gone."[55] A generation gap yawned.

✄✄✄ *If I do get a Victory medal, it should be for fighting the Army all these years.*
— Merle Egan Anderson[56]

What's more, it was hard for some of the women not to feel that they were returning to an ungrateful nation. The United States government did not choose to provide treatment to overseas women war workers for injuries to their health sustained as a result of their service. The Women's Overseas Service League and other pressure groups eventually persuaded veterans' hospitals to admit army nurses—but not other women who had served overseas, even though some had worked side by side with the army nurses.

Not until 1977 did the Signal Corps telephone operators finally win their prolonged battle for recognition as veterans and entitlement to veterans' benefits. During the war the army had failed to define their legal status, but many of the women had clearly understood themselves to be enlisting in the military. Their uniforms, their discipline, their susceptibility to orders all strengthened this belief. They were sworn into the armed forces with the same oath administered to the troops; they enlisted for the duration and served as members of the army, and were subject to court martial under the Code of Military Justice: one woman was in fact court-martialed and sent back to the States for discharge. As Grace Banker testified: "Once when some of us saluted the General [Pershing] as he passed by he turned to Colonel B. and said 'Those girls are real soldiers.' "[57]

Although some of them, like Louise Barbour, insisted that their service was its own reward, women like Grace Banker and Merle Anderson carried on the struggle for an incredible half a century. In 1977, the Congress finally steeled itself to acknowledge their veterans' status—along with that of the WASPs (Women's Airforce Service Pilots) of World War II. Since the youngest of the telephone operators was then almost eighty, none of them could get to Washington to celebrate.

The almost fourth-dimensional sense of power and service which sustained such women is gone. They are physically and nervously drained to the dregs, yet they don't dare to stop and rest; that means reflection.

—Elizabeth Shepley Sergeant[58]

But the postwar depression which some women war workers shared with many soldiers cannot be attributed solely to the familial and national situations to which they returned, disoriented. It encompassed a sense of loss of the intensity and excitement of wartime life, "those days . . . when you saw everything, and felt everything, and got so much out of mere living!"[59] Mary Lee writing home at the end of May 1919 complained: "I wish something would *happen*. This is the last little gasp of war, and it *is* fun if you are right up where things are happening. I suppose the Germans will sign peace tomorrow and life will start again on the dull slothfulness of another era of peace and prosperity."[60] And Elizabeth Shepley Sergeant asked, "What is to become of all of us? We might have been in a closed sack for four years. A giant hand has unloosed the string that binds it. Tossed us free into space where we sprawl and kick and choke, because we have so much air to breathe. Surprised, aghast. Michelangelo should be here to paint us in these catastrophic attitudes."[61]

Their depression began before they came home. "Just after the celebrating of the signing of the armistice," wrote the journalist Clara Savage Littledale, "there came a terrific slump. Everything seemed to be so absolutely all-over. . . . A strange kind of depression set in. Almost everyone felt it and could hardly speak for gloom. Of course it was a natural reaction after being keyed-up to war-pitch for so long."[62]

Mary Lee's autobiographical novel *"It's a Great War!"* unforgettably depicts a ship in a French port loaded with veterans, military and civilian, female and male; at the loading dock military police in small boats circled it continuously to prevent suicides.

Eunice Tietjens documents the widespread malaise in her account of her trip home in January 1919: "Never have I seen a group so psychologically confused and uprooted . . . the whole boatload of us. Almost everyone felt that he had been miscast in his activities, almost nobody knew how to begin civilian life again. Every one of us was fit for the psychoanalysts. I met casually in the Red Cross party two tall unusual-looking girls, twins, named Cromwell. I was not thinking of the art of writing, and it did not occur to me that one of them was the young and very talented poet Gladys Cromwell, some of whose poems we had published in *Poetry* [of which Tietjens had been an editor]. They seemed even more upset than the rest of us. . . . the next morning . . . I learned that we had stopped because the Cromwell girls had committed suicide. I talked to the American doughboy who had seen them go. He said that he had been on the lower deck . . . which was deserted by all but the two girls and himself, as it was dinner time. The two were talking together by the rail. Presently they withdrew a little from it and then, to his horror, he saw one of them break into a run, flip over the rail and leap into the water. The doughboy shouted and ran towards the spot. But the second was too quick for him and went over after her sister. The first, who must have been the poet, went over without a sound, but the second screamed as she jumped, and screamed again as she drifted past in the water. . . . I believe that every one of us on that boat might have done the same."[63]

The survivors, those whom depression attacked less cataclysmically, those who eventually coped with it more or less satisfactorily, found themselves ambivalent. Their records from the thirties up through the eighties exhibit their contradictory feelings as they looked back on their war service—"A mixture of sadness, horror, and joy," as Viola May Burleson put it. "Sadness that so many young men should have to go out to die. . . . The horror of seeing humanity slaughter each other. The joy of being able to 'do my bit.' "[64] No one recorded a wish that she had not gone to war. Almost to a woman, they took pride in what they had done.

One way and another, they accepted the failure of the war in its professed purposes. They consoled themselves that they had done what they could. "Can the elation of THEN," asked Mary Sample, a canteen worker, "be reconciled to the disillusionment of AFTER and the half-satisfied, half-cynical acceptance of NOW? It was a tremendous experience. I had not tried anything very big before. For the first time in my life I bumped up against something entirely too big for me to lick. In my efforts to make at least a scratch on the surface I often found myself doing more than I had ever thought possible, physically, and my Celtic capacity for enthusiasm and idealism knew no bounds. But it was always getting 'nipped' by carping criticism, cases of buck-passing, wire-pulling, little straws which prepared me for acceptance of the fact that this war had not ended war. But there was a gain: We had *meant* to end it; we had *tried* our utmost, according to the light we then saw."[65]

They underestimated their achievement. The efforts of the peace workers could not stop World War I, let alone wipe war from the face of the earth, but they did contribute to the creation of the League of Nations and the United Nations: they did more than dream such things could be. The alleviation of suffering and misery earns scant attention in the histories men write, but it matters. Into a world with "neither joy, nor love, nor light,/Nor certitude, nor peace, nor help for pain," the American women throughout the war and after it brought hope and cheer and surcease.

As individuals they had gained lifelong friendships, friendships based on common concerns, common endeavors, and mutual respect. When convention and affection silenced them to others, they could confide in those who had seen what they had seen. As a natural outcome, "to keep alive the spirit that prompted overseas service," in 1921 they founded the Women's Overseas Service League, composed, writes Helene M. Sillia, their historian, "of women who were originally selected for ability and for character as well and who were then flung headlong into an experience such as no women, of the modern world at least, have ever before undergone. They returned from that adventure with the conviction that they had by it been set apart. . . . that the country for which they were willing to sacrifice so much still demanded their devotion and service."[66]

And women through their war work had grown, matured. But despite the number of first-time experiences and the frequency of the women's comments on the self-confidence and heightened self-respect they gained from tackling jobs they didn't think they could handle, the records reveal little about the permanence of such changes. Alice Lord O'Brian, who hesitated in 1917 to assume the direction of a canteen but in 1919 took on what was described to her as "the worst job in France," refurbishing and running an old Parisian hotel for enlisted men on leave, and who was twice decorated by the French, conceptualized herself differently after the war than before. But of what happened to the newly gained self-respect on her return to Buffalo, we know nothing. The notes in *Over Here*, a publication of the Women's Overseas Service League, reveal that in the twenties members were leading lives much like those of other women: wedding and birth announcements figure more prominently than notices of professional advancement.

Their experience in Europe during World War I, while it demonstrated unanticipated strength, endurance, and courage, revolutionized neither the women who went overseas nor society. Lots of women believed that "proving themselves" would establish them as political and economic equals. Prophecies of millennial changes abounded. Mabel Potter Daggett in 1916 declared to her editor at the *Pictorial Review*, "Look! . . . See the message in the sky written in letters of blood, above the battlefields of Europe. There it is, the promise of freedom for women!"[67] And Eva Perry Moore wrote in 1919: "Women have proved their worth in new fields of activity; they have developed unknown qualities of leadership and management which will not be allowed to lie dormant. . . ."[68] In 1921 the YMCA's official war history declared that "The traditional relationship between fighting men and women was directly challenged in this war by the women themselves. . . . Wherever men were, there were women also, taking their full share of what was to be done and meeting emergencies with no hampering preconceptions as to what was and what was not their proper function."[69] On June 30, 1926, the *Omaha Bee*, searching for the accolade, editorialized that "the overseas girl was one of the boys"—praise which *Carry On* thought ". . . about the finest thing we could have said about us."[70]

Now and then, it's true, the war experience turned a woman around, as with Edith Nourse Rogers, whose overseas and domestic war service converted her from a socialite to a member of the House of Representatives with special interest in veterans' affairs. Once in a while a woman found war service that furthered her career, as with the economist Hazel Kyrk, whose work as a statistician with the American Division of the Allied Maritime Transport Council furnished material for her doctoral dissertation. Here and there the exigencies of the war opened a door to new skills and new professions, like training as laboratory or bacteriological technicians and the development of occupational and physical therapy, but by and large the war did not create new career potentials for women.[71] For individual women and for women as a group the war experience did intensify the movement toward a changed status—just as it and the performance of American women at home helped the already swelling suffrage movement to crest.[72] It was no epiphany, but it did broaden minds and open vistas.

The changes in women's fashions offer a paradigm for the changes in women's status. The American women in Serbia who cut each other's hair because they could not keep long hair clean and free from nits, the women who hemmed up their skirts to keep them out of the European mud, the chauffeuses who wore pants to repair their cars simply hastened the move to more practical and less constricting clothing already initiated late in the nineteenth century when women began to ride bicycles and swim.

Sailing with the Peace Ship turned Rebecca Shelley into a radical pacifist, but she would never have gone had she not imaginatively and vigorously created her own opportunity. Nurses who served in Serbia and Siberia went on to work in China and the Near East, but they had already selected themselves for the Mercy Ship adventure. Dr. Esther Lovejoy spent most of her postwar life with the American Women's Hospitals which she had helped to create, but she already had behind her a colorful career. Julia Stimson and Carrie Hall rose to the top of their profession, but before the war they had already been distinguished nursing administrators.

Experience overseas for some women accelerated their acceptance of the general cultural shift from romanticism to realism, from nineteenth-century to twentieth-century values. The sculptor Gertrude Vanderbilt Whitney's experience in founding and running a hospital in France in 1914–15 "changed the character of her sculpture" by convincing her "that suffering and heroism were not abstractions to be treated symbolically but terrible realities which demanded direct expression in art. . . ."[73] Juliet Goodrich, ex-debutante, canteen worker, and nurse's aide, wrote of her coming home "not merely to a changed self, but to a changed world. The old rigid shell of society had cracked. There was a feeling of freedom abroad, and while other people were scolding about the oppressiveness of the income tax, and the awful extortions of the laboring man, I found myself more comfortable, more at home than in my old environment, feeling the new world, for all its dark problems, fuller of promise, fuller of hope than the old."[74]

Interestingly enough, what the women had done in the war overseas and at home did startle some men in the American military into attention. In 1924 a paper submitted at the Army War College at Washington Barracks advocated immediate planning for the utilization of women in the military in any future war, arguing not only that women do some jobs, like running a telephone switchboard, better than men, but also that the women would otherwise insist on participating on their own terms—especially now that they had the vote. Appended was a questionnaire sent by the Secretary of War to various army commands saying that "in the next war" it will be necessary to use women in order to conserve manpower and promote efficiency, and "because women will not be satisfied if they are not permitted to serve in an emergency."[75]

Indeed the American military, wary of the forthrightly pacifist and antimilitarist stand of the major women's organizations between the wars, appointed a civilian "Director of Women's Programs," Anita Phipps. To the consternation of the military establishment, in 1926 she came up with a plan for a women's service corps. The War

Department rejected it out of hand. In 1928 another plan for a women's corps developed by Major Everett S. Hughes provided that women would be given full, not simply auxiliary, military status. Somehow or other it simply vanished into the files, not to resurface until after the Women's *Auxiliary* Army Corps of World War II had already become a reality. Nor did either of these plans head off heated debate in World War II about the entrance of women into the armed forces.

Many of the best and the brightest of the World War I generation of women found their way to service in Europe: service to the cause of peace, service to the ideal of democracy, service to the United States of America, service to menfolk. They found the satisfactions of work in the public sphere, high adventure, and the ability to endure discomfort, danger, and sometimes death. These were their achievements, and these their rewards in "The Great War." While at its end the woman who had served overseas might still personally feel "crowned with her glorious French achievement" and vaunting "the usual scalps at her belt,"[76] the public soon forgot her contribution, and her government chose not to reward it. Her deeds were largely written out of history. Her daughters could hardly build on her accomplishments, for they did not know them. Instead in World War II they were doomed to meet the same opposition, endure the same treatment, and entertain the same false hopes of earning new status for women by their contributions.

The mills of women's history grind all too slowly. But fortunately, the women who went overseas in World War I left their own testaments, to survive in the recesses of archives and libraries, and finally to speak for them here.

APPENDIX A

Numbers of American Women in Europe in War-Connected Activities, 1914–18

To TRY TO ESTIMATE the total number of American women overseas in World War I induces frustration. No single reliable source of information exists. Some organizations have gone out of existence, their records long since lost. Some have partial or unreliable records: as close to World War I as 1930, the War Department told a representative of the Women's Overseas Service League that "no woman served in the war except Army nurses and a few Signal Corps women!" In professions like journalism, no one ever kept count. Often records did not distinguish between women who served during the war and those who went over during the years immediately after the war. Anecdotal evidence suggests that medical aides may have equaled in numbers the registered nurses, but it's impossible even to estimate that figure in any reliable way. Many women undoubtedly appear in more than one count, since some small organizations worked under the aegis of the American Red Cross, and women transferred rather freely.

However, the American Red Cross estimates about 10,000 nurses overseas, and records 4,610 American women engaged in relief work in Europe. The YWCA employed 433 women abroad; the Salvation Army, 109; the YMCA, 3,480. James W. Evans and Gardner L. Harding tally 658 women among the entertainers who went overseas—though some 593 of these are included in the YMCA figure. The Quakers report 40 women in France in November 1918; 6 American Quaker women worked in Russia; the Quakers probably also had American women in England. Thousands of American women also served overseas under the auspices of about fifty other American and forty-five foreign agencies and war organizations.

About 230 women went as telephone operators with the Signal Corps, and the Quartermaster Corps employed 120 women overseas. According to *Carry On* (August 1930), about 135 women worked overseas as bacteriologists and laboratory assistants. Laura B. Hoppin's list of physical-therapy and occupational-therapy aides shows about 150 sent overseas during the war. The American Women's Hospitals dispatched about 350 women doctors overseas for their own units, and certified another 100 to the Red Cross, but some of these may not have gone until after the war; on the other hand some doctors who went refused to register with the gender-segregated AWH, and AWH also sent doctors to the Rockefeller Institute, the British Expeditionary Force in Egypt, refugee hospitals in Serbia, the Smith College unit, and the Commission for the Prevention of Tuberculosis in France. Forty-seven women pacifists sailed as delegates to the International Congress of Women, and at least a like number on the Ford Peace Ship. None of these figures count the American expatriates who devoted themselves to war work, the American missionaries already abroad who intermittently engaged in war relief, the women who established their own individual enterprises, or the many itinerants who now and then volunteered.

Alma Lutz, coworker with Harriot Stanton Blatch and editor of *With Love, Jane: Letters from American Women on the War Fronts*, in 1945 estimated that some 10,400 Army nurses served in England, France, Italy, Belgium, Siberia, and Occupied Germany, a figure close to the 10,000 we got from the American Red Cross. Navy nurses served in England, Ireland, Scotland, and on the coast of France. A few women members of the United States Naval Reserve served in France; 1 in Puerto Rico; others in Guam, the Panama Canal Zone, and Hawaii. About 1,000 women Civil Service employees, Lutz says, served overseas with the American Army in Ordnance, the Quartermaster Corps, the Treasury Department, and the Secret Service. Lutz's figures *may* include the 230 women telephone operators who served with the Signal Corps.

Ruth Eleanor McKee, who, in collaboration with Alice Fleenor Sturgis, did careful research for their book *Three Daughters*, estimated that 22,000 American women worked in Europe during the war. Unfortunately, she did not elaborate on the bases for that figure.

The *Omaha Bee* on June 3, 1923, estimated that about 24,000 women had served overseas. *Carry On*, in August 1925, stated the total number of women who served overseas at 25,000. But in November 1924, *Carry On* had quoted an Associated Press dispatch dated November 15, 1924, which said: "Approximately 90,000 women served with the United States army overseas, but that included welfare workers, clerks, telephone and telegraph operators, dieticians, cooks, employees in the reclamation service, and others. . . ."

On balance, 25,000 seems a realistic, conservative figure.

APPENDIX B

World War I Chronology

Events in SMALL CAPITALS *pertain directly to American women overseas.*

1914

June 28: Assassination of Austrian Archduke Francis Ferdinand at Serajevo, by a Serbian.

July 28: Austria-Hungary declares war on Serbia.

Aug. 1: Germany declares war on Russia.

Aug. 3: Germany declares war on France. German troops enter Belgium.

Aug. 4: Great Britain declares war on Germany.

Aug. 6: Austria-Hungary declares war on Russia.

Aug. 7: First British troops land in France.

Aug. 8: Serbia at war with Germany.

Aug. 12: England at war with Austria-Hungary.

Aug. 23: Battle at Mons, Belgium, forces British to join retreat of all Allied lines.

Sept. 3: Paris placed in state of siege; government transfers to Bordeaux.

Sept. 6–10: Battle of the Marne; German advance toward Paris stopped.

Sept. 9: ARC HOSPITAL UNIT SAILS FOR SERBIA.

Sept. 12: Trench warfare begins.

Sept. 14: ARC MERCY SHIP (S.S. *RED CROSS*) SAILS FOR EUROPE WITH HOSPITAL UNITS FOR WARRING NATIONS.

Nov. 15: Deadlock on western front begins; endures with little change for almost four years.

1915

Feb. 2: Britain begins blockade of shipments of grain and flour shipments to Germany.

Feb. 4: Germany declares submarine zone around British Isles; neutral ships advised of danger. United States protests, Feb. 19.

Apr. 15: First zeppelin raid on Paris.

Apr. 22–May 8: Germans use gas for first time.

Apr. 28: INTERNATIONAL CONGRESS OF WOMEN OPENS AT THE HAGUE.

May 7: S.S. *Lusitania* sunk by German submarine.

May 23: Italy declares war on Austria-Hungary and begins invasion.

Aug. 4–6: German aircraft bomb English towns.

Aug. 15: Allied aircraft bomb Karlsruhe, Germany.

Oct. 4: Franco-British forces land at Salonika, Greece, to support Serbian resistance to Austrian-German-Bulgarian offensive.

Oct. 11: ARC RECALLS MERCY SHIP UNITS, BUT MANY NURSES REMAIN IN EUROPE UNDER OTHER AUSPICES.

Oct.–Nov.: Serbia overrun by Central Powers, its army retreating across frontier into Albania.

Dec. 4: FORD PEACE SHIP CARRYING PEACE ADVOCATES SAILS ON CHARTERED STEAMER *OSCAR II* FOR EUROPE.

1916

Jan. 21: Battle of Verdun begins.

Jan. 29–31: Zeppelins bomb Paris and English towns.

July 1: Allied offensive begins at the Somme, continues until November.

Aug. 28: Italy declares war on Germany.

Nov. 7: Woodrow Wilson reelected President of United States.

1917

Jan. 31: Germany resumes unrestricted submarine warfare.

Feb. 3: United States breaks diplomatic relations with Germany.

Feb. 28: The Zimmermann Telegram affair.

Mar. 11: Revolution breaks out in Petrograd, Russia.

Mar. 12: Tsar Nicholas abdicates Russian throne. First Provisional Government formed.

Apr. 6: United States declares war on Germany.

May 8–19: FIRST CONTINGENTS OF ARC BASE HOSPITALS SAIL FOR EUROPE, ASSIGNED TO BEF.

May–June: French troops mutiny.

June–July: FIRST YMCA CANTEENS IN FRANCE OPENED.

June 12–29: Greece enters war against Germany.

June 13: General Pershing and staff arrive in Paris.

June 17: Russian Duma votes in favor of an immediate offensive against

Germany. On July 1 the Russian offensive begins in Galicia, led by Kerensky, minister of war.

June 26: First American troops arrive in France.

July 14–19: Political crisis in Germany over peace demands.

July 19–26: Russian armies mutiny and retreat. Kerensky becomes premier of provisional government.

Oct. 24–Nov. 23: Austro-German offensive in Italy; Italian forces are routed at Caporetto.

Nov.: EAGLE HUT (YMCA SOLDIERS' CLUB) OPENS IN LONDON.

Nov. 8–14: Second Russian revolution, led by Bolsheviks (Lenin and Trotsky), overthrowing Kerensky government.

Dec. 4–7: United States declares war on Austria-Hungary.

1918

Jan.–Feb.: Strikes in Austria and Germany in favor of peace, aggravated by food shortage.

Feb. 11: Russian government (Bolshevik) declares end of war with Germany without signing a peace treaty.

Feb. 15: FIRST LEAVE CENTER FOR U.S. TROOPS OPENS AT AIX-LES-BAINS

Feb. 18–19: Germany resumes hostilities against Russia, leading to signing of peace treaty at Brest-Litovsk.

Mar. 6: FIRST UNIT OF TELEPHONE OPERATORS SAILS FOR FRANCE.

Mar. 21: Beginning of German offensive along a fifty-mile line.

June 3–6: American troops check German advance at Château-Thierry and Neuilly.

July 16: Ex-Tsar Nicholas of Russia is executed along with his family.

July 18: Allied armies (including U.S. units) launch successful counterattacks that continue throughout the summer.

Sept. 12–16: U.S. Army carries out its first great offensive, wiping out the St. Mihiel salient; the first battle in France in which U.S. Army fights under the American flag.

Oct. 23: United States announces that 2 million American soldiers have sailed for overseas service, about half since July 1.

Nov. 3: Mutiny spreads throughout German fleet and naval bases.

Nov. 9: Kaiser Wilhelm abdicates.

Nov. 11: German delegates sign an armistice agreement. End of hostilities.

NOTES

CHAPTER 1
The Entrepreneurial War

1. Margaret Deland, *Small Things* (New York: D. Appleton and Co., 1919), 8.

2. Marie Van Vorst, *War Letters of an American Woman* (New York: John Lane Co., 1916), 94–96.

3. Nancy Woloch, *Women and the American Experience* (New York: Alfred A. Knopf, 1984), 269.

4. Judith Freeman Clark, *Almanac of American Women in the 20th Century* (New York: Prentice Hall Press, 1987), 28.

5. James R. McGovern, "The American Woman's Pre–World War I Freedom in Manners and Morals," *Journal of American History* LV (September 1968): 323.

6. L[inus] P[ierpont] Brockett and Mary C. Vaughan, *Woman's Work in the Civil War: A Record of Heroism, Patriotism and Patience* (Philadelphia: Zeigler, McCurdy & Co., 1867), 67–68.

7. Mary Elizabeth Massey, *Bonnet Brigades* (New York: Alfred A. Knopf, 1966), 65–86 passim.

8. Ibid., xiv, 52.

9. Brockett and Vaughan, 751.

10. Jeanne Holm, *Women in the Military: An Unfinished Revolution* (Novato, Calif.: Presidio Press, 1982), 8.

11. Barbara Jean Steinson, "Female Activism in World War I: The American Women's Peace, Suffrage, Preparedness, and Relief Movements, 1914–1919" (Ph.D. diss., University of Michigan, 1977), 328.

12. Ida Clyde Gallagher Clarke, *American Women and the World War* (New York: D. Appleton and Co., 1918), 510.

13. Mabel Potter Daggett, *Women Wanted: The Story Written in Blood Red Letters on the Horizon of the Great War* (New York: George H. Doran Co., 1918), 11.

14. Marian Baldwin, *Canteening Overseas* (New York: The Macmillan Co., 1920), 12.

15. David M. Kennedy, *Over Here: The First World War and American Society* (New York: Oxford University Press, 1980), 216.

16. Margaret Deland, quoted in an undated article from an unidentified newspaper clipping in Cordelia Cree Papers, Military History Institute, Carlisle Barracks, Pa.

17. See Appendix A.

18. This list is not exhaustive. We have drawn it from records of individual women who worked in Europe during World War I.

19. Women's Overseas Service League, *Carry On* IX (February 1930).

20. Women's Overseas Service League, "YMCA in the Far East," in *Lest We Forget . . . : A History of the Women's Overseas Service League*, ed. by Helene M. Sillia (privately printed, n.p., 1978), 253.

21. Mary Heaton Vorse, *A Footnote to Folly: Reminiscences of Mary Heaton Vorse* (New York: Farrar and Rinehart, 1935), 125.

22. Mary Williams Dewson, letter of March 1, 1918, Mary Williams Dewson Papers, Schlesinger Library, Radcliffe College.

23. Esther Root and Marjorie Crocker, *Over Periscope Pond: Letters from Two American Girls in Paris, October 1916–January 1918* (Boston: Houghton Mifflin Co., 1918), 55.

24. Rosalie Slaughter Morton, *A Woman Surgeon: The Life and Work of Rosalie Slaughter Morton* (New York: Frederick A. Stokes Co., 1937), 281.

25. Margaret Mayo, *Trouping for the Troops: Fun-Making at the Front* (New York: George H. Doran Co., 1919), 37.

26. Mary Roberts Rinehart, *My Story: A New Edition and Seventeen New Years* (New York: Rinehart & Co., 1948), 545.

27. Esther Pohl Lovejoy, *Certain Samaritans* (New York: The Macmillan Co., 1933), 11.

28. *A Red Triangle Girl in France* (New York: George H. Doran Co., 1918), 62. See also Mary Louise Rochester Roderick, *A Nightingale in the Trenches* (New York: Vantage Press, 1966), 18: ". . . imagine my astonishment at running into my two cousins, Mary Louise ('Ezze') and Lee Rochester, from New York, during the raid and in semi-darkness."

29. Chloe Owings, unpublished autobiography, 92, Chloe Owings Papers, Schlesinger Library, Radcliffe College.

30. Ruth Holden, letter of January 4, 1916, Ruth Holden Papers, Schlesinger Library, Radcliffe College.

31. Juliet Goodrich, unpublished autobiographical essay, 8, Juliet T. Goodrich Papers, Schlesinger Library, Radcliffe College.

32. Elizabeth Shepley Sergeant, *Shadow-Shapes: The Journal of a Wounded Woman, October 1918–May 1919* (Boston: Houghton Mifflin Co., 1920), 33.

33. Julia C. Stimson, *Finding Themselves: The Letters of an American Army Chief Nurse in a British Hospital in France* (New York: The Macmillan Co., 1918), 3.

34. Sergeant, 211.

35. Letter from Richard C. Cabot to Charles G. Stockton, July 4, 1917, Charles G. Stockton Papers, Schlesinger Library, Radcliffe College; and Anna Holman Papers, Schlesinger Library.

36. Rinehart, 134–35.

37. Van Vorst, 200.

38. Gertrude F. Atherton, *The White Morning: A Novel of the Power of the German Women in Wartime* (New York: Frederick A. Stokes Co., 1918), 7–8.

39. Roderick, 24, 28.

40. Lovejoy, *Certain Samaritans*, 28f.

41. Goodrich, unpublished autobiography, 10, Juliet T. Goodrich Papers.

42. Adele Hunton and Kathryn Johnson, *Two Colored Women with the American Expeditionary Forces* (New York: AMS Press, 1971, reprint of 1920 edition), 23.

43. Atherton, *The White Morning*, 50.

44. This journey paled into insignificance in Miller's memory beside her odyssey after the war in charge of the nursing service to repatriate seriously wounded soldiers, which took her

23,000 miles from Tiumen to Vladivostok to Kobe, Japan, to Honolulu to San Francisco to Newport, Virginia, to Brest, France, through France, Belgium, Austria, Switzerland, and Czechoslovakia in "8 horses and 20 men [sic]" railroad cars to Prague, Bohemia. "Our casualties included:— One on the Pacific Ocean, one crossing the United States, one on the Atlantic, and one in Brest, France." "With the Red Cross in Siberia," Women's Overseas Service League, Lest We Forget, 249–51 passim.

45. YWCA, War Work Bulletin nos. 17 and 18 (February 5, 1918).

46. Virginia Crocheron Gildersleeve, Many a Good Crusade: The Memoirs of Virginia Crocheron Gildersleeve (New York: The Macmillan Co., 1954), 122.

47. Elizabeth Ashe, Intimate Letters from France during America's First Year of War (San Francisco: Philopolis Press, 1918), 34.

48. Holden, letter of June 7–20, 1916.

49. Holden, letter of July 20, 1916.

50. Mary Lee, letter of May 27, 1918, Mary Lee Papers, Schlesinger Library, Radcliffe College.

51. Stimson, 170.

52. Letter of November 12, 1918, Vassar Unit for Service Abroad File, Vassar College Library.

53. Winsor School, The Overseas War Record of the Winsor School, 1914–1919 (privately printed, n.d.), 88.

54. Carrie May Hall, letter of October 22, 1918, Carrie May Hall Papers, Schlesinger Library, Radcliffe College.

55. Alice Lord O'Brian, No Glory: Letters from France 1917–1919 (Buffalo, N.Y.: Airport Publishers, 1936), 61–62.

56. Winsor School, 76–78 passim.

57. Winsor School, 55.

58. Hall, undated letter, probably summer of 1917.

59. YWCA, War Work Bulletin no. 20 (February 22, 1918).

CHAPTER 2
Common Experiences

1. Irene Wilkinson O'Connor, papers of Irene Wilkinson O'Connor, Military History Institute, Carlisle Barracks, Pa.

2. Mary Williams Dewson, Mary Williams Dewson Papers, Schlesinger Library, Radcliffe College. For a description of the rubber suit, see Albert R. Lamb, The Presbyterian Hospital and the Columbia-Presbyterian Medical Center, 1868–1943 (New York: Columbia University Press, 1955), 112.

3. Marion Baldwin, Canteening Overseas, 1917–1919 (New York: The Macmillan Co., 1920), 7.

4. Mount Holyoke Alumnae Quarterly, January 1919, 234. For vivid descriptions of flu on shipboard, see Willa Sibert Cather, One of Ours (New York: Alfred A. Knopf, 1922), and Ruth Eleanor McKee in collaboration with Alice Fleenor Sturgis, Three Daughters (Garden City, N.Y.: Doubleday, Doran & Co., 1938).

5. Mrs. J. Borden Harriman, From Pinafores to Politics (New York: Henry Holt & Co., 1923), 288–89.

6. Edith Gratie Stedman, undated letter of Atlantic crossing (Fall 1917), Edith Gratie Stedman Papers, Schlesinger Library, Radcliffe College.

7. YWCA, War Work Bulletin no. 37 (August 16, 1918).

8. Stedman, letters of January 1918 and March 2, 1918.

9. Dewson, letter of April 7, 1918.

10. Susan Ware, Partner and I: Molly Dewson, Feminism, and New Deal Politics (New Haven: Yale University Press, 1987), 82.

11. Stedman, letter of May 26, 1918.

12. *Indiana Women in the World War*, comp. by Past Presidents' Parley (American Legion Auxiliary, Dept. of Indiana, 1936–38), I: 40.

13. Lavinia L. Dock, Sarah Elizabeth Pickett, Clara D. Noyes, Fannie F. Clement, Elizabeth G. Fox, Anna R. Van Meter, *A History of American Red Cross Nursing* (New York: The Macmillan Co., 1922), 489–90.

14. Women's Overseas Service League, "With the Red Cross in Siberia," *Lest We Forget . . . A History of the Women's Overseas Service League*, ed. by Helene M. Sillia (privately printed, n.p., 1978), 250.

15. Mary Smith Churchill, *You Who Can Help: Paris Letters of an American Army Officer's Wife, August, 1916–January, 1918* (Boston: Small, Maynard & Co., 1918), 98–99, 111–12.

16. Mary King Waddington, *My War Diary* (New York: Charles Scribner's Sons, 1918), 284.

17. Margaret Sanger, *An Autobiography* (New York: Dover Publications, 1971; reprint of W.W. Norton edition of 1938), 131.

18. Baldwin, 16.

19. Marie Van Vorst, *War Letters of an American Woman* (New York: John Lane Co., 1916), 159.

20. Elisabeth Marbury, *My Crystal Ball: Reminiscences* (New York: Boni and Liveright, 1923), 155.

21. E. M. Tenison, *Louise Imogen Guiney: Her Life and Works, 1861–1920* (London: The Macmillan Co., 1923), 247, 280.

22. Harriman, 247.

23. Ruth Holden, Ruth Holden Papers, Schlesinger Library, Radcliffe College.

24. Jessica L. Payne, "What I Saw in England and France," [Brooklyn] *Ea-gle Library* XXXI, no. 199 (November 1916): 3–4.

25. Harriman, 247.

26. Mildred Aldrich, *On the Edge of the War Zone: From the Battle of the Marne to the Entrance of the Stars and Stripes* (London: Constable and Co., 1918), 157.

27. Ruth S. Farnam, *A Nation at Bay* (Indianapolis: Bobbs-Merrill Co., 1918), 133–34.

28. Gertrude F. Atherton, *The Living Present* (New York: Frederick A. Stokes & Co., 1917), 117–18.

29. Adele Louise Happock, Adele Louise Happock Papers, Military History Institute, Carlisle Barracks, Pa.

30. Stedman, letter of February 22, 1918.

31. Agnes Gilson Bignell, to her mother, August 13, 1918, Agnes Gilson Bignell Papers, Courtesy of Wellesley College Archives, Wellesley, Mass.

32. Stedman, letter of February 22, 1918.

33. Jean Chalon, *Portrait of a Seductress: The World of Natalie Barney* (New York: Crown Publishers, 1979), 123, 123 n. 2.

34. R. W. B. Lewis, *Edith Wharton: A Biography* (New York: Harper & Row, 1975), 385.

35. Esther Pohl Lovejoy, *The House of the Good Neighbor* (New York: The Macmillan Co., 1919), 160–61.

CHAPTER 3
To the Rescue

1. Ruth Pierce, *Trapped in "Black Russia": Letters, June–November, 1915* (Boston and New York: Houghton Mifflin Co., 1918).

2. Inez Irwin, unpublished diary, 170, Inez Irwin Papers, Schlesinger Library, Radcliffe College. But see the accounts of "Josephine Therese" and Mary Ethel McAuley in chapter 8.

3. Sylvia Beach, *Shakespeare and Company* (New York: Harcourt Brace & Co., 1959), 11, 13–14.

4. Ruth Holden, letter of November 15, 1914, in Ruth Holden Papers, Schlesinger Library, Radcliffe College.

5. Lucy Biddle Lewis, letter to family dated May 15, 1915, Biddle MSS(C), Friends' Historical Library, Swarthmore, Pa.

6. American Board of Commissioners for Foreign Missions, Balkan Mission, "General Report of Monastir Station and Girls Boarding School for the Years 1915–1916," Houghton Library, Harvard University.

7. Galina Gorokhoff, ed., *Love Locked Out: The Memoirs of Anna Lea Merritt with a Checklist of Her Works* (Boston: Museum of Fine Arts, n.d.), 220, 222–23.

8. Isadora Duncan, *My Life* (New York: The Liveright Pub. Corporation, 1966; reprint of Boni and Liveright 1927 ed.), 308, 310.

9. Mabel Dodge Luhan, *Movers and Shakers* (Albuquerque: University of New Mexico Press, 1985; originally published as volume 3 of *Intimate Memories* [New York: Harcourt, Brace, 1936]), 295.

10. Jean Chalon, *Portrait of a Seductress: The World of Natalie Barney* (New York: Crown Publishers, 1979), 122–31 passim. See also George Wickes, *The Amazon of Letters: The Life and Loves of Natalie Barney* (New York: G. P. Putnam's Sons, 1976), 141.

11. Mary Dexter, letter of May 28, 1915, to "Aunt K.," Papers of Mary Dexter, Schlesinger Library, Radcliffe College.

12. Winsor School, *The Overseas War Record of the Winsor School, 1914–*

1919 (privately printed, n.p., n.d.), 69, 70.

13. Elisabeth Marbury, *My Crystal Ball: Reminiscences* (New York: Boni and Liveright, 1923), 93–94.

14. Gertrude F. Atherton, *Adventures of a Novelist* (New York: The Liveright Pub. Corporation, 1932), 509.

15. Mary King Waddington, *My War Diary* (New York: Charles Scribner's Sons, 1917), 20.

16. Ibid., 181, 182.

17. Gertrude F. Atherton, *The Living Present* (New York: Frederick A. Stokes Co., 1917), 128.

18. Waddington, 292.

19. R. W. B. Lewis, *Edith Wharton: A Biography* (New York: Harper & Row, 1975), 368.

20. Ibid., 371.

21. Ibid., 384, 374.

22. Charles M. Bakewell, *The Story of the American Red Cross in Italy* (New York: The Macmillan Co., 1920), 9, 98, 139.

23. Janet Scudder, *Modeling My Life* (New York: Harcourt, Brace and Co., 1925), 274–76.

24. Ibid., 276, 277.

25. Mary Dexter, *In the Soldier's Service: War Experiences of Mary Dexter, England, Belgium, France, 1914–1918* (Boston: Houghton Mifflin Co., 1918), 102.

26. Katherine Blake, *Some Letters Written to Maude Gray and Marian Wickes, 1917–1918* (New York: privately printed, 1920).

27. Edith O'Shaughnessy, *My Lorraine Journal* (New York: Harper and Bros. [c. 1918]), 9, 10.

28. Mary Smith Churchill, *You Who Can Help: Paris Letters of an American Army Officer's Wife, August, 1916–January, 1918* (Boston: Small, Maynard & Co., 1918), 58, 59.

29. Ibid., 77–81 passim.

30. Carrie May Hall: "Tell the women to make 'Blighty' bags! We use them here by the bale. When a man is reduced to a stretcher and is passed through the field ambulance on to a casualty clearing station and then after hours or perhaps days to a base hospital he wants something to hold his little treasures, all that he has left when his clothes are taken away and he is put to bed. These bags are about 9 x 12 some a little larger—some a little smaller with a tape run in the top and a piece of white paper or cambric stitched on one side as a sort of name plate. The bags are made of everything under the sun—plain or figured or striped or spotted—calico or cretonne or gingham or satine—the gayer the better." Letter of December 2, 1917, Carrie May Hall Papers, Schlesinger Library, Radcliffe College.

31. Churchill, 103–4.

32. Ibid., 117–18.

33. Ruth S. Farnam, *A Nation at Bay: What an American Woman Saw and Did in Suffering Serbia* (Indianapolis: The Bobbs-Merrill Co., 1918), 8.

34. Alexis Kara-Georgevitch, *For the Better Hour* (London: Constable and Co., 1917), 146–53.

35. Farnam, 8–194, passim. See especially 8, 67, 91–92, 147, 152–53, 167–68, 183–84, 188, 191, 192, 193–94. Tempting as it is to smile at Farnam's self-aggrandizement and to flinch at her bloodthirst, it's only fair to say that a trip to the front in Serbia was not the kind of tour, laced with champagne, that Edith O'Shaughnessy describes. Getting to Serbia at all was difficult and life threatening; anyone traveling the path Farnam describes encountered real hardships.

36. Women's Overseas Service League, Helene M. Sillia, ed., *Lest We Forget . . . : A History of the Women's Overseas Service League* (privately printed, n.p., 1978), 1.

37. Charlotte Kellogg, *Women of Belgium; Turning the Tragedy to Triumph*, 4th ed. (New York: Funk & Wagnalls Co., 1917). Kellogg was the only woman member of the Commission for Relief in Belgium, chaired by Herbert Hoover.

38. Henrietta B. Ely, speech of February 1915, Henrietta B. Ely Papers, Archives, Miss Porter's School, Farmington, Conn.

39. Chloe Owings, ARCH report of October 21, 1916, quoted in Chloe Owings's unpublished autobiography, "Living through Covered Wagon to Space Ship Age or Life Is a Cooperative," 97, Chloe Owings Papers, Schlesinger Library, Radcliffe College.

40. Gertrude F. Atherton, *Life in the War Zone* (New York: System Printing Co., 1916), 22.

41. Ibid., 21.

42. Alice B. Toklas, *The Alice B. Toklas Cook Book* (New York: Harper & Row, 1954), 57, 59.

43. Ibid., 62–64, 72.

44. Amy Owen Bradley, *Back of the Front in France: Letters from Amy Owen Bradley, Motor Driver of the American Fund for French Wounded* (Boston: W. A. Butterfield, 1918), letter of April 21, 1918.

45. Ibid., letter of November 25, 1917.

46. Ibid., letters of November 30, 1916, and November 10, 1917.

47. American Red Cross, *Red Cross Bulletin* no. 22 (August 31, 1918), table of organization of the ARC Commission for France.

48. Fisher Ames, Jr., *American Red Cross Work Among the French People* (New York: The Macmillan Company, 1921), 13.

49. Lewis, 405.

50. Elizabeth H. Ashe, *Intimate Let-*

ters from France During America's First Year of War (San Francisco: Philopolis Press, 1918), 57.

51. Bakewell is an excellent source for the Italian activities of the ARC in World War I.

52. Ibid., 36–37.

53. Ibid., 107.

54. Ibid., 148, 169.

55. Indiana Women in the World War, comp. by Past Presidents' Parley (American Legion Auxiliary, Dept. of Indiana, 1936–1938) I: 34.

56. Quoted in Susan Ware, Partner and I: Molly Dewson, Feminism, and New Deal Politics (New Haven: Yale University Press, 1987), 73.

57. Ibid., 76 n. 8.

58. Mary Williams Dewson, letters of April 7, 1918, and July 3, 1918, Mary Williams Dewson Papers, Schlesinger Library, Radcliffe College.

59. Dewson, letter of September 3, 1918.

60. Ware, 80, 82.

61. Dewson, letter of September 3, 1918.

62. Ibid.

63. Rufus M. Jones, A Service of Love in War Time: American Friends' Relief Work in Europe, 1917–1919 (New York: The Macmillan Co., 1920), 140.

64. Ibid., 192, 196, 238.

65. Ibid., 137–38.

66. Charles Evans, letter of April 25, 1918, in Biddle MSS(W), Friends' Historical Library, Swarthmore, Pa.

67. Mary Elizabeth Duguid, letters of August 21, 1917, September 5, 1917, Thanksgiving 1917, Spring 1918 (?), Elkinton Papers, Friends' Historical Library, Swarthmore, Pa.

68. Duguid, letter of March 8, 1918, and Charles Evans, letter of April 25, 1918.

69. Mary Hoxie Jones, Swords into Ploughshares: An Account of The Ameri-can Friends' Service Committee 1917–1937 (Westport, Conn.: Greenwood Press, 1971; reprinted from the edition of 1937), 37.

70. Lydia Lewis [Rickman], letter, Intelligencer LXXIV, no. 34: 779. John Forbes, American Friends and Russian Relief 1917–1927 (Philadelphia, 1952), provides an overview of the Friends' work in Russia in World War I.

71. Lydia Lewis [Rickman], letter, Intelligencer LXXIV, no. 34: 779.

72. Anna Haines, undated letter, Intelligencer LXXV, no. 2: 27.

73. Emilie Bradbury, Anna Haines, and Lydia Lewis Rickman, unidentified extracts from their letters. Intelligencer LXXV, no. 34: 539.

74. John Rickman, letters to his mother, March 18 and 22, 1918, Biddle MSS(C), Friends' Historical Library, Swarthmore, Pa. Parenthetical remarks in quotation handwritten rather than typed; internal evidence suggests they were added later.

75. Esther White, letter of October 1, 1918, Intelligencer LXXVI, no. 2: 24.

76. Ibid., 24–25.

77. Lydia Lewis Rickman, letters of March 22, 1918, and May 22, 1918, Intelligencer LXXV, no. 33: 522.

78. Anna J. Haines, letter, Intelligencer LXXVI, no. 36: 569.

79. Mount Holyoke Alumnae Quarterly, April 1918, 43–46, and January 1919, 257.

80. The Red Cross Bulletin no. 40 (September 30, 1918).

81. Harriet Boyd Hawes, quoted in Louise Elliott Dalby's "An Irrepressible Crew": The Smith College Relief Unit (Northampton, Mass.: Friends of the Smith College Library, 1968), 15. The letters of many of the workers in the Smith College Relief Unit are in the Sophia Smith Collection at Smith College. Professor Dalby's excellent and useful

work not only records the deeds but also captures the spirit of the unit.

82. Ruth Louise Gaines, *The Ladies of Grécourt: The Smith College Unit in the Somme* (New York: E. P. Dutton, 1920), 81–82.

83. YMCA, *War Work Bulletin* no. 51 (December 6, 1918).

84. Marie Wolfs, letter of October 10, 1917, quoted in Dalby, 30.

85. Ibid., 29.

86. Wolfs, letter of January 26, 1918, quoted in Dalby, 42.

87. Frances Valentine, letter of December 31, 1917, quoted in Dalby, 39.

88. "A Working Visit with the Smith College Girls at Grécourt," *Literary Digest* LVI (March 23, 1918): 54.

89. Wolfs, letter of October 10, 1917, quoted in Dalby, 29.

90. Catherine Hooper, letter of November 24, 1917, quoted in Dalby, 32–33.

91. Wolfs, letter of December 13, 1917, quoted in Dalby, 33.

92. Wolfs, letter of January 26, 1918, quoted in Dalby, 42.

93. Wolfs, letter of February 5, 1918, quoted in Dalby, 52.

94. Wolfs, letter of December 13, 1918, quoted in Dalby, 53–54.

95. Elizabeth Bliss, letter received by her mother May 13, 1918, quoted in Dalby, 59. Dalby errs in attributing this letter to Frances Valentine. Correction supplied by Maida Goodwin, Archives Specialist, Smith College Archives, Smith College.

96. Elizabeth Bliss, diary, quoted in Dalby, 57.

97. Frances Valentine, letter of April 1, 1918, quoted in Dalby, 61.

98. Ibid., 63.

99. Ibid., 67.

CHAPTER 4
Binding Up the Wounds

1. Elizabeth H. Ashe, *Intimate Letters from France During America's First Year of War* (San Francisco: Philopolis Press, 1918), 28. This quotation describes Ashe's professional response as Chief Nurse of the Children's Bureau of the American Red Cross to a hospital run by males alone.

2. Elisabeth Marbury, *My Crystal Ball: Reminiscences* (New York: Boni and Liveright, 1923), 273.

3. Mary Roberts Rinehart, *Kings, Queens and Pawns* (New York: George H. Doran Co., 1915), 354, 359.

4. Lavinia L. Dock, Sarah Elizabeth Pickett, Clara D. Noyes, Fannie F. Clement, Elizabeth G. Fox, and Anna R. Van Meter, *A History of American Red Cross Nursing* (New York: The Macmillan Co., 1922), 162–63.

5. Ibid., 168.

6. Ibid., 173.

7. "American Women's Hospital No. 2 in the Advanced Area," *Bulletin* of the American Women's Hospitals I, no. 1 (October 1918): 6.

8. Madeleine Zabriski Doty, *Short Rations: Experiences of an American Woman in Germany* (New York: A. L. Burt Co., 1917), 58.

9. Eunice Tietjens, *The World at My Shoulder* (New York: The Macmillan Co., 1938), 153.

10. Mrs. Theodore Roosevelt, Jr., *The Day Before Yesterday: Reminiscences of Mrs. Theodore Roosevelt, Jr.* (Garden City, N.Y.: Doubleday & Co., 1959), 100–101.

11. Juliet Goodrich, unpublished typescript, Juliet T. Goodrich Papers, Schlesinger Library, Radcliffe College.

12. Laura Jayne Bucknell Loyson (Mme. Paul Hyacinthe Loyson), letter of May 25, 1915, Wellesley College Archives, Box 1, 1VW. World War I.

13. Winsor School, *The Overseas War Record of the Winsor School, 1914– 1919* (privately printed: Boston: Winsor School Graduate Club, n.d.), 85–86.

14. Elsie de Wolfe, *After All* (New York: Harper and Bros., 1935), 181.

15. Katharine Foote, *88 Bis and V.I.H.: Letters from Two Hospitals by an American V.A.D.* (Boston: The Atlantic Monthly Press, 1919), 70, 93.

16. Ashe, 62.

17. Mary Dexter, letter of June 18, 1915, Mary Dexter Papers, Schlesinger Library, Radcliffe College.

18. Inez Irwin, unpublished autobiography, Inez Irwin Papers, Schlesinger Library, Radcliffe College, 379– 80. As so often in World War I sources, the woman described is unidentified. But internal evidence and correlation with other sources make Simmonds's identity almost a certainty.

19. Ashe, 41.

20. Monica Krippner, *The Quality of Mercy: Women at War in Serbia 1915– 1918* (Newton Abbot, London: David & Charles, 1980), 174.

21. Ashe, 29.

22. Ethel Polk-Peters, "Autobiographical Sketch," *Medical Review of Reviews* (August 1935).

23. D'Andigne's addendum to Gertrude Atherton, *The Living Present* (New York: Frederick A. Stokes & Co., 1917), 302, 303.

24. *"Mademoiselle Miss": Letters from an American Girl Serving with the Rank of Lieutenant in a French Army Hospital at the Front* (Boston: W. A. Butterfield, 1916), 10, 16–17, 19, 25.

25. Ruth Holden, letters to "Louise" of December 3, 1915, December 11, 1915, and January 29, 1916, Ruth Holden Papers, Schlesinger Library, Radcliffe College.

26. Holden, letter to "Louise" of November 7, 1916.

27. Holden, letter to father, February 3–16, 1917, Ruth Holden Papers.

28. Marie Van Vorst, *War Letters of an American Woman* (New York: John Lane Co., 1916), 62–63.

29. Florence Billings, newspaper clipping, Redlands, n.d., among papers of Florence Billings (1879–1959), Sophia Smith Collection, Smith College.

30. Van Vorst, 79–80.

31. Julia C. Stimson, *Finding Themselves: The Letters of an American Army Chief Nurse in a British Hospital in France* (New York: The Macmillan Co., 1918), 87, 102.

32. Esther Pohl Lovejoy, *The Certain Samaritans* (New York: The Macmillan Co., 1933), 6–7.

33. Ibid., 7.

34. YWCA, *War Work Bulletin* 27 (April 12, 1918): 3. National Board Archives, New York.

35. Lovejoy, *Certain Samaritans*, 7.

36. Rosalie Slaughter Morton, *A Woman Surgeon: The Life and Work of Rosalie Slaughter Morton* (New York: Frederick A. Stokes Co., 1937), 275.

37. Lovejoy, *Certain Samaritans*, 13.

38. Ibid., 16–18, passim.

39. Ibid., 22.

40. Ibid., 23.

41. Morton, 282.

42. Carrie May Hall, letters of May 4, 1918, and August 9, 1918, Carrie Hall Papers, Schlesinger Library, Radcliffe College. For the transfer of hospitals from one authority to another, see also Portia Kernodle, *The Red Cross Nurse in Action, 1882–1948* (New York: Harper and Bros., 1949), 156–57. The situation was complicated. Some hospitals administered by the Red Cross had mostly Red Cross personnel, except perhaps for some army doctors and orderlies, but admitted U.S. and other Allied troops.

Other Red Cross hospitals, known as "military hospitals," served only American troops and were under the direction of the U.S. Army, though the nurses were usually Red Cross.

43. Fisher Ames, Jr., *American Red Cross Work Among the French People* (New York: The Macmillan Company, 1921), 25–26.

44. See Kernodle, 166ff. Kernodle is also a good source on the multitudinous other activities of the Red Cross, like its Bureau of Refugees and Relief, its Bureau of Tuberculosis, its work with the repatriated, etc. Charles M. Bakewell, *The Story of the American Red Cross in Italy* (New York: The Macmillan Co., 1920) is also helpful in this regard.

45. Ashe, 44, 48–49.

46. Ibid., 54–55, 70–71, 103.

47. Morton, 272.

48. Letter from executive secretary of AWH to Dr. Regina Flood Keyes, August 20, 1918, AWH Historical Materials, 1:2, Archives, Medical College of Pennsylvania. This letter mentions "at least 100" such women; in our judgment the figure is low.

49. Morton, 279, 282.

50. AWH, *Bulletin* of The American Women's Hospitals I, no. 1 (October 1918): 10, 11.

51. Tietjens, 157.

52. Alfreda Withington, *Mine Eyes Have Seen: A Woman's Saga* (New York: E. P. Dutton, 1941), 199.

53. Ibid., 181.

54. Ibid., 187.

55. Ibid., 211–12.

56. Morton, 215, 252.

57. Ruth A. Parmelee, "Reminiscences of Twenty Years in the Near East," *Medical Review of Reviews* (August 1935): 377–405.

58. "5/26/18: Howard University graduate to go to France. Dr. Mary L. Brown has been commissioned to go to France, according to Mrs. Katherine D. Tillman of the NAACP. Dr. Brown took the medical course at Howard University and postgraduate work at Edinburgh." Press Releases, World War I, 1914–1918, Committee on Public Information, Division on Women's War Work, Vertical Files, Schlesinger Library, Radcliffe College. Howard University confirms Dr. Brown's graduation, but has no other information about her. Nor can the NAACP offer more.

59. Lovejoy, *Certain Samaritans*, 25.

60. AWH, report in *Bulletin* of the American Women's Hospitals I, no. 2 (January 1919).

61. Winsor School, 54–55.

62. Mrs. J. Borden Harriman, *From Pinafores to Politics* (New York: Henry Holt and Co., 1923), 291.

63. Winsor School, 20–21.

64. Claudia M. Oakes, *U.S. Women in Aviation Through World War I* (Washington, D.C.: Smithsonian Institution Press, 1978), 37. The YMCA enlisted women in its ambulance corps: see Hazel Hulva's records in *Indiana Women in the World War*, comp. by Past Presidents' Parley, American Legion Auxiliary, Dept. of Indiana, 1936, I: 32.

65. Winsor School, 71–72.

66. Mary Dexter, *In the Soldier's Service: War Experiences of Mary Dexter, England, Belgium, France, 1914–1918* (Boston: Houghton Mifflin Co., 1918), 137–38, 153, 178.

67. Ibid., 151, 153.

68. Ibid., 139, 146, 149.

69. Women's Overseas Service League, Helene M. Sillia, ed., *Lest We Forget . . . A History of the Women's Overseas Service League* (privately printed, n.p., 1978), 217.

70. Ibid., 219.

71. Ashe, 117.

72. "Civilian Reporting for Duty,"

in Women's Overseas Service League, *Lest We Forget*, 245–46.

73. Edith Holt Bloodgood, ed., in collaboration with Rufus Graves Mather, *First Lady of the Lighthouse: A Biography of Winifred Holt Mather* (New York: The Lighthouse, New York Association for the Blind, 1952), 81.

74. Ashe, 69, and "Artist Who Made New Faces for Old," in Women's Overseas Service League, *Lest We Forget*, 239–40.

75. Bloodgood, 82, 86.

76. Ibid., 90.

77. Theodore W. Koch, *Books in the War: The Romance of Library War Service* (New York: Houghton Mifflin Co., 1919), 346–47.

78. Laura B. Hoppin, ed., *History of the World War Reconstruction Aides: Being an account of the activities and whereabouts of Physio Therapy and Occupational Therapy Aides who served in U.S. Army Hospitals in the United States and in France during the World War* (Millbrook, N.Y.: William Tyldsley, 1933), 76.

79. Lena Hitchcock's story in Women's Overseas Service League, *Lest We Forget*, 220.

80. Hoppin, 27–28.

81. Ibid., 65.

82. Women's Overseas Service League, *Lest We Forget*, 255–56.

83. Hoppin, 76–77.

84. Letter of Dr. Frankwood E. Williams, Associate Medical Director for the National Committee for Mental Hygiene, in Hoppin, 76–77.

85. Dexter, *In the Soldier's Service*, 209.

86. Ibid., 103, 105–6, 114, 120.

87. Ashe, 97.

88. *I Saw Them Die: Diary and Recollections of Shirley Millard* (New York: Harcourt, Brace, and Co., 1936), 83.

89. Webster's letter from Beauvais quoted in Ashe, 106–7.

90. Olivia E. Hamilton, letter of June 9, 1916, Olivia E. Hamilton Papers, Schlesinger Library, Radcliffe College, 29.

91. Ashe, 101. Susan Armeny's paper, "The Responses of Organized Women and Women Physicians to World War I," delivered at the Conference on Women in the Health Professions, Boston College, November 15, 1980, and now on file in the Archives of the Pennsylvania College of Medicine, discusses the opposition of some nurses to the use of aides on the grounds that they were insufficiently trained. Physicians, on the other hand, generally supported their use. Note, however, that Ashe in her powerful position as Chief Nurse of the ARC Children's Bureau warmly endorsed the aides.

92. Elizabeth Shipley Sergeant, *Shadow-Shapes: The Journal of a Wounded Woman, October 1918–May 1919* (Boston: Houghton Mifflin Co., 1920), 10–11.

93. See Kernodle, 163, and Dock, 625.

94. Hall, letter of April 8, 1918, to Elizabeth C. Burgess.

95. See the Committee on Public Information, press releases for April 19, 1918, and May 4, 1918, from Division on Women's War Work, Vertical Files, Schlesinger Library, Radcliffe College. See also Jeanne Holm, *Women in the Military: An Unfinished Revolution* (Novato, Calif.: Presidio Press, 1982), 17, 108.

96. Alma Lutz, coll. and ed., *With Love, Jane: Letters from American Women on the War Fronts* (New York: The John Day Co., 1945), 194–95.

97. Hall, letter of June 6, 1917.

98. "*Mademoiselle Miss*," 33.

99. Winsor School, 52.

100. See *The Story of U.S. Army Base*

Hospital No. 5: By a Member of the Unit (Cambridge, Mass.: The University Press, 1919), chapter 3, and Albert R. Lamb, *The Presbyterian Hospital and the Columbia-Presbyterian Medical Center, 1868–1943* (New York: Columbia University Press, 1955). See also Hall, letter of April 8, 1918, to Elizabeth C. Burgess; and Sophie C. Winton Papers, Military History Institute, Carlisle Barracks, Pa.

101. Item on Ellen Bradley, *Carry On* (May 1959).

102. Dock, 516–17.

103. Stimson, 142, 134.

104. Ashe, 112–13.

105. Eleanor Lee, *History of the School of Nursing of the Presbyterian Hospital* (New York: G. P. Putnam's Sons, 1942), 112–13.

106. Report of Ruth Cushman, in Dock, 655.

107. Report of Katheryn A. Leverman, in Dock, 657–58.

108. Frank Freidel, *Over There: The Story of America's First Great Overseas Crusade* (Boston: Little, Brown and Co., 1964), 266–67.

109. Report of Florence Missimer, quoted in Dock, 746.

110. Mary Elderkins's report, in Dock, 753–54.

111. American Red Cross, *The Work of the American Red Cross* (Washington, D.C., 1917), 94. See also the reference to this raid in *The Story of U.S. Army Base Hospital No. 5*, 46–47.

112. Dock, 456, and Lamb, 117.

113. Dock, 222.

114. Ibid., 185.

115. Ernest Bicknell, *In War's Wake, 1914–1915* (Washington, D.C.: American National Red Cross, 1936), 154.

116. Dock, 188.

117. Ibid., 189.

118. Mabel T. Boardman, *Under the Red Cross Flag at Home and Abroad* (Philadelphia: J. B. Lippincott Co., 1915, 1917), 208.

119. Dock, 179.

120. Ibid., 187–88.

121. Ibid., 217–18.

122. Ibid., 491.

123. Ibid., 744.

124. Ellen N. LaMotte, *The Backwash of War* (New York: G. P. Putnam's Sons, 1934), 19. Charles V. Genthe describes LaMotte's book as the most bitterly disillusioned of all the war narratives he examined. *American War Narratives, 1917–1918: A Study and Bibliography* (New York: D. Lewis, 1969), 101.

125. Dock, 449.

126. Ibid., 499.

127. Hamilton, 21–22.

CHAPTER 5
Aid and Comfort

1. ". . . a commanding officer stated that his men were more contented and more easily handled since the unprecedented innovation of women in the camp. . . ." Evangeline Booth and Grace Livingston Hill, *The War Romance of the Salvation Army* (Philadelphia: J. B. Lippincott Co., 1919), 60. Cf. "The bull was accompanied by six cows. . . . their presence was the best guarantee of the bull's good conduct." Dorothy L. Sayers, *Busman's Honeymoon* (New York: Avon Books, 1968), 197.

2. Amelia Peabody Tileston and Her Canteens for the Serbs, with outline of her life by Mary Wilder Tileston (Boston: Houghton Mifflin Co., 1919) 122.

3. Ibid., 17.

4. Ibid., 105.

5. Ibid., 112, 115–16. The story of Flora Sandes is an epic in itself. She stayed on in Yugoslavia after the German occupation of World War II. By then a feisty old lady, she daunted even the Nazis. See her book, *The Autobiography of a Woman Soldier: A Brief Record of Adventure with the Serbian Army, 1916–1919* (New York: Frederick A. Stokes Co., n.d.).

6. Edith Gratie Stedman, papers of Edith Gratie Stedman, Schlesinger Library, Radcliffe College.

7. Maurice Francis Egan and John B. Kennedy, *The Knights of Columbus in Peace and War.* 2 vols. (New Haven, Conn.: Knights of Columbus, 1920) I: 378. But "29 April 1918: Three women are with the party which recently arrived in France as an advance guard of the American Catholic War Workers sent over by the Knights of Columbus," Press Releases, World War I, 1914–1918, Committee on Public Information, Division on Women's War Work, Vertical Files, Schlesinger Library, Radcliffe College.

8. Booth and Hill, 202–3.

9. Egan and Kennedy, I: 375–76.

10. [Young Men's Christian Association], *Service with Fighting Men: An Account of the Work of the American Young Men's Christian Association in the World War.* 2 vols. (New York: Association Press, 1924) I: 101; II: 56–57.

11. Ibid., I: 258. See also Mary Ross Hall and Helen Firman Sweet, *Women in the YMCA Record* (New York: Association Press, 1947), 75.

12. The Salvation Army, *The War Cry*, no. 1898 (February 16, 1918): 12.

13. Herbert A. Wisbey, Jr., *Soldiers Without Swords: A History of the Salvation Army in the United States* (New York: The Macmillan Co., 1955) 166.

14. Booth and Hill, 44.

15. Seymour J. Currey, *Illinois Activities in the World War, Covering the Period from 1914 to 1920.* 3 vols. (Chicago: Thomas B. Poole Co., 1921) II: 550–51.

16. Booth and Hill, 53.

17. YMCA, *Service to Fighting Men*, General Order no. 26, August 28, 1917, II: Appendix II, 459.

18. The YMCA tried to give away contributed cigarettes and charge only for those that the Y had bought, but in the field the complicated accounting broke down; in any case the general public, civilian and military, failed to understand the policy. Variations in the prices of food from one hut to another further confused the servicemen. The women workers frequently wrote of their dislike of charging servicemen for these small comforts; sometimes they defied the regulations and gave away what they were supposed to sell.

19. See Frank Freidel, *Over There: The Story of America's First Great Overseas Crusade* (Boston: Little, Brown and Co., 1964), 299–302. The women and men who represented the YMCA during the war held a variety of religious views, from fundamentalists to liberals. And, like the rest of the nation, the organization suffered the stresses and strains of chauvinism and wartime propaganda. If the universities were banning the teaching of German from their classrooms, if editors gullibly published every story of Hunnish atrocities concocted by British propaganda, if the United States population generally took seriously such ideas as a "war to end war," it's less surprising that the YMCA descended to such barbarisms as distributing pamphlets on preferred methods of bayoneting and abandoned qualms about smoking and the breaking of the Sabbath.

20. Stedman, letter dated January 1918.

21. In August 1918 this regulation was modified to permit the service of women with brothers in the military, provided the women signed a pledge not

to try to see those brothers *under any circumstances* and not to marry overseas.

22. *A Red Triangle Girl in France* (New York: George H. Doran Co., 1918), 139–40.

23. "How Overseas Canteen Workers Are Selected," *The Index*, August 7, 1918. See the file of Cordelia Cree, Military History Institute, Carlisle Barracks, Pa.

24. Claudia M. Oakes, *U.S. Women in Aviation Through World War I* (Washington, D.C.: Smithsonian Institution Press, 1978), 21.

25. Katherine Morse, *The Uncensored Letters of a Canteen Girl* (New York: Henry Holt and Co., 1920), 63.

26. Newspaper clipping, source and date questionable, possibly Hatfield, Mass., March 25, 1918, in papers of Florence Billings, Sophia Smith Collection, Smith College. See also Mrs. J. Borden Harriman, *From Pinafores to Politics* (New York: Henry Holt and Co., 1923), 291.

27. "Mrs. Belmont Tiffany Tells of Woman's Work Behind the Front," *Literary Digest* LVI (March 2, 1918): 47ff.

28. Booth and Hill, 55.

29. Mrs. Theodore Roosevelt, Jr., *Day Before Yesterday: The Reminiscences of Mrs. Theodore Roosevelt, Jr.* (Garden City, N.Y.: Doubleday & Co., 1959), 85.

30. Ibid., 111.

31. Marian Baldwin, *Canteening Overseas 1917–1919* (New York: The Macmillan Co., 1920), 90, 91–92.

32. Adriana Studebaker of the Smith College Relief Unit, quoted in *Indiana Women in the World War*, 2 vols., comp. by Past Presidents' Parley (American Legion Auxiliary, Dept. of Indiana, 1936–38), I: 61.

33. Roosevelt, 93.

34. Booth and Hill, 240, 244–45.

35. Ibid., 94.

36. Morse, 5–6.

37. Ibid., 5–6. She's quite right about the magnificence of her posters, for the French employed some of their finest artists to design them. Miss Porter's School in Farmington, Conn., has a small collection of these works of art, the gift of an alumna who served overseas.

38. Juliet Goodrich, unpublished manuscript, in Juliet T. Goodrich Papers, Schlesinger Library, Radcliffe College, 9.

39. Alice Lord O'Brian, *No Glory: Letters from France 1917–1919* (Buffalo, N.Y.: Airport Publishers, 1936), 40, 52, 59–60.

40. Ibid., 149. Years later Hannah Hofman said "she not only had no desire to *fraternize* with doughnuts but also lost her taste for pies." "Salvation Army Lassie," in Women's Overseas Service League, *Lest We Forget . . . : A History of the Women's Overseas Service League*, ed. by Helene M. Sillia (privately printed; n.p., 1978), 264.

41. Booth and Hill, 78.

42. "Mrs. Belmont Tiffany Tells of Woman's Work Behind the Front."

43. YMCA, *Service with Fighting Men* II: 59 n. 1.

44. Goodrich, unpublished autobiography, 9.

45. "Soda Fount Angel," in Women's Overseas Service League, *Lest We Forget*, 245.

46. Eleanor Barnes, ARC hospital recreation worker, "Overseas Women— In the Memory of One," in Women's Overseas Service League, *Lest We Forget*, 237.

47. Booth and Hill, 257.

48. Katherine Mayo, *"That Damn Y": A Record of Overseas Service* (Boston: Houghton Mifflin Co., 1920), 321–22.

49. Indiana Women in the World War, II: 39.

50. Winsor School, *The Overseas War Record of the Winsor School, 1914–1919* (Boston: Winsor School Graduate Club, n.d.), 76.

51. Red Triangle Girl, 110–11.

52. Stedman, letter of January 6, 1918.

53. Letter from Catherine Hooper, December 14, 1917, quoted in Louise Elliott Dalby, *"An Irrepressible Crew"* : *The Smith College Relief Unit* (Northampton, Mass.: Friends of the Smith College Library, 1968), 35.

54. YMCA, *Service with Fighting Men* II: 84.

55. Sara Frances Jones, YMCA worker, in Women's Overseas Service League, *Lest We Forget*, 223.

56. Laurence Stallings, *The Doughboys* (New York: Popular Library, 1964), 297.

57. Winsor School, Elizabeth Potter, report in *Winsor School*, 76.

58. Red Triangle Girl, 101.

59. Booth and Hill, 13.

60. YMCA, *Service with Fighting Men* II: 136.

61. Booth and Hill, 167.

62. Ibid., 251–54 passim.

63. Women's Overseas Service League, *Carry On*, VIII (May 1929): 24.

64. Baldwin, 129–58 passim.

65. YMCA, *War Work Bulletin*, issued by the War Work Council, National Board of the YWCA, special issue, n.d., National Board Archives, New York.

66. "The other day one of our nurses had news of the death of a member of her family and there was not a place in the hospital where she could go to be quiet. All sixty-six of us live together in one big ward. The whole hospital was so crowded that we finally had to get everybody out of the linen room and shut her in there so that she could have her cry out by herself." YWCA, *War Work Bulletin* no. 25 (March 29, 1918).

67. Jean S. Cavers's report to National Board, April 1, 1918, Records Files Collection, YWCA, National Board Archives, New York.

68. YWCA, *War Work Bulletin* no. 49 (November 22, 1918). Compare Mary Dingman's report of February 8, 1918, in which she speaks of the relief of the male officers when the YWCA found housing for a handful of women stenographers and clerks in army offices when their units moved. Records Files Collection.

69. YWCA, report to National Board, August and September 1918, from G. E. MacArthur, and Report to National Board, March 1918, from Perrie Jones, Records Files Collection.

70. YWCA, *War Work Bulletin* no. 40 (September 20, 1918).

71. YWCA, *War Work Bulletin* no. 17 and 18 (February 5, 1918).

72. YWCA, *War Work Bulletin* no. 28 (April 19, 1918).

73. YWCA, *War Work Bulletin* no. 36 (August 2, 1918).

74. YWCA, *War Work Bulletin* no. 17 and 18 (February 5, 1918), and no. 27 (April 12, 1918).

75. YWCA, *War Work Bulletin* no. 30 (May 3, 1918).

76. YWCA, *War Work Bulletin* no. 32 (May 31, 1918).

77. Ibid.

78. YWCA, *Report of the Overseas Committee of the War Work Council, 1917–1920*, Records Files Collection, 65.

79. YWCA, report of July 1918 to National Board, Records Files Collection.

80. YWCA, report of August 1918 to National Board, Records Files Collection.

81. YWCA, report of July 1918 to National Board, Records Files Collection.

82. YWCA, *Report of the Overseas Committee*, 72.

83. Boies's story has been ably narrated by her granddaughter, Elizabeth Leighton, in "A Woman's Mission to Revolutionary Russia: Bessie Boies Cotton and the Young Women's Christian Association," unpublished honors thesis, Mount Holyoke College, 1983.

84. YWCA, *War Work Bulletin* no. 20 (February 22, 1918).

85. YWCA, *Report of the Overseas Committee*, 74.

86. YWCA, *War Work Bulletin* no. 19 (February 15, 1918).

87. YWCA, *War Work Bulletin* no. 20 (February 22, 1918).

88. YWCA, letter of January 20, 1918, quoted in *War Work Bulletin* no. 32 (May 31, 1918).

89. YWCA, report to National Board, March 4, 1918, quoted in Leighton, 47.

90. Ibid., 46–47.

91. "When the Czechs took Samara Miss Dickerson was for a time entirely cut off from the rest of the body and the Soviet." YWCA, *War Work Bulletin* no. 54 (January 3, 1919).

92. Leighton, 60.

93. Ibid., 61.

94. Ibid., 63–64.

95. Ibid., 65.

96. The American-born Countess Laura de Grozdawa Tarcyznourcz, spelled Turczynowicz in her book *When the Prussians Came to Poland: The Experiences of an American Woman During the German Invasion* (New York: G. P. Putnam's Sons, 1916), had escaped from Poland after six months in 1915 of virtual imprisonment there, during which she involuntarily entertained General von Hindenburg, who used her house as his headquarters. In 1917 she had begun recruiting in America 500 Polish women to go to France as a sister army to the Polish troops, proposing for their training an intensive course based on the YWCA six-months' nursing course, modified to suit the Polish women. YWCA, *War Work Bulletin* no. 20 (February 22, 1918).

97. "Librarian Overseas," in Women's Overseas Service League, *Lest We Forget*, 260. Burton Stevenson inaugurated this highly successful program. "As word spread of the new service, the Paris Library was deluged with requests. Mrs. Stevenson, who supervised the mailing department, started with a staff of two persons in September 1918." Arthur P. Young, *Books for Sammies, The American Library Association and World War I* (Pittsburgh: Beta Phi Mu, 1981), 70.

98. When the government agreed to give draft exemptions to men of the seven welfare groups, at least one librarian objected: "I urgently request our Headquarters to ask General Crowder to instruct Draft Boards not to honor this exemption claim. Let's not become more and more effeminate. We men have much to overcome as Librarians, and we need help rather than hindrance." Lloyd W. Josselyn, librarian at Camp Johnston, Fla. quoted in Young, *Books for Sammies*, 33.

99. William Orr, Educational Director of the YMCA, said that books can show men why they are fighting and how to fight. If the soldier was struck by the horrors of trench warfare, books, teachers, lecturers, and entertainers will "bring up his strength of body and mind and spirit so that he shall fittingly go on to complete the grim business." "A stirring appeal [was] sent us for books by a commander of stevedores in one of these port cities. He wanted recreation books to combat the social evil. . . . they were the best antidote." M. Llewellyn Raney, "The A.L.A. Follows the Flag Overseas," *Bulletin of the American Library Association* XII (September 1918): 95, 85.

100. "Women and the Work They Do," *War Library Bulletin* (January 1918): 9, Item 533 in American Library Association, Library War Service Correspondence, XXXIX: Miscellaneous Information, 1917–1921.

101. A.L.A. Library War Service Correspondence XXXIX: 532, 529–531. In response to Winser, Putnam said that several women were already serving as unpaid assistants in the camp libraries. Young, *Books for Sammies*, 34.

102. Proceedings of annual meeting in *Bulletin of the American Library Association* XII (September 1918): 285.

103. American Library Association, Library War Service Correspondence XXXIX: 536.

104. *Bulletin of the American Library Association* XII (September 1918): 88–89.

105. Mrs. Watson's story appears in a copy of an item in the *Kernersville News* for November 6, 1958 in the Charlotte G. Light Chilson Papers, Military History Institute, Carlisle Barracks, Pa.

106. Caption under picture facing p. 329 in Theodore W. Koch, *Books in the War: The Romance of Library War Service* (New York: Houghton Mifflin Co., 1919).

107. *Bulletin of the American Library Association* XIII (May 1919): 158.

108. Orlando C. Davis, *Bulletin of the American Library Association* XIII (May 1919): 304.

109. Arthur P. Young, "The American Library Association and World War I," unpublished Ph.D. dissertation, University of Illinois, 1976, 176.

110. "Report of A.L.A. Representa-

tives in Europe," Paris, April 5, 1920, *Bulletin of the American Library Association* XIV (July 1921): 239, and "The Headquarters Library," *Bulletin of the American Library Association* XIII (May 1919). "Staff members, who worked indefatigably to get the library, included Mrs. Burton Stevenson; Mary J. Booth, Illinois State Normal School Library; Mrs. Frederick Palmer, wife of the famous war correspondent; and Elizabeth G. Potter, Oakland (California) Public Library." Young, *Books for Sammies*, 67. The physical description of the library appears in "Librarian Overseas," Women's Overseas Service League, in *Lest We Forget*, 260; this article focuses on Louise Prouty, who also worked there.

111. "Historical Sketch A.L.A. War Service from January 1, 1919, to November 2, 1920, prepared at request of War Department," 72–73.

112. Report from Herbert Putnam, General Director, War Service Committee, Paris, May 28, 1919, "Report of A.L.A. Representatives in Europe," *Bulletin of the American Library Association* XIV (July 1921): 248.

113. Elsie Janis, *The Big Show: My Six Months with the American Expeditionary Forces* (New York: Cosmopolitan Book Corp., 1919), 135.

114. *Indiana Women in the World War*, I: 54.

115. Margaret Mayo, *Trouping for the Troops: Fun-Making at the Front* (New York: George H. Doran Co., 1919), 18–21. The heading of this chapter section belongs to this delightful book.

116. Ibid., 30, 31.

117. Janis, 6–8.

118. James M. Evans and Gardner L. Harding, *Entertaining the American Army: The American Stage and Lyceum in the World War* (New York: Association Press, 1921), 258.

119. Ibid., 145.

120. Mayo, 28–29.

121. Evans and Harding, 135.

122. Janis, 53.

123. Ibid., 19.

124. Evans and Harding, 74.

125. Janis, 192, xi, xii.

126. Evans and Harding, 77.

127. Ibid., 39–40.

128. Mary Louise Rochester Roderick, *A Nightingale in the Trenches* (New York: Vantage Press, 1966), 24, 165–66. It's only fair to add Evans and Harding's comment that Rochester [later Roderick] was "one of the real musical discoveries of the War" and "her brief account of some of her early experiences reveals a loyal and intrepid soldier . . . ," 29.

129. President Wilson opposed his daughter's going to France to sing for the soldiers on the grounds that such a venture put undue responsibility on the French government and added one more mouth to feed. Edith Wilson, *My Memoirs* (Indianapolis: Bobbs-Merrill Co., 1938), 161.

130. Evans and Harding, 104.

131. Ibid., 62, 58.

132. Ibid., 86.

133. Mayo, 13, and Janis, 1.

134. Janis, 63.

135. Evans and Harding, 73.

136. *The Tacoma Sunday Ledger-News Tribune*, Tacoma, Washington, November 7, 1937.

137. Evans and Harding, 98, 97, 99–100.

138. Ibid., 139.

139. Ibid., 122.

140. From "Soldiers, Come Back Clean," in Ella Wheeler Wilcox, *Hello, Boys!* (London: Gay and Hancock, 1919), 39–40.

141. Baldwin, 81.

142. Evans and Harding, 229.

143. Ibid., 157.

144. Mayo, 76.

145. Evans and Harding, 101.

146. Ibid., 133.

147. Janis, 158.

148. Mayo, 84–85.

149. Evans and Harding, 137.

150. Janis, 10–11.

151. Ibid., 93–94.

152. Ibid., 66, 103.

153. *The Tacoma Sunday Ledger-News Tribune*, November 7, 1937.

154. Mayo, 48–49.

155. Ibid., 57.

156. Illustration in Evans and Harding.

157. Mayo, 141–43.

158. Ibid., 57.

159. Janis, 83.

160. Mayo, 113–15.

161. Roderick, 184.

CHAPTER 6
The Black Record

1. Adele Hunton and Kathryn Johnson, *Two Colored Women with the American Expeditionary Forces* (New York: AMS Press, 1920, 1971), 157. Like so many books of the period, Hunton and Johnson's work often frustrates the researcher. Conflicts in memory between the authors appear; evidently they did not try to reconcile differences. And all too often they omitted dates and jumbled time. Nonetheless the book is invaluable, for the uniqueness of its information and the passion that informs it.

2. The record of the black soldiers has fortunately survived in works like Charles H. Williams's *Negro Soldiers in World War I: The Human Side* (New York: AMS Press, 1923, 1970, earlier titled *Sidelights on Negro Soldiers*), Emmet J. Scott's *Official History of the American Negro in the World War* (New York:

Arno Press, 1969 reprint of 1919 edition), and Gerald W. Patton's *War and Race: The Black Officer in the American Military, 1915–1941* (Westport, Conn.: Greenwood Press, 1981). Williams not only consulted documents but also interviewed thousands of black soldiers. Even World War I fiction scants black participation: "As we look back over the many novels about the war with their variety of plots and characters, it is highly surprising that only five present any discussion of the black in World War I." Philip E. Hager and Desmond Taylor, *The Novels of World War I: An Annotated Bibliography* (New York: Garland Publishing Co., 1981), 8.

3. Hunton and Johnson, 125.

4. Ibid., 184–85.

5. Ibid., 15.

6. Ibid., 85.

7. See chapter 4 above, p. 98, and p. 302, note 58.

8. Hunton and Johnson, p. 135, and Alice Dunbar-Nelson's chapter on "Negro Women in War Work" in Scott, 379. For the history of black nurses in the American military, see also Williams, 122–23; Darlene Clark Hine, "Mabel K. Staupers and the Integration of Black Nurses into the Armed Forces," in *Black Leaders of the Twentieth Century*, ed. by John Hope Franklin and August Meier (Urbana: University of Illinois Press, 1982), 246–55 passim; and Joanna Schneider Zangrando and Robert L. Zangrando, "ER and Black Civil Rights," in *Without Precedent: The Life and Career of Eleanor Roosevelt*, ed. Joan Hoff-Wilson and Marjorie Lightman (Bloomington: Indiana University Press, 1984), 57.

9. Hunton's life is outlined in *Profiles of Negro Womanhood: 20th Century* II, ed. by Sylvia G. L. Dannett, in *Negro Heritage Library* (New York: M. W. Lads, 1964).

10. Hunton and Johnson, 23–24.

11. Ibid., 138.

12. Ibid., 145.

13. Ibid., 213–14.

14. Ibid., 150.

15. Ibid., 96.

16. Williams, 243–44.

17. Hunton and Johnson, 156–57.

18. Williams, 110.

19. Hunton and Johnson, 32, 23.

20. Ibid., 162.

21. Ibid., 102–3.

22. Ibid., 97.

23. *A Red Triangle Girl in France* (New York: George H. Doran Co., 1918), 124.

24. Marian Baldwin, *Canteening Overseas 1917–1919* (New York: The Macmillan Co., 1920), 82.

25. Elsie Janis, *The Big Show: My Six Months with the American Expeditionary Forces* (New York: Cosmopolitan Book Corp., 1919), 195–96.

26. Ella Wheeler Wilcox, *Hello, Boys!* (London: Gay and Hancock, 1919), 59–60.

27. Hunton and Johnson, 20.

28. *Profiles of Negro Womanhood*, 204.

29. Hunton and Johnson, 152, 22.

30. Ibid., 182.

CHAPTER 7
The Hello Girls

1. (June 1918), quoted in press release from the U.S. Army Signal Center and School, Fort Monmouth, N.J., March 24, 1972.

2. James Guthrie Harbord, *The American Army in France, 1917–1919* (Boston: Little, Brown and Co., 1936), 166.

3. Rheta Childe Dorr, *A Soldier's Mother in France* (Indianapolis: Bobbs Merrill Co., 1918), 216.

4. Published in the *Los Angeles Times;* cited in A. Lincoln Lavine, *Circuits of Victory* (Garden City, N.Y.: Doubleday, Page & Co., 1921), 271.

5. Lavine, 279.

6. Louise C. Barbour, unpublished typescript, in Louise Barbour Papers, Schlesinger Library, Radcliffe College; and Lavine, 275ff.

7. Grace Banker (Paddock), "I Was a Hello Girl," *Yankee Magazine* (March 1974). Hereafter cited as Banker.

8. " 'Hello Girls' Going Over There," *Literary Digest* LVI, April 6, 1918.

9. Isaac F. Marcosson, *S.O.S.: America's Miracle in France* (New York: John Lane Co., 1919), 116.

10. Barbour, unpublished typescript.

11. Barbour, letter of November 25, 1918, and unpublished typescript.

12. Banker, 68.

13. Barbour, unpublished typescript.

14. Banker, 68.

15. Barbour, unpublished typescript.

16. Ibid.

17. Indiana Women in the World War, 2 vols., comp. by Past Presidents' Parley, American Legion Auxiliary, Dept. of Indiana, 1936–38 I: 76.

18. Quoted by Frank Freidel, *Over There: The Story of America's First Great Overseas Crusade* (Boston: Little, Brown and Company, 1964), 105.

19. "My Experiences with the Signal Corps," in Women's Overseas Service League, *Lest We Forget . . . : A History of the Women's Overseas Service League,* ed. by Helene M. Sillia (privately printed, n.p., 1978), 259–60 passim.

20. Barbour, letter to mother, November 25, 1918.

21. YWCA, Lula Frick Taylor's report of September 1918 to National Board, Records Files Collection, National Board Archives, New York.

22. YWCA, Ruth Frances Woodsmall's report of September 1–October 1, 1918, to National Board.

23. Barbour, unpublished typescript.

24. Banker, 102.

25. Lavine, 564–65.

26. Banker, 103–4.

27. Barbour, letter of November 25, 1918.

28. Paula M. Cheatham, "The Army's Forgotten Women," unpublished typescript, Military History Institute, Carlisle Barracks, Pa., 4.

29. Lavine, 491.

30. Banker, 71, 104.

31. Lavine, 492–93.

32. Banker, 102.

33. Lavine, 494.

34. Berthe M. Hunt, quoted in Lavine, 564.

35. Barbour, letter to mother, November 25, 1918.

36. Banker, 107.

37. "Memento of the Telephone Operating Unit, Signal Corps, Christmas, France, 1918," Archives of the American Telephone and Telegraph Company, New York City, World War I Collection.

CHAPTER 8
The Reporters

1. Carita Spencer, *War Scenes I Shall Never Forget,* 3d ed. (New York: Carita Spencer, 1916), 17.

2. Mrs. J. Borden Harriman, *From Pinafores to Petticoats* (New York: Henry Holt and Co., 1923), 251.

3. Spencer, 28.

4. Josephine Therese, *With Old*

Glory in Berlin (Boston: The Page Co., 1918), 89.

5. Ibid., 161–62.

6. Ibid., 169, 177.

7. Ibid., 182, 187.

8. Ibid., 197, 221–22, 256, 259–60.

9. Glenna L. Bigelow, *Liège on the Line of March, An American Girl's Experiences When the Germans Came Through Belgium* (New York: John Lane Co., 1918), 44, 47, 49.

10. Ibid., 130–31, 136.

11. Mildred Aldrich, *On the Edge of the War Zone: From the Battle of the Marne to the Entrance of the Stars and Stripes* (London: Constable and Co., 1918), 30.

12. Ibid., 9.

13. Ibid., 24.

14. Ibid., 108, 72, 82–83.

15. Ibid., 173–74.

16. Ibid., 90, 93–94. "Germany's wilful destruction is on a pre-conceived plan—a racial principle. The more races she can reduce and enfeeble the more room there will be for her. Germany wants Belgium—but she wants as few Belgians as possible. So with Poland, and Servia, and north-east France. She wants them to die out as fast as possible. It is a part of the programme of a people calling themselves the elect of the world—the only race, in their opinion, which ought to survive." Ibid., 159. "You are going to come some day to the opinion I hold—that if we want universal peace we must first get rid of the race that does not want it or believe in it." Ibid., 160. It must be remembered that by this juncture Aldrich, much as she underplayed the hardships she experienced, had gone through two winters of monotony, deprivation, and bad war news, with little of the intellectual stimulation that her career had brought her. On the other hand, her sentiments were far from unique.

17. Ibid., 258.

18. This story is told in Frances W. Huard, *My Home in the Field of Honour* (New York: George H. Doran Co., 1916).

19. Phillip Knightley, *The First Casualty: From the Crimea to Vietnam: The War Correspondent as Hero, Propagandist, and Myth Maker* (New York: Harcourt Brace Jovanovich, 1975), 126–27. Books on the journalism of World War I have usually ignored the women who reported it. Emmet Crozier in his *American Reporters on the Western Front: 1914–1918* (New York: Oxford University Press, 1959) registered only a couple of ineffectual females. Knightley mentioned only one. Whitman Bassow in *The Moscow Correspondents* (New York: William Morrow and Co., 1988) had similar problems. Fortunately Ishbel Ross in *Ladies of the Press: The Story of Women in Journalism by an Insider* (New York: Arno Press, 1974; reprint of Harper and Bros. edition of 1936) has added numbers to the roster, and some of the women journalists have recorded their own stories.

20. Gertrude F. Atherton, *Life in the War Zone* (New York: System Printing Co., 1916), 1–17 passim.

21. Ellen N. LaMotte, *The Backwash of War* (New York: G. P. Putnam's Sons, 1934), vii–viii.

22. Ibid., 107, 109.

23. Ibid., 130–31.

24. Lavinia L. Dock, Sarah Elizabeth Pickett, Clara D. Noyes, Fannie F. Clement, Elizabeth G. Fox, and Anna R. Van Meter, *History of American Red Cross Nursing* (New York: The Macmillan Company, 1922), 175.

25. Madeleine Zabriskie Doty, *Short Rations: Experiences of an American*

Woman in Germany (New York: A. L. Burt Co., 1917), 169.

26. *Women of the World's Greatest Newspaper* (Chicago: Public Service Office of the *Chicage Tribune*, 1927), 4.

27. Inez Irwin, unpublished autobiography, Inez Irwin Papers, Schlesinger Library, Radcliffe College, 375. See also Ross, 368–69, and *Leslie's Photographic Review of the Great War*, ed. Edgar Allen Forbes (New York: Leslie-Judge Co., 1920), pages not numbered.

28. Heywood Hale Broun, *Whose Little Boy Are You? A Memoir of the Broun Family* (New York: St. Martin's Press, 1983), 62.

29. Clara Savage Littledale, letter of December 2, 1918, Clara Savage Littledale Papers, Schlesinger Library, Radcliffe College.

30. Rheta Childe Dorr, *A Soldier's Mother in France* (Indianapolis: Bobbs Merrill Co., 1918), 2–3.

31. Anna Steese Richardson, "Overseas with the A.E.F.," *McCall's Magazine*, Oct. 1918, 6. For a similar incident, see Margaret Mayo, *Trouping for the Troops: Fun-Making at the Front* (New York: George H. Doran Co., 1919), 17–19.

32. Gertrude F. Atherton, *The Living Present* (New York: Frederick A. Stokes Co., 1917), xi, 37–40 passim.

33. Jessica Lozier Payne, "What I Saw in England and France," *Eagle Library* XXXI, no. 199 (November, 1916): 7, 8.

34. Inez H. Irwin, unpublished diary, Inez Irwin Papers, 428–29.

35. Doty, *Short Rations*, 121–22.

36. Ibid., 30–32, 35, 38.

37. Ibid., 90.

38. Ibid., 129–30 passim.

39. Ibid., 157.

40. Ibid., 226–27.

41. Mary Ethel McAuley, *Germany in War Time: What an American Girl Saw and Heard* (Chicago: The Open Court Publishing Co., 1917), 100. McAuley's remarks on the reading material available to the Germans in wartime are engrossing. "One of the most surprising things that was printed was Zimmermann's letter to Mexico. It came out in all the papers, for Zimmermann thought that the best thing to do was to publish it. It was not very popular with the German people." (100) Barbara Tuchman's *The Zimmermann Telegram* (New York: Ballantine Books, 1959, 1966) is an accessible work on this extraordinary ploy which so influenced Wilson's action in involving the United States in World War I. McAuley also comments that English newspapers were much read in Germany, and that American papers were readily available up until the end of April 1917.

42. Ibid., 7–9 passim.

43. Ibid., 20–21.

44. Ibid., 87.

45. Ibid., 143–44.

46. Ibid., 289–90.

47. Ibid., 148–49.

48. Ibid., 207, 211, 213–14.

49. Information on suppression of McAuley's book comes from Mr. David Koch, Archivist of Special Collections at the University of Southern Illinois, where the records of the Open Court Publishing Company are deposited. The owner of the company was of German descent, and a daring and innovative publisher, whose letters to McAuley directly state his sympathies with Germany.

Appendix II of Arthur P. Young's *Books for Sammies* (Pittsburgh: Beta Phi Mu, 1981) lists "Books and Pamphlets Banned by the War Department." It includes Emily G. Balch's *Approaches to the Great Settlement* and Madeleine Doty's *Short Rations*.

50. See Marian Baldwin, *Canteening*

Overseas, 1917–1919 (New York: The Macmillan Co. 1920), 121–23.

51. Eunice Tietjens, *The World at My Shoulder* (New York: The Macmillan Co., 1938), 137, 141.

52. Ibid., 151.

53. Mary Dexter, *In the Soldier's Service: War Experiences of Mary Dexter, England, Belgium, France, 1914–1918* (Boston: Houghton Mifflin Co., 1918), 170.

54. Elizabeth Shepley Sergeant, *Shadow-Shapes: The Journal of a Wounded Woman, October 1918–May 1919* (Boston: Houghton Mifflin Co., 1920), 20, 12–13. Parts of this book were first published in *The New Republic* during 1917 and 1918.

55. Mary Roberts Rinehart, *My Story: A New Edition and Seventeen New Years* (New York: Rinehart & Co., 1948), 146–47.

56. Ibid., 149.

57. Ibid., 153.

58. Ibid.

59. Ibid., 158. This adviser became the Henri of Rinehart's novel *The Amazing Interlude* (New York: The Review of Reviews Corp., 1917).

60. Rinehart, *My Story*, p. 160.

61. Ibid., 163, 165. Knightley, 85, notes the military reluctance *initially*, in 1914, to allow any correspondent, man or woman, at the front. The newspapers of course were eager to cover the war, but Lord Kitchener "was determined not to have them in France at any price. The Regular Army officers tended to agree with him." In time this attitude changed, as far as male journalists were concerned, when the military realized the potential benefit to them of feeding the correspondents the news they wanted the public to receive.

62. Rinehart, *My Story*, 180, 182. Rinehart adapted this incident for use in her novel *The Amazing Interlude*.

63. Rinehart, *My Story*, 189–90.

64. Ibid., 192.

65. Madeleine Zabriskie Doty, *Behind the Battle Line: Around the World in 1918* (New York: The Macmillan Co., 1918), 41.

66. February according to the old Russian calendar, March according to the Western calendar. Henceforth we will follow the Western calendar.

67. Rheta Childe Dorr, *A Woman of Fifty* (New York: Arno Press, 1980; reprint of Funk & Wagnalls edition of 1924), 319.

68. Bessie Beatty, *The Red Heart of Russia* (New York: The Century Co., 1918).

69. For biographical information see Virginia Gardner, *"Friend and Lover": The Life of Louise Bryant* (New York: Horizon Press, 1982).

70. Louise S. Bryant, *Six Red Months in Russia* (New York: Arno Press and The New York Times, 1970; reprint of George H. Doran Co. 1918 edition).

71. Doty, *Battle Line*, 29, 95, 47, and 51.

72. Bryant, *Six Red Months*, xi ff.

73. Doty, *Battle Line*, 44, 49, 50.

74. Beatty, 28.

75. Dorr, *Inside the Russian Revolution*, 1–2. It's difficult to square Dorr's statements about her political convictions one with another. In her autobiographical *A Woman of Fifty* (New York: Arno Press, 1980, reprint of Funk and Wagnalls edition of 1924), 313–14, Dorr explains that with the outbreak of World War I she found that she had lost interest in women's causes. "I couldn't think what was the matter with me. All my life I had devoted myself to women and children without distinction of race or color. Now I seemed to care less for women and children of any race than I did for the men who were fighting Germans. . . . I read every line of war news, and noth-

ing else in the papers had the least interest for me except the pictures of English women in overalls working in docks and shipyards and in every kind of war-munitions factories. One day, looking at a page of these pictures, the explanation suddenly dawned on me. I had widened my interest to include both men and women who were doing together the only work the world called for at that hour. The class war I had begun to fight in childhood was over. The thing I had long dreamed of had happened— women had broken into the human race!" (313–14) Quite probably her decision to campaign for the Republicans in 1916 stemmed in part from her hawkish opposition to Wilson, who was then campaigning on the slogan "He kept us out of war."

76. Dorr, *Inside the Russian Revolution*, 2, 231, 233, 243.

77. Bryant, *Six Red Months*, 161.

78. Doty, *Battle Line*, 46, 45.

79. Ibid., 44.

80. Bryant, *Six Red Months*, 47.

81. Beatty, 224.

82. Ibid., 156–57, 162.

83. Bryant, *Six Red Months*, 80.

84. Beatty, 204.

85. Ibid., 207, 213.

86. Ibid., 216–17.

87. Bryant, *Six Red Months*, 87.

88. Doty, *Battle Line*, 49.

89. Bryant, *Six Red Months*, 178, 179–80.

90. Ibid., 189–90.

91. Ibid., 191–92.

92. Beatty, 316.

93. Ibid., 28, 29, 31.

94. Bryant, *Six Red Months*, 48–49.

95. Dorr, *Inside the Russian Revolution*, 6, 16.

96. Ibid., 173.

97. Beatty, 46.

98. Ibid., 40.

99. Ibid., 446.

100. Dorr, *Inside the Russian Revolution*, ix.

101. Beatty, 357–58.

102. Ibid., 357.

103. Bryant, *Six Red Months*, 169–70. Maria Spiridonova at seventeen while still a student became a terrorist and assassinated the tyrant Governor Luzhenovsky of Tambov, a peasant nemesis; she was arrested, sexually assaulted, and tortured, but met her sufferings with dignity. Bryant admired this heroine of American militant feminists and spoke of her as the most powerful woman in all Russia. Gardner, 92. Doty, *Battle Line*, 55, reported a different answer from Spiridonova: "The reason more Bolshevik women aren't prominent is because they haven't the strength or the training and they aren't practical. But it will come one day."

104. Dorr, *Inside the Russian Revolution*, 194–95, 197.

105. Doty, *Battle Line*, 120–21.

106. Ibid., 119.

107. Bryant, *Six Red Months*, 219.

108. Ibid., 214–16 passim.

109. Beatty, 92, 114.

110. Dorr, *Inside the Russian Revolution*, 50.

111. Beatty, 101, 105.

112. Information and quotations from Dorr in this narration of her travels with Botchkareva are drawn from *Inside the Russian Revolution*, 60–69.

113. Beatty, 98–99.

114. Ibid., 109.

115. Dorr, *Inside the Russian Revolution*, 74.

116. Beatty, 110.

117. Dorr, *Inside the Russian Revolution*, 78.

118. Bryant, *Six Red Months*, 212.

119. Beatty, 112–14 passim.

120. Bryant, *Six Red Months*, 124.

121. Ibid., 134.

122. Ibid., 268.

123. Doty, *Battle Line*, 136.

124. Beatty, 480.

CHAPTER 9
The Novelists

1. Edith Wharton, *The Marne* (New York: D. Appleton and Co., 1919), 43–44.

2. Several bibliographies survey World War I novels: Stanley Cooperman's *World War I and the American Novel* (Baltimore: Johns Hopkins Press, 1967); Charles V. Genthe's *American War Narratives, 1917–1918: A Study and Bibliography* (New York: D. Lewis, 1969); Myron J. Smith, Jr.'s *War Story Guide: An Annotated Bibliography of Military Fiction* (Metuchen, N.J.: The Scarecrow Press, 1980); and especially Philip E. Hager and Desmond Taylor's *The Novels of World War I: An Annotated Bibliography* (New York: Garland Publishing Co., 1981).

Hager and Taylor, 5, remark on the difference between the critical perception and the characteristics of popular literature: "Many of the critical assessments of World War I literature suggest that the fiction written during the early part of the 1914–1918 period was prowar; that later fiction was characterized by disenchantment, and finally, by revulsion and outrage at the waste of human life and the folly of war. . . . However, our reading and examination of all the novels that deal with the war or some aspect of it reveal a different composite picture."

3. Anna Robeson Brown Burr, *The House on Charles Street* (New York: Duffield and Co., 1921), 65.

4. Willa Cather, *One of Ours* (New York: Alfred A. Knopf, 1922, 1940), 229.

5. Ibid., 248, 375.

6. Ibid., 419–20.

7. Ibid., 409.

8. Ibid., 459.

9. Wharton, *A Son at the Front* (New York: Charles Scribner's Sons, 1923).

10. Ibid., 76, 90, 390–91, 193–94.

11. Ibid., 371–72.

12. Gertrude Atherton, *The White Morning: A Novel of the Power of the German Women in Wartime* (New York: Frederick A. Stokes Co., 1918), 47, 2, 43.

13. Barbara W. Tuchman, *The Zimmermann Telegram* (New York: Ballantine Books, 1959, 1966), 2.

14. Marice Rutledge (Marice Gibson Hale), *Children of Fate* (New York: Frederick A. Stokes Co., 1917). Born Mary Louise Gibson, by marriage she became successively Marie Louise Goetchius; then Marie Louise Van Saanen Algi; then Mrs. Gardiner Hale; then Mme Obri. She wrote fiction under the names of Marice Hale, Rutledge Hale, and Marice Rutledge. This colorful American woman, full of improbable stories about her European adventures, is described by the journalist Inez H. Irwin in her unpublished autobiography, Irwin Papers, Schlesinger Library, Radcliffe College, 50–51.

15. Rutledge, 86–89 passim, 272.

16. Ibid., 94–95.

17. Dorothy Canfield (Fisher), *The Deepening Stream* (New York: Harcourt, Brace & Co., 1930).

18. Ibid., 242, 243.

19. Ibid., 327–28.

20. Mary Lee, *"It's a Great War!"* (Boston: Houghton Mifflin Co., 1929).

21. The prize sharer, William T. Scanlon, wrote *God Have Mercy on Us*, based on his experiences in the Marine Corps.

22. Lee, 343–44.

23. Ibid., 259. Ellipses in the original.

24. Ibid., 337.

25. Ibid., 467–68. The Y canteen workers, that is, are like frontier women, in that they keep men from abandoning completely the standards of civilization. Or, to put it in the terms John Keegan uses in *The Face of Battle*, they draw the war experience and the peace experience a little closer together. Some might suggest that women thus enable the continuation of war; others might wonder whether without women men at war would descend into complete bestiality.

26. Lee, 530, 574.

27. Ruth Eleanor McKee, in collaboration with Alice Fleenor Surgis, *Three Daughters* (Garden City, N.Y.: Doubleday, Doran & Co., 1938).

28. Ibid., 153.

29. Ibid., 471.

30. Ibid., 478.

31. Ibid., 531.

CHAPTER 10
The Women's War Against War

1. Vida Dutton Scudder, *On Journey* (New York: E. P. Dutton, 1937), 280–81.

2. Jane Addams, *The Second Twenty Years at Hull-House, September 1909 to September 1929* (New York: The Macmillan Co., 1930), 117–18.

3. Mercedes M. Randall, *Improper Bostonian: Emily Greene Balch* (New York: Twayne Publishers, 1964), 134.

4. R. L. Duffus, *Lillian Wald, Neighbor and Crusader* (New York: The Macmillan Co., 1938), 148.

5. Randall, 147.

6. Leonora O'Reilly, "Report on the International Congress of Women" in *Proceedings of the Fifth Biennial Convention of The National Women's Trade Union League of America, New York City, June 7–12, 1915*, 7.

7. Ibid., 1.

8. Letter of April 22, 1915, in Barbara Sicherman, *Alice Hamilton, A Life in Letters* (Cambridge: Harvard University Press, 1984).

9. Randall, 151.

10. O'Reilly, 1, 3.

11. Margaret Sanger, *An Autobiography* (New York: Dover Publications, 1971; reprint of W. W. Norton edition of 1938), 149.

12. Balch, in Jane Addams, Emily G. Balch, and Alice Hamilton, *Women at the Hague: The International Congress of Women and Its Results* (New York: Garland Publishing Co., 1972; reprint of 1915 edition), 14. "Base and silly" was a phrase Theodore Roosevelt used to describe pacifist efforts.

13. Lucy Biddle Lewis, letter of April 26, 1915, Biddle MSS, Friends' Historical Library, Swarthmore, Pa.

14. Randall, 159.

15. Ibid., Introduction, 1.

16. Letter of Alice Hamilton, May 5, 1915, in Sicherman, 190.

17. Alice Hamilton, *Exploring the Dangerous Trades: The Autobiography of Alice Hamilton, M.D.* (Boston: Northeastern University Press, 1985, reprinted from 1943 ed.), 165–66.

18. Ibid., 167, 168–69. See also letter from Hamilton, May 16, 1915, in Sicherman, 192.

19. Hamilton, *Autobiography*, 174–75.

20. Addams, in Addams, Balch, and Hamilton, 96. Mary Louise Degen, *The History of the Women's Peace Party* (New York: Burt Franklin Reprints, 1974; reprint of Johns Hopkins Press edition of 1939), identifies the speaker as the German Foreign Minister von Jagow.

21. Balch, in Addams, Balch, and Hamilton, 53.

22. Hamilton, 172.

23. Addams, in Addams, Balch, and Hamilton, 66, 67–68, 70.

24. Ibid., 75.

25. Ibid., 127.

26. Ibid., 98.

27. Hamilton, 211.

28. Quoted in Randall, 212.

29. The critical meeting between Schwimmer and Ford was also attended by Louis Lochner. In her interview with Barbara J. Steinson of November 1974 (Rebecca Shelley Papers, Bentley Library, University of Michigan, Ann Arbor, Mich), Shelley said, "I immediately on my return from [the International Congress at] the Hague was inspired to get to Ford. And that inspiration came in part from Angela [Morgan, another delegate] and her basic belief, of course she was a theosophist and a spiritualist and a Christian Socialist." Janet Reedy's synopsis of Shelley's life (also in the Shelley Papers, Bentley Library), 11, reports: "Staying at Angela Morgan's boarding house, kneeling beside her bed in prayer one day, [Shelley] received a clear call: 'Go to Ford.' "

The definitive work on the Peace Ship is Barbara S. Kraft's *The Peace Ship: Henry Ford's Pacifist Adventure in the First World War* (New York: Macmillan Publishing Co., 1978). Burnet Hershey's *The Odyssey of Henry Ford and the Great Peace Ship* (New York: Taplinger, 1967) is a breezy firsthand account. Lella Secor Florence's *The Ford Peace Ship and After* in *We Did Not Fight* (New York: Burt Franklin Reprints, 1974; reprint of Cobden-Sanderson's 1935 edition) helpfully presents the point of view of a journalist converted to pacifism by the experience.

30. Degen, 132–33. Kraft's account differs in detail: Ford told Wilson he was backing the women's mediation plan and hiring a ship to take a large delegation to Europe, asking Wilson to appoint the members of the delegation; that evening Ford chartered space.

31. Quoted in Kraft, 77.

32. Hershey, 205, and *Women of the World's Greatest Newspaper* (Chicago: Public Service Office of the Chicago Tribune, 1927), 44–45.

33. Hershey, 68.

34. Florence, 281–82.

35. Ida M. Tarbell, *All in the Day's Work: An Autobiography* (New York: The Macmillan Co., 1939), 313. Although then and later many questioned whether Addams simply used her health to disguise her discomfort with the whole enterprise, the weight of the evidence strongly indicates a sincere intention to sail. See, for example, Ida M. Tarbell, who refused Addams's urging to go: ". . . Miss Addams called me up, and for a half-hour we argued the matter on the telephone. All I could say was: 'If you see it you must go, Miss Addams. I don't see it and I can't. . . .' We were to talk it over in the morning, but that night they took her to Chicago, hurried her into a hospital. She was very ill. . . . Years after, I asked her, 'Would you have gone if you had not been ill?' 'I certainly should,' she said. 'There was a chance, and I was for taking every chance.' " Tarbell, 312–13. Allen F. Davis says that three days before the sailing date Addams became seriously ill with what was later diagnosed as tuberculosis of the kidney. *American Heroine: The Life and Legend of Jane Addams* (New York: Oxford University Press, 1973), 238.

36. Eleanor Flexner's foreword to Florence, xi.

37. Florence, 275–76, 281–84 passim.

38. Ibid., 281–84 passim.

39. Randall, 213.

40. Kraft, 271.

41. Balch, in Addams, Balch, and Hamilton, 109.

42. Davis, 226. "We certainly were told that regular rations of rum are served on the English side and that before a bayonet charge the Germans give a mixture containing sulphuric ether and the French absinthe." Letter from Alice Hamilton to Jane Addams, July 20, 1915, Sicherman, 195. "The men are filled with rum and ether before the bayonet charges." Marice Rutledge, *Children of Fate* (New York: Frederick A. Stokes Co., 1917), 88. ". . . the tradition of every attack being a double tot of rum beforehand." Robert Graves, *Good-bye to All That*, 2d ed. (Garden City, N.Y.: Doubleday & Co., 1957), 151.

43. Letter to *The Rochester Herald*, quoted by Davis, 229. See also Addams, *The Second Twenty Years*, 131–32.

CHAPTER 11
The Front as Frontier

1. Mary Lee, "Young America," published in an unidentified and undated journal, 599 in file of Dorothy Lee Mills Young, Military History Institute, Carlisle Barracks, Pa.

2. Elizabeth Shepley Sergeant, *Shadow-Shapes: The Journal of a Wounded Woman, October 1918–May 1919* (Boston: Houghton Mifflin Co., 1920), 215–16.

3. W. P. B., "The Salvation Army and Its Work in the World's War," *The Mess Kit* I: no. 7 (September 1919): 4. A copy of this article is in the papers of Helen Sparks, Salvation Army worker, in the Military History Institute, Carlisle Barracks, Pa.

4. Clara Savage Littledale, "The First Word from France," *Good Housekeeping* (October 1918), 39.

5. Katherine Duncan Morse, *The Uncensored Letters of a Canteen Girl* (New York: Henry Holt and Co., 1920), 265.

6. *A Red Triangle Girl in France* (New York: George H. Doran Co., 1918), 12.

7. Samuel H. Ranck, "A Librarian's Job in Base Section #1, France," *Bulletin of the American Library Association* XIII (May, 1919): 299.

8. Ruth Eleanor McKee, *Three Daughters* (Garden City, N.Y.: Doubleday, Doran & Co., 1938), 342. McKee's research was so impeccable that it's quite possible that this is an actual incident related to her by a woman who witnessed it.

9. Elsie Janis, *The Big Show: My Six Months with the AEF* (New York: Cosmopolitan Book Corp., 1919), 223–24.

10. Quoted in William L. O'Neill, *Everyone Was Brave: The Rise and Fall of Feminism in America* (Chicago: Quadrangle Books, 1969), 190.

11. *Red Triangle Girl*, 77–79 passim.

12. *Indiana Women in the World War*, 2 vols., comp. by Past Presidents' Parley (American Legion Auxiliary, Dept. of Indiana, 1936–38) I: 58.

13. "A Prize Specimen of Wounded Hero," *The World Wars Remembered: Personal Recollections of Heroes, Hello Girls, Flying Aces, Prisoners, Survivors, and Those on the Home Front, from the Pages of Yankee Magazine* (Dublin, N.H.: Yankee, Inc., 1979), 99.

14. Oleda Joure Christedes Papers, Military History Institute, Carlisle Barracks, Pa.

15. Women's Overseas Service League, *Lest We Forget*, 224.

16. Ruth Holden, Ruth Holden Papers, Schlesinger Library, Radcliffe College.

17. Women's Overseas Service League, *Carry On* VII (August 1929): 11, and Claudia M. Oakes, *United States*

Women in Aviation Through World War I (Washington, D.C.: Smithsonian Institution Press, 1978), 21.

18. Eleanor B. Kilham, *Letters from France: 1915–1919* (Salem, Mass.: no publisher given, 1941), 11.

19. Harriot E. S. Blatch, *Mobilizing Woman-Power* (New York: The Woman's Press, 1918), 131–33. Oakes, 21, also notes the tendency of every country, but especially Britain and the United States, to underemploy its best women as waitresses, floor scrubbers, and drivers, rejecting the skills of the trained and educated.

20. Louise C. Barbour, Louise Barbour Papers, Schlesinger Library, Radcliffe College.

21. Paper by Paula M. Cheatham. "The Army's Forgotten Women," in papers of Josephine Davis Gray, Military History Institute, Carlisle Barracks, Pa.

22. Christedes Papers.

23. The Cordelia Cree Papers at the Military History Institute at Carlisle Barracks, Pa., contain letters, alternately indignant and heartbroken, from Norris and Jones to "Miss Smith," defending their YMCA work. Jones sailed for France October 4, 1918, and worked during the war in Cherbourg at wet and dry canteens and at a rest camp. Norris served only after the war. Jones and Norris were particularly hurt that their good work of several months was ignored by the YMCA because of their AWOL two weeks: they had not realized that their offense would be viewed so seriously. For a discussion of such problems, see [Young Men's Christian Association], *Service with Fighting Men: An Account of the Work of the Young Men's Christian Association in the World War*, 2 vols. (New York: The Association Press, 1924) I: 481. At war's end the YMCA delivered more than 21,000 certificates of honorable service to its women and men workers, denying them to only 319 men and 80 women. Grounds for denial were serious moral offenses (no women were cited for these), inefficiency, refusal to obey orders, going AWOL. *Service with Fighting Men* I: 507–8.

24. Lavinia L. Dock, Sarah Elizabeth Pickett, Clara D. Noyes, Fannie F. Clement, Elizabeth G. Fox. and Anna R. Van Meter, *History of American Red Cross Nursing* (New York: The Macmillan Co., 1922), 213.

25. *Red Triangle Girl*, 144, 97.

26. Margaret Deland, *Small Things* (New York: D. Appleton and Co., 1919), 145–47 passim, 275.

27. Margaret Deland, letter of December 21, 1920, Margaret Deland Papers, Schlesinger Library, Radcliffe College.

28. *Indiana Women in the World War* I: 13–14.

29. David R. Francis, *Russia from the American Embassy, 1916–1918* (New York: Arno Press, 1970; reprint of Charles Scribner's Sons edition of 1921), 11.

30. Vera B. Whitehouse, *A Year as a Government Agent* (New York: Harper & Bros., 1920), 101.

31. Marie Van Vorst, *War Letters of an American Woman* (New York: John Lane Co., 1916), 74.

32. Janis, 127, 77.

33. Katherine Mayo, *"That Damn Y": A Record of Overseas Service* (Boston: Houghton Mifflin Co., 1920), 194–95.

34. Kilham, letter of September 9, 1915, 14. Kilham was a physician.

35. Julia C. Stimson, *Finding Themselves: The Letters of an American Army Chief Nurse in a British Hospital in France* (New York: The Macmillan Co., 1918), 79.

36. *The Service Star* VI, no. 2 (February 1923); the *Omaha World Herald* for November 11, 1922; and Selfridge's

obituary in the *Chicago Tribune*, reprinted in Muriel Beadle's *The Fortnightly of Chicago: The City and Its Women: 1873–1973*, ed. Fanny Butcher (Chicago: Henry Regnery Co., 1973).

37. Women's Overseas Service League, *Lest We Forget*, 2.

38. *Indiana Women in the World War* I: 60.

39. Mildred B. Byers and Mary Gruetzman, papers, Military History Institute, Carlisle Barracks, Pa.

40. Rosalie Slaughter Morton, *A Woman Surgeon: The Life and Work of Rosalie Slaughter Morton* (New York: Frederick A. Stokes Co., 1937), 380.

41. Elizabeth Campbell Bickford, unpublished typescript, 2 and 11, and letter of July 29, 1981, to James A. Kegel, Elizabeth Campbell Bickford Papers, Military History Institute, Carlisle Barracks, Pa.

42. *Indiana Women in the World War* I: 19.

43. Marian V. Dunn Adams, Marian V. Dunn Adams Papers, Military History Institute, Carlisle Barracks, Pa.

44. Morton, 276.

45. Alice Lord O'Brian, *No Glory: Letters from France, 1917–1919* (Buffalo, N.Y.: Airport Publishers, 1936), 8, 141, 152–53.

46. *Indiana Women in the World War* I: 25.

47. Ibid., 32.

48. *Those War Women by One of Them* (New York: Coward McCann, 1929), 280.

49. Gertrude Stein, *Wars I Have Seen* (New York: Random House, 1945), 212–13.

50. "Women War Workers of the World: Number Two in the Series," *The Touchstone* III, no. 6 (September 1918), 508.

51. *Mount Holyoke Alumnae Quarterly*, April 1918, 45.

52. Clara Savage Littledale, letter of December 2, 1918, Clara Savage Littledale Papers, Schlesinger Library, Radcliffe College.

53. Edith Gratie Stedman, letter of May 26, 1918, Edith Gratie Stedman Papers, Schlesinger Library, Radcliffe College.

54. Carrie May Hall, letter of July 24, 1917, Carrie May Hall Papers, Schlesinger Library, Radcliffe College.

55. Morton, 347.

56. Merle Egan Anderson, Merle Egan Anderson Papers, Military History Institute, Carlisle Barracks, Pa. Anderson spearheaded the efforts to obtain recognition as veterans for the Signal Corps telephone operators.

57. Grace Banker, "I Was a 'Hello Girl,' " *Yankee Magazine* (March 1974), 68.

58. Sergeant, *Shadow-Shapes*, 187.

59. Letter from Margaret Deland, November 19, 1923, in Edith Gratie Stedman Papers.

60. Lee, "Young America."

61. Sergeant, *Shadow-Shapes*, 81.

62. Littledale, letter of December 2, 1918.

63. Eunice Tietjens, *The World at My Shoulder* (New York: The Macmillan Co., 1938), 174.

64. *Indiana Women in the World War* I: 10.

65. Ibid., 53–54.

66. Women's Overseas Service League, *Lest We Forget*, 2.

67. Mabel Potter Daggett, *Women Wanted: The Story Written in Blood Red Letters on the Horizon of the Great War* (New York: George H. Doran Co., 1918), 2.

68. *Vassar Quarterly* (November 1919), 31.

69. YMCA, *Service with Fighting Men* I: 100 and II: 65.

70. Women's Overseas Service League, *Carry On* (August 1926).

71. Morton, 282. See also Preston William Slosson, *The Great Crusade and After: 1914–1928* (New York: The Macmillan Co., 1930), 131–32; Judith Freeman Clark, *Almanac of American Women in the 20th Century* (New York: Prentice Hall Press, 1987), 28; Nancy Woloch, *Women and the American Experience* (New York: Alfred A. Knopf, 1984), 389; Gail Braybon and Penny Summerfield, *Out of the Cage: Women's Experiences in Two World Wars* (London: Pandora Press, 1987), 2; *Behind the Lines: Gender and the Two World Wars*, ed. by Margaret Randolph Higgonet, Jane Jenson, Sonya Michel, and Margaret Collins Weitz (New Haven: Yale University Press, 1987), introduction, and Joan W. Scott's essay "Rewriting History"; Barbara J. Steinson, "The 'Mother Half of Humanity': American Women in the Peace and Preparedness Movements in World War I," in *Women, War and Revolution*, ed. by Carol R. Berkin and Clara Lovett (New York: Holmes and Meier, 1980), 276.

72. James R. McGovern, "The American Woman's Pre–World War I Freedom in Manners and Morals," *Journal of American History* LV (September 1968): 315–33.

73. Notable American Women 1607–1950: A Biographical Dictionary, 3 vols., ed. by Edward T. James, Janet Wilson James, and Paul S. Boyer (Cambridge, Mass.: The Belknap Press of Harvard University Press, 1971), III: 602.

74. Juliet Goodrich, Juliet T. Goodrich Papers, Schlesinger Library, Radcliffe College.

75. The Army War College, Washington Barracks, D.C., Memorandum for the Director G-1 Division, the Army War College. Subject: "The Utilization of Women in the Military Service in Time of War." Dec. 23, 1924. Submitted by D. M. Ashbridge, Major C.A.C. Military History Institute, Carlisle Barracks, Pa. The appended questionnaire was distributed by order of the secretary of war, November 10, 1924. See also Brig. Gen. A. J. Bowley, A.C. of S., G-1, "Work of the Personnel Division of the War Department General Staff." Lecture delivered at the Army War College, Washington, D.C., October 1, 1929. Military History Institute, Carlisle Barracks, Pa.

76. Sergeant, *Shadow-Shapes*, 168.

BIBLIOGRAPHY

Fiction and Poetry

Aldridge, John W. *After the Lost Generation: A Critical Study of the Writers of Two Wars*. Freeport, N.Y.: Books for Libraries Press, 1971; reprint of 1951 edition.

Andrews, Mary Raymond Shipman. *The Forge in Which the Soul of a Man Was Tested*. 1915.

Ascher, Carol, Louise DeSalvo, and Sara Ruddick. *Between Women: Biographers, Novelists, Critics, Teachers and Artists Write about Their Work on Women*. Boston: Beacon Press, 1984.

Atherton, Gertrude F. *The White Morning: A Novel of the Power of the German Woman in Wartime*. New York: Frederick A. Stokes Co., 1918.

Beaumann, Nicola. *A Very Great Profession: The Woman's Novel 1914–1939*. London: Virago Press, 1983.

Bennett, Mildred R. *The World of Willa Cather*. New York: Dodd, Mead & Co., 1951.

Bergonzi, Bernard. *Heroes' Twilight: A Study of the Literature of the Great War*. New York: Coward-McCann, 1965.

Brown, E. K. [and Leon Edel]. *Willa Cather: A Critical Biography*. New York: Alfred A. Knopf, 1953.

[Burr, Anna Robeson Brown.] *The House on Charles Street*. New York: Duffield and Co., 1921.

Cadogan, Mary, and Patricia Craig. *Women and Children First: The Fiction of Two World Wars*. London: Victor Gollancz, 1978.

Cather, Willa. *One of Ours*. New York: Alfred A. Knopf, 1922, 1940.

Chartres, Annie Vivanti. *The Outrage*. New York: Alfred A. Knopf, 1918.

Cooperman, Stanley. *World War I and the American Novel*. Baltimore: Johns Hopkins University Press, 1967.

Cru, Jean Horton. *War Books: A Study in Historical Criticism*. Edited and partially translated by Stanley J. Pincetl, Jr., and Ernest Marchand. San Diego: San Diego State Univ. Press, c. 1976.

Day, Dorothy. *The Eleventh Virgin*. New York: Albert and Charles Boni, 1921.

Dillon, Mary. *Comrades*. New York: The Century Co., 1918.

Divine, Charles. *Cognac Hill*. New York: Payson and Clarke, 1927.

Fetterley, Judith. *The Resisting Reader: A Feminist Approach to American Fiction*. Bloomington: Indiana University Press, 1978.

[Fisher], Dorothy Canfield. *The Day of Glory*. New York: Henry Holt and Co., 1919.

———. *The Deepening Stream*. New York: Harcourt, Brace and Co., 1930.

———. *A Harvest of Stories*. New York: Harcourt, Brace and Co., 1927, 1956.

———. *Home Fires in France*. New York: Henry Holt & Co., 1918.

Genthe, Charles V. *American War Narratives, 1917–1918: A Study and Bibliography*. New York: D. Lewis, 1969.

Gilbert, Sandra M. "Soldier's Heart: Literary Men, Literary Women, and the Great War." *Signs* 8 (Spring 1983): 442–50.

Gold, Henry G. "The Great War: A Literary Perspective." *Parameters* XVII (Summer 1987): 86ff.

Hager, Philip E., and Desmond Taylor. *The Novels of World War I: An Annotated Bibliography*. New York: Garland Publishing Co., 1981.

Huard, Frances W. *Lilies, White and Red*. New York: George H. Doran, 1919.

Johnston, Annie Fellows. *Georgina's Service Stars*. New York: Britton Publishing Co., 1918.

Klein, Holger, ed. *The First World War in Fiction: A Collection of Critical Essays*. New York: Barnes and Noble, 1976.

Lee, Mary. *"It's a Great War!"* Boston: Houghton Mifflin Co., 1929.

McKee, Ruth Eleanor, in collaboration with Alice Fleenor Sturgis. *Three Daughters*. Garden City, N.Y.: Doubleday, Doran & Co., 1938.

Montague, Margaret P. *England to America*. New York: Doubleday, Page, 1920.

Paul, Elliott. *The Amazon*. New York: Horace Liveright, 1930.

Reilly, Catherine W., ed. *Chaos of the Night: Women's Poetry and Verse of the Second World War*. London: Virago Press, 1984.

———. *Scars Upon My Heart: Women's Poetry and Verse of the First World War*. London: Virago Press, 1981.

Rinehart, Mary Roberts. *The Amazing Interlude*. New York: The Review of Reviews Corp, 1917.

Rutledge, Marice (Marice Gibson Hale). *Children of Fate*. New York: Frederick A. Stokes Co., 1917.

Sedgwick, Anne Douglas. *The Little French Girl*. Boston: Houghton Mifflin Co., 1924.

Sherwood, Margaret. *The Worn Doorstep*. Boston: Little, Brown and Co., 1916.

Smith, Helen Zenna (Evadne Price). *"Not so Quiet . . .": Stepdaughters of War*. London: Albert E. Marriott, 1930.

Smith, Myron J., Jr. *War Story Guide: An Annotated Bibliography of Military Fiction*. Metuchen, N.J.: The Scarecrow Press, 1980.

Walsh, Thomas Jeffrey. *American War Literature: 1914 to Vietnam*. New York: St. Martin's Press, 1982.

Washington, Ida H. *Dorothy Canfield Fisher: A Biography*. Shelburne, Vt.: The New England Press, 1982.
Wharton, Edith. *The Marne*. New York: D. Appleton and Co., 1919.
———. *A Son at the Front*. New York: Charles Scribner's Sons, 1923.
Wilcox, Ella Wheeler. *Hello, Boys!* London: Gay and Hancock, 1919.
Wylie, Ida A. R. *Towards Morning*. London: John Lane Co., 1918.

Memoirs and Biographies

Adams, Marian V. Dunn. Papers. Military History Institute, Carlisle Barracks, Pa.
Addams, Jane. *The Second Twenty Years at Hull-House, September 1909 to September 1929, With a Record of a Growing World Consciousness*. New York: The Macmillan Co., 1930.
Aldrich, Mildred. Papers. Schlesinger Library, Radcliffe College.
———. *A Hilltop on the Marne*. Boston: Houghton Mifflin Co., 1915.
———. *On the Edge of the War Zone: From the Battle of the Marne to the Entrance of the Stars and Stripes*. London: Constable and Co., 1918.
———. *The Peak of the Load*. Boston: Small, Maynard & Co., 1918.
American Women's Overseas Service League Scrapbook. MS 1262. Nebraska State Historical Society Library, Lincoln, Nebr.
Anderson, Merle Egan. Papers. Military History Institute, Carlisle Barracks, Pa.
Ashe, Elizabeth. *Intimate Letters from France during America's First Year of War*. San Francisco: Philopolis Press, 1918.
Atherton, Gertrude F. *Adventures of a Novelist*. New York: The Liveright Publishing Corp., 1932.
———. "A German Letter." *New York Times*, November 28, 1914.
———. *Life in the War Zone*. New York: System Printing Co., 1916.
———. *The Living Present*. New York: Frederick A. Stokes & Co., 1917.
Baldwin, Marian. *Canteening Overseas, 1917–1919*. New York: The Macmillan Co., 1920.
Ballou, Jenny. *Period Piece, Ella Wheeler Wilcox and Her Times*. Boston: Houghton Mifflin Co., 1940.
Banker, Grace. "I Was a 'Hello Girl.' " *Yankee Magazine*, March 1974.
Barbour, Louise C. Papers. Schlesinger Library, Radcliffe College.
Beach, Sylvia. *Shakespeare and Company*. New York: Harcourt Brace & Co., 1959.
Beatty, Bessie. *The Red Heart of Russia*. New York: The Century Co., 1918.
Bickford, Elizabeth Campbell. Papers. Military History Institute, Carlisle Barracks, Pa.
Bigelow, Glenna L. *Liège on the Line of March, An American Girl's Experiences When the Germans Came Through Belgium*. New York: John Lane Co., 1918.

Bignell, Agnes Gilson. Papers. World War I Collection. Wellesley College Archives.

Billings, Florence. Papers. Sophia Smith Collection, Smith College.

Blake, Katherine. *Some Letters Written to Maude Gray and Marian Wickes, 1917–1918.* New York: privately printed, 1920.

Blatch, Harriot E. S., and Alma Lutz. *Challenging Years: Memoirs of Harriot Stanton Blatch.* New York: G. P. Putnam's Sons, 1940, 1976.

Bloodgood, Edith Holt, ed., in collaboration with Rufus Graves Mather. *First Lady of the Lighthouse: A Biography of Winifred Holt Mather.* New York: The Lighthouse, New York Association for the Blind, 1952.

Botchkareva, Maria. *Yashka, My Life as Peasant, Officer and Exile.* Set down by Isaac Don Levine. New York: Frederick A. Stokes Co., 1919.

Bradbury, Emilie. Letter, *Intelligencer* LXXV, nos. 11, 34.

Bradley, Amy Owen. *Back of the Front in France: Letters from Amy Owen Bradley, Motor Driver of the American Fund for French Wounded.* Boston: W. A. Butterfield, 1918.

Brittain, Vera. *Testament of Youth.* New York: Wideview Books, 1980; reprint of Victor Gollancz edition of 1933.

Broun, Heywood Hale. *Whose Little Boy Are You? A Memoir of the Broun Family.* New York: St. Martin's Press, 1983.

Bryant, Louise S. Papers. Sophia Smith Collection, Smith College.

———. *Six Red Months in Russia: An Observer's Account of Russia Before and During the Proletarian Dictatorship.* New York: Arno Press and The New York Times, 1970; reprint of George H. Doran Co. edition of 1918.

Burton, Margaret E. *Mabel Cratty, A Leader in the Art of Leadership.* New York: The Women's Press, 1929.

Byers, Mildred B. Papers. Military History Institute, Carlisle Barracks, Pa.

Carry On. Publication of The Women's Overseas Service League. 1922–1988.

Chalon, Jean. *Portrait of a Seductress: The World of Natalie Barney.* New York: Crown Publishers, 1979.

Cheatham, Paula M. Papers. Military History Institute, Carlisle Barracks, Pa.

Chilson, Charlotte G. Light. Papers. Military History Institute, Carlisle Barracks, Pa.

Christedes, Oleda Joure. Papers. Military History Institute, Carlisle Barracks, Pa.

Churchill, Mary Smith. *You Who Can Help: Paris Letters of an American Army Officer's Wife, August, 1916–January, 1918.* Boston: Small, Maynard & Co., 1918.

Clark, Rosamond. Papers. Schlesinger Library, Radcliffe College.

Clark, Timothy R., ed. *The World Wars Remembered: Personal Recollections of Heroes, Hello Girls, Flying Aces, Prisoners, Survivors, and Those on the Home Front, from the Pages of Yankee Magazine.* Dublin, N.H.: Yankee, Inc., 1979.

Coale, Edith. Letters, *Intelligencer* LXXV, no. 4: 60.

Cree, Cordelia. Papers. Military History Institute, Carlisle Barracks, Pa.

Davis, Allen F. *American Heroine: The Life and Legend of Jane Addams.* New
    York: Oxford University Press, 1973.
Deland, Margaret. Papers. Schlesinger Library, Radcliffe College.
———. *Golden Yesterdays.* New York: Harper and Bros., 1941.
———. *Small Things.* New York: D. Appleton and Co., 1919.
de Wolfe, Elsie. *After All.* New York: Harper and Bros., 1935.
Dewson, Mary Williams. Papers. Schlesinger Library, Radcliffe College.
Dexter, Mary. Papers. Schlesinger Library, Radcliffe College.
———. *In the Soldier's Service: War Experiences of Mary Dexter, England, Bel-
    gium, France, 1914–1918.* Boston: Houghton Mifflin Co., 1918.
Dorr, Rheta Childe. *Inside the Russian Revolution.* New York: The Macmillan
    Co., 1917.
———. *A Soldier's Mother in France.* Indianapolis: Bobbs Merrill Co., 1918.
———. *A Woman of Fifty.* New York: Arno Press, 1980; reprint of Funk &
    Wagnalls edition of 1924.
Doty, Madeleine Zabriskie. Papers. Sophia Smith Collection, Smith College.
———. *Behind the Battle Line: Around the World in 1918.* New York: The
    Macmillan Co., 1918.
———. *Short Rations: Experiences of an American Woman in Germany.* New
    York: A. L. Burt Co., 1917.
Draper, Ruth. *The Art of Ruth Draper: Her Dramas and Characters, with a Memoir
    by Morton Dauwen Zabel.* Garden City, N.Y.: Doubleday and Co., 1960.
Dryden, Elizabeth. *Paris in the Herrick Days.* Paris: Dorbon-Ainé, 1915.
Duffus, R. L. *Lillian Wald, Neighbor and Crusader.* New York: The Macmillan
    Co., 1938.
Duguid, Mary and William. Letters. Elkinton Papers, Friends' Historical Li-
    brary, Swarthmore, Pa.
Duncan, Isadora. *My Life.* New York: The Liveright Pub. Corp., 1966; reprint
    of Boni and Liveright edition of 1927.
Ely, Henrietta B. Papers. Archives of Miss Porter's School, Farmington, Conn.
Farmborough, Florence. *With the Armies of the Tsar, A Nurse at the Russian
    Front, 1914–1918.* New York: Stein and Day, 1975.
Farnam, Ruth S. *A Nation at Bay: What an American Woman Saw and Did in
    Suffering Serbia.* Indianapolis: Bobbs-Merrill Co., 1918.
Farrell, John C. *Beloved Lady: A History of Jane Addams' Ideas on Reform and
    Peace.* Baltimore: Johns Hopkins University Press, 1967.
"Fine Fighting Spirit Shown in Letters from the Front," *Literary Digest* LVI
    (January 19, 1918): 48f.
Fitzgerald, Alice Louise Florence. *The Edith Cavell Nurse from Massachusetts:
    A Record of One Year's Personal Service with the B.E.F. . . . . 1916–1917.*
    Boston: W. A. Butterfield, 1917.
Florence, Barbara Moench, ed. *Lella Secor, A Diary in Letters, 1915–1922.* New
    York: Burt Franklin, 1978.
Florence, Lella Secor. *The Ford Peace Ship and After.* Reprint of memoir in

Julian Bell, ed. *We Did Not Fight, 1914–1918*. New York: Burt Franklin Reprints, 1974; reprint of Cobden-Sanderson edition of 1935.

[Foote, Katharine.] *88 Bis and V.I.H.: Letters from Two Hospitals by an American V.A.D.* Boston: The Atlantic Monthly Press, 1919.

Gaines, Anna J. Letters, *Intelligencer* LXXV, nos. 2, 27; no. 34: 539; LXXVI, no. 36: 569.

Gardner, Mary Sewall. Papers. Schlesinger Library, Radcliffe College.

Gardner, Virginia. *"Friend and Lover": The Life of Louise Bryant*. New York: Horizon Press, 1982.

Gildersleeve, Virginia Crocheron. *Many a Good Crusade: The Memoirs of Virginia Crocheron Gildersleeve*. New York: The Macmillan Co., 1954.

Goldman, Emma. *My Disillusionment in Russia*. Gloucester, Mass.: Peter Smith, 1983; reprint of Harper and Row edition.

Goodrich, Juliet T. Papers. Schlesinger Library, Radcliffe College.

de Gramont, E., Ex-Duchesse de Clermont-Tonnerre. *Years of Plenty*. Translated by Florence and Victor Llona. New York: Jonathan Cape & Harrison Smith, 1929.

Graves, Robert. *Good-bye to All That*. 2d ed., rev. Garden City, N.Y.: Doubleday & Co., 1957.

Gray, Josephine Davis. Papers. Military History Institute, Carlisle Barracks, Pa.

Gruetzman, Mary. Papers. Military History Institute, Carlisle Barracks, Pa.

Haines, Anna J. Letter in *Intelligencer* LXXV, no. 2 (January 12, 1918).

Hale, Nancy. *Mary Cassatt: A Biography of the Great American Painter*. Garden City, N.Y.: Doubleday & Co., 1975.

Hall, Carrie May. Papers. Schlesinger Library, Radcliffe College.

Hamilton, Alice. "At the War Capitals," *Survey* XXXIV (August 7, 1915): 417–22.

———. *Exploring the Dangerous Trades: The Autobiography of Alice Hamilton, M.D.* Boston: Northeastern University Press, 1985; reprint of 1943 edition.

Hamilton, Olivia E. Papers. Schlesinger Library, Radcliffe College.

Hancock, Joy Bright. *Lady in the Navy*. Annapolis: Naval Institute Press, 1972.

Happock, Adele Louise. Papers. Military History Institute, Carlisle Barracks, Pa.

Harbord, James Guthrie. *Leaves from a War Diary*. New York: Dodd, Meade & Co., 1926.

Harriman, Mrs. J. Borden (Florence Jaffray Hurst Harriman). *From Pinafores to Politics*. New York: Henry Holt and Co., 1923.

Harrison, Florence Louise. Papers. Schlesinger Library, Radcliffe College.

Head, Lydia Bush-Brown. Papers. Sophia Smith Collection, Smith College.

Hoff-Wilson, Joan, and Marjorie Lightman, eds. *Without Precedent: The Life and Career of Eleanor Roosevelt*. Bloomington: Indiana University Press, 1984.

Holden, Ruth. Papers. Schlesinger Library, Radcliffe College.

Holman, Anna Elizabeth. Papers. Schlesinger Library, Radcliffe College.

Holt, Winifred. See Bloodgood, Edith Holt.

Huard, Frances W. *My Home in the Field of Honour*. New York: George H. Doran Co., 1916.

Hudson, Elisabeth. Papers. Archives of Miss Porter's School, Farmington, Conn.

Hunt, Emily F. Papers. Schlesinger Library, Radcliffe College.

Hunton, Adele, and Kathryn Johnson. *Two Colored Women with the American Expeditionary Forces*. New York: AMS Press, 1920, 1971.

Hutton, I. Emslie. *With a Woman's Unit in Serbia, Salonika and Sebastopol*. London: Williams & Norgate, 1928.

Indiana Women in the World War. 2 vols. Compiled by Past Presidents' Parley, American Legion Auxiliary, Dept. of Indiana, 1936–38.

Irwin, Inez. H. Papers. Schlesinger Library, Radcliffe College.

Janis, Elsie. *The Big Show: My Six Months with the AEF*. New York: Cosmopolitan Book Corp., 1919.

Kara-Georgevitch, Princess Alexis. *For the Better Hour*. London: Constable and Co., 1917.

Karr, Jean. *Grace Livingston Hill, Her Story and Her Writings*. New York: Greenberg Publishers, 1948.

Keyes, Regina Flood. Letter, *Bulletin* of The American Women's Hospitals I, no. 1 (October 1918): 10, 11.

Kilham, Eleanor B. *Letters from France: 1915–1919*. Salem, Mass.: no publisher given, 1941.

King, Hazel, ed. *One Woman at War, Letters of Olive King 1915–1920*. Carleton, Victoria: University of Melbourne Press, 1986.

Lambie, Margaret. *Verdun Experiences*. Washington, D.C.: The Current Press, 1945.

LaMotte, Ellen N. "An American Nurse in Paris," *Survey* XXXIV (1915): 333.

———. *The Backwash of War*. New York: G. P. Putnam's Sons, 1934.

Lee, Helena Crummett. Papers. Schlesinger Library, Radcliffe College.

Lee, Mary. Papers. Schlesinger Library, Radcliffe College.

Leighton, Elizabeth. "A Woman's Mission to Revolutionary Russia: Bessie Boies Cotton and the Young Women's Christian Association." Unpublished honors thesis, Mount Holyoke College, 1983.

Lewis, Lucy Biddle. Papers in Biddle MSS(C), Friends' Historical Library, Swarthmore, Pa.

Lewis, Lydia. See Lydia Lewis Rickman.

Lewis, R. W. B. *Edith Wharton: A Biography*. New York: Harper and Row, 1975.

Literary Digest LVI (March 23, 1918).

Littledale, Clara Savage. Papers. Schlesinger Library, Radcliffe College.

Lovejoy, Esther Pohl. *Certain Samaritans*. New York: The Macmillan Co., 1933.

———. *The House of the Good Neighbor*. New York: The Macmillan Co., 1919.

Loyson, Laura Jayne Bucknell. Letter in Wellesley College *News'* Sources. World War I Collection. Wellesley College Archives.

Luhan, Mabel Dodge. *Movers and Shakers.* Albuquerque: University of New Mexico Press, 1985. Originally published as volume 3 of *Intimate Memories,* New York: Harcourt, Brace, 1936.

Lutes, Della Thompson. *My Boy in Khaki: A Mother's Story.* New York: Harper and Bros., 1918.

Lutz, Alma, ed. *With Love, Jane: Letters from American Women on the War Fronts.* New York: The John Day Co., 1945.

McAuley, Mary Ethel. *Germany in War Time: What an American Girl Saw and Heard.* Chicago: The Open Court Publishing Co., 1918.

MacKay, Helen G. *Journal of Small Things.* New York: Duffield and Co., 1917.

Macnaughtan, Sarah. *A Woman's Diary of the War.* New York: E. P. Dutton, 1916.

"Mademoiselle Miss": Letters from an American Girl Serving with the Rank of Lieutenant in a French Army Hospital at the Front. Boston: W. A. Butterfield, 1916.

Marbury, Elisabeth. *My Crystal Ball: Reminiscences.* New York: Boni and Liveright, 1923.

Mayo, Margaret. *Trouping for the Troops: Fun-Making at the Front.* New York: George H. Doran Co., 1919.

Mellow, James R. *Charmed Circle: Gertrude Stein and Company.* New York: Avon Books, 1974.

Merritt, Anna Lea. *Love Locked Out: The Memoirs of Anna Lea Merritt with a Checklist of Her Works.* Edited by Galina Gorokhoff. Boston: Museum of Fine Arts, n.d.

Millard, Shirley. *I Saw Them Die: Diary and Recollections of Shirley Millard.* New York: Harcourt, Brace, and Co., 1936.

[Morse, Katherine Duncan.] *The Uncensored Letters of a Canteen Girl.* New York: Henry Holt and Co., 1920.

Mortimer, Maud. *A Green Tent in Flanders.* Garden City, N.Y.: Doubleday, Page & Co., 1917.

Morton, Rosalie Slaughter. *A Woman Surgeon: The Life and Work of Rosalie Slaughter Morton.* New York: Frederick A. Stokes Co., 1937.

"Mrs. Belmont Tiffany Tells of Woman's Work Behind the Front," *Literary Digest* LVI (March 2, 1918): 47ff.

Noyes, Frances Newbold. *My A.E.F., A Hail and Farewell.* New York: Frederick A. Stokes Co., 1920.

O'Brian, Alice Lord. *No Glory: Letters From France, 1917–1919.* Buffalo, N.Y.: Airport Publishers, 1936.

O'Connor, Irene Wilkinson. Papers. Military History Institute, Carlisle Barracks, Pa.

O'Shaughnessy, Edith L. *My Lorraine Journal.* New York: Harper and Bros. [c. 1918].

One Woman's War. New York: The Macaulay Co., 1930.

Owings, Chloe. Papers. Schlesinger Library, Radcliffe College.

Paddock, Grace Banker. See Grace Banker.

Parmelee, Ruth A. "Reminiscences of Twenty Years in the Near East," *Medical Review of Reviews* (August 1935): 377–405.

Parsons, Mrs. William Barclay [and others]. *War Letters 1917–1919.* Boston: privately printed, 1921.

Payne, Jessica L. "What I Saw in England and France." Brooklyn, N.Y.: [Brooklyn] *Eagle Library* XXXI, no. 199 (November 1916): 3–8.

Peat, Louisa Watson. *Mrs. Private Peat, by Herself.* Indianapolis: The Bobbs-Merrill Co., 1918.

Pierce, Ruth. *Trapped in "Black Russia": Letters, June–November, 1915.* Boston and New York: Houghton Mifflin Co., 1918.

Polk-Peters, Ethel. "Autobiographical Sketch," *Medical Review of Reviews,* August 1935.

Randall, Mercedes M. *Improper Bostonian: Emily Greene Balch.* New York: Twayne Publishers, 1964.

A Red Triangle Girl in France. New York: George H. Doran Co., 1918.

Reedy, Janet. Synopsis of life of Rebecca Shelley. Rebecca Shelley Papers, Bentley Library, University of Michigan, Ann Arbor, Mich.

Richardson, Anna Steese. "Overseas with the A.E.F." *McCall's Magazine,* October 1918.

Rickman, John. Letters, March 18 and 22, 1918, Biddle MSS(C), Friends' Historical Library, Swarthmore, Pa.

———. "Commonplaces in Buzuluk." *Atlantic Monthly,* March 1919.

———, and Lydia Lewis Rickman. "Picture of Russian Peasant Life in the Period August 1916–September 1918," and other papers, including "Conditions in Eastern Siberia and Manchuria in the Autumn of 1918" and *An Eyewitness from Russia* (London: People's Russian Information Bureau, 1917). Biddle MSS(C) at Friends' Historical Library, Swarthmore, Pa.

Rickman, Lydia Lewis. Letters, reprinted in *Intelligencer* LXXIV, no. 4: 825; no. 34: 539, 540, 779; LXXV, no. 33: 522.

Rinehart, Mary Roberts. *Dangerous Days.* New York: George H. Doran Co., 1919.

———. "For King and Country," serial in *Saturday Evening Post,* beginning April 17, 1915.

———. *My Story. A New Edition and Seventeen New Years.* New York: Rinehart & Co., 1948.

Roderick, Mary Louise Rochester. *A Nightingale in the Trenches.* New York: Vantage Press, 1966.

Rogers, Edith Nourse. Papers. Schlesinger Library, Radcliffe College.

Roosevelt, Mrs. Theodore, Jr. *Day Before Yesterday: The Reminiscences of Mrs. Theodore Roosevelt, Jr.* Garden City, N.Y.: Doubleday & Co., 1959.

Root, Esther, and Marjorie Crocker. *Over Periscope Pond: Letters from Two*

American Girls in Paris, October 1916–January 1918. Boston: Houghton Mifflin Co., 1918.

Sandes, Flora. *The Autobiography of a Woman Soldier: A Brief Record of Adventure with the Serbian Army, 1916–1919.* New York: Frederick A. Stokes Co., n.d.

Sanger, Margaret. *An Autobiography.* New York: Dover Publications, 1971; reprint of W. W. Norton edition of 1938.

[Schwimmer] *Rosika Schwimmer: World Patriot: A Biographical Sketch.* Endorsed by Marguerite Gobat, Lida Gustava Heymann, Lola Maverick Lloyd, Eugenie Miskolczy Meller, Mevr. R. van Wulfften Palthe Broese van Groenau, Naima Sahlbom (N.p.: International Committee for World Peace Prize Award to Rosika Schwimmer, 1937).

Scudder, Janet. *Modeling My Life.* New York: Harcourt, Brace and Co., 1925.

Scudder, Vida Dutton. *On Journey.* New York: E. P. Dutton, 1937.

Secor, Lella. See Lella Secor Florence.

Secrest, Meryle. *Between Me and Life: A Biography of Romaine Brooks.* Garden City, N.Y.: Doubleday and Co., 1974.

Sedgwick, Anne Douglas. *A Portrait in Letters.* Edited by Basil de Sèlincourt. Boston: Houghton Mifflin Co., 1936.

Sergeant, Elizabeth Shepley. *Shadow-Shapes: The Journal of a Wounded Woman, October 1918–May 1919.* Boston: Houghton Mifflin Co., 1920.

Shaw, Anna. Papers. Friends' Historical Library, Swarthmore, Pa.

Shelley, Rebecca, with Barbara J. Steinson. Typescript of oral history of Rebecca Shelley. November, 1974. Bentley Library, University of Michigan, Ann Arbor, Mich.

Shortall, Katherine, *A "Y" Girl in France: Letters of Katherine Shortall.* Boston: R. G. Badger, [c. 1919].

Sicherman, Barbara. *Alice Hamilton, A Life in Letters.* Cambridge: Harvard University Press, 1984.

Sinclair, May. *A Journal of Impressions in Belgium.* New York: The Macmillan Co., 1915.

Sparks, Helen. Papers. Military History Institute, Carlisle Barracks, Pa.

Speakman, Marie Anna. *Memories.* Wilmington, Del.: The Greenwood Bookshop, 1927.

Spencer, Carita. *War Scenes I Shall Never Forget.* 3d ed. New York: Carita Spencer, 1916.

Stanley, Monica. *My Diary in Serbia.* London: Simkin, Marshall, Hamilton, Kent & Co., 1916.

Stedman, Edith Gratie. Papers. Schlesinger Library, Radcliffe College.

Stein, Gertrude. *Wars I Have Seen.* New York: Random House, 1945.

Sterne, Elaine, ed. *Over the Seas for Uncle Sam.* New York: Britton Publishing Co., 1918.

Stillman, Ruth. Papers. Archives of Miss Porter's School, Farmington, Conn.

Stimson, Julia C. *Finding Themselves: The Letters of an American Army Chief*

Nurse in a British Hospital in France. New York: The Macmillan Co., 1918.

Stockton, Lucy. Charles G. Stockton Papers. Schlesinger Library, Radcliffe College.

Tarbell, Ida. *All in the Day's Work: An Autobiography.* New York: The Macmillan Co., 1939.

Tenison, E. M. *Louise Imogen Guiney: Her Life and Works, 1861–1920.* London: The Macmillan Co., 1923.

Therese, Josephine. *With Old Glory in Berlin.* Boston: The Page Co., 1918.

Those War Women, By One of Them. New York: Coward-McCann, 1929.

Thurstan, Violetta. *The Hounds of War Unleashed.* St. Ives, Cornwall: United Writers Publications, 1978.

Tietjens, Eunice. *The World at My Shoulder.* New York: The Macmillan Co., 1938.

Tileston, Amelia Peabody. *Amelia Peabody Tileston and Her Canteens for the Serbs*, with an outline of her life by Mary Wilder Tileston. Boston: Houghton Mifflin Co., 1919.

Toklas, Alice B. *The Alice B. Toklas Cook Book.* New York: Harper & Row, 1954.

———. *What Is Remembered.* New York: Holt, Rinehart and Winston, 1963.

Turczynowicz, Laura de Grozdawa. *When the Prussians Came to Poland: The Experiences of an American Woman During the German Invasion.* New York: G. P. Putnam's Sons, 1916.

Uncensored Letters of a Canteen Girl. See Katherine Duncan Morse.

Van Vorst, Marie. *War Letters of an American Woman.* New York: John Lane Co., 1916.

Vorse, Mary Heaton. *A Footnote to Folly: Reminiscences of Mary Heaton Vorse.* New York: Arno Press, 1980; reprint of Farrar and Rinehart edition of 1935.

Waddington, Mary King. *My War Diary.* New York: Charles Scribner's Sons, 1918.

"War Letters of an American Woman," *Outlook* CXIII (August 1916): 794–99, 863–68.

War Nurse, The True Story of a Woman Who Lived, Loved and Suffered on the Western Front. New York: Cosmopolitan Book Corp., 1930.

A War Nurse's Diary: Sketches from a Belgian Field Hospital. New York: The Macmillan Co., 1918.

Ware, Susan. *Partner and I: Molly Dewson, Feminism, and New Deal Politics.* New Haven: Yale University Press, 1987.

Warwick, Frances Evelyn (The Countess of Warwick). *A Woman and the War.* New York: George H. Doran Co., 1916.

Wharton, Edith. *The Letters of Edith Wharton.* Edited by R. W. B. and Nancy Lewis. New York: Charles Scribner's Sons, 1988.

Wheelwright, Julie. "Flora Sandes—Military Maid," *History Today* XXXIV (March 1989): 42ff.

White, Esther M. Letter, *Intelligencer* LXXVI, no. 2: 24–25.

Whitehouse, Vira B. *A Year as a Government Agent*. New York: Harper & Bros., 1920.

Wickes, George. *The Amazon of Letters: The Life and Loves of Natalie Barney*. New York: G. P. Putnam's Sons, 1976.

Wilcox, Ella Wheeler. *The Worlds and I*. New York: Arno Press, 1980; reprint of George H. Doran edition of 1918.

Wilson, Edith. *My Memoirs*. Indianapolis: Bobbs-Merrill Co., 1938.

Winsor School. *The Overseas War Record of the Winsor School, 1914–1919*. Boston: Winsor School Graduate Club, n.d.

Winton, Sophie C. Papers. Military History Institute, Carlisle Barracks, Pa.

Withington, Alfreda. *Mine Eyes Have Seen: A Woman Doctor's Saga*. New York: E. P. Dutton & Co., 1941.

Woodsmall, Ruth. Papers. Sophia Smith Collection, Smith College.

Young, Dorothy Lee Mills. Papers. Military History Institute, Carlisle Barracks, Pa.

Organizations

Ahern, Mary Eileen, "A.L.A. News from Overseas," *Bulletin of the American Library Association* XIII (May 1919): 312.

American Board of Commissioners for Foreign Missions. Balkan Mission. "Report of Women's Work in Samokov and Sofia for 1914–15"; "General Report of Monastir Station and Girls Boarding School for the years 1915–16." Archives of American Board of Commissioners for Foreign Missions, Houghton Library, Harvard University.

American Friends Service Committee. *Bulletin No. 16, June 1, 1917–May 31, 1918*. Friends' Historical Library, Swarthmore, Pa.

———. *The Story of the American Friends Service Committee 1917–1952*. (AFSC, n.p., n.d.)

American Library Association. *Bulletin of the American Library Association XII* (September 1918): 88–89.

———. *Handbook of ALA War Service Personnel*. ALA Archives, University of Illinois.

———. "The Headquarters Library," *Bulletin of the American Library Association* XIII (May 1919).

———. "Historical Sketch A.L.A. War Service from Jan. 1, 1919, to Nov. 2, 1920," prepared at request of War Department. ALA Archives, University of Illinois.

———. Library War Service Correspondence XXXIX: 536. ALA Archives, University of Illinois.

———. *Library War Service Reports*. ALA Archives, University of Illinois.

———. *Proceedings* of annual meeting in *Bulletin of the American Library Association* XII (September 1918): 285.

——. "Report of A.L.A. Representatives in Europe." *Bulletin of the American Library Association* XIV (July 1921): 239.

——. "Women and the Work They Do," *War Library Bulletin* (January 1918): 9, item 533, in American Library Association, Library War Service Correspondence XXXIX: Miscellaneous Information, 1917–1921. ALA Archives, University of Illinois.

American Red Cross. *Annual Reports, 1914–1919.*

——. *Bulletin.* No. 22 (August 31, 1918).

——. *Bulletin.* No. 40 (September 30, 1918).

——. *Instructions and Information for Red Cross Workers in France.* Bureau of the Secretary General, ARC in France, Paris: April 1, 1918.

——. *The Work of the American Red Cross.* Washington, D.C.: American Red Cross, 1917.

——. *The Work of the American Red Cross, Report by the War Council of Appropriations and Activities from Outbreak of War to November 1, 1917.* Washington, D.C.: American Red Cross, 1919.

——. *The Work of the American Red Cross During the War, A Statement of Finances and Accomplishments for the Period July 1, 1917, to February 28, 1919.* Washington, D.C.: American Red Cross, October 1919.

——. *The Work of the American Red Cross: A Statement of Its War Time Activities Throughout the World.* Washington, D.C.: American Red Cross, December 1, 1918.

American Telephone and Telegraph Company Archives. World War I Collection.

American Women's Hospitals. *Bulletin* I, no. 1 (October 1918) and no. 2 (January 1919).

American Women's Hospitals. Letter of Executive Secretary, August 20, 1918. American Women's Hospitals Historical Materials, 1:2. Archives, Medical College of Pennsylvania.

Ames, Fisher, Jr. *American Red Cross Work Among the French People.* New York: The Macmillan Co., 1921.

Aynes, Edith. *From Nightingale to Eagle: The Army Nurses' History.* New York: Prentice-Hall, 1973.

Bakewell, Charles M. *The Story of the American Red Cross in Italy.* New York: The Macmillan Co., 1920.

Bicknell, Ernest. *In War's Wake, 1914–1915.* Washington, D.C.: American National Red Cross, 1936.

Boardman, Mabel T. *Under the Red Cross Flag at Home and Abroad.* Philadelphia: J. B. Lippincott Co., 1915, 1917.

Booth, Evangeline, and Grace Livingston Hill. *The War Romance of the Salvation Army.* Philadelphia: J. B. Lippincott Co., 1919.

Bulson, Florence I. "Michigan State Federation of Women's Clubs and the Great War," *Michigan History Magazine* III (1919): 564ff.

Committee on Public Information, Division on Women's War Work. Press

Releases, World War I, 1914–1918. Vertical Files, Schlesinger Library, Radcliffe College.

Concerning Base Hospital No. 5. A Book Published for the Personnel of Base Hospital No. 5. France, 1918–19. Boston: Barta Press, n.d.

Dalby, Louise Elliott. *"An Irrepressible Crew": The Smith College Relief Unit.* Northampton, Mass.: Friends of the Smith College Library, 1968. The Sophia Smith Collection, Smith College Library.

Davis, Donald, and Eugene P. Trani. "The American YMCA and the Russian Revolution," *Slavic Review* 33 (September 1974): 469–91.

Davis, Orlando C. Report in *Bulletin of the American Library Association* XIII (May, 1919): 304.

Davison, Henry P. *The American Red Cross in the Great War.* New York: The Macmillan Co., 1919.

Dickinson, Asa Don. Report in *Bulletin of the American Library Association* XIII (May 1919): 158.

Dock, Lavinia L., Sarah Elizabeth Pickett, Clara D. Noyes, Fannie F. Clement, Elizabeth G. Fox, and Anna R. Van Meter. *A History of American Red Cross Nursing.* New York: The Macmillan Co., 1922.

Egan, Maurice Francis, and John B. Kennedy. *The Knights of Columbus in Peace and War.* 2 vols. New Haven, Conn.: Knights of Columbus, 1920.

Engelman, Morris. *Four Years of Relief and War Work by the Jews of America, 1914–1918: A Chronological Review.* New York, 1918.

Engert, Roderick. "Signal Corps Female Telephone Operators in World War I." Washington, D.C.: U.S. Army Center of Military History, March 22, 1979.

Evans, Charles. Letter of April 25, 1918. Biddle MSS(W), Friends' Historical Library, Swarthmore, Pa.

Evans, James M., and Gardner L. Harding. *Entertaining the American Army: The American Stage and Lyceum in the World War.* New York: Association Press, 1921.

Forbes, John. *American Friends and Russian Relief 1917–1927.* Philadelphia, 1952: reprint from the *Bulletin* of Friends' Historical Association, Spring and Autumn Nos., 1952.

———. *The Quaker Star Under Seven Flags, 1917–1927.* Philadelphia: University of Pennsylvania Press, 1962.

Friends Reconstruction Unit 1918–1920. "Assignments of Members of the American Friends Reconstruction Unit, January 1, 1918." Biddle MSS, Friends' Historical Library, Swarthmore, Pa.

Fry, Anna Ruth. *A Quaker Adventure: The Story of Nine Years' Relief and Reconstruction.* New York: Frank Maurice, 1927.

Gaines, Ruth Louise. *Helping France: The Red Cross in the Devasted Area.* New York: E. P. Dutton, 1919.

———. *The Ladies of Grécourt: The Smith College Unit in the Somme.* New York: E. P. Dutton, 1920.

Hall, Constance. Scrapbook of Children of the Frontier. Constance Hall Papers. Schlesinger Library, Radcliffe College.

Hall, Mary Ross, and Helen Firman Sweet. *Women in the YMCA Record*. New York: Association Press, 1947.

Holt, Winifred. *A Report to the Committee for Men Blinded in Battle, Hon. John H. Finley, Acting President, Along with Accounts of the Opening of the Phare at Sèvres, Christmas at the Phare in Paris, New Year's at the Phare in Paris*. Paris: The Committee for Men Blinded in Battle, May 1918.

Hoover, Herbert. *An American Epic. II: Famine in Forty-five Nations. Organization behind the Front, 1914–1923*. Chicago: Henry Regnery Co., 1960.

Hoppin, Laura B., ed. *History of the World War Reconstruction Aides: Being an account of the activities and whereabouts of Physio Therapy and Occupational Therapy Aides who served in U.S. Army Hospitals in the United States and in France during the World War*. Milbrook, N.Y.: W. Tyldsley, 1933.

"How Overseas Canteen Workers Are Selected." *The Index*, August 7, 1918.

James, Bessie R. *For God, For Country, For Home: The National League for Women's Service, A Story of the First National Organization of American Women Mobilized for War Service*. New York: G. P. Putnam's Sons, 1920.

James, Marquis. *A History of the American Legion*. New York: William Green, 1923.

Jones, Lester Martin. *Quakers in Action*. New York: The Macmillan Co., 1929.

Jones, Mary Hoxie. *Swords into Ploughshares: An Account of the American Friends' Service Committee, 1917–1937*. Westport, Conn.: Greenwood Press, 1937, 1971.

Jones, Rufus M. *The American Friends in France, 1917–1919*. Edited by Donald S. Howard. New York: Russell Sage Foundation, 1943.

———. *A Service of Love in War Time: American Friends' Relief Work in Europe, 1917–1919*. New York: The Macmillan Co., 1920.

Kernodle, Portia. *The Red Cross Nurse in Action, 1882–1948*. New York: Harper and Bros., 1949.

Koch, Theodore W. *Books in the War: The Romance of Library War Service*. New York: Houghton Mifflin Co., 1919.

Lamb, Albert R. *The Presbyterian Hospital and the Columbia-Presbyterian Medical Center, 1868–1943*. New York: Columbia University Press, 1955.

Lee, Eleanor. *History of the School of Nursing of the Presbyterian Hospital*. New York: G. P. Putnam's Sons, 1942.

Mayo, Katherine. *"That Damn Y" : A Record of Overseas Service*. Boston: Houghton Mifflin Co., 1920.

Moorland, Jesse E. "The Y.M.C.A. with Colored Troops," *Southern Workman* 48 (April 1919): 171–75.

Mount Holyoke Alumnae Quarterly. April 1918 and January 1919.

National League for Women's Service *Monthly Bulletin* I–II (1917–19).

O'Reilly, Leonora. "Report on the International Congress of Women" in *Proceedings of the Fifth Biennial Convention of The National Women's Trade Union League of America, New York City, June 7–12, 1915*.

Putnam, Herbert. "Report of A.L.A. Representatives in Europe." *Bulletin of the American Library Association* XIV (July 1921): 248.

Ranck, Samuel H. "A Librarian's Job in Base Section #1, France." *Bulletin of the American Library Association* XIII (May 1919).

Raney, M. Llewellyn. "The A.L.A. Follows the Flag Overseas." *Bulletin of the American Library Association* XII (September 1918).

Reed College. *War Work for Women: Training of Reconstruction Aides for Military Hospitals*. Portland, Ore.: Reed College, 1918.

Salvation Army. *The War Cry*. 1917–1918.

Seton, Grace Thompson. "Le Bien-Etre du Blessé: Woman's Motor Unit of New York Women's City Club Report December 1917–1919." 1919.

The Story of U.S. Army Base Hospital No. 5, By a Member of the Unit. Cambridge, Mass.: The University Press, 1919.

Thomison, Dennis. *A History of the American Library Association, 1876–1972.* Chicago: American Library Association, 1978.

U.S. Army Signal Center and School, Ft. Monmouth, N.J., Press Release #2037286, 1972.

"Vassar Alumnae in Foreign Service," in *Vassar College Bulletin* VIII, no. 3 (May 1919).

Vassar Quarterly (November 1919).

Vassar Unit for Service Abroad. Papers. Vassar College Library.

"The Vassar Unit for Service Abroad under the American Red Cross." N.d., n.p. Brochure in Vassar College Library.

"What the Salvation Army Has Done," *Literary Digest* LVI (March 16, 1918): 38f.

Winser, Beatrice. Letters, February 20, 1918, to Newton D. Baker; April 28, 1918, to Herbert Putnam. ALA Library War Service Correspondence XXXIX: 529–32.

Wisbey, Herbert A., Jr. *Soldiers Without Swords: A History of the Salvation Army in the United States.* New York: The Macmillan Co., 1955.

Women's Overseas Service League. *Lest We Forget . . . : A History of the Women's Overseas Service League.* Edited by Helene M. Sillia. Privately printed, 1978.

———. Scrapbook. Nebraska State Historical Society MS 1262, Lincoln, Neb.

"A Working Visit with the Smith College Girls at Grécourt," *Literary Digest* LVI (March 23, 1918): 53ff.

W.P.B. "The Salvation Army and Its Work in the World's War," *The Mess Kit* I, no. 7 (September 1919): 4.

Young, Arthur P. "The American Library Association and World War I." Unpublished Ph.D. diss., University of Illinois, 1976.

———. *Books for Sammies, The American Library Association and World War I.* Pittsburgh: Beta Phi Mu, 1981.

Young, Geoffrey W. *A Story of the Work of the Friends' Ambulance Unit Oct. 1914–Feb. 1915.* London: Newnham, Cowell and Griper, 1915.

[Young Men's Christian Association.] *Service with Fighting Men: An Account of the Work of the American Young Men's Christian Association in the World War.* 2 vols. New York: Association Press, 1924.

Young Women's Christian Association. *Report of the Overseas Committee of the War Work Council, 1917–1920*, prepared by Helen Hendricks [1921?], Records Files Collection, National Board Archives, New York.
———. Reports to National Board, Records Files Collection, National Board Archives, New York.
———. *War Work Bulletin*, 1917–19. Publication of the War Work Council, National Board of the YWCA, National Board Archives, New York.
———. "The Work of Colored Women." 1919.

Reference Works

Bassow, Whitman. *The Moscow Correspondents*. New York: William Morrow & Co., 1988.
Beadle, Muriel. *The Fortnightly of Chicago: The City and Its Women: 1873–1973*. Edited by Fanny Butcher. Chicago: Henry Regnery Co., 1973.
Boucher, François, and Frances Wilson Huard, comps. *American Footprints in Paris: A Guidebook of Historical Data Pertaining to Americans in the French Capitol from the Earliest Days to the Present Times*. New York: George H. Doran Co., 1921.
Chicago Tribune. Women of the World's Greatest Newspaper. Chicago: Public Service Office of the *Chicago Tribune*, 1927.
Clark, Judith Freeman. *Almanac of American Women in the 20th Century*. New York: Prentice Hall Press, 1987.
Crozier, Emmet. *American Reporters on the Western Front 1914–1918*. New York, Oxford University Press, 1959.
Curti, Merle. *American Philanthropy Abroad: A History*. New Brunswick: Rutgers University Press, 1963.
Edwards, Julia. *Women of the World, The Great Foreign Correspondents*. Boston: Houghton Mifflin Co., 1988.
Franklin, John Hope, and August Meier, eds. *Black Leaders of the Twentieth Century*. Urbana, Ill.: University of Illinois Press, 1982.
Hoehling, A. A. *Women Who Spied: True Stories of Feminine Espionage from the American Revolution to the Present Day*. New York: Dodd, Mead and Co., 1967.
Hutton, Joseph Bernard. *Women in Espionage*. New York: The Macmillan Co., 1971.
McCullough, Joan. *First of All: Significant "Firsts" by American Women*. New York: Holt, Rinehart and Winston, 1980.
Mead, Kate. *Medical Women of America*. New York: Froben Press, 1933.
Morton, Brian N. *Americans in Paris: An Anecdotal Street Guide*. Ann Arbor, Mich.: The Oliva & Hill Press, 1984.
Nims, Marion R. *Woman in the War: A Bibliography*. Washington: Government Printing Office, 1918.
Notable American Women 1607–1950: A Biographical Dictionary. 3 vols. Edited

by Edward T. James, Janet Wilson James, and Paul S. Boyer. Cambridge, Mass.: The Belknap Press of Harvard University Press, 1971.

Notable American Women, The Modern Period, a Biographical Dictionary. Edited by Barbara Sicherman and Carol Hurd Green. Cambridge, Mass.: The Belknap Press of Harvard University Press, 1980.

Oakes, Claudia M. *U.S. Women in Aviation Through World War I.* Washington, D.C.: Smithsonian Institution Press, 1978.

Profiles of Negro Womanhood, II, 20th Century. Edited by Sylvia G. L. Dannett, in *Negro Heritage Library.* New York: M. W. Lads, 1964.

Prominent Women of Illinois, 1885–1932. Chicago: The Illinois Women's Press Association, 1932.

Ross, Ishbel. *Ladies of the Press: The Story of Women in Journalism by an Insider.* New York: Arno Press, 1974; reprint of Harper and Bros. edition of 1936.

Schlipp, Madelon Golden, and Sharon M. Murphy. *Great Women of the Press.* Carbondale, Ill.: Southern Illinois University Press, 1983.

Women and War

Addams, Jane, Emily G. Balch, and Alice Hamilton. *Women at the Hague: The International Congress of Women and its Results.* New York: Garland Publishing Co., 1972; reprint of 1915 edition.

Armeny, Susan. "The Responses of Organized Women and Women Physicians to World War I," delivered at the Conference on Women in the Health Professions, Boston College, November 15, 1980. Archives, Pennsylvania College of Medicine.

Ashbridge, D. M. "The Utilization of Women in the Military Service in Time of War." Paper submitted to the Army War College, December 23, 1924. Military History Institute, Carlisle Barracks, Pa.

Berkin, Carol R. and Clare A. Lovett, eds. *Women, War and Revolution.* New York: Holmes & Meier, 1980.

Binkin, Martin, and Shirley Bach. *Women and the Military.* Washington, D.C.: Brookings Institution, 1977.

Blatch, Harriot E. S. *Mobilizing Woman-Power.* New York: The Woman's Press, 1918.

Bowley, A. J. "Work of the Personnel Division of the War Department General Staff." Lecture at the Army War College, Washington Barracks, D.C., October 1, 1929. Military History Institute, Carlisle Barracks, Pa.

Braybon, Gail. *Women Workers in the First World War: The British Experience.* London: Croom Helm; Totowa, N.J.: Barnes & Noble, 1981.

———, and Penny Summerfield. *Out of the Cage: Women's Experiences in Two World Wars.* London: Pandora Press, 1987.

Brockett, L[inus] P[ierpont], and Mary C. Vaughan. *Woman's Work in the Civil War, A Record of Heroism, Patriotism and Patience.* Philadelphia: Ziegler, McCurdy & Co., 1867.

Burnett-Smith, A. *As Others See Her: An Englishwoman's Impressions of the American Woman in War Time.* Boston: Houghton Mifflin Co., 1919.

Bussey, Gertrude, and Margaret Tims. *Pioneers for Peace: Women's International League for Peace and Freedom, 1915–1965.* London: Allen and Unwin, 1980.

Cheatham, Paula M. "The Army's Forgotten Women." Papers of Josephine Davis Gray, Military History Institute, Carlisle Barracks, Pa.

Clappison, Gladys (Bonner). *Vassar's Rainbow Division.* Ames, Iowa, 1964.

Clarke, Ida Clyde Gallagher. *American Women and the World War.* New York: D. Appleton and Co., 1918.

Costello, John. *Virtue Under Fire: How World War II Changed Our Social and Sexual Attitudes.* Boston: Little, Brown and Co., 1985.

Daggett, Mabel Potter. *Women Wanted: The Story Written in Blood Red Letters on the Horizon of the Great War.* New York: George H. Doran Co., 1918.

Dalby, Louise Elliott. "The Great War and Women's Liberation." Skidmore College Faculty Research Lecture, 1970.

Degen, Mary Louise. *The History of the Women's Peace Party.* New York: Burt Franklin Reprints, 1974; reprint of Johns Hopkins Press edition of 1939.

Degler, Carl N. *At Odds: Women and the Family in America from the Revolution to the Present.* New York: Oxford University Press, 1980.

DePauw, Linda Grant. *Founding Mothers: Women of America in the Revolutionary Era.* Boston: Houghton Mifflin Co., 1975.

Dessez, Eunice C. *The First Enlisted Women 1917–18.* Philadelphia: Dorrence & Co., 1955.

Evans, Elizabeth. *Weathering the Storm: Women of the American Revolution.* New York: Scribners, 1975.

Forster, Margaret. *Significant Sisters: The Grassroots of Active Feminism, 1839–1939.* New York: Alfred A. Knopf, 1985.

Frois, Marcel. *La Santé et le Travail des Femmes pendant la Guerre.* Publications de la Dotation Carnegie pour la Paix Internationale. Paris: Les Presses Universitaires de France, 1926.

Fournier, Donna. "The Forgotten Enlisted Women of World War I," *The Retired Officer* 20 (October 1984).

Giddings, Paula. *When and Where I Enter: The Impact of Black Women on Race and Sex in America.* New York: William Morrow and Co., 1984.

Ginsburgh, Robert. "Daughters of Valor." *American Legion Magazine*, May 1939.

" 'Hello Girls' Going Over There," *Literary Digest* LVI (April 6, 1918): 80.

Hewitt, Linda L. "Woman Marines in World War I." Washington, D.C.: History and Museum Division, HQ U.S. Marine Corps, 1974.

Higonnet, Margaret Randolph, et al., eds. *Behind the Lines: Gender and the Two World Wars.* New Haven: Yale University Press, 1987.

Hine, Darlene Clark, "Mabel K. Staupers and the Integration of Black Nurses into the Armed Forces." In *Black Leaders of the Twentieth Century*, edited by John Hope Franklin and August Meier. Urbana: University of Illinois Press, 1982.

Hitchcock, Nevada D. "The Mobilization of Women," *Annals of the American Academy of Social and Political Sciences.* LXXVIII (July 1918): 24–31.

Holm, Jeanne. *Women in the Military: An Unfinished Revolution.* Novato, Calif.: Presidio Press, 1982.

Huard, Frances W. *With Those Who Wait.* New York: George H. Doran Co., 1918.

Kaufman, Ruth Wright. "The Woman Ambulance Driver in France," *The Outlook* CXVII (October 1917): 170–72.

Kellogg, Charlotte (Hoffman). *Women of Belgium; Turning the Tragedy to Triumph.* 4th ed. New York and London: Funk & Wagnalls Co., 1917.

Kerber, Linda. *Women of the Republic.* Chapel Hill, N.C.: University of North Carolina Press, 1980.

Krippner, Monica. *The Quality of Mercy: Women at War in Serbia 1915–1918.* Newton Abbot, London: David & Charles, 1980.

Laffin, John. *Women in Battle.* London: Abelard-Schuman, 1967.

Lapinska, Melanie, and Lady Muir Mackenzie. "Women Doctors: An Historic Retrospect." *The Overland Monthly* LXVII, Second Series (January–June 1916): 117–21.

McCulloch, Rhoda. *The War and the Woman Point of View.* New York: Association Press, 1920.

Macdonald, Sharon, Pat Holden and Shirley Ardener, eds. *Images of Women in Peace and War: Crosscultural and Historical Perspectives.* Madison: University of Wisconsin Press, 1988.

McGovern, James R. "The American Woman's Pre–World War I Freedom in Manners and Morals." *Journal of American History* LV (Sept. 1968): 315–333.

McLaren, Barbara. *Women of the War.* New York: George H. Doran Co., 1918.

Malan, Nancy E. "How 'Ya Gonna Keep 'Em Down?: Women and World War I," *Prologue: The Journal of the National Archives* V, no. 4 (Winter 1973): 209–54.

Marwick, Arthur. *Women at War 1914–1918.* Glasgow: Fontana, 1977.

Massey, Mary Elizabeth. *Bonnet Brigades.* New York: Alfred A. Knopf, 1966.

Medical Review of Reviews. August 1935. Third Woman's Issue.

Mitchell, David. *Monstrous Regiment: The Story of the Women of the First World War.* New York: The Macmillan Co., 1965.

Norton, Mary Beth. *Liberty's Daughters.* Boston: Little, Brown and Co., 1980.

"Nurses of America, Your Country Needs You," *The Touchstone* III, no. 3 (June 1918): 215–18.

O'Neill, William L. *Everyone Was Brave: The Rise and Fall of Feminism in America.* Chicago: Quadrangle Books, 1969.

O'Reilly, Leonora. "Report on the International Congress of Women." *Pro-*

ceedings of the Fifth Biennial Convention of the National Women's Trade Union League of America, New York City, June 7–12, 1915.

Press Releases, Committee on Public Information, Division on Women's Work. Vertical Files, Schlesinger Library, Radcliffe College.

Reifert, Gail, and Eugene Dermody. *Women Who Fought: An American History.* Norwalk, Calif.: Dermody, 1978.

Report of the International Congress of Women. The Hague, 1915.

Ruutz-Rees, Caroline. "The Mobilization of American Women." *The Yale Review* N.S. VII (1918): 801–18.

Shorer, Michele. "Roles and Images of Women in WWI Propaganda." *Politics and Society* V (1975): 469–86.

Smith, Annie S. *As Others See Her: An Englishwoman's Impressions of the American Women in Wartime.* Boston: Houghton Mifflin Co., 1919.

Sochen, June. *Herstory: A Woman's View of American History.* New York: Alfred Publishing Co., 1974.

———. *Movers and Shakers: American Women Thinkers and Activists, 1900–1970.* New York: Quadrangle Press, 1973.

———. *The New Woman: Feminism in Greenwich Village, 1910–1920.* New York: Quadrangle Press, 1972.

Solomon, Barbara Miller. *In the Company of Educated Women: A History of Women and Higher Education in America.* New Haven: Yale University Press, 1985.

Steinson, Barbara Jean. *American Women's Activism in World War I.* New York: Garland Press, 1988.

———. "Female Activism in World War I: The American Women's Peace, Suffrage, Preparedness, and Relief Movements, 1914–1919." Ph.D. diss. Ann Arbor, Mich., 1977.

———. "The 'Mother Half of Humanity': American Women in the Peace and Preparedness Movements in World War I," in *Women, War and Revolution,* edited by Carol R. Berkin and Clara M. Lovett. New York: Holmes and Meier, 1980.

Stiehm, Judith Hicks, ed. *Women and Men's Wars.* Oxford: Pergamon Press, 1983.

Tingley, Elizabeth and Donald F. *Women and Feminism in American History.* Detroit: Gale Research Co., 1981.

Villard, Henry S. "A Prize Specimen of Wounded Hero." *The World Wars Remembered: Personal Recollections of Heroes, Hello Girls, Flying Aces, Prisoners, Survivors, and Those on the Home Front, from the Pages of Yankee Magazine.* Dublin, N.H.: Yankee, Inc., 1979.

Whitney, Janet Payne. "The Women Behind the Guns," *The Independent* XCII (October, November, December 1917): 22–23, 50.

Willenz, June A. *Women Veterans: America's Forgotten Heroines.* New York: Continuum, 1983.

Williams, Beryl. "Kollontai and After: Women in the Russian Revolution." In *Women, State and Revolution: Essays on Power and Gender in Europe Since*

1789, edited by Sian Reynolds. Amherst: University of Massachusetts Press, 1987.

Wiltsher, Anne. *Most Dangerous Women, Feminist Peace Campaigns of the Great War.* London: Pandora Press, 1985.

Woloch, Nancy. *Women and the American Experience.* New York: Alfred A. Knopf, 1984.

"Woman's Work in the World War: Motor Society Means Wider Opportunities for Those Who Cannot Fight." *Motor Age* XXXI (April 26, 1917): 32–33.

"Women Doctors' Wonderful Work Amid War's Horrors," *Literary Digest* LVI (February 16, 1918): 40ff.

"Women War Workers of the World: The Amazing Results of Their Organizations and Individual Efforts," *The Touchstone* III, no. 5 (August 1918): 412–19, 456; no. 6 (September 1918): 508–14.

"Women's Organizations for War Work," *The Touchstone* III, no. 4 (July 1918): 339–40.

"Women's Work in War-Time," *Literary Digest* L (June 26, 1915): 1533.

Wylie, Ida A. R. "An Englishwoman Visits America in France." *Good Housekeeping,* November 1917, 37ff.

"Yeomanettes of World War I," *U.S. Naval Institute Proceedings* LXXXIV (1957): 1338–45.

Yost, Edna. *American Women of Nursing.* Philadelphia: J. B. Lippincott Co., 1947.

World War I

Army Times Editors. *A History of the United States Signal Corps.* New York: Army Times Publishing Co., 1961.

Barbeau, Arthur E., and Florette Henri. *The Unknown Soldiers: Black American Troops in World War I.* Philadelphia: Temple University Press, 1974.

Coffman, Edward M. *The War to End All Wars: The American Military Experience in World War I.* New York: Oxford University Press, 1968.

Crozier, Emmet. *American Reporters on the Western Front, 1914–1918.* New York: Oxford University Press, 1959.

Currey, J. Seymour. *Illinois Activities in the World War, Covering the Period from 1914 to 1920.* 3 vols. Chicago: Thomas B. Poole Co., 1921.

Dos Passos, John. *Mr. Wilson's War.* Garden City, N.Y.: Doubleday, 1962.

Ecksteins, Morris. *Rites of Spring: The Great War and the Birth of the Modern Age.* Boston: Houghton Mifflin Co., 1989.

Egan, Eleanor Franklin. "War Notes on the Golden Horn." *Saturday Evening Post,* October 23, 1915, through November 20, 1915.

Ferro, Marc. *The Great War, 1914–1918.* London: ARK Paperbacks, 1987.

Foner, Jack D. *Blacks and the Military in American History.* New York: Praeger, 1974.

Francis, David R. *Russia from the American Embassy, 1916–1918*. New York: Arno Press, 1970; reprint of Charles Scribner's Sons edition of 1921.

Freidel, Frank. *Over There: The Story of America's First Great Overseas Crusade*. Boston: Little, Brown and Co., 1964.

Fussell, Paul. *The Great War and Modern Memory*. New York: Oxford University Press, 1975.

Harbord, James Guthrie. *The American Army in France, 1917–19*. Boston: Little, Brown and Co., 1936.

Henri, Florette, and Richard Stillman. *Bitter Victory: A History of Black Soldiers in World War I*. Garden City, N.Y.: Doubleday and Co., 1970.

Herman, Sondra R. *Eleven Against War: Studies in American Internationalist Thought, 1898–1921*. Stanford, Calif.: Hoover Institution Press, 1969.

Hershey, Burnet. *The Odyssey of Henry Ford and the Great Peace Ship*. New York: Taplinger, 1967.

Hirschfeld, Magnus. *The Sexual History of the World War*. New York: Falstaff Press, 1937.

Holmes, Richard. *Acts of War: The Behavior of Men in Battle*. New York: Free Press, 1985.

Jeffreys-Jones, Rhodri J. *American Espionage: From Secret Service to CIA*. New York: The Free Press, 1977.

Kennedy, David M. *Over Here: The First World War and American Society*. New York: Oxford University Press, 1980.

Knightley, Phillip. *The First Casualty: From the Crimea to Vietnam: The War Correspondent as Hero, Propagandist, and Myth Maker*. New York: Harcourt Brace Jovanovich, 1975.

———. *The Second Oldest Profession: Spies and Spying in the Twentieth Century*. New York: W. W. Norton & Co., 1986.

Kraft, Barbara S. *The Peace Ship: Henry Ford's Pacifist Adventure in the First World War*. New York: Macmillan Publishing Co., 1978.

Lattimore, Florence L. "Aboard the Oscar II." *Survey*, January 15, 1916, 457–60.

Lavine, A. Lincoln. *Circuits of Victory*. Garden City, N.Y.: Doubleday, Page & Co., 1921.

Leed, Eric J. *No Man's Land: Combat and Identity in World War I*. Cambridge: Cambridge University Press, 1979.

Leslie's Photographic Review of the Great War. Edited by Edgar Allen Forbes. New York: Leslie-Judge Co., 1920.

Littledale, Clara Savage. "The First Word from France." *Good Housekeeping*, Oct. 1918, 38ff.

———. "Helping Out in France." *Good Housekeeping*, Nov. 1918, 22ff.

———. "Where Glory Shone About." *Good Housekeeping*, Dec. 1918, 22ff.

Luebke, Frederick C. *Bonds of Loyalty: German-Americans and World War I*. DeKalb, Ill.: Northern Illinois University Press, 1974.

McClellan, Edwin North. *The United States Marine Corps in the World War*.

Washington, D.C.: Historical Branch, G-3 Division Headquarters, U.S. Marine Corps, 1968; reprint of 1920 edition.

Marcosson, Issac F. *S.O.S.: America's Miracle in France*. New York: John Lane Co., 1919.

Marshall, S. L. A. *World War I*. Boston: Houghton Mifflin Co., 1964.

May, Henry F. *The End of American Innocence: A Study of the First Years of Our Own Time, 1912–1917*. New York: Oxford University Press, 1979.

Moley, Raymond, Jr. *The American Legion Story*. New York: Duell, Sloan and Pearce, 1966.

Moskin, J. Robert. *The U.S. Marine Corps Story*. New York: McGraw-Hill Book Co., 1977.

Nalty, Bernard. *Strength for the Fight, A History of Black Americans in the Military*. New York: Free Press, 1986.

Palmer, Frederick. *America in France*. Westport, Conn.: Greenwood Press, 1975; reprint of Dodd, Mead & Co. edition of 1918.

Panichas, George, ed. *The Promise of Greatness: The War of 1914–1918*. New York: John Day, 1968.

Patton, Gerald W. *War and Race: The Black Officer in the American Military, 1915–1941*. Westport, Conn.: Greenwood Press, 1981.

Peterson, H. C., and Gilbert C. Fite. *Opponents of War, 1917–1918*. Madison, Wis.: University of Wisconsin Press, 1957.

Potter, Elizabeth Gray. "Just Babies, But Victims of the Hun's Brutality." *Woman's Home Companion*, October 1918, 40ff.

Richardson, Anna Steese. "The Game of Keeping Fit." *Woman's Home Companion*, October 18, 1918.

———. "Overseas with the A.E.F." *McCall's Magazine*, October 1918.

———. Article in *War Work Bulletin* no. 37 (August 16, 1918).

Rickards, Maurice. *Posters of the First World War*. New York: Walker & Co., 1968.

Rinehart, Mary Roberts. *Kings, Queens and Pawns*. New York: George H. Doran Co., 1915.

———. "Queen Mary of England." *Saturday Evening Post*, June 19, 1915.

———. "The Queen of the Belgians." *Saturday Evening Post*, July 3, 1915.

———. "The Red Badge of Mercy." *Saturday Evening Post*, July 31, 1915.

———. "A Talk with the King of the Belgians." *Saturday Evening Post*, April 13, 1915.

Roth, Jack J., ed. *World War I: A Turning Point in Modern History*. New York: Alfred A. Knopf, 1967.

Scott, Emmett J. *Scott's Official History of the American Negro in the World War*. New York: Arno Press, 1919, 1969.

Sergeant, Elizabeth Shepley. "Y.M.C.A. and A.E.F." *New Republic* XV (June 22, 1918): 228–31.

Sharpe, Henry G. *The Quartermaster Corps in the Year 1917 in the World War*. New York: Century Co., 1921.

Slosson, Preston William. *The Great Crusade and After: 1914–1928*. New York: The Macmillan Co., 1930.

Smith, Daniel M. *The Great Departure: The United States and World War I, 1914–1920*. New York: John Wiley and Sons, 1965.

Stallings, Laurence. *The Doughboys*. New York: Popular Library, 1964.

Stokesbury, James L. *A Short History of World War I*. New York: William Morrow and Co., 1981.

Tuchman, Barbara W. *The Guns of August*. New York: Dell Publishing Co., 1962.

———. *The Zimmermann Telegram*. New York: Ballantine Books, 1959, 1966.

Wharton, Edith. *Fighting France from Dunkerque to Belfort*. Westport, Conn.: Greenwood Press, 1974; reprint of Scribner's edition of 1915.

Williams, Charles Halston. *Negro Soldiers in World War I: The Human Side*. New York: AMS Press, 1970; reprint of 1923 edition; first titled *Sidelights on Negro Soldiers*.

Williams, Ennion G. "Physicians as a Factor in National Efficiency." *Annals of the American Academy of Social and Political Science* LXXVIII (July 1918): 41–47.

Wohl, Robert. *The Generation of 1914*. Cambridge, Mass.: Harvard University Press, 1979.

ACKNOWLEDGMENTS

Illustrations

Our thanks to:

The Metropolitan Museum of Art, New York, N.Y., for permission to reproduce a picture of a motor corps uniform donated by Jane Darlington Irwin.

The Morris Library, Southern Illinois University at Carbondale, for permission to reproduce the dust jacket of Mary McAuley's *Germany in War Time*.

The National Archives, for permission to reproduce pictures of the Signal Corps telephone operators' quarters, American Fund for French Wounded motor corps women, a railroad station platform in France, Salvation Army women making pies, Ruth Law, and a poster warning against women spies.

Miss Porter's School, Farmington, Conn., for permission to reproduce a sketch of the American canteen at Epernay and two sketches from Ruth Stillman's autograph book.

The National Board of the Young Women's Christian Association of the United States of America, for permission to reproduce their poster "Back Our Girls Over There, United War Work Campaign," copyright by the YWCA of the U.S.A., held in perpetuity.

UPI/Bettmann Newsphotos, for permission to reproduce photographs of Madeleine Doty, Mrs. Burden Turner, a Salvation Army woman sewing, Elsie Janis, Louise Bryant, and a Red Cross nurse in the Armistice celebration.

The National Council of the Young Men's Christian Associations, for permission to reproduce drawings from James M. Evans and Gardner L. Harding, *Entertaining the American Army: The American Stage and Lyceum in the World War*.

Quotations

Our thanks to:

Charles D. Adams, for permission to quote his mother, Marian V. Dunn Adams.

American Board of Commissioners for Foreign Missions and Houghton Library, Harvard University, for permission to quote from the A.B.C.F.M. papers.

American Legion Auxiliary of Indiana, for permission to quote from *Indiana Women in the World War*.

American Library Association Archives at the University of Illinois at Urbana/Champaign, for permission to quote from the ALA files.

Archives and Special Collections on Women in Medicine, Medical College of Pennsylvania, for permission to quote from the American Women's Hospitals files.

The Bentley Historical Library, University of Michigan, Ann Arbor, for permission to quote from Rebecca Shelley's interview with Barbara J. Steinson, and from Janet Reedy's synopsis of Rebecca Shelley's life.

Mildred Brown Byers, for permission to quote her.

Paula M. Cheatham, for permission to quote from her speech on women who have served the United States.

Frances E. Collins, for permission to quote from the poetry of Ella Wheeler Wilcox.

Constable Publishers, for permission to quote from Mildred Aldrich, *On the Edge of the War Zone: From the Battle of the Marne to the Entrance of the Stars and Stripes*.

Friends' Historical Library of Swarthmore College, Swarthmore, Pa., for permission to quote Mary Elkinton Duguid, Charles Evans, Lucy Biddle Lewis, and John Rickman.

Garland Publishing Co., for permission to quote from Jane Addams, Emily G. Balch, and Alice Hamilton, *Women at the Hague: The International Congress of Women and Its Results*.

Joyce Goodrich, for permission to quote from the papers of Juliet T. Goodrich.

Rush G. Hamilton, for permission to quote from Alice Hamilton, *Exploring the Dangerous Trades: The Autobiography of Alice Hamilton, M.D.*

Harper & Row, for permission to quote from Grace Livingston Hill and Evangeline Booth, *The War Romance of the Salvation Army*. Copyright 1919 by Grace Livingston Hill. Reprinted by permission of Harper & Row, Publishers, Inc.

Harvard University Press and the Trustees of Amherst College, for permission to quote from Emily Dickinson, *The Poems of Emily Dickinson*, Thomas H. Johnson, ed., Cambridge, Mass.: The Belknap Press of Harvard University Press, copyright 1951, © 1955, 1979, 1983 by the President and Fellows of

Harvard College. Reprinted by permission of the publishers and the Trustees of Amherst College.

Henry Holt and Company, Inc., for permission to quote from Mary Roberts Rinehart, *My Story: A New Edition and Seventeen New Years*. Copyright 1931, 1948 by Mary Roberts Rinehart. Copyright © 1976 Frederick R. Rinehart and Alan G. Rinehart. Reprinted by permission of Henry Holt and Company, Inc.

Alfred A. Knopf, Inc., for permission to quote from Willa Cather's *One of Ours*. Copyright 1922 by Willa Cather and renewed 1950 by Edith Lewis, Executrix, and City Bank Farmers Trust Co. Reprinted by permission of Alfred A. Knopf, Inc.

Trustees of Mount Holyoke College, for permission to quote from the honors thesis of Elizabeth Leighton.

Irene Wilkinson O'Connor, for permission to quote her.

The Open Court Publishing Company, for permission to quote from Mary Ethel McAuley, *Germany in War Time: What an American Girl Saw and Heard*.

Mary T. Samuel, for permission to quote Mary Gruetzman.

The Schlesinger Library, Radcliffe College, for permission to quote from the Louise Barbour papers, the Mary Williams Dewson papers, the Margaret Deland papers, the Mary Dexter papers, the Juliet T. Goodrich papers, the Carrie May Hall papers, the Olivia E. Hamilton papers, the Ruth Holden papers, the Inez H. Irwin papers, the Mary Lee papers, the Clara Savage Littledale papers, the Chloe Owings papers, the Edith Gratie Stedman papers, and the Charles G. Stockton papers.

Helene M. Sillia of the Women's Overseas Service League, for permission to quote from *Lest We Forget . . . : A History of the Women's Overseas Service League*.

Smith College Archives, Smith College, for permission to quote from Louise Elliott Dalby, *"An Irrepressible Crew": The Smith College Relief Unit*.

Vassar College Library, for permission to quote from a letter of Lida A. Little.

Thomas S. Walker, for permission to quote from Mary Lee, *"It's a Great War!"*

The Wellesley College Archives, for permission to quote from the Agnes Gilson Bignell papers and from Laura Jayne Bucknell Loyson.

The National Council of Young Men's Christian Associations, for permission to quote from James M. Evans and Gardner L. Harding, *Entertaining the American Army: The American Stage and Lyceum in the World War*.

The National Board of the Young Women's Christian Association of the United States of America, for permission to quote from the YWCA archives.

INDEX

Abbott, Grace, 248
Adams, Marian V. Dunn, 274
Addams, Jane:
  criticism of, 10, 262
  Ford Peace Ship and, 258, 259
  international women's congress
    chaired by, 248, 249, 251
  mediation plan and, 258, 260, 261
  on peace delegation, 252–53, 254,
    255, 256
  on popular reaction to war, 247
AEF, see American Expeditionary
  Force
AFFW, see American Fund for French
  Wounded
AFSC, see American Friends Service
  Committee
Air Force, U.S., 232
air raids, 27, 28, 34, 116
ALA, see American Library
  Association
Alcott, Louisa May, 6
Aldrich, Mildred, 36, 192–94
Allchin, Marion F., 143–44
Allies, American commitment to, 4, 10
Allison, Grace, 116–17
Amazing Interlude, The (Rinehart), 232
ambrine cure, 82
ambulances, 85, 99–101
American Ambulance, 9, 35, 39, 51,
  56, 87–88
American Board of Commissioners for
  Foreign Missions, 35
American Committee for Devastated
  France, 91, 96

American Convalescent Homes, 42
American Expeditionary Force (AEF),
  61, 122–23, 177
  see also specific services
American Federation of Labor, 248
American Friends Service Committee
  (AFSC):
  establishment of, 63
  British Quakers and, 64
  proselytizing prohibited for, 63, 65
  in Russian service, 66–71
American Fund for French Wounded
  (AFFW), 44–45, 51, 52–53, 56,
  73, 90, 94
American Hostels for Refugees, 41
American Huguenot Committee, 50
American Legion, 240
American Library Association (ALA),
  149–54
American Red Cross (ARC), 54–62
  age limits of, 15–16
  AWH units requested by, 91
  black nurses ignored by, 169–70
  bureaucracy of, 43, 61
  Casualty Bureau of, 53
  chief nurse of, 88
  Children's Bureau of, 21, 56, 93–94
  criticism of, 55
  diverse services offered by, 54–55
  in England, 35
  expansion of, 55
  female physicians deployed by, 96,
    97
  French table of organization for, 54
  Home Service of, 58–59

352